Functions of the Brain

Considering how computational properties of the brain inform cognitive functions, this book presents a unique conceptual introduction to cognitive neuroscience. This essential guide explores the complex relationship between the mind and the brain, building upon the authors' extensive research in neural information processing and cognitive neuroscience to provide a comprehensive overview of the field.

Rather than providing detailed descriptions of different cognitive processes, *Functions of the Brain: A Conceptual Approach to Cognitive Neuroscience* focuses on how the brain functions using specific processes. Beginning with a brief history of early cognitive neuroscience research, Kok goes on to discuss how information is represented and processed in the brain before considering the underlying functional organization of larger-scale brain networks involved in human cognition. The second half of the book addresses the architecture of important overlapping areas of cognition, including attention and consciousness, perception and action, and memory and emotion.

This book is essential reading for upper-level undergraduates studying Cognitive Neuroscience, particularly those taking a more conceptual approach to the topic.

Albert Kok is Emeritus Professor at the University of Amsterdam, the Netherlands. He is a former member of the Board of Directors of the Society of Psychophysiological Research (SPR, USA) and Chairman of the Society of Psychonomics in the Netherlands.

Functions of the Brain

A Conceptual Approach to Cognitive Neuroscience

Albert Kok

LONDON AND NEW YORK

First published 2020
by Routledge
2 Park Square, Milton Park, Abingdon, Oxon OX14 4RN

and by Routledge
52 Vanderbilt Avenue, New York, NY 10017

Routledge is an imprint of the Taylor & Francis Group, an informa business

© 2020 Albert Kok

The right of Albert Kok to be identified as author of this work has been asserted by him in accordance with sections 77 and 78 of the Copyright, Designs and Patents Act 1988.

All rights reserved. No part of this book may be reprinted or reproduced or utilised in any form or by any electronic, mechanical, or other means, now known or hereafter invented, including photocopying and recording, or in any information storage or retrieval system, without permission in writing from the publishers.

Trademark notice: Product or corporate names may be trademarks or registered trademarks, and are used only for identification and explanation without intent to infringe.

British Library Cataloguing-in-Publication Data
A catalogue record for this book is available from the British Library

Library of Congress Cataloging-in-Publication Data
Names: Kok, A. (Albert), author.
Title: Functions of the brain : a conceptual approach to cognitive neuroscience / Albert Kok.
Description: Milton Park, Abingdon, Oxon ; New York, NY : Routledge, 2020. | Includes bibliographical references and index.
Identifiers: LCCN 2019018192 (print) | LCCN 2019022025 (ebook) | ISBN 9780429451171 (ebook) | ISBN 9781138323681 (hbk : alk. paper) | ISBN 9781138323834 (pbk : alk. paper) | ISBN 9780429451171 (ebk)
Subjects: LCSH: Brain. | Cognitive neuroscience.
Classification: LCC QP376 (ebook) | LCC QP376 .K634 2020 (print) | DDC 612.8/2—dc23
LC record available at https://lccn.loc.gov/2019018192

ISBN: 978-1-138-32368-1 (hbk)
ISBN: 978-1-138-32383-4 (pbk)
ISBN: 978-0-429-45117-1 (ebk)

Typeset in Optima
by Apex CoVantage LLC

Contents

About the author	xiv
Preface	xv

1 The birth of cognitive neuroscience — 1

Introduction	1
The development of cognitive neuroscience	2
Behaviorism	2
Cognitive psychology	4
Cognitive neuroscience	5
Cognitive neuroscience triangle	6
Behavior	6
Computations	7
Brain	8
The mind-brain	9
A simple neurocognitive model	9
Decomposing the mind-brain	12
The global-local debate	14
Lashley and Penfield	15
Domain specificity and more	17
Connectivity and the local-global controversy	18
Methods in cognitive brain research	18
Event-related potentials (ERPs)	19
Imaging the structure and function of the brain (MRI, fMRI)	21
Lesion studies	22
Neural network modeling	24
Brain connectivity studies	25
Structural connectivity	26
Functional connectivity	26
Effective connectivity	28
Contribution to cognitive neuroscience	30

2 Introducing the brain: from synapse to networks — 32

- Introduction — 32
- Gross anatomy and function of the brain — 33
  - Cerebral cortex — 33
    - Spatial divisions — 35
    - Primary and secondary areas — 36
    - Connections — 38
    - Prefrontal cortex — 38
    - Evolution — 40
  - Limbic system — 43
    - Anatomy and function — 43
    - Cingulate gyrus — 43
    - Hippocampus — 44
    - Amygdala — 45
    - Septum — 46
    - Insula — 46
  - Basal ganglia — 47
    - Function — 47
    - Motor memory — 47
    - Motivation — 48
  - Thalamus and hypothalamus — 49
  - Brainstem — 50
    - Reticular formation — 50
    - Tectum and tegmentum — 52
    - Dopamine pathways — 52
    - Cerebellum — 53
    - Medulla and pons — 53
- Connections in the brain: from neurons to networks — 54
  - Micro-level: neurons and synapses — 56
    - Growth and development — 57
    - Topographic, horizontal and vertical organization — 59
    - Cortical layers and columns — 60
  - Local networks in the cortex — 63
  - Subcortical nuclei — 64
  - Large-scale networks — 65
    - Imaging techniques — 66
    - Linking structural to functional networks — 68
    - Modeling functional networks — 69
    - Communication efficiency — 71
    - Cortical-subcortical networks — 71

Laterality and the brain	72
Introduction	72
Anatomy and functions of the cerebral hemispheres	73
Symmetries	73
Connections of the corpus callosum	75
Function of callosal connections	77
Evolutionary perspectives	78
Symmetry	79
Asymmetry	79
Control functions	80
Handedness and language development	80
Split-brain studies	82
Generativity and syntax	84
Varieties of laterality	85
What is lateralized?	86

3 Representation, computing and control — 89

Introduction	89
A catalog of representations	91
State of the brain	91
Functional cerebral space	92
Complex representations	94
Conceptual knowledge	94
Action representations	96
Dispositional representations	97
Self-representations	97
Codes in the brain	98
Local coding	98
Vector coding	98
How does the brain solve the binding problem?	101
Binding units	102
Interaction	103
Synchronicity	103
Top-down influences	104
Synchronicity in imaging networks	105
Computations in the brain	105
Information processing models	106
Input functions	107
Central functions	107
Input-output translation	109

CONTENTS

Output functions	111
Connectionist models	111
Pattern-association networks	112
Analyzing the functional properties of networks	114
Computational modeling	115
Control functions of the brain	115
Automatic control	116
Attentional and executive control	116
Putting it together: hierarchical distributed networks	118
The flexibility of neurocognitive networks	119

4 Activation, attention and awareness — 122

Introduction: the hierarchy of activation, attention and awareness	122
Neurobiology of activation	126
Introduction	126
Thalamic nuclei	127
Thalamocortical circuits (gate system)	128
Extrathalamic pathways (gain system)	129
Activation and stress	129
Attention: manifestations, varieties and methods	131
Selection as the core element of attention	131
The manifestations of selective attention	132
Reflexive and voluntary attention	133
Reflexive attention	134
Voluntary attention	134
Bottleneck versus resource theories	139
Filter models	139
Resource models	140
Early versus late selection	141
Is spatial attention special?	142
Feature integration	143
Attentional neglect	144
Memory and attention	146
Neurobiology of attention	148
Mechanisms of expression and control	150
Expression mechanisms	151
Control mechanisms	154
Role of the thalamus	156
Role of the superior colliculus	157
Role of higher centers	158

	Empirical studies: ERP and fMRI	159
	Determining the direction of visual-spatial attention	161
	Complex cognitive tasks: ERP studies	161
	Cognitive control: the role of frontal cortical areas	162
Awareness and consciousness		164
	Manifestations of consciousness	165
	Alertness	165
	Orienting	166
	Focused attention and working memory	166
	The self	167
	The unrestrained mind	168
	Default network	168
	Salience network	169
	Validating the salience network	169
	Constraints of task-free states of the brain	172

5 Perception and action — 176

Introduction		176
Visual perception		177
	From eye to brain: geniculostriate and tectopulvinary routes	177
	Geniculostriate route	178
	Tectopulvinary route	179
	Further stations in the visual cortex, dorsal and ventral routes	181
	Visual illusions	182
	Higher-order vision	183
	How the senses interact	186
	Crossmodal plasticity in sensory deprived subjects	186
	Memory for faces	188
	Senses mislead	189
Action systems		190
	Introduction: the hierarchical structure of the motor system	190
	Subcortical organization and circuits	192
	Complex and motor loops	192
	Inhibitory circuits between basal ganglia and cortex	193
	Cortical organization: three systems of motor control	196
	SMA: the action programming system	197
	Premotor cortex: the instructions-generating system	198
	Motor cortex: the movement execution system	198
From perception to action		200
	Introduction	200

	Perception-action cycle	202
	Response competition and affordance	203
	The role of the parietal cortex revisited	206
	Oculomotor pathways	208
Time perception		213
	Scalar expectancy theory (SET)	214
	Neural models of timing	215
	Striatal Beat Frequency Model (SBF)	215
	Aging and time perception	217

6 Memory systems — 220

Introduction: the multiple manifestations of memory	220
Memory depends on functional cerebral space	222
Anterior-posterior axis	222
Left-right hemispheres	223
Cortical-subcortical connections	224
Memory also depends on the state of the brain	224
Short-term versus long-term memories	224
Explicit versus implicit memory	225
The 'ins' and 'outs' of memory: encoding and retrieval	225
Encoding	226
Forms of retrieval	226
Retrieval and forgetting	228
Memory and the brain: varieties of memory	229
Long-term memory	229
Declarative (explicit) memory	230
Non-declarative (implicit) memory	231
Short-term memory as an activated subset of long-term memory	232
Sensory memory and priming (route 1)	234
Short-term memory as a portal to long-term memory (route 2)	234
Working memory (route 3)	234
Working memory	235
Executive control	238
Encoding and retrieval in explicit memory	238
Prefrontal cortex	239
Medial temporal regions	241
Encoding and the hippocampus	241
Retrieval and the hippocampus	242
Reinstatement or transformation	242
Explicit memory: circuits, deficits and mechanisms	243
The binding role of the medial temporal region	243

The circuitry of consolidation and retrieval	245
The time course of consolidation	246
Differential role of anterior and posterior zones of the hippocampal formation	248
Schema updating	249
Memory guided behavior	251
Relational memory	252
False memories	253
The cellular basis of explicit learning	254
Long-term potentiation	254
Associative LTP	256
The role of NMDA receptors	257
Amnesia and deficits in consolidation	258
Patient studies	259
Animal studies of amnesia	262
Cortical lesions	264
Semantic dementia	264
Agnosia	264
Frontal lesions	267
Implicit memory: priming, learning and mechanisms	267
Priming	268
Priming and habituation	268
Characteristics of positive priming	268
Right-hemisphere and priming	271
Habit learning	271
Sensorimotor learning	271
Role of basal ganglia	272
The time course of skill learning	272
Cellular processes of elementary learning	276
Habituation	276
Sensitization	277
Classical conditioning	277

7 Emotions — 280

Introducing emotions	280
Classification of emotions	281
Valence and intensity	281
The level of organization: primary versus secondary emotions	283
Level of experience: explicit or implicit	284
Subprocesses of emotion	285

Emotion and cognition	285
Interactive model	285
The function and expression of emotions	287
The relationship between feelings and bodily reactions	288
Feelings as the cause of bodily reactions	288
Feelings as the result of bodily reactions	289
Feelings and bodily reactions emitted as parallel reactions	289
A parallel hierarchical model	290
Learning emotions	292
What triggers an emotion?	292
Positive and negative reinforcers	293
A classification of emotions based on reinforcers	294
Primary and secondary reinforcers	295
The drive for curiosity and information seeking	296
Implicit emotional learning	297
Augmented startle	297
Fear conditioning: direct and indirect afferent routes	299
Affective priming	300
Explicit emotional learning	301
Neuroaffective networks	303
Components of the neuroaffective network	304
Structure and function of the amygdala	304
Orbitofrontal cortex	307
Anterior cingulate cortex	309
Where do emotional memories reside?	310
Explicit affective memory	310
Reconsolidation	311
Implicit affective memory	313
Pattern association networks in the amygdala	313
Back projections	315
Circuits of primary and secondary emotions	315
Primary emotions	315
Secondary emotions	316
Emotions and decision making	317
Somatic markers	317
Reinforcement guided decisions	319
Neurotransmitters and emotions	321
Medial forebrain bundle	321

Locus coeruleus-noradrenergic system	322
Dopamine and emotions	323
Enhancement of positive reinforcers	323
Emotional learning and dopamine	324
Depression: the role of noradrenaline, serotonin and stress hormones	325
Noradrenaline	325
Serotonin	326
Stress hormones	326
Summarizing neurotransmitters and depression	327
Depression and disturbed functional connectivity in the brain	328
Epilogue	*331*
References	*334*
Index	*365*

About the author

Albert Kok is Emeritus Professor from the University of Amsterdam. He studied at Leiden University where he obtained his Master degree in 1966. Until 1971 he worked as research assistant at respectively the Laboratory for Ergonomic Psychology (TNO) in Amsterdam and the Department of Clinical and Industrial Psychology of the University of Utrecht. His early research was committed to developing measures of mental workload using performance and autonomic physiological measures. In 1971 he moved to the Psychonomic Department of the Free University of Amsterdam where he finished this thesis in 1976. His work as Assistant Professor concerned application of electrophysiological measures (ERPs) in information processing paradigms. In 1986 he was appointed professor in Physiological Psychology at the Psychonomic Department of the University of Amsterdam. In the period until his retirement in 2004 he was involved in lecturing graduate students in Cognitive Neuroscience as well as establishing with his research team an international network for Cognitive Neuroscience. In his later work and publications on selective attention and response inhibition electrophysiological measures were supplemented with functional imaging of the brain. Albert Kok is strongly committed to the interaction of Cognitive Psychology with Neuroscience. The present book is a reflection of his research interest as well as his lecturing activities during his academic years. He is a former member of the Board of Directors of the Society of Psychophysiological Research (SPR, USA) and former chairman of the Societies of Psychophysiology and Psychonomics in the Netherlands.

Preface

Probably the best-known quote in cognitive neuroscience came from cognitive scientist Marvin Minsky (1985), who stated: 'the mind is what the brain does'. Its implication is clear: those who seek to understand the mind should turn to the brain for the real answers. A groundbreaking insight from modern neuroscience that seemed to provide at least the beginning of a solution to the philosophical paradox was that the brain is not just an organ, but also a biophysical network in which mental states emerge from the interaction between multiple physical and functional levels. Still, cognitive scientists are struggling with the question how the human mind relates to that biophysical entity. How did 'we', that is our identity, feelings and thoughts, emerge from that lump of billions of neurons and their connections? How realistic is the assumption of modern cognitive neuroscience that human cognition can indeed be 'mapped' to our brains?

This book is not intended to answer all these questions, some of which have strong philosophical connotations. Neither is it my intention to present a detailed overview of various methods, theories and functions of the brain in relation to cognition. Instead, I have chosen to focus on some principal elements underlying the 'mind-brain' relationship, meaning cognitive functions as far as they depend on the computational properties of the brain. After sketching the 'birth' of cognitive neuroscience and presenting a simple model of mind-brain interactions in Chapter 1, I focus in Chapter 2 on the principles underlying the neural organization of the brain, including microscopic as well as macroscopic levels. Chapter 3 deals with some elementary 'building blocks' of the mind-brain relating to the question how information is represented and processed in the brain at a computational level, and outlines some principles underlying the functional organization of large-scale brain networks that are also applicable to human cognition.

Chapters 4 to 7 elaborate the building blocks and network principles discussed in the earlier chapters, and the way neural systems are connected with one another in functional brain space. Here I shall primarily use a systems-oriented approach, and address more broadly the functional architecture of four important overlapping domains of cognition. The chapters include in successive order: attention and consciousness, perception and action, memory and emotion. The reader may wonder why language, a topic generally included in textbooks dealing with the mind-brain relationship, is missing. Although language functions are also firmly rooted in the structures of the brain, there was a good reason to not include it in the book. Most important was that a treatise on the unique and intricate qualities of language would be slightly out of context of the present book, dealing primarily with more elementary forms of cognitive functions that humans share with other higher mammals. Chapter 2 however will discuss some aspects of language, while focusing on the laterality of brain functions.

I am grateful to 'critical friends' John Polich, Axel Mecklinger, Martin Eimer and Jaap Murre who were helpful with their constructive comments on earlier drafts of the book. In particular I'd like to thank my wife and loving companion Ite Rümke for her support in scrutinizing the manuscript, and her numerous valuable suggestions to improve my writings.

1 The birth of cognitive neuroscience

CONTENTS

- ▶ Introduction
- ▶ The development of cognitive neuroscience
- ▶ The mind-brain
- ▶ Methods in cognitive brain research

Introduction

Cognitive psychology is committed to the study of cognition, a domain traditionally considered as the 'home base' of functions like perception, attention, memory, language and consciousness. Human cognition, the 'knowing part' of our mind is nonetheless functionally related to another domain of the human mind, emotion, even though they correspond with different divisions of the brain. Emotions and its 'feeling part' color cognitive processes and events that we experience or recall. In turn, cognitive processes can influence and control emotional processes. When faced with uncertainty, human organisms will not only engage areas in the brain that developed relatively late in the course of evolution, like the neocortex. Even complex decisions may then appeal to evolutionarily old structures in the limbic system that regulate affective processes. The fusion between rational and irrational processes that often underlies human social decision making (Tversky & Kahneman, 1981; Damasio, 1994) indicates that human emotions and their underlying mechanisms are essential elements to be considered in the study of human cognition.

The central issue addressed in the present chapter is how we can conceptualize the relationship between mind and brain and their constituting parts. This will necessarily lead us back to some questions that were initially raised in cognitive psychology as well as in neuroscience, but later were reunited in cognitive neuroscience.

Our daily behavior depends to a large extent on the amalgam of cognitive and emotional functions, glued together in the seamless unity of our conscious or unconscious mind. Nonetheless, the principal task of cognitive psychology is not to understand the workings of the 'full mind' as represented in our daily experiences, but rather to unravel its covert structure and functional sub-components.[1] For example, recognizing a familiar face might be dissected into two subcomponents: analyzing its perceptual features (the shape of face, eyes and mouth), and the subsequent search for a match of the perceptual image with representations stored in long-term memory. The temporal aspects of these processes are also a crucial part of the unraveling process: does the analysis of perceptual characteristics precede recognition, or do both processes run in parallel?

Current investigators of the human mind will probably accept the idea that cognitive and emotional processes arise from the complex machinery of the brain, which in turn is the product of successive adaptations during a long biological evolution. But for over a century, cognitive psychology and neuroscience were strictly separate research domains. This 'separation of disciplines' has a long history with interesting cyclic trends. For example, at the end of the 19th century psychologists were particularly interested in the integration of physiology and psychology. In fact, psychology began as Physiological Psychology. Both Wilhelm Wundt and William James, the founders of experimental psychology in Europe and the United States respectively, were fascinated by the question how properties of the brain and mind were related to one another (Boring, 1929). But in the following decades, the interest of psychologists shifted gradually towards the subjective quality of the human mind with introspection as their major tool, to subjectively experience or 'understand' mental states.

The development of cognitive neuroscience

Modern cognitive neuroscience, a core issue of the present book, did not drop from heaven but evolved in the 20th century as the product of some crucial steps in the history of the scientific study of the human mind. The brief historical perspective presented ahead may clarify why a central notion of cognitive neuroscience that the 'mind is a product of brain', developed relatively late in the 20th century.

Behaviorism

In the mid-20th century behaviorism was the first step in the transition of a predominantly subjective psychology into an objective science of behavior. Since it abandoned all 'mentalist' concepts and methods as introspection, it became known as 'black-box' psychology, psychology without a mind (Figure 1.1).

Behaviorists placed much emphasis on changes in behavior caused by external stimuli and rewards, which they regarded as the central subject of scientific research. Physiology, as manifested in the activity of muscles and the autonomic nervous system, was reinstated, providing as it did a valuable source of information of the body's reflexive responses to external stimuli. A second important spin-off of behaviorism was research techniques, like classical and instrumental conditioning, which were ideally suited for application in experimental animal research. Even today, conditioning remains the principal tool in neurobiology to study 'cognition', i.e. elementary learning and memory processes in animals. The rationale of behaviorism was that knowledge of the laws of behavior of laboratory animals could also be useful to gain insight into cognitive learning in humans.

In this respect, behaviorism came much closer to principles of evolutionary thinking, as represented in Darwin's theory of natural selection (Darwin, 1859), than earlier,

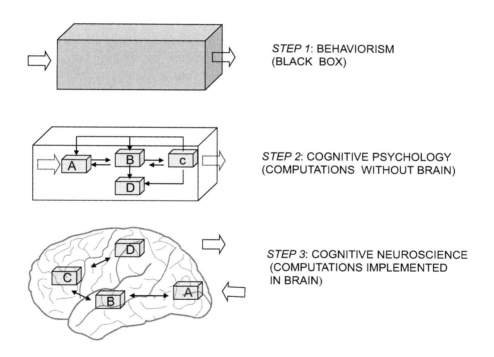

FIGURE 1.1
Three steps in the development of cognitive neuroscience. Step 1, Behaviorism as a reaction to the predominantly subjective character of psychology. Step 2, the rebirth of Cognitive Psychology is accompanied by a renewed interest in processes within the black box, but with no reference to the brain. Step 3: Cognitive Neuroscience describes mental processes at the level of the mind as well as the brain.

more cognitively oriented movements in psychology like Gestalt psychology and Jean Piaget's fundamental theory of development.

Cognitive psychology

The second crucial step in the development of cognitive neuroscience took place in the early 1960s. It was the renewed interest in higher mental processes, a movement also known as a cognitive revival or 'shift'. The central mission of the new cognitive psychology or 'cognitivism' was to fill the mental vacuum created by behaviorism: cognitive psychology re-opened the black box by paying attention to the higher mental processes as the hidden causes of behavior.

But it also appeared that the practitioners of this new cognitive psychology showed little interest in the neural substrates of human behavior. It remained typically a 'dry mind' approach of psychology, as Kosslyn and Koenig (1992) characterized it so aptly it in their seminal introductory book. A possible reason why is that research into physiological processes was still strongly associated with the behaviorist tradition. Another factor was that cognitive psychology was predominantly 'functionalistic', i.e. primarily focused on functions and its manifestations in behavior, rather than its neural substrate. The functionalistic character of this new cognitive psychology was also clearly manifested in the frequent use of the computer as a metaphor – or model – of mental processes.

Indeed, the computer invented by two brilliant pioneers, Alan Turing and John von Neumann, now emerged as a powerful tool that allowed to formulate more precisely theories of brain functioning. A device invented by Turing called 'Turing machine' provided the basic ingredients of a computer program. A Turing machine is an idealized and amazingly simple computing device consisting of a read/write head (or 'scanner') with a paper tape passing through it. The tape is divided into squares, each square bearing a single symbol '0' or '1'. The machine changes symbols by deleting or changing its content. The tape is the machine's general-purpose storage medium, serving both as the vehicle for input and output and as a working memory for storing the results of intermediate steps of the computation. Turing's abstract conceptualization of a computing system also formed the framework of von Neumann's design of the architecture of the electronic digital computer with parts consisting of a processing unit, and mass storage unit and input and output mechanisms. This system contained all the elements necessary to describe a basic information processing system as implemented in cognitively oriented models.

Another area of research becoming an essential element of cognitive psychology from the 1950s onwards was the information processing approach. The main focus of information processing theories in psychology concerned isolating information processing stages that reflected successive transformations of information, flowing from stimulus to a motor response. Its principal initiators were Broadbent (1958), Sternberg (1969) and Atkinson and Shiffrin (1968). Sternberg's approach focused primarily on the analysis of choice reaction task measures, with no direct reference to the brain. The statistical relationship between task variables affecting performance, in fact, served as the primary tool to isolate stages as independent ('additive') factors. Information processing paradigms, typically accompanied by diagrams of 'arrows and boxes' stimulated a renewed interest in mental chronometry, as initially conceived by the Dutch optical physiologist Donders (1869). This held in particular for the timing of processes, like early and late selection in selective attention tasks, and processes like stimulus evaluation, decision and memory search and response preparation in choice reaction and memory search tasks (Sternberg, 1969; Sanders, 1983; Shiffrin & Schneider, 1977).

Cognitive neuroscience

At the end of the 20th century cognitive experimental psychologists started using a new version of the choice reaction task called 'conflict' task, supplemented with physiological measures like the electromyogram (muscle activity) of the involved lower arm, and the Lateralized Readiness Potential (LRP; an electrophysiological scalp-recorded measure of the brain reflecting motor preparation). In the conflict paradigm the target (for example a central arrow or bracket sign) is flanked by non-target stimuli which correspond either with the same directional response as the target (congruent flankers, e. g. > > > > >), or with the opposite response (incongruent flankers < < > < <), or with neither (neutral flankers, e.g. x x > x x) (Eriksen & Eriksen, 1974). Incongruent targets typically elicited longer Rts than neutral or congruent trials. Physiological results obtained with the paradigm provided additional insights into the serial versus parallel nature of information processes. Incongruent stimulus elicited 'incorrect' muscle and motor activity of the brain, before the occurrence of the overt correct button press response. The combined use of behavioral and psychophysiological measures thus suggested a parallel activation of stimulus and response related information channels.

Another area in which behavioral and electrical recordings of brain activity contributed to elucidating the neural mechanism underlying mental processes was that of selective human attention. The studies were particularly useful because they revealed an essential function of human spatial attention in increasing the 'sensory gain' of perceptual processes in a relatively early phase of the processing sequence. This effect became apparent in the enhancement of early scalp-recorded brain potentials (P1, N1), elicited by visual stimuli presented at attended relative to unattended locations of the subject's visual field (Mangun & Hillyard, 1995; Desimone & Duncan, 1995).[2]

These studies foreboded the birth of cognitive neuroscience, a discipline which took the characteristics of the brain into account when describing the characteristics of the human mind. One might say that opening the black box of behaviorism not only brought back the mind but also revealed the organ that produced the mind: the human brain. Unlike the mind, the brain and its networks are physical substances obeying the same physical laws as other physical substances (see Figure 1.1 lower panel). Mental processes could now be described concurrently at both the mental and neural levels, with the human brain serving as the 'organ' or biological hardware, in which the mental software was implemented.

In addition to electrophysiological measures, a new and powerful tool, functional imaging (fMRI) of the blood flow within the brain, allowed to further explore the spatial characteristics of large-scale networks, activated during performance of a cognitive task (see Gazzaniga et al., 2002 for an early overview). Cognitive researchers gradually became more inclined to consider neural constraints in the modeling of mental processes, i.e. the limiting conditions imposed by the central nervous system as the neural substrate of the human mind. This research included animal studies focusing on neural processes at the micro level, using micro-electrodes to probe action and synaptic potentials reflecting the transmission of information in the brain. At the macro level, cognitive activity as regulated by larger functional units and networks in the brain now also became an essential element in the theorizing of cognitive psychologists.

Cognitive neuroscience triangle

For many years cognitive psychology had successfully examined human behavior using computer modeling and refined cognitive task paradigms, leading to new insights into the structure of the human mind, without any thought of the brain. Similarly, in the domain of neuroscience animal studies had yielded significant new findings relating to brain structures and mechanisms with no direct reference to cognitive processes and theories. Neurophilosopher Patricia Churchland was one of the first who advocated a 'co-evolutionary' research ideology. Neuroscience needs psychology to know 'what the brain does', and to better understand the specific nature of its processes. In turn, psychology also needs neuroscience to understand 'what the system does'. Cognitive research will thus profit most from research that considers all these factors together. A similar view was expressed by Kosslyn and Koenig (1992), who schematized the central mission of cognitive neuroscience as a triangle (see Figure 1.2), with the corners representing respectively behavior, computations and the brain.

Behavior

The top of the triangle is formed by behavior, which also includes its underlying covert cognitive functions (in short: cognition). As clarified in the preceding paragraphs, studies of human behavior had a long tradition with behaviorism restricted to overt behavior, and cognitive psychology focusing on the human mind and its inner workings.

THE BIRTH OF COGNITIVE NEUROSCIENCE

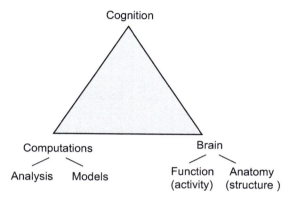

FIGURE 1.2
The triangle of cognitive neuroscience. Insights into the functional architecture of cognition are derived concurrently from computational analyses and models, and the analysis of neural substrates and connections of the brain.
Source: Adapted from Kosslyn & Koenig (1992).

This gradually led to the development of methods and models to examine the possible structures and computational processes underlying cognition.

Computations

Computations (literally: calculations) relate to the processing structures that take place between input and output, that might or might not relate to brain structures. Some examples follow here.

A first example is the attempt of early experimental psychologists to isolate primary components of information processing, with no reference to the brain. Studies of serial processing stages (Sternberg, 1969), components of selective attention (Posner & Cohen, 1984), mental-rotation (Shepard & Cooper, 1982) and memory search (Shiffrin & Schneider, 1977) serve to illustrate this critical epoch in experimental psychology. In contrast with the notion of serial processing derived from these studies, other researchers, for instance McClelland (McClelland & Rumelhart, 1988) developed models that emphasized the parallel (simultaneous) organization of processing components.

Later, Posner and Raichle (1994) were able to link three crucial stages of visual attention to a posterior attention network in the brain. In their view attention operated like a 'mental spotlight' with three subcomponents: 'disengage', 'move' and 'engage'. Studies of patients with specific brain lesions made it possible to localize these three components in three specific areas of the posterior attention network (see also Figure 1.3).

Computer simulations are a second example of a way to explore the fictional properties of mind and brain. In the language of computers, computations are described as

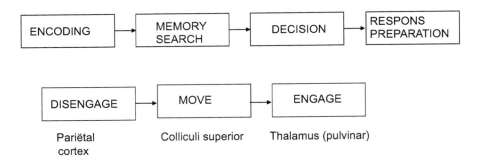

FIGURE 1.3
Two models of information processing stages based on specific processing components developed in the early years of cognitive science. Top: Sternberg's stage model based on analysis of reaction times. Bottom: Posner's components model of the posterior attention system.

algorithms: systematic and explicit steps, used in a computer program to solve specific problems or to simulate specific activities within a complex system. A more recent spin-off of computer models is artificial intelligence (AI) networks, resting on the idea that intelligent behavior arises by combining simple operations that can be programmed on a computer. AI proved to be highly useful in the design of intelligent machines or 'robots'. However, they could also serve to build models of biological information processing networks that mimic neural processes, like recognition of photographs of actual human faces. These artificial neural networks should not be confused with real networks of the brain, with neurons that use synaptic potentials and neurotransmitters to communicate within larger functional networks. Nevertheless, some of these more cognitively inspired computer models have proven useful to assist cognitive neuroscientists. They may, for example, be helpful to unravel what the brain 'does', and to verify to what extent a machine like a brain could generate cognitive processes as conceptualized in more formal computing models.

Brain

The brain is a dynamical system of enormous complexity, which is estimated to have around 10^{12} neurons and 10^{15} synapses, with a time scale of neuronal events in the millisecond range. The brain is also considered to be the causal machine of overt human behavior, as well as the covert processes that together constitute our 'mind'. As will be elaborated in the following chapters, the interest of cognitive neuroscientists in the brain concerned not so much its microstructures, but rather the larger functional aggregates of neurons and their connections. Large-scale functional networks are composed of smaller entities, called 'nodes' or 'hubs', corresponding with local clusters of nerve cells that in turn are connected to other local clusters. Large-scale distributed networks are not restricted to regions in the neocortex, but also include structures in the limbic system and brain stem, with important nuclei clustering in the hippocampus and basal ganglia. In summary: computational analysis and computer modeling are not just refined tools to analyze or simulate elements of cognitive systems, but also serve to explore how these elements function in networks of the brain as the machinery that produces cognition.

The mind-brain

Mental processes are the product of the brain: 'the mind is what the brain does'. Rather than conceiving mind and brain as separate entities as in dualism, the 'mind-brain' conceptualization considers them as two aspects of the same thing, or two points on a continuum (Llinás & Churchland, 1996). It is like the color of an object that can be described in physical terms as the spectral composition of light, or in physiological terms as activation of color-specific areas in the retina and visual cortex by a bright stimulus. This dual-aspect theory does not follow the reductionist's account that in due time brain concepts might replace mind concepts, and make references to mental phenomena as separate entities superfluous. The following paragraphs focus in more detail on models and basis research strategies used to unravel the complex relationship between cognition and the human brain.

A simple neurocognitive model

Figure 1.4 depicts a simple hierarchical model illustrating how the relationship between mind and brain can be conceptualized at different levels of the system. The model represents in a compact and eclectic way the views expressed in various introductory handbooks of cognitive neuroscience. It does nevertheless raise philosophical questions about the direct way it addresses the long-debated mind-brain relationship.[3]

Some neuroscientists do indeed believe that brain-scans will reveal the ultimate truth about the structure and mechanisms of the mind. However, others have argued that by relying merely on functional imaging of the brain, neuroscience might slip back into a new phrenology (Uttal, 2001). Indeed, the view shared by most cognitive neuroscientists is that insights from cognitive psychology will remain crucial to understand what the brain does in a computational sense, and to frame appropriate research questions. Cognitive theories will thus remain useful in the construction of cognitive tasks, specifically designed to engage the brains networks and to clarify their role in functions like memory, attention and consciousness.[4] However, as will be pursued in the paragraphs that follow, the first requisite is to trace down the more primary components of the cognitive system that are specific enough to be operationally defined in the context of these

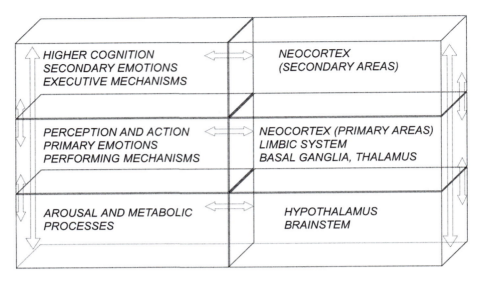

FIGURE 1.4
Simplified model of the 'mind-brain' with higher-order and lower-order levels connected via reciprocal vertical pathways (vertical arrows). Horizontal arrows illustrate the connections between mind and brain at each level of the hierarchy. Higher mental processes are assumed to depend on neural structures at the highest level of the neocortex, as well as structures at the lower levels, such as the limbic system and even the brainstem.

experimental paradigms. This approach necessarily implies some form of reduction of more complex functions. A second assumption of the mind-brain model is that mind and brain share the same hierarchical architecture, with various levels communicating via reciprocal vertical connections. For example, arousal mechanisms at lower 'drive' levels play an important role in the modulation of higher mental processes such as consciousness and attention (the left column in Figure 1.4). In turn, higher 'executive' processes can modulate processes like perception and motor skills at lower levels. The neural system (depicted in the right column of Figure 1.4) displays a similar hierarchical organization with the neocortex, limbic system and brainstem at different and reciprocally connected levels. Finally, the horizontal arrows are the most crucial element in the model, suggesting a close connection between mental and neural levels. Using the computer metaphor, we might say that the mental processes are 'implemented' in the neural structures at the same level of organization.

This principle works in two directions. Processes like memory, attention and consciousness are primarily dependent on neural structures at the highest level. However, due to the vertical organization principle, the same functions also depend on structures at the lower levels such as the limbic system and the brainstem. Consciousness, for example, can be described as 'capacity for self-reflection', a function that we tend to locate in the higher association areas in the brain. But it is also the ability to focus

THE BIRTH OF COGNITIVE NEUROSCIENCE

BOX 1.1 DESCARTES: DUALIST AND GENIUS

Descartes (1596–1650), the most famous representative of dualism, saw the mind as a non-physical entity, and thus believed that its functions proceeded independently of the brain. Descartes' significance is his insight that mind and body should interact somewhere in the human brain, and he even invented in his imagination the location were this should take place. The most likely candidate was a small organ, the pineal gland located just behind the optic chiasm of the visual system (see insert). 'It is rather the innermost part of the brain, which is a certain very small gland situated in the middle of the brain's substance and suspended above the passage through which the spirits in the brain's anterior cavities communicate with those in its posterior cavities'.*

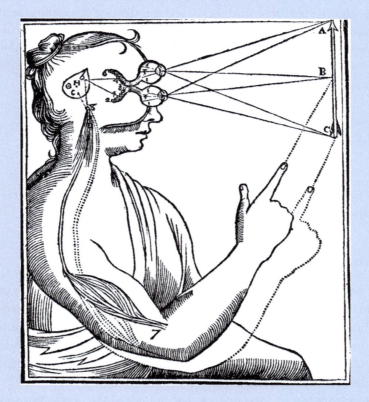

Visual impressions entered the pineal gland via small openings ('pores') where they released 'animal spirits' stored in empty spaces, which subsequently activated the muscles via tubes. The pineal gland produced conscious experiences and guided voluntary movements, such as pointing at objects in the visual environment

continued

> that attracted our attention. By claiming the pineal gland as a central organ of coordination, Descartes produced a crude prototype of modern 'homuncular' theories, assuming that some area or network in the brain (presumably the prefrontal cortex) would be the locus of executive functions involved in conscious control. The core of Descartes' argument of an independent immaterial mind was later revived in theories of cognitivists like Chomsky and Fodor, convicted that knowledge of the brain would not be of great help to unravel the complexity of the mind, in particular the use and production of language (Smith Churchland, 2002; Pinker, 1997).
>
> By creating a sharp conceptual boundary between the immaterial soul and a physical body, including the brain, Descartes spared the Christian dogma of the immortality and irreducibility of the human soul. Critics of Descartes may have not fully realized that this also paved the way for a scientific study of the human brain, and its associated mental functions. It is sometimes speculated that if Descartes had lived in the age of computers, and had not experienced the moral coercion of the Church, his theory would have had a less dualistic character with a more materially based mind.
>
> * René Descartes (1662). *Le Traité de l'Homme*. Florens Schuyl, Leiden.

attention or mental alertness, functions that have been shown to depend on structures at lower levels of the brain like the thalamus and brainstem, respectively.

Decomposing the mind-brain

The human brain has evolved from more simple forms of life in a mllion years of evolution, during which old and new neural systems gradually started to work together. Examining how the mind has gradually developed from these more primitive nervous systems is one way to unravel the complex structure of the human mind (Plotkin, 1997). The ultimate goal of this exercise is to obtain a better understanding of the interaction between body and mind. Churchland and Sejnowski (1992) called this a 'reductive integration' of psychology and neurobiology. Reduction relates to the process which gradually transforms psychological concepts so that they become compatible with principles derived from neurobiology. Cognition as a global theoretical concept thus needs to be decomposed into scientifically tractable subdomains that are 'specific enough to be operationally defined in the context of an experimental paradigm and which can be tied to specific measures of cognitive and neural function' (Spunt & Adolphs, 2017).

A preliminary question might be: does the mind have a structure? Our intuition would probably tell us no, because everyday experience teaches us that the mind functions as a unit without boundaries that separate processes. Riding a bicycle in Amsterdam, for example, requires that I move my legs and pay close attention to the traffic while I navigate through the maze of narrow streets. Nevertheless, I have no awareness that I am using certain motor, perceptual or memory functions. The seamless quality of everyday experience does tell us something important, namely that different parts of our mind work together in unison. And because my experiences are causally linked to my brain, dedicated areas in the brain must also work in synchrony with the flow of perceptual, memory and motor processes. Taken from this perspective, mental structures are like brain structures: they relate to different components at the structural levels or separate divisions of the brain, but functionally they are closely tied together.

BOX 1.2 REDUCTIONISM OR REDUCTION?

Critics of reductionism have argued that the human mind is too complex and too varied to be reduced to a number of basic biological mechanisms. Neurophilosopher Patricia Churchland (1986), however, argued that instead of using reductionism (which as an 'ism' evokes a negative association like materialism or capitalism), the term 'reduction' might be more suitable to describe the mission of cognitive neuroscience. My former professor in Experimental Psychology at the University of Leiden, John van de Geer spoke of 'ontologizing of methodological questions'. Studying the behavior of rats or pigeons (like many psychologists did in those days) does not imply that we consider man equal to rat or pigeon. Animal research was (and still is) a valuable tool to gain insight into basic mechanisms underlying learning, selective attention and emotions that humans share with animals. Reduction is, in fact, a basic principle in science, as it should be in psychology or psychiatry. For example, there are solid arguments for reducing (or rather: conceptualizing) a complex phenomenon like attention to a selection mechanism or 'filter' that passes or enhances relevant information and blocks irrelevant information. Potential defects of this filter mechanism may very well underlie certain behavioral disorders such as schizophrenia or hyperactivity, as a result of which impressions permanently flood the brain from the outside world. In this hypothetical case, the complex theory of 'attention' is reduced to a simpler psychological theory 'filtering mechanism'.

Interestingly, there is evidence to suggest that such a mechanism possibly exists in the brain. The thalamus behaves like a selective filter and forms a crucial element of attention in its more complex manifestations (LaBerge, 1995). The advantage is that one can now examine the same mechanism from a broader and more unified theoretical perspective, encompassing psychology as well as neurobiology.

Communication dynamics of large-scale networks in the brain provide the basis for the interactions between these subdomains of cognition.

These examples suggest that natural complex behavior and its underlying subjectively experienced processes are not the ideal starting point for scientists interested in unraveling the human mind and its neural underpinnings. They must first attempt to 'dissect' this behavior in more specific functions. Neurophysiologist Arbib formulated the two steps of the dissection process, namely structural decomposition (isolating brain structures) followed by functional decomposition (isolating related subprocesses). The keyword here to integrate these isolated functions is *connectivity*, i.e. networks of physical connections between large numbers of neuronal elements. At the structural level, connectivity reflects the anatomical relationship between neural elements; that is, their synaptic connections or inter-regional projections. They provide their basic 'skeleton' or 'wiring diagram'. Functional connectivity, by contrast, describes the temporal coherence, often expressed in a set of pair-wise statistical dependencies between the time-courses of neurophysiologic signals, recorded from individual neural elements.

Figure 1.5 schematically presents the organization of cognition and brain. The cognitive domain is dissected into some global functions, which in turn contain smaller units – the local functions and underlying mechanisms. Notice that these local functions are postulated to exist within global functions that were already widely accepted as being structurally different from another. The same principle holds for the brain's architecture that follows a similar hierarchical stratification, running from the brain to large-scale networks, to local networks.[5] Similar to the mind-brain model presented earlier, Figure 1.5 depicts a parallel organization of the two domains and their respective subcomponents. It implies a functional relationship between various levels: the brain with cognition, large-scale networks with global functions, and local networks with local functions. For example, perception, memory and motor systems correspond to three global networks of the brain. However, at more specific levels, the neural elements of these networks receive their specific functional status. For example, if global network 1 represents the visual cortex, it can be structurally dissected into three local networks subserving perception of color, form and movement respectively. When we now follow a moving colored ball with our eyes, these three local functions of visual perception become implemented in their respective local networks in the visual cortex.

The global-local debate

The struggle between localized and distributed accounts of how cognitive functions are represented in the brain has persisted in the history of cognitive neuroscience for at least 200 years. It started with Franz Joseph Galls' phrenology (Gall & Spurzheim, 1810–1819) and found its current 'niche' in functional imaging of the brain. The debate is dominated by the question of to what extent cognitive functions are global (or neurally distributed) or specific (or neurally localized).

THE BIRTH OF COGNITIVE NEUROSCIENCE

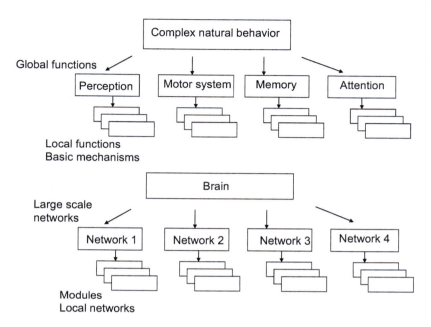

FIGURE 1.5
Schematic view of the parallel organization of complex natural behavior in global and local functions, and the brain in large-scale and local networks. Global functions are supposed to correspond to global (large-scale) networks, and local functions to local (or modular) networks.

Lashley and Penfield

One of the early proponents of the global position was Karl Lashley (1929), whose work has been crucial for scientific research into the neural basis of memory: the search for the 'engram'. An engram is a memory trace or impression from a specific event or perceived image in the brain, like a footstep that leaves a print in the snow. Lashley found that if rats learned to solve a particular problem in a maze, their learning performance (the number of attempts needed to learn a route in the maze) depended proportionally on the size of the experimentally applied cortical lesion, rather than the specific location of the lesion in the brain. One may now argue that solving a maze problem depends on many separate but functionally related local neural events that occupy a relatively large area in the brain. Lashley also formulated two related principles based on his experiments; mass action: the brain functions as an integrated whole, and equipotentiality: different areas in the brain have identical functions. He was right concerning the first, but wrong concerning the second principle.

Lashley's 'global' theory has often been contrasted with that of another pioneer, the neurologist Penfield (Penfield & Jasper, 1954; Penfield & Perot, 1963). Penfield used electrical stimulation of the temporal lobe of epileptic patients under surgery and local anesthesia, which to his surprise elicited particular memory associations, like faces of known persons or images from the environment. These findings suggested that impressions were stored at very specific locations in the temporal lobe, just like sounds or images are stored on specific sections of an audio or video recorder. However, later studies led to a different interpretation of these early findings.

Hebb's theory of the reverberating circuits (Hebb, 1949), published in the late forties, meant a big step forward in the theory of the neural basis of memory. According to Hebb the mental image of a visual object like a triangle will be stored in a neuroelectrical network of brain cells, called a 'reverberating circuit', distributed over a relatively large area in the brain (Figure 1.6). With repeated presentation, the triangle will gradually become consolidated in the memory system, by strengthening the synapses that connect more distributed nerve cells and local networks. This principle became known as 'Hebb's rule': the strength of synaptic connections between two nerve cells a and b will gradually increase by repeated and concurrent activation of the postsynaptic membrane of cell a and the presynaptic membrane of cell b.

After the consolidation of its connections, stimulation of a single cell in a network might then suffice to 'ignite' the entire network. Hebb's theory of the reverberating

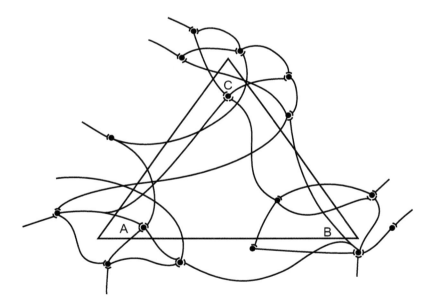

FIGURE 1.6
Example of a 'Hebbian' network. When looking at the individual angles (A, B and C) of the triangle, the synaptic connections of neurons (or local networks of neurons) associated with each of the angles are strengthened. Later, the three corners (and their local networks) will form connections in a distributed network, which corresponds to a more abstract spatial representation of the triangle as a whole.
Source: Adapted from Posner & Raichle (1994).

circuits also opened a way to reconcile the local and global position. For example, the principle of distributed storage could also explain the phenomenon of specific memory representations as described by Penfield. Stimulation of a specific area in the temporal cortex of his patients would not remain restricted to that area, but automatically extend to a much larger network in the temporal cortex

Hebb's theory had a great impact on modern theories on how the brain stores information during explicit or implicit learning (further pursued in Chapter 6). Empirical support and concurrent stronger neural underpinning of his theory were later found in the discovery of long-term potentiation (Bliss & Lømo, 1973, see Chapter 6), demonstrating that learning in experimental animals corresponds with neurochemical modifications in the synapses in the hippocampus of the brain.

Domain specificity and more

Decomposition of the cognitive domain not only holds for global functions that we already knew are separate, and which even constitute separate chapters in introductory handbooks of cognitive psychology. It also holds for smaller structures within these functions. Evidence supporting this functional parcellation came (among others) from studies of brain-damaged patients showing that a highly localized lesion might damage a part of a function, but not eliminate the complete function. The unraveling process also implied that the mind and its components were no longer seen as something mystical, but rather as the product of algorithms referred to earlier. Algorithms are formal operations carried out on syntactically structured representations, i.e. structures that contain information in a symbolic form.

A related and increasingly important concept that emerged in cognitive as well as neural science became *domain specificity*, implying that some aspects of information processing are specialized for particular types of stimuli or a particular type of information (e. g. color, shape, pitch, or perhaps even human faces, e.g. Kanwisher, 2000). Domain-specific structures are often seen as the opposite of central systems like memory, executive functions and attention, that are thought to be domain non-specific.

Cognitivism played an essential role in the unraveling of subcomponents of cognition and the underlying mechanisms, but did so without any thought of or consideration for the brain. Cognitive scientist Jerry Fodor (Fodor, 1985, 2000; Coltheart 1999) initially introduced the concept of domain specificity and its structural processing components, called modules. Domain specificity has since his seminal work been invoked to explain a range of cognitive phenomena, and has been a hallmark of theories of cognitive as well as neural architecture. In Fodor's view modules depended on two principles: informational encapsulation (the modules received restricted information from other modules) and cognitive impenetrability (the modules could not be influenced by top-down cognition). However, in contrast with the view that domain-specificity only concerns peripheral modules that serve to provide inputs to a domain-general central system, more recent theories now accept the view that domain specificity also applies to modular components involved in more central coordinating activities. Thus, a milder 'new look' replaced Fodor's more rigid conceptualization of modules (Shallice, 1984; Spunt & Adolphs, 2017). According to this view, separate modules (and their neural counterparts) could also be functionally related. Importantly, their specific quality could even be 'multifunctional', and recruited in functionally different networks, like letters in a crossword puzzle.

Connectivity and the local-global controversy

Both cognitivism and neuroscience became dominated by theoretical models of neural architectures known as connectionist networks.[6] Network theories, in particular, have been successful in bridging the gap between local and global theories of brain functioning, by emphasizing connectivity rather than isolated areas in the brain. Connectivity relates to the numerous white-matter tracts that allow transmission of neural information between cortical areas. By contrast to modules that show a strong local connectivity and clustering, large-scale networks connect localized cortical regions over relatively long distances. A simple example is a road map of a country where various routes and highways connect larger cities and smaller villages via dense local connections (van den Heuvel, 2009). Cognitive neuroscience research had so far focused on identifying the function of separate brain regions. Recent advances though, have led to thinking about the brain consisting of interacting sub-networks that can be identified by examining connections across the whole brain.

Brain activity is local as well as global, and the keyword that integrates these two principles is distributed processing. Local specialized processes and their respective local networks – or modules – are the building stones of large-scale networks. By addressing how connectivity mediates both segregation and integration, network approaches not only reconciled these seemingly opposing perspectives; they also suggested that their coexistence is fundamental for brain function (Sporns, 2014).

In summary, complex functions when unraveled may, in fact, reveal a pattern of local networks that are spread out over large areas of the brain. Dividing the mind and brain into distinct structures with distinct functions raises the question of which part of the mind (or brain) brings all the parts together. Such a supervisory coordinating system should be ideally located in the center of networks connecting more discrete areas receiving input from many sub-areas.

Methods in cognitive brain research

A number of brain-oriented research techniques have proven to be particularly suitable for application in human cognitive research. They included the EEG (electroencephalogram), the ERP (event-related potential), MRI (magnetic resonance imaging), functional MRI (fMRI) and studies of brain lesions in neurological patients. A relatively new avenue of research called functional connectivity imaging (fcMRI) emerged, committed to examining the brain's connectivity architecture and how the different regions in the brain communicate with one another. Cognitive neuroscience has also profited from computer modeling of neural networks and methods that aimed at describing complex processes at the computational level, and validating assumptions derived from empirical methods like functional imaging. A brief overview of these methods follows.

Event-related potentials (ERPs)

ERPs represent the electric activity of the brain that is recorded from the scalp and triggered by specific events like stimuli or movements. ERPs are often averaged over a series of trials, and assumed to reflect electrical potentials originating from sources directly under the scalp, or 'smeared out' potentials from more distant sources that are simultaneously active.

ERPs have been a valuable tool used by clinicians as well as cognitive researchers, because they reflect brain activity that provides a window into perceptual, cognitive and motor processes during performance of a cognitive task (Kutas & Hillyard, 1980; Donchin, 1981; Hillyard et al., 1995; Polich & Kok, 1995; Kok, 2001, see also Handy, 2004). Early components in the time range 0–150 ms are taken to reflect 'exogenous' factors, i.e. sources that are primarily related to sensory processing. Longer latency potentials are seen as reflecting 'endogenous' sources, i.e. processes related to the variation of the state of a subject depending on the demands of a cognitive task. Their high temporal resolution made them especially useful to examine processes taking place in the millisecond range.

BOX 1.3   CAN P300 READ OUR MIND?

An ERP component perhaps attracting most attention from researchers since its discovery by Samuel Sutton (Sutton et al., 1965), is the P300 (or P3) component. P300 is a positive peak in the electrical activity of the brain, occurring at about 300 milliseconds after the presentation of the stimulus. P300 appears to be sensitive (amongst other things) to the familiarity of certain events, for example, when a picture of a familiar object is inserted randomly in a series of pictures of unfamiliar objects. The familiar object will then 'match' with a representation in the corresponding long-term memory (LTM) that generates

continued

P300. One might say that P300 'reads the mind', since it is sensitive to the activated content of LTM, and thus able to reveal specific hidden knowledge. This aspect of P300 has been used by Larry Farwell (2012) to develop a clever lie detection procedure based on the principle of guilty knowledge.* Suppose a thief steals an amount of 1200 Euro, and during interrogation is asked to watch a sequence of slides showing pictures of all sorts of amounts: 500, 1000, 1200, 300 Euro. It is then likely that P300 shows up in his brain recordings, when the thief sees the 'guilty' amount of 1200 Euro. Farwell spoke of 'brain fingerprinting': P300 acts as a thumbprint of the brain, because it is capable of detecting specific hidden knowledge stored in the brain of the subject's memory system.

*For a more recent and general overview of concealed knowledge methods, see Rosenfeld J.P. (Ed.) 2018. *Detecting concealed information and deception: recent developments.* London: Academic Press.

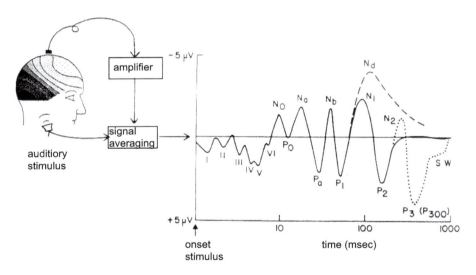

FIGURE 1.7
Idealized representation of an average ERP, elicited by acoustic stimuli. Very early or 'exogenous' auditory components (indicated by Roman numerals) represent 'brain-stem' potentials originating from the afferent auditory neural pathways. The following components P1, N1, P2, N2 and P3 arise in the cortex, referred to as 'endogenous' components since they are particularly sensitive to the demands of the cognitive task.
Source: From: Hillyard (1993).

The electrical fields that generate these potentials presumably behave as 'equivalent dipoles'. For example, an equivalent dipole could reflect the summated activity of a bundle of pyramidal cells that exhibit a similar vertical orientation to the skull. They might also form the geometric center or 'center of gravity' of a relatively large electrical field or network in the brain. In an attempt to localize the source of scalp-recorded potentials, ERP researchers are confronted with the inverse problem: the source must be computed backward from the scalp recording to the brain's deeper layers that generate these potentials.

A mathematical technique called spatial-temporal dipole modeling has been applied with relative success to determine areas in the brain that might be critical for generating these potential fields (Scherg & von Cramon, 1985, but see also Handy, 2004, for a more extensive overview). Another drawback in the interpretation of ERPs derived from averaged stimulus-locked waveforms is that of variability of the latency ('jitter') of individual waveforms across trials. Latency jitter smears, or blurs, averaged ERPs and – depending on the experimental condition – can obscure or mimic amplitude differences. Mathemathical techniques can be used to correct for the variability of the single-trial latencies (Ouyang et al., 2016).

Related to the EEG is the magnetoencephalography or MEG. MEG represents magnetic fields perpendicular to electrical currents. These fields are generated by the apical dendrites of pyramidal neurons in the sulci of the brain, running parallel to the scalp. An advantage of MEG is that the magnetic fields are not distorted by tissues between the source and the scalp. A drawback is that magnetic fields are very weak, requiring superconducting quantum interference devices (SQUIDS) to detect the fields. MEG signals evoked by stimuli can be averaged over a series of trials as with ERPs, in which case they are called event-related related fields (ERFs).

Imaging the structure and function of the brain (MRI, fMRI)

New non-invasive methods allowed gaining more insight into functions of the brain using in vivo mapping of its activity. They included MRI (magnetic resonance imaging) and fMRI (functional magnetic imaging). MRI provides a structural 3D map of neurons (grey matter) and their connections (white matter). It is based on measuring magnetic properties of hydrogen nuclei in brain tissue, and its acquisition usually follows three separate steps. First, initially randomly organized hydrogen molecules (or: protons) are aligned by applying a strong magnetic field. Second, by applying a brief radio signal the molecules start to rotate or spin to a new position (called precess) and subsequently return to their original position (called relax). The relaxation process will then produce a weak magnetic signal that is picked up by the scanner (in so-called T1-weighted images).

By applying different radio signals, neural tissue can be characterized by two different relaxation times – T1 and T2. T1 (longitudinal relaxation time) is the time constant which determines the rate at which excited protons return to equilibrium. It is a measure of the time taken for spinning protons to realign with the external magnetic field. T2 (transverse relaxation time) is the time constant which determines the rate at which excited protons reach equilibrium or go out of phase with each other. It is a measure of the time taken for spinning protons to lose phase coherence among the nuclei spinning perpendicular to the main field.

fMRI, or functional imaging, is derived from the same machine that extracts MRI images, but provides a more dynamic picture of the brain in an active state. It is based on hemodynamics, which are local changes in cerebral blood flow in the arteries of the brain. Hemoglobin is a substance of the blood that absorbs oxygen. When oxygen is absorbed it becomes deoxygenated, which is more sensitive or paramagnetic than oxygenated blood. When brain regions become activated, more blood will flow in these areas, which changes the ratio between oxygenated and deoxygenated blood. This process, called the BOLD (Blood Oxygenation Level Dependent) effect, is subsequently picked up by the detectors in the MRI machine and displayed as T2-weighted images in the period when the MRI signal is decaying. In the brain's resting state BOLD fMRI time series typically show low-frequency oscillations of around 0. 01–0.1 Hz (Cordes 2005), of which the specific origin remains unknown (e.g. Heeger & Ress, 2002). Modern application of fMRI allows to time-lock the BOLD signals to specific single events, like with ERPs, and then average the signals over repetitions of a number of these events. Another advantage is that experimental (task related) and control trials can be presented randomly, thus minimizing the confound with variation in attentional and arousal states that may occur in blocked presentations.

Lesion studies

Neuropsychology is a field of psychology that examines deficits in cognitive functions in brain-damaged patients by using cognitive tests or experimental approaches. Numerous neuropsychological studies have been performed on patients who had suffered brain damage as a result of an accident, a brain hemorrhage or a brain tumor. Anatomical measures of brain structures (MRI) are often used to determine with greater precision the regions of the brain that could have caused the behavioral deficit.

Neuropsychological findings have proven to be one of the most informative sources of areas in the brain that, when damaged, affect functions like attention, memory and language. An essential tool in neuropsychological research into the consequences of brain damage for behavior is the *double dissociation* between performances in cognitive tests. For example, damage in the left frontal area (called the Broca area) was often found to lead to impairments in speech (motor aphasia) but not to disturbances in the understanding of language (see Figure 1.8). In another group of patients with damage in the left posterior area (called the Wernicke area), the same language test will show the opposite pattern: an almost intact performance in the speech test, but a poor performance in the test for language comprehension (sensory aphasia). With double dissociation, the researcher has stronger proof that specific areas in the brain correspond with specific task components than with single dissociation.

Transcranial magnetic stimulation (TMS) is a relatively recent device in the toolbox of cognitive neuroscience that fits in the tradition of neuropsychology, with its emphasis on the damaging effects of traumatic lesions of cognitive functioning. TMS is called a 'virtual lesion' method: it uses a magnetic coil which emits a very brief but powerful magnetic pulse that is relatively safe for patient or subject (Pascual-Leone et al., 1994; Siebner, 2000).

When the pulse is applied to a critical region, it will temporarily disrupt ongoing or externally evoked neural activity. For example, when applied to regions critical for speech production it could lead to a momentary arrest of speech.

Different types of TMS (single-pulse, paired-pulse, repetitive) will interfere with higher brain functions that depend on neuronal networks close to the skull. Behavioral TMS effects on the brain are usually short-lived, and their underlying mechanisms are not yet wholly understood (Rossini & Rossi, 2007). For example, single-pulse TMS might affect ongoing (task-relevant) neuronal activity by initially synchronizing the action potentials of many neurons, followed by long-lasting inhibition (Siebner, 2009). If TMS

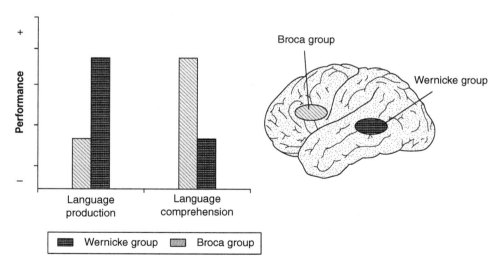

FIGURE 1.8
Hypothetical example of double dissociation. The Wernicke group (Wernicke area damaged) scores low in language comprehension, but standard in language production. The Broca group (Broca area damaged) shows the reversed image.

THE BIRTH OF COGNITIVE NEUROSCIENCE

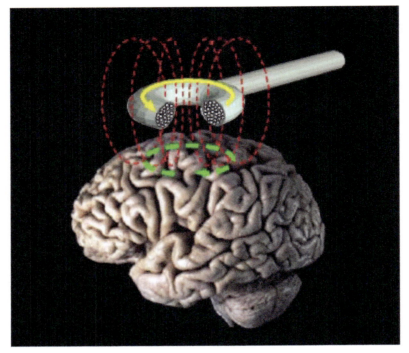

FIGURE 1.9
A magnetic coil placed close to the skull emits a pulse that activates a neighboring area in the cortex below the skull, such as the motor or visual area. Although the scope of TMS is limited, it may be a useful contribution to probe processes that depend on structures close to the skull.
Source: Public Domain, NIH.

alters a cognitive task performance, it could be taken as a sign that the stimulated brain region is causally involved in that task (Zieman, 2010).

Neural network modeling

There remains a gap separating models of the brain as a computational machine and computational models of neuronal dynamics per se, such as models of brain function and biophysics (Friston & Dolan, 2010). The term 'neural network' suggests that such networks depend on properties of the brain. Neural networks, though, are often software applications that are used to simulate the behavior of artificial or real biological neural networks. Their goal might be to simulate mental processes like reading or writing, learning, or recognizing objects, which are subsequently implemented in machines performing basic tasks like face or voice recognition or reading. Unlike the stages that characterize symbolic information processing models, much more

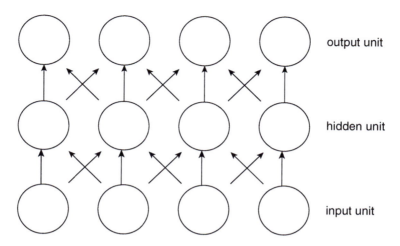

FIGURE 1.10
Example of a simple three-layer neural network, an input device, a hidden unit and an output unit. This network model only contains 'forward' connections. Other models also use 'recurring' or 'feedback' connections.

emphasis is placed on parallel processing, which explains their being labeled originally as parallel distributed processing (PDP) systems. In PDP systems the flow of information depends on layers of connections between elementary and identical units that together serve to simulate functions without any reference to theories of mental functioning.

Modern sequels of PDP systems are artificial intelligence (AI) and artificial neural networks (ANNs), some of which possibly are vaguely inspired by biological neural networks. AI systems can learn (that is: progressively improve performance on) tasks by using real-life examples, generally without task-specific programming. For example, in image recognition, they learn to identify images that contain cats by analyzing example images that have been manually labeled as 'cat' or 'no cat' and using the results to identify cats in other images. They do this without any a priori knowledge about cats – that they have fur, tails, whiskers and cat-like faces, for instance. Instead, they evolve their own set of relevant characteristics from the learning material they process.

Brain connectivity studies

The study of connectivity, that is to say the structural and functional connections between networks of the brain, is essential for understanding how the brain works as an integrated whole. Connectivity appears in three guises: a structural, functional and effective one. Structural connectivity concerns mapping of connection paths (white matter), while functional connectivity concerns the statistical relationship between time series of neuronal activity of different elements of the brain. Effective connectivity denotes the directional or causal relationship between these elements. I will briefly discuss each of these methods next.

Structural connectivity

The short and long connection paths (white matter) in the brain can be mapped using an MRI–based technique called tractography. Tractography is a modeling technique used to extract the fiber tracks in the brain from diffusion-weighted imaging (DWI). DWI is sensitive to the diffusion of water molecules in the brain (Mori, 2007). DWI represents the raw data (diffusion maps in a bunch of different directions). When used to calculate tensors (matrices that summarize the diffusion pattern in each voxel), tractography allows to infer the presence of white matter fibers. The resulting tractogram, or diffusion tensor images (DTI), presents a 3D image of long connections of nerve fibers – the white matter trajectories – as well as the more complex short connections between different structural and subcortical areas. In neural systems that communicate via electrochemical transmission, minimizing the number of synapses between any two neuronal elements (that is, their path length) is intuitively more efficient. Longer paths are more susceptible to noise, are more likely to involve a greater number of distinct processing steps, incur longer transmission delays and are energetically (metabolically) more 'expensive' (Koenigsberger et al., 2017). Thus a longer path length between two neural elements will also lead to weaker functional interactions. Combined analyses of structural and functional networks, obtained from resting brain fMRI, have shown that the presence and strength of structural connectivity between two nodes is correlated with the strength of their mutual functional relationship (Honey et al., 2009). Researchers used diffusion tensor imaging to track the movements of water through 82 separate areas of the brain and their interconnecting neurons. They found 12 areas of the brain that had significantly more connections than all the others, both to other regions and among themselves. These 'rich clubs' have the 'privilege' to accept only preprocessed, high-order information, rather than raw incoming sensory data (van den Heuvel & Sporns, 2011).

Functional connectivity

Functional connectivity (also denoted as fcMRI) is based on analyses of an association matrix. It is a mathematical representation of the network, containing all pair-wise correlations between nodes in the network. The overall connectivity of the brain can be visualized with this method using a connectivity matrix that shows the strength of all connections between selected regions within the brain (see Box 1.4).

In order to define the functional connections of networks in the brain, it is necessary to compute cross-correlations (or the coherence) between fMRI time series (BOLD signals) in predefined regions of interest (ROI's). The analyses, also called *seed-based* or *ROI-based* functional connectivity, typically use a voxel-wise approach, which allows a fine-grained analysis of the brain's structure (a voxel covers a region of about four cubic millimeters, comprising around 600.000 neurons). In seed analysis, one uses a priori determination of regions, which is often based on a hypothesis, or prior results. Task-dependent fMRI, for example, is often used to select a seed region of interest as a template for the resting-state time-series. The time series of the seed voxels are then correlated with the resting-state time-series in a certain region. A high correlation between the time-series of voxel i and voxel j is reflecting a high level of functional connectivity between these task-free and task-relation regions (van den Heuvel & Hulshoff Pol, 2010). A disadvantage of an ROI–driven approach is its dependence on the selection of seeds, which makes it vulnerable to bias (Lv et al., 2018).

BOX 1.4   GLOSSARY OF TERMS AND TECHNIQUES USED IN NETWORK MODELING

▶ Blood-oxygen-level-dependent (BOLD) signal: a measure of metabolic activity in the brain based on the difference between oxyhemoglobin and deoxyhemoglobin levels arising from changes in local blood flow. It forms the basis of fMRI.

▶ Functional connectivity (fcMRI): based on the computation of cross-correlations (or coherence) between fMRI time series (BOLD signals) in predefined regions of interest (ROI's; see also seed-based analysis).

▶ Diffusion-based (or tensor) tractography: a class of noninvasive magnetic resonance techniques that trace fiber bundles (white matter tracts) in the human brain in vivo, based on properties of water molecule diffusion in the local tissue microstructure.

▶ Granger causality analysis (GCA): a statistical method applied to the brain, measures the degree of predictability of temporal changes in one brain area that can be attributed to those in another area.

▶ Dynamic causal modeling (DCM): statistical analysis technique based on bilinear dynamic models, for making inferences about the effects of experimental manipulations on inter-regional interactions in latent neuronal signals.

▶ Effective connectivity: another term for DCM.

▶ General linear model (GLM): a mathematical technique aiming to predict the variation of a dependent variable in terms of a linear combination (weighted sum) of several reference functions.

continued

> - Graph theory: a mathematical technique used to express a complex network as a graph G = (V, E), with V the collection of nodes and E the collection of connections ('edges") between the nodes.
> - Independent component analysis (ICA): a computational technique that separates a multivariate signal into additive components, based on the assumption that the components arise from statistically independent non-Gaussian sources.
> - Statistical Parametric Mapping (SPM): standard statistical package used to test hypotheses about functional imaging data.
> - Seed-based (ROI) analysis: a method that utilizes a priori selection of specific areas in the brain. It uses a voxel-wise approach (a voxel covers a region of about four cubic millimeters), which allows a fine-grained analysis of the brain.

An alternative is a data-based approach called Independent Component Analysis (ICA). ICA is normally applied without any a priori assumptions and is not confined to selected specific regions, but extracts all detectable networks within the brain. It is also an effective method to reduce the staggering amount of correlation data. ICA is a mathematical technique similar to principal components analysis that serves to reduce a large set of correlated neural signals to a smaller set number of independent ('non-Gaussian') spatiotemporal components (Seeley et al., 2007; Beckmann et al., 2005).

Another method used to provide information on patterns of connectivity in complex networks is Graph Theory. Graph Theory was initially used to examine properties of networks like the Internet or aircraft flight patterns. It also allows decomposing the characteristics of complex biological networks, at the level of global and local connectivity (Bullmore & Sporns, 2009). When applied to fcMRI signals it uses the association matrix, now transformed ('thresholded') into a binary connectivity matrix.

Effective connectivity

Functional connectivity as described in Box 1.4 is an observable phenomenon quantified with measures of statistical dependencies between BOLD signals. ICA and Graph Theory are typical examples of techniques used to assess intrinsic brain networks. As such they are neutral or 'agnostic' concerning the direction of the information flow in the brain, or the causality and direction of connections. Another important application of network models concerns their role to map causal dependencies among neural events, summarized as the 'effective connectivity' of networks (Valdez-Sosa, 2011; Friston, 2011).

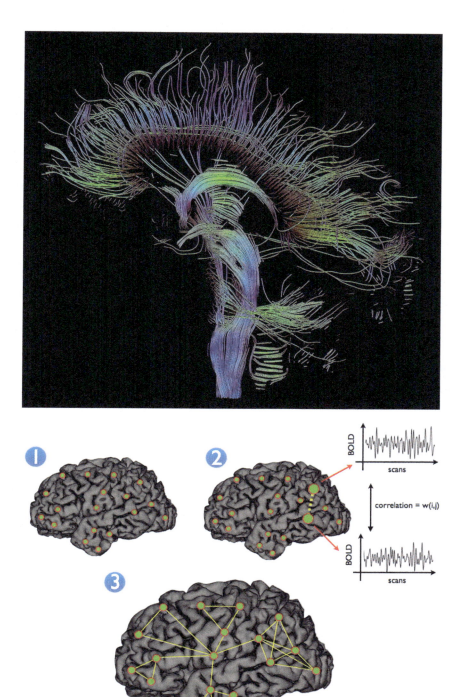

FIGURE 1.11

Upper: Structural connectivity: tractography provides a three-dimensional structural map ('skeleton') of the short and long-range connections in the brain (by Thomas Schultz, Creative Commons, Share Alike, CC BY-SA 3.0). Lower: Functional connectivity: Step 1, selection of ROIs (Regions of Interest), Step 2, Calculation of coherence between BOLD time-series, Step 3, Network with all functional links between ROIs.

Source: Adapted with permission from van den Heuvel (2009).

Several methods have been proposed for effective connectivity analysis, including structural equation modeling, multivariate autoregressive modeling, dynamic Bayesian models, bilinear dynamic systems, switching linear dynamic systems and dynamic causal modeling (see Smith et al., 2011 for a more detailed overview). Two popular methods using directional measures include Granger Causality Analysis (GCA) and Dynamic Causal Modeling (DCM). GCA provides a generic statistical tool to characterize directed functional interactions from time-series data, applied in neuroscience and neuroimaging (Seth et al., 2015). It implements a statistical, predictive notion of causality, whereby causes precede and help to predict their effects. In particular high-resolution data obtained from electrical or magnetic recordings of continuous neural activity are well suited to GCA.

Although dynamical causal modeling (DCM) is based on biophysical non-functional data, some models may use neurally plausible schemes (for instance, a scheme that follows a sequence of information processing stages) as biophysical modeling to explain empirical data. The basic idea behind DCM is that neural activity propagates through brain networks as in an input-output system, where unobservable (hidden) neural dynamics mediate causal interactions. For example, DCM applied on fcMRI signals has been used to test hypotheses about particular changes in intrinsic and extrinsic connectivity that meditate fMRI responses, to identify the locus of attentional modulation (Friston & Dolan, 2010).

Contribution to cognitive neuroscience

So far, large-scale network analysis of structural and functional connectivity has given only limited insight into the mechanisms by which neuronal systems compute, that is, the rules underlying the transformation and encoding of neural response patterns in both local and distributed circuits (see Sporns, 2014 for a review). The reason might be that in the past the primary focus has been on network studies of task-free or resting functional brain connectivity (Raichle et al., 2001; Greicius, 2003). Future work could broaden the range of applications by developing network models for task-evoked functional connectivity. For example, some interesting work on modeling of specific cognitive operations has revealed large-scale networks involved in memory recollection (Fornito et al., 2012) and cognitive control (Cole et al., 2012, 2013). The latter study also revealed the central role of the prefrontal cortex and the frontoparietal network as flexible hub regions in cognitive control.

Notes

1   The terms function and process will be used indiscriminately throughout this book to refer to dynamic properties of the cognitive as well as the neural systems. The term structure refers to

2　A brief introduction to these measures, in particular the event-related potentials (ERPs) of the brain, is provided in the methods section further along, and in Chapter 4 dealing with selective attention.

3　By using the term 'mind-brain' I follow Patricia Churchland's original description of mental phenomena as products of the brain, which she referred to as 'Mind in Brain' (Churchland, 1986).

4　Contrasting with this view, Shulman & Rothman (2019), recently proposed a Non-cognitive Behavioral Model (NBM) which correlates observed human behavior directly with measured brain activity without making assumptions about intervening cognitive processes. NBM attempts to derive cognitive models empirically from imaging and other direct measurements of brain activity, instead of cognitive and computational models of mental activity.

5　A recent study using multi-modal magnetic resonance images succeeded to delineate even 180 areas per hemisphere of the cortex, bounded by sharp changes in cortical architecture, function, and connectivity (Glasser et al., 2016).

6　Brain connectivity networks in the present context are not to be confused with Artificial Neural Networks and Artificial Intelligence Modeling that are related to computer simulation with no direct reference to the brain. See the following methods section for further clarification.

2 | Introducing the brain: from synapse to networks

CONTENTS

- ▶ Introduction
- ▶ Gross anatomy and function of the brain
- ▶ Connections in the brain: from neurons to networks
- ▶ Laterality and the brain

Introduction

In the previous chapter we stated that cognitive functions are not unitary but involve more specific or local functions. Similarly, in the neural domain gross dissection of the brain reveals that it is certainly not equipotential, but that different parts do different things. Like cognition, the brain has a distinct hierarchical architecture, running from global to local networks, connected by numerous reciprocal pathways. Importantly, the brain's structural organization creates conditions that also affect its functional architecture. The present chapter considers the anatomy of the brain from two different hierarchical perspectives. The first part describes the brain's global architecture and subdivisions, starting with the phylogenetically newer neuroanatomical systems and their evolution, and working down to older systems and their component structures, nuclei and circuits. The second part follows the same strategy but in reversed order, with emphasis on the connections between various parts of the brain. It starts at the micro level, describing synapses, local networks and some basic principles of coding in neural networks and then works up to larger structural and functional networks at the macro level. Laterality of brain functions is the third and final section of this chapter, dealing with the anatomical and functional specializations of the two cerebral hemispheres.

Gross anatomy and function of the brain

The vertical hierarchical classification of the brain follows its phylogenesis, in other words the successive evolutionary stages and adaptations in the development of the brain, during which its networks increased drastically in complexity and size. In line with its evolution, the brain's architecture is often described in terms of three gross anatomical divisions, ranging from the human forebrain to midbrain and brainstem, with each division incorporating subdivisions and their respective anatomical structures.

One of the great challenges within an evolutionary scenario is to understand the separation between the mushroom-shaped cerebral cortex and lower structures, like the basal ganglia, hippocampus and cerebellum. A general accepted theory is that the lower structures represent older, more primitive versions of the cortex that gradually changed their roles with the rapid expansion of the cerebral cortex in higher mammals. Their primary function could then have gradually transformed into 'support organs' or, in terms of Gerald Edelman, 'appendages' of the cerebral cortex serving the ordering of input and output to and from the cortex (Edelman, 1992). The principal function of the hippocampus, for example, with its extensive connections to other brain regions, is to regulate input from the sensory organs to the posterior and temporal cortices, in particular the storage of explicit long-term memories.

The intimate connections between hippocampus and hedonic centers such as the hypothalamus and amygdala could have evolved to control affective input to the medial frontal cortex. Similarly, the massive long-range connections between basal ganglia, cerebellum and cortex could have become crucial in assisting motor output and planning of movements, initiated in the motor centers of the anterior cortex, albeit on different timescales.

In successive order the next sections focus on the major subdivisions of the brain as depicted in Figure 2.1 (Figures 2.3 and 2.4 present a more detailed view of the anatomical details). The forebrain (also called prosencephalon) contains two divisions – cerebrum (or telencephalon) and diencephalon. The cerebrum consists of two symmetrical hemispheres that contain respectively the cerebral cortex (meaning 'bark' like the bark of a tree) and two core structures, the limbic system and basal ganglia. The thalamus and hypothalamus are the major structures of the diencephalon. The brainstem refers to phylogenetically older structures ranging in respective order from the mesencephalon (midbrain) to the metencephalon to the myelencephalon.

Cerebral cortex

The term 'cerebral cortex' or 'neocortex' refers to the part of the forebrain that developed late in the phylogeny. It consists of a thin layer of gray matter, the name given to the dense collection of nerve cells in the brain. A nerve cell, or neuron, has a cell body,

INTRODUCING THE BRAIN

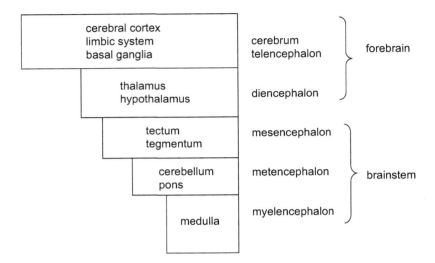

FIGURE 2.1
Sketch of the brain, with corresponding divisions and subdivisions.

dendrites and axons. In the center of the cell, called the nucleus, we find the chromosomes, strands of DNA that carry genetic information. Dendrites are treelike branches (derived from the Greek 'dendron' which means tree) that serve as essential recipients of information. Axons, in turn, are long slender tubes that carry information from the cell body to the terminal buttons. Its underlying signal is called the action potential. The synapse is the junction between the terminal button of an axon and the membrane (dendrite) of another neuron. The synapse uses a chemical substance called neurotransmitter that either has a facilitatory or an inhibitory effect on another neuron.

The cortical layer is compressed into a relatively small surface with various windings (gyri) and grooves (fissures or sulci, see Figure 2.3). Sulci are the small grooves and fissures the big grooves. Spread in a flat plane, the cortex of an adult person might cover a field of about 45 square meters. Most neurons of the cortex are pyramidal cells and spiny stellate cells. Even more numerous than neurons are the glial cells that can take different forms and functions, and have a supportive function, like repair and the formation of myelin. Myelin is a sheet of fatty substance that is wrapped around the axons and is found in the brain as well as in the peripheral nervous system. Neurons vary in shape depending on their functional role as sensory, motor, pyramidal neuron or local interneuron.

Not all axons contain myelin, but if they do, it enhances the speed of transmission of action potentials by a principle called saltatory (jump-wise) conduction. In the long efferent axons of motor neurons projecting to the spinal cord, myelin facilitates the speed and efficiency of motor behavior. Damage to, and 'wear and tear' of the myelin sheet is found in a neurological disease called multiple sclerosis, but could also lead to more benign symptoms such as the gradual slowing of cognitive and motor functions in old age.

The brain contains a series of interconnected chambers called ventricles that are filled with cerebrospinal fluid. The fluid is manufactured by the choroid plexus, a tissue with a rich blood supply. The largest ventricles are the first and second lateral ventricles, connected with the third ventricle. The cerebral aqueduct connects the third with the fourth ventricle deep in the brain.

Spatial divisions

To facilitate navigation in the cerebrum it is customary to divide its three-dimensional space into three planes. The coronal plane divides the brain in a frontal (anterior) and back (posterior) section, the sagittal plane in a left and right section and the horizontal plane in an upper and lower section (Figure 2.2). The terms dorsal and ventral relate to the geometry of a four-legged animal (like a dog) where dorsal refers to the back (upper) and ventral to the belly (under) side of the body. The terms lateral and medial refer to the outer and inner (or central) surfaces of the two hemispheres. Each hemisphere is divided in four gross anatomical areas: the frontal, parietal, temporal and occipital lobes (Figure 2.3). The central sulcus separates the frontal lobe from the parietal lobe, and the lateral sulcus separates the frontal lobe from the temporal lobe. Finally, the occipital lobes are located at the most posterior end of the posterior cortex. Within each lobe there are many functionally specific areas segregated into motor areas, areas for specific sensory modalities and 'association' areas that mediate higher-order functions and often combine different modalities.

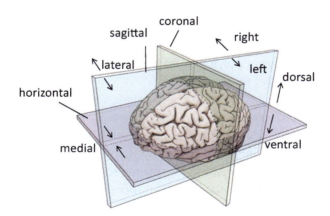

FIGURE 2.2
Sections of the brain (sagittal, coronal, horizontal and medial). Left/right refers to the left and right hemispheres in the horizontal plane, ventral/dorsal to the upper and lower sections in the sagittal plane and lateral/medial to the outer and inner surfaces of the cortex in the coronal plane.

> ## BOX 2.1 FOUR SIGNIFICANT AREAS IN THE CEREBRAL CORTEX, WITH THEIR GLOBAL FUNCTIONS
>
> ▶ Frontal area: action and planning of movement, language (speech: left hemisphere), inhibition of irrelevant or inappropriate behavior, internal control of attentional processes and working memory.
>
> ▶ Parietal area: somatic-sensory perception, integration of sensory information, spatial orientation to environmental cues and identification of the location of objects in the environment.
>
> ▶ Temporal area: auditory perception, identification of objects in the environment, consolidation and storage of memory representations and language (comprehension, left-hemisphere).
>
> ▶ Occipital area: visual perception.

Primary and secondary areas

The precentral gyrus and postcentral gyrus, located anterior and posterior to the central sulcus, are the locations of the primary motor and somatosensory areas respectively. The primary visual area lies at the back of the occipital lobe and the auditory projection area in the superior temporal lobe (Figure 2.3). Another important division in the neocortex is that between primary and secondary areas. Primary areas (another name is sensory or unimodal cortex) include the previously mentioned four projection areas. The primary visual pathway, for example, sends detailed maps of retinal positions via the lateral geniculate nucleus of the thalamus to the primary visual cortex. The secondary areas, also referred to as association or polymodal cortex, are folded around the primary areas, and account for about 75% of the total cortex.

Their function is not exclusively sensory and motor, but also the integration of information. Integration could refer to the level of processing (integration of stimuli from multiple sensory modalities to meaningful entities), as well as to the level of storage of information in higher-order memory representations.

The term 'association cortex' rests on the assumption that its primary function is to connect sensory and motor areas. As such it is responsible for the 'deeper' processing of information coming from the cortical sensory areas, after which it is transmitted to the memory or action-related areas in the brain. Neurons in the association areas also participate in functional networks, on a larger scale than the local networks of primary sensory areas.

The medial-sagittal section of the brain (Figure 2.4) displays the major structures of the neocortex, the diencephalon and the midbrain.

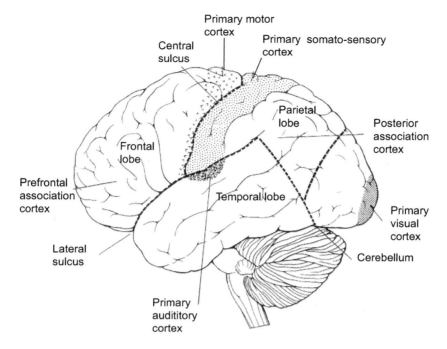

FIGURE 2.3
Lateral view of the human neocortex with major gyri, sulci and lobes. The temporal lobe contains the superior, middle and inferior temporal gyri. Precentral and postcentral gyri are located in front of and behind the central sulcus. The lateral sulcus separates the frontal lobe from the temporal lobe.

Source: From Kandel et al. (1991).

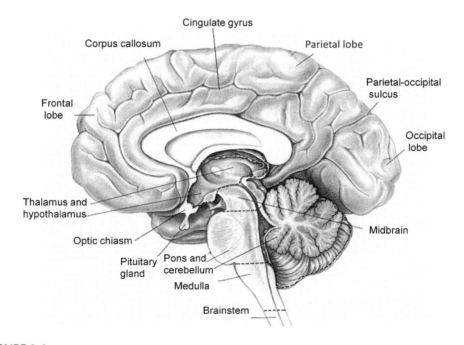

FIGURE 2.4
Medial-sagittal view of the human brain displaying the major structures of the right half of the neocortex, diencephalon and the midbrain.

Source: From Kandel et al. (1991).

Connections

The cortex contains various types of connections, labeled afferent (receiving) and efferent (sending), as well as excitatory and inhibitory pathways. Adjacent cortical areas are often connected by forward and backward connections depending on the site of origin: a projects forwards to area b, and receives information backwards from b.

Globally, the bundles of myelinated fibers form three types of tracts: association tracts (within each hemisphere), commissural tracts (between the hemispheres) and projection tracts (between cortex and subcortical structures). The most conspicuous part of the commissural tracts is the central portion called the corpus callosum, forming the main central 'bridge' between the two hemispheres. A large gyrus forms its roof, called the cingulate gyrus (Figure 2.4). Association tracts are further subdivided according to the areas that they connect. For example, the posterior part of the parietal cortex is connected via long myelinated fibers with two areas in the anterior motor area, involved in the programming of motor activity. They include the supplementary motor area (the medial section) and premotor cortex (the lateral section).

Messages from the brain to the spinal cord serve to control muscles and are organized into two paths: the dorsolateral tract (also called the pyramidal tract) that leaves the primary motor cortex, and the ventromedial tract that originates from many parts of the cerebral cortex. The dorsolateral path controls movements in peripheral areas such as the hands, arms and the feet and crosses from one side of the brain to the opposite side of the spinal cord. Axons of the ventromedial tract project to both sides of the spinal cord and control the muscles of the neck, shoulders and trunk.

Prefrontal cortex

Humans and geat apes share a large prefrontal cortex (Semendeferi et al., 2002). In humans the prefrontal cortex globally contains three sub-areas, the dorsal and the ventral prefrontal cortex and the orbitofrontal cortex (Figure 2.5). Each area contains a

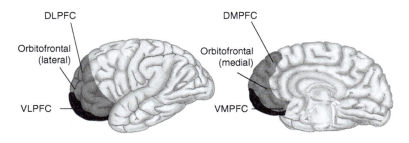

FIGURE 2.5
Subdivisions of the prefrontal cortex. Left: lateral view with VLPFC (ventrolateral prefrontal cortex, DLPFC (dorsolateral prefrontal cortex) and orbitofrontal cortex (lateral). Right: medial view with DMPFC (dorsomedial prefrontral cortex), VMPFC (ventromedial prefrontal cortex) and orbitofrontal cortex (medial).

lateral and medial part. The dorsolateral prefrontal cortex (DLPFC) has many output connections with the premotor region, area 8 (also known as the frontal eye fields) and the oculomotor system (colliculi superior). Its main inputs come from the parietal region, which plays a vital role in processing spatial information from the outside world. The dorsomedial prefrontal cortex (DMPFC) lies medially in the prefrontal cortex.

The second important area is the ventral prefrontal cortex, subdivided into a lateral part, the ventrolateral prefrontal cortex (VLPFC) and a medial part, the ventromedial prefrontal cortex (VMPFC). The main cortical input connections of the ventrolateral section come from the temporal cortex, necessary for processing object information. VMPFC has many direct connections with areas involved in the regulation of instinctive behavior and emotions, e.g. the amygdala and the hypothalamus. The third and most frontally located part of the prefrontal cortex is the orbitofrontal cortex (orbis = eye chamber). This area is connected to the amygdala via reciprocal connections, while mainly output connections have been identified with the hypothalamus. The ventromedial region is vital for the regulation of autonomous physiological processes like heart rate, respiratory and blood pressure.

BOX 2.2   THE PREFRONTAL CORTEX

The prefrontal cortex is often associated with complex unitary functions, although the nature of these functions remained poorly understood. Concepts like 'higher order processing' and 'executive functions' only added to the confusion about the precise role of its component processes (Wagner et al., 2001). Functional imaging of the brain, however, has contributed in various ways to unravel its functional organization. This has revealed that the unique function of the prefrontal cortex lies in its hierarchical organization, involving long-range connections with the perceptual and motoric association areas, the limbic system, basal ganglia, thalamus and brainstem. These circuitries originate in different sections of the prefrontal cortex to control, activate, inhibit and coordinate activities in more remote areas of the brain. Prefrontal patients are often capable to solve problems or tasks that require convergence on a single solution, but have much more difficulty with tasks offering a variety of different solutions, called *divergent thinking* by J. Guilford (1967). Disturbances in the higher control or executive functions of the prefrontal cortex not only occur after lesions in the frontal cortex itself, but also after lesions in the lower parts of the brain, which may include lesions in the dorsomedial nucleus of the thalamus, the caudate nucleus and structures in the brainstem such as reticular formation. Also, multifocal partial lesions in white matter (which as such may not lead to cognitive impairment) can lead to disorders in executive functions caused by an impaired connectivity of the involved networks.

Evolution

The human brain is an amazingly complex system that evolved from natural selection and successive adaptations during the long course of evolution. The hierarchical structure of the brain, already manifested in its gross anatomical divisions, reflects how complex systems are built upon, incorporate and even recruit older systems. Complex traits can only have evolved as part of a gradual evolutionary acquisition, a step by cumulative step process (see also Simon, 1962 for a general overview of complex systems).

Any theory claiming that the human brain and its product, the mind, have a supranatural origin proves to be less compelling than the theory stating that they are the inevitable product of natural selection. Cognitive researchers may find it difficult to understand how evolutionary principles can help to unravel the roots of human consciousness, memory or human affective processes. But why, for example, do people remember frequent or recent events better than infrequent or more remote ones? Or why are they so good at recognizing faces or facial expressions?

Why can certain emotional stimuli give rise to physiological responses without any conscious perception? Why has language developed in such complexity in humans, and not – or to a much lesser extent – in non-humans?

One idea is that the brain, like most complex biological systems, has resulted from selection processes in which multiple, often competing, traits and constraints must be satisfied simultaneously (Bullmore & Sporns, 2012). With the brain being a product of evolution, it is not surprising to find many similarities between cognitive functions as expressed in humans and non-human species. Even intelligence, often seen as a human

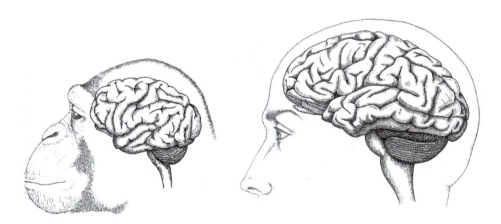

FIGURE 2.6
Cerebrum of chimpanzee and man drawn on the same scale. The prefrontal cortex, assumed to be the site of planning and coordination of actions, has developed most conspicuously in man.

Source: Adapted from Hubel (1979). With kind permission of the artist Patricia J. Wynne.

quality par excellence, might not be as uniquely human as assumed in mainstream psychology. Natural selection ascribes all successful adaptations of living species to their unique and complex niches, which in turn are examples of sophisticated, complex and 'clever' forms of behavior.

Intelligent behavior of animals is not only manifested in its sometimes-striking resemblance to the way humans behave. In the millions of years of evolution, many animal species have developed refined specific perceptual and cognitive abilities to adapt to their sophisticated worlds. Think not only of chimpanzees and bonobos, who resemble us in various ways, but also of dolphins, parrots, sheep, wasps, bats and whales. Or of the accurate navigational skills enabling birds and sharks to travel thousands of miles to reach their respective destinations. Perhaps the traditional view that living species on earth represent a cognitive ladder with man on top is incorrect; it is more like a bush, with cognition taking different forms that are often incomparable to ours.

Of course there also are boundaries that separate humans from other smart mammals. Some might even feel that the specific development of *H. Sapiens* deserves the qualification 'cognitive revolution' (Harari, 2014). Indeed, in a relatively short period, human beings made a huge leap forward to the top of the food chain. This development may have resulted in a relatively fast expansion of specific anatomical structures in the brain, such as the prefrontal cortex (Passingham, 1982, 2002).

This development is also known as encephalization, defined as the amount of brain mass related to an animal's total body mass. Primates, as well as humans, are traditionally seen as having developed large brains as a response to their more cognitively demanding niches. Charles Darwin was already aware of its importance. In 1891 he wrote: 'no one, I presume, doubts that the large proportion which the size of man's brain bears to his body, compared to the same proportion in the gorilla or orang, is closely connected with his mental powers.' In a similar vein, cognitive neuroscientist Richard Passingham developed an index that allowed comparing the evolutionary expansion of different structures in the human brain with that of non-human primates. This showed that for the neocortex the increase in volume was about 3.2 times greater than for primates of the same body weight (Figure 2.7), suggesting that brain mass has been an essential factor in the emergence of the unique cognitive ability of humans. However, the larger brain relative to the body in humans may have resulted not only from the faster growth rate of their brain, but also from a slower growth rate of their body, relative to primates.

For phylogenetically old areas like the brainstem, the increase was relatively small. The diencephalon, with thalamus and hypothalamus, showed a stronger increase. For the hippocampus, cerebellum and neocortex, the brain expansion was greatest. Surprisingly, this could indicate that the cerebellum was involved in the development of higher cognitive functions. Passingham also found evidence that the human brain has proportions one would predict by extrapolating the trend of earlier primate brain expansions. More simply: human brains mirror the architecture of large-brained primates (Donald, 1991).

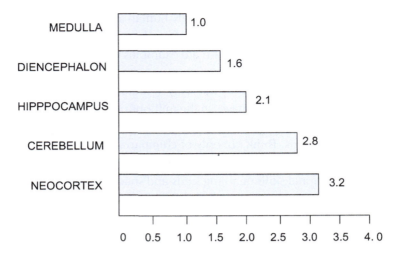

FIGURE 2.7
Expansion of specific parts of the human brain with its evolution, according to Passingham. The numbers reflect the size of certain parts of the brain, relative to the size of the same areas in non-human primates of the same body weight. The value 3.2 for the neocortex means that humans have 3.2 times as much brain volume as primates of the same weight.

Source: Adapted from Donald (1991).

BOX 2.3 BIGGER BRAIN ALSO SMARTER BRAIN?

When comparing brains of different species, behavioral biologists often use relative brain size: this is brain size corrected for body mass. On the relative scale humans, dolphins and great apes score higher than the elephant, which has the largest brain of all land mammals. Even birds with their super tiny brains have developed astonishingly complex ways to adapt and survive in their environment. Now how can such a tiny brain be so smart? A recent study published by the research team of Pavell Nemec* from Prague sheds some new light on this interesting problem. They compared the brains of different mammals and birds with the same brain size. They found that bird brains have more neurons (nerve cells) than mammalian brains and even primate brains of similar mass. So it is not brain size per se that determines smart or intelligent behavior, but the density or the number of nerve cells packed in some regions of the brain.

For many years psychologists and biologists have taken the view that firm boundaries separate behavior of man and animal. Indeed, man has developed advanced technologies and can plan, use complex grammar in his speech and has developed a sense of self. However, it looks as if these traditional views are

continued

> corroding. The primatologist Frans de Waal raised the intriguing question of if we 'are smart enough to know how smart animals are'. Instead of trying to prove humanity's superiority, let's use our big brains to comprehend the world as experienced by other species.
>
> Sources: Jerison (1973), Emery, (2016). *Olkowicz et al. (2016).

Limbic system

The primary structures in the limbic systems are the hippocampus ('seahorse'), amygdala (almond-shaped nuclei), hypothalamus (literally: under the thalamus), septum (fence) and cingulate gyrus (belt-shaped winding).

Anatomy and function

The limbic system is considered to be phylogenetically older than the surrounding neocortex, the reason why some of its parts are called archicortex or paleocortex ('old cortex'). It forms an annular layer ('limbus') around the brain stem, at the transition between the diencephalon and telencephalon (Figure 2.8). The ring-like structure of the limbic system is most pronounced in the cingulate gyrus, a band of cortex running from anterior to posterior, and the parahippocampal gyrus that contains the hippocampus. Notice that classification by anatomical criteria is not always sufficient to describe functional roles. The typical shape of the limbic system does not necessarily imply a close functional relationship between its parts.

For example, some parts of the limbic system like the hippocampus and the thalamus are not exclusively involved in the regulation of emotion. In turn, the network in the brain that regulates affective processes is not limited to structures in the limbic system, but also involves ventromedial regions in the prefrontal cortex.

Cingulate gyrus

The cingulate gyrus (or gyrus cinguli) is a part of the mesocortex (the transition area between the neocortex and the paleocortex) that – like the neocortex – has six granular layers and is divided in a posterior and anterior part. The posterior part of the cingulate gyrus is part of the limbic lobe and forms a central node in the resting state or 'default' mode network' of the brain (see Chapter 4). The anterior part is called the anterior cingulate area. It acts as a kind of interface between the frontal cortical areas and the limbic system. The dorsal (middle) part, the 'cognitive division', is associated

INTRODUCING THE BRAIN

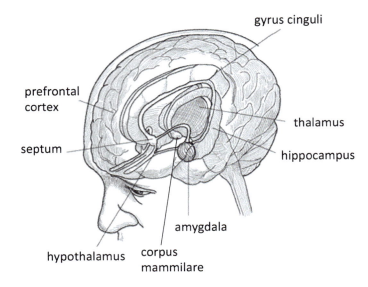

FIGURE 2.8
View of some structures belonging to the limbic system.
Source: Adapted from: Bloom & Lazerson (1988).

with the control of cognitive processes and has many connections with the dorsal part of the prefrontal cortex. The frontal part, the 'affective division' is involved in emotional control and has links to the limbic system and the orbital-prefrontal cortex. Damasio (1994) calls it a 'fountainhead' region, a source of energy for internal as well as external actions (see Figure 7.10. in the Emotion chapter for a more detailed description of these subdivisions).

Hippocampus

The hippocampus is a distinct macroscopic structure, sited deeper in the temporal brain, that follows the C-shape geometry of the limbic system. In humans it is usually dived in three parts; the anterior (ventral), posterior (dorsal) and intermediate section. It is considered to be part of the old evolutionary cortex of the limbic system that also shows a horizontal layering of neurons. The hippocampus is essential for capturing and consolidating new episodic information in sections of the memory system, called declarative or explicit memory. It receives input from virtually all cortical areas including the hypothalamus, amygdala and ventral medial prefrontal cortex (the ventral section). The dorsal section has many 'place cells' (i.e. cells that code for spatial locations), and is believed to connect to parts of the cortex involved in spatial memory. Its various sections and functions, as well as long-term potentiation (LTP), the neurochemical principle underlying the process of consolidation, are further discussed in Chapter 6 (Memory).

BOX 2.4   SEX AND THE BRAIN

The human brain is a sexually dimorphic organ, shaped by sex-specific selection pressures. A robust finding of many studies is that men on the average have a larger volume of grey and white matter than women (Ritchie et al., 2018). The same holds for comparisons at the subregional level, in structures such as the hippocampus, striatum, amygdala and the thalamus. Women on the other hand have a higher thickness of cortical tissue than men. But despite these consistent sex-linked patterns in gross brain anatomy, researchers using functional and structural imaging of the brain also found considerable overlap between men and women in brain volume and cortical thickness, similar as for their height. Furthermore, when corrected for total brain volume, regional differences in volume are strongly attenuated, suggesting that these effects are, to a large extent, a byproduct of an overall bigger male brain (McCarthy & Arnold, 2011; Ruigrok et al., 2014).

Very early in life androgens act to masculinize various human behavior. Masculinization and defeminization are separate hormonally driven processes. They organize the neural substrate to promote male-typic behaviors while suppressing female-typic behaviors. In men these are controlled by *testosterone* and the enzyme *aromatase* that transforms testosterone into *estradiol*. Feminization of the brain in women on the other hand, is the default process that occurs in the absence of high levels of gonadal steroids, testosterone in particular, during a perinatal sensitive period. Testosterone is also present in women, produced primarily in their ovaries and adrenal glands.

Gonadal effects are not the only cause of sexual differentiation in the brain. Studies of rodents have revealed that genes encoded on the X or Y chromosome also have a sex-specific complement that provides a direct genetic pathway to sexual differentiation. For example, the mammalian Y chromosome was found to contain a dominant testis-determining gene, that was later identified as *Sry*18. These genetic effects occur at the top of the molecular cascade that differentiates testicular from ovarian development. This gene might be responsible for the cascade of developmental events that cause bodies and brains to take on male characteristics. A possible implication being that the brains of males differ from those in females, by virtue of differences in their sex chromosome complement, interacting with gonadal effects.

Amygdala

The amygdala is essential for the regulation of emotional behavior – especially when it concerns primary and innate emotions such as fear – but also for the affective 'coloring' of cognitive processes. Like the hippocampus, it is located deep in the temporal lobes of each hemisphere and is subdivided into some smaller nuclei. The amygdala is also essential in detecting fearful or threatening stimuli. Chapters 6 and 7 will deal with more specific aspects of the hippocampus and amygdala in connection with memory and emotional processes.

Septum

The septum (Latin for 'fence') controls basic instinctive drives, like thirst and sexual reactions. Feelings of euphoria often accompany stimulation of this area. It is an essential site in the so-called self-stimulation experiments with rats.

Insula

The insula (Latin for 'island') or insular cortex lays hidden deep in the temporal cortex in the medial wall of the lateral sulcus. It is also considered to be a part of the limbic system. Its functions are not yet clear, since the region is often associated with a variety of conditions. Examples are the somatosensory and taste perception, motor control, self-awareness and emotional functions. Functional imaging studies have identified parts of the insula as core structures of a large-scale network called the salience network.

BOX 2.5 STRUCTURES AND NUCLEI OF THE BASAL GANGLIA

- ▶ Basal ganglia, proper: collection of nuclei in the forebrain involved in control of movement and selection of actions, with the striatum and globus pallidus as the major nuclei folded around the thalamus.
- ▶ Basal ganglia, functional: also involve subthalamic nuclei and substantia nigra.
- ▶ Pars compacta: nuclei within the substantia nigra that produce dopamine.
- ▶ Striatum ('striped area'): the largest structure of the basal ganglia. It is divided into the ventral and a dorsal striatum, based upon its function and connections.
- ▶ Dorsal striatum: composed of the caudate nucleus and the putamen, which together are part of a complex loop controlling planning and execution of movement.
- ▶ Ventral striatum, also called nucleus accumbens: part of the mesocortical dopamine pathway involved in reinforcement of behavior.

continued

> - Caudate nucleus: has an elongated C shaped structure, and involves regulation in planning of movement together with the premotor areas. The amygdala lies at its tail end.
> - Putamen: a large round structure lateral in the basal ganglia, and part of the motor loop, involved in the regulation of movements and working together with the caudate nucleus.
> - Globus pallidus (Latin for 'pale globe'), also known as paleostriatum or dorsal *pallidum*: a structure medially in the basal ganglia. Divided in globus pallidus interna (GPi) and globus pallidus externa (GPe). Both regions acquire input from the putamen and caudate and communicate with the subthalamic nucleus.
> - Internal capsule: a bundle of white matter that separates the dorsal striatum from the caudate nucleus and the putamen.

Basal ganglia

The basal ganglia are a highly complex structure in the lower forebrain. They consist of three primary nuclei: the globus pallidus, the caudate nucleus and the putamen (Figure 2.9). In a functional sense, the subthalamic nucleus and substantia nigra in the brainstem also belong to the basal ganglia. Putamen and caudate nucleus together are called neostriatum, while the term striatum ('striped area') refers to the neostriatum and globus pallidus. The nucleus accumbens (Latin for 'lying against'), adjacent to the septum, is also considered to be part of the basal ganglia. Another name is paleostriatum or ventral striatum, while the neostriatum is called dorsal striatum (see Box 2.4 for a summary of these structures).

Function

An essential function of the basal ganglia is the control of movements, in particular in establishing a state of balance between inhibition and excitation of the motor regions. Control takes place in various subcortical-cortical circuits that receive input from broad regions of the cortex, and then loop back to the cortex via the ventral nuclei of the thalamus (see Chapter 5 for more details).

Motor memory

The basal ganglia too are involved in skill learning. As such they are essential for the consolidation of several aspects of movements in the 'motor memories', located in the

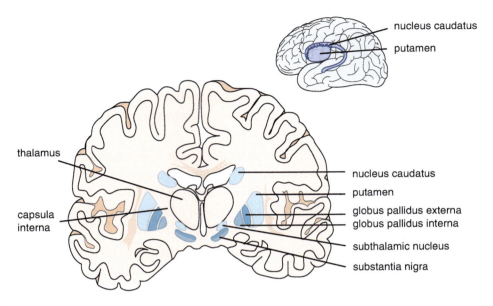

FIGURE 2.9
Left section: Coronal section of the basal ganglia with the caudate nucleus, globus pallidus and putamen. Also shown are the thalamus, subthalamic nucleus and substantia nigra. Upper right section: lateral 3D view of basal ganglia.

secondary motor cortices. Motor memory also includes motor programs and precalculated instructions that guide and produce specific movements when activated. The involvement of the basal ganglia in skill learning is reminiscent of the role of the hippocampus in consolidating perceptual information in declarative memory, sited in the temporal cortices.

Motivation

Another vital role of the basal ganglia concerns the participation of specific nuclei that regulate the motivational or 'drive' state of the cortex via neurotransmitter circuits. The ventral striatum (also known as nucleus accumbens) has many dopaminergic receptors and is part of the mesolimbic dopamine system. This system is essential for regulating the effect of reinforcers on behavior, similar to the effect of natural rewards like food, water and sex. Also, self-administration of certain drugs specifically depends on the mesolimbic system. The neostriatum receives input from dopaminergic systems like the substantia nigra and ventral tegmentum in the brainstem that modulate activation of the motor system, probably in an antagonistic fashion (see Box 2.6 and Figure 2.12 further ahead for a more detailed view of the dopamine pathways).

Dopamine released in the motor system affects performing skills (e.g. a forehand smash in tennis). In Parkinson's patients, a dramatic loss of dopaminergic fibers

INTRODUCING THE BRAIN

(originating in a group of nuclei called pars compacta, and projecting to the striatum) is often the cause of motor disturbances. These may become manifest in lack or clumsiness of movement (hypokinesia) and slowness of body movements and speech (bradykinesia).

Thalamus and hypothalamus

Thalamus and hypothalamus together form the diencephalon, the second major division of the forebrain. The thalamus lies in the center of the basal ganglia and consists of two small symmetrical egg-shaped structures connected via a bridge of grey matter called massa intermedia. It contains many distinct nuclei, among which the pulvinar, anterior, ventral and dorsal nuclei function as relay stations in several thalamocortical pathways (Figure 2.10). Some nuclei in the thalamus, like the lateral (LGN) and medial (MGN) geniculate, function primarily as sensory relay stations where afferent

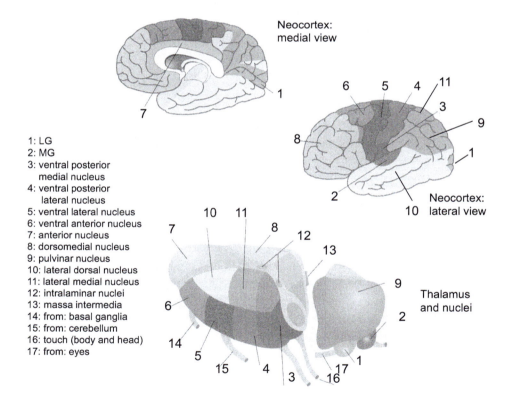

1: LG
2: MG
3: ventral posterior medial nucleus
4: ventral posterior lateral nucleus
5: ventral lateral nucleus
6: ventral anterior nucleus
7: anterior nucleus
8: dorsomedial nucleus
9: pulvinar nucleus
10: lateral dorsal nucleus
11: lateral medial nucleus
12: intralaminar nuclei
13: massa intermedia
14: from: basal ganglia
15: from: cerebellum
16: touch (body and head)
17: from: eyes

FIGURE 2.10
Thalamic nuclei and their projections to the medial and lateral surfaces of the cortex (LG lateral geniculate, MG medial geniculate).
Source: Adapted from Carlson (2002).

information from sensory organs passes on its way to the primary cortical projection areas. For example, the retinogeniculate-cortical path, also called the primary visual pathway, connects specific points of the retina with layer 4 of the LGN and the visual cortex. Other nuclei in the thalamus are involved in top-down control of sensory information via cortical-thalamic pathways. For example, the pulvinar connects via a triangular circuit with the posterior parietal cortex and a secondary visual area called V4, where it controls selective inhibition in conditions of voluntary visual spatial attention. Another corticothalamic pathway involves a loop between the mediodorsal nuclei of the thalamus and the dorsolateral prefrontal cortex (see Chapter 4).

The hypothalamus is a core area consisting of a variety of nuclei, lying directly beneath the thalamus against the wall of the third ventricle. The hypothalamus contains high levels of noradrenaline. It regulates body temperature and basic motivational processes like flight and fight behavior, eating, drinking and sexual behavior. It is also responsible for releasing stress hormones in the adrenal gland through the nearby pituitary. The hypothalamus has numerous connections with the amygdala and the cingulate gyrus in the limbic system, but also with structures in the ventromedial (lower middle) portions of the prefrontal brain. Together, these areas constitute a large-scale network responsible for the regulation of primary and secondary emotions.

Brainstem

The brainstem, with tectum and tegmentum, cerebellum ('little brain'), pons and medulla is the evolutionarily oldest part of the brain (see Figure 2.11).

Reticular formation

The brainstem also contains a diffuse and elongated network of nuclei and nerve fibers referred to as reticular formation. The reticular formation (called RAS: Reticular Activation System) is not anatomically well defined and extends from the thalamus to the spinal cord. Traditionally it has been subdivided into an ascending and a descending part. The ascending reticular activating system, known as ARAS, consists of two different pathways (Magoun, 1952). The extrathalamic route arises from nuclei in the brain stem that produce neurotransmitters arising from cholinergic, glutamatergic, noradrenergic and dopaminergic nuclei. A second thalamic pathway projects via nonspecific nuclei of the thalamus to the cortex. The descending part of the RAS (called DRAS) regulates the state of motor neurons in the spinal cord via reticulo-striatal tracts. After its initial discovery by Moruzzi and Magoun in the 1950s the unitary role of the RAS in controlling the arousal state of the cortex and motor system has been questioned and described as being either too complicated to study or as an undifferentiated part of the brain with no organization at all.

BOX 2.6 DOPAMINE PATHWAYS AND NUCLEI

Various pathways regulate the flow of dopamine to the cortex:

- ▶ The nigrostriatal, mesolimbic and mesocortical pathways together form the medial forebrain bundle, a bundle of nerve fibers projecting to the frontal brain.
- ▶ The nigrostriatal pathways have their origin in the substantia nigra (in a nucleus called pars compacta). Their fibers project via the dorsal striatum to motor regions in the frontal cortex that control motor activity.
- ▶ The mesolimbic pathway, sometimes referred to as the reward pathway, arises in the ventral tegmentum and then connects via nuclei of the amygdala and ventral striatum to the cingulate cortex.
- ▶ The mesocortical pathway also arises in the ventral tegmentum, and then projects directly to the orbitofrontal cortex. See also Figure 2.12.

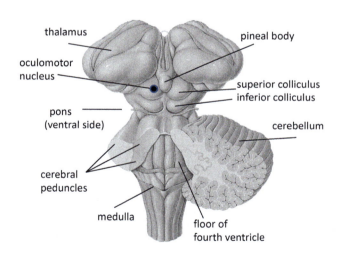

FIGURE 2.11
Dorsal view of the brainstem with (from bottom to top) medulla, pons and tectum containing the four colliculi. The egg-shaped thalamus on top is considered to be part of the forebrain. Cranial nerves and pons are located at the ventral side of the brainstem. The cerebellum is located at the level of the brainstem, but considered to be a functionally separate and unique structure. Also not visible is the reticular formation, which consists of a diffuse elongated formation of nerve fibers connecting a multitude of small nuclei.

INTRODUCING THE BRAIN

Tectum and tegmentum

The tectum (Latin for 'roof') and tegmentum (Latin for 'veil') are two structures of the midbrain. The tectum covers the dorsal portion and the tegmentum, the largest ventral part of the midbrain. The dorsal portion is at the same level as the superior colliculus, containing visuomotor neurons. A horizontal section of the tectum of the midbrain reveals that these neurons have relays in the superior colliculi. For auditory functions, the relays are situated in the inferior colliculi. A pathway called the tectopulvinar route, arising from the superior colliculi and projecting via the thalamus to the parietal cortex, is considered to be an old evolutionary route in the control of spatial orientation and its related eye-movements. Horizontal sections of the tegmentum reveal several nuclei like the substantia nigra, red nucleus and ventral tegmentum with widespread modulatory projections to the cortex, using the transmitter dopamine.

Dopamine pathways

The nigrostriatal pathway primarily regulates motor functions via relays in the dorsal striatum (Figure 2.12). The functions of the mesolimbic and mesocortical pathways mainly concern controlling emotional and attentional processes. Deregulation of the mesolimbic pathway plays a significant role in the development and maintenance of

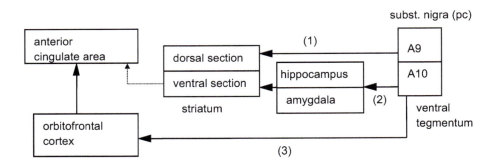

1 = nigrostriate system
2 = mesolimbic system
3 = mesocortical system

FIGURE 2.12
Sketch of three dopaminergic pathways. A9 and A10 indicate cell groups located in dorsal and ventral tegmentum, respectively. Both areas are involved in dopamine production, but have a different effect on the striatum and the frontal cortical areas.

addiction. Malfunctioning of the mesocortical pathways is often reflected in pathological states of the brain, like schizophrenia (in particular its 'negative symptoms') and attentional deficits.

Cerebellum

The cerebellum ('small brain') consists of separate groups of neurons located in the cerebellar cortex that have a unique structure, and contain four pairs of deep nuclei and white matter. In a way, its divisions resemble those of the forebrain's cerebral hemispheres. The cerebellum contains many parallel grooves that reflect a continuous thin layer of tissue tightly folded in the style of an accordion. Within this thin layer, there are several types of neurons with a highly regular arrangement, the most important being large Purkinje cells with rich dendrite arbors and a significant number of smaller granule cells.

The function of the cerebellum is indirect control of movement via a cerebellar-cortical loop that runs via the thalamus to the motor cortex, supplementing the two basal ganglia-cortical loops that will be discussed in greater detail in Chapter 5. Its control concerns the timing of movement, as well as the smooth execution of successive short-lasting movements. The cerebellar-cortical loop probably has several functions. One is timing and coordination of movements and balance between body limbs. The cerebellum is also involved in motor learning and considered to be a site of motor memories. Studies have further suggested a cognitive 'executive' role for the cerebellar-cortical loops that could include aspects of working memory for the timing of movements.

Medulla and pons

Close to the cerebellum are the medulla ('marrow') and pons ('bridge'). In the brainstem, the medulla forms the most caudal part, and the pons a large bulge. Both areas contain nuclei that regulate vital functions such as heart rate, breathing, swallowing and the sleep-wake cycle. Structures in the pons further play a role in regulating the startle reaction, and the state of arousal of the cortex via neurotransmitters. An important nucleus in the pons is the locus coeruleus; the source of widespread noradrenergic projections to hypothalamus, thalamus, hippocampus and neocortex, where they modulate the excitability of cells (see also Box 2.7). Other nuclei are the raphe nuclei that produce serotonin (5-HT). Raphe nuclei contain the rostral nuclei of the pons and the lower caudal nuclei of the medulla. The primary targets of the rostral nuclei are areas in the cortex, thalamus and striatum. Both sets of nuclei are often seen as parts of the reticular activation system, introduced earlier in this chapter.

> ### BOX 2.7 MAJOR NEUROTRANSMITTERS OF THE BRAIN
>
> The family name of compounds with a similar molecular structure:
>
> - Amino acids:
>   - Glutamate, principal excitatory neurotransmitter, with nuclei widespread in the brain and spinal cord.
>   - GABA, principal inhibitory neurotransmitter, with nuclei widespread in the brain and spinal cord.
>   - Glycine, an inhibitory neurotransmitter with nuclei in the brainstem, spinal cord.
> - Acetylcholine (Ach):
>   - Primary neurotransmitter in the central nervous system with nuclei in the dorsal pons, basal forebrain and medial septum. Behavior: REM sleep, learning, memory, movements (via the release in peripheral neuromuscular synapses).
> - Monoamines:
>   - Catecholamines (subclass):
>   - Dopamine (DA). Nuclei: substantia nigra (Pc). Behavior: motor system, motivation.
>   - Noradenaline (NA) (norepinephrine NE). Nuclei: locus coeruleus. Behavior: arousal, vigilance.
>   - Adrenaline (A) (epinephrine). Nuclei: Adrenal medulla. Behavior: stress, arousal, vigilance.
>   - Indolamines (subclass):
>   - Serotonin (5HT). Nuclei: raphe nuclei in the midbrain, pons and medulla. Behavior: mood states, REM sleep, dreaming, arousal.

Connections in the brain: from neurons to networks

We are born with a brain with a fixed maximum number of cells. The brain is not a diffuse network of arbitrarily connected nerve cells, but a system with a high degree of structural organization. Also, the white matter tracts that connect nerve cells are not randomly arranged, but follow the topographical organization of structurally and functionally distinct regions. Among other things, this is manifested by the fact that neurons do not connect to all other neurons, but often show clusters of locally dense connections with neurons nearby.

The brain as a whole functions as a 'super-system' that integrates different organizational levels, ranging from minimally small units (the micro-level) to larger units (the macro-level: see Figure 2.13). Nerve tracts (bundles of axons covered with myelin) provide the long-range pathways connecting regions that are more widely apart (Figure 2.14). The

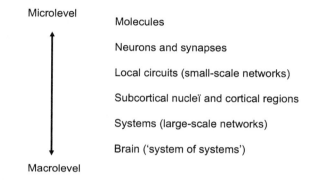

FIGURE 2.13
Structural organization levels of the brain running from systems at the micro to macro level. Connections between neurons are formed in increasingly complex patterns starting with neurons and synapses, to local cortical circuits and subcortical nuclei, to large-scale networks.

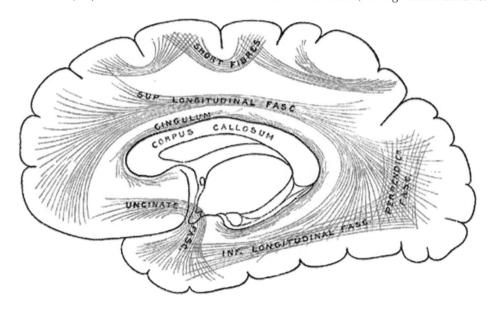

FIGURE 2.14
Major long-range association fibers running within the cerebral hemispheres, connecting the posterior and anterior regions in the cerebrum. The superior and inferior longitudinal fasciculi and the cingulum.

Source: Gray Atlas, nr 751.

INTRODUCING THE BRAIN

next sections will first consider structures and functions at the micro-level of the brain, (as manifested in neurons and local networks), and then proceed to networks at a larger scale.

Micro-level: neurons and synapses

At the microscopic level the cell body of a neuron and its branching structures called dendrites and axons (with its branches called collaterals) form the basic unit of communication in the nervous system. The dendrite of a neuron receives multiple input axons of other neurons. When their summed potentials are large enough to depolarize the cell membrane, they elicit an action potential that propagates along the axon to its terminal buttons (Figure 2.15). Then, at the end of the axon, there is a spectacular alteration of the membrane permeability, called synaptic transmission. When the action potential arrives at the presynaptic membrane, it triggers the opening of voltage-gated Ca^{2+} channels increasing the intracellular Ca^{2+} concentration.

This process, in turn, triggers the fusion of some synaptic vesicles within the presynaptic membrane resulting in a release of neurotransmitters into the synaptic cleft, the space between the pre- and postsynapse (Figure 2.16). Here they bind to receptors on

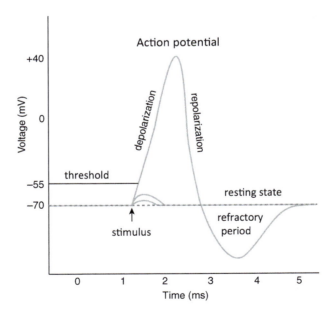

FIGURE 2.15
The action potential is released when a depolarizing current reaches the firing threshold of an axon. This process is followed by a rapid inflow of sodium (Na^+) ions and outflow of potassium (K^+) ions through the cell membrane.

the post-synaptic membrane that generate two forms of synaptic potentials, excitatory postsynaptic potentials (EPSPs) and inhibitory postsynaptic potentials (IPSPs). EPSPs depolarize the membrane and move it closer to the threshold of the action potential. IPSPs hyperpolarize the membrane and move it farther away from the threshold. In order to depolarize a neuron enough to cause an action potential, there must be enough EPSPs to both counterbalance the IPSPs and depolarize the membrane from its resting membrane potential to its threshold. Importantly, synaptic potentials are not only effective at the level of local individual neurons. They also provide a mechanism for reconfiguring neural circuits, by 'leaking' of electrical activity in a local synapse to coupled neurons dictated by the synchronous timing of potentials (Alcami & Pereda, 2019). As such, electric synapses contribute to synaptic integration at more global level of neural circuits.

Growth and development

Genetic codes determine to a large extent the organization of the central nervous system as maintained across generations. Nonetheless, there is significant variability in neural organization, even among individuals with the same genetic properties, like identical twins. The number of synaptic connections, as well as the patterns of axonal connections make this apparent. In the early fetal period many nerve cells migrate from the ventricles through glia cells to the brain's cortex. A set of genes, called the genetic envelope, largely determines this process (Changeux, 1985) that controls the division, migration and differentiation of nerve cells as well as the onset of their spontaneous activity (Kostovic et al., 2014).

The ventricles play a vital role in the migration process because they contain a kind of 'map' of the neural pathways and their destinations in the cortex to where the nerve cells migrate. For example, one zone determines migration to the visual cortex, another zone migration to the frontal cortex. Building the structure of the cerebral cortex starts with the lower layers and ends with the higher layers.

The growth of new brain cells and their interconnections (synapses, dendrites and axons) occurs mainly before birth and in early childhood. At the end of pregnancy, there is a period of exuberant growth of synapses, with a 'big bang', starting around the moment of birth. The peak of synaptic connections then occurs around the second year of life. In the first two years of life, there is a rich branching ('arborization') of dendrites, followed by a process of synaptic growth. This involves the formation of new synapses as well as elimination ('pruning') of superfluous synapses in childhood (Figure 2.17). Findings further suggest that the dynamic process of overconnectivity followed by pruning also operates at the systems level and helps to reconfigure and rebalance cortical and subcortical connectivity in the developing brain (Uddin et al., 2010). Lack of synchronicity between pairs of neurons could be a causal factor in the elimination of

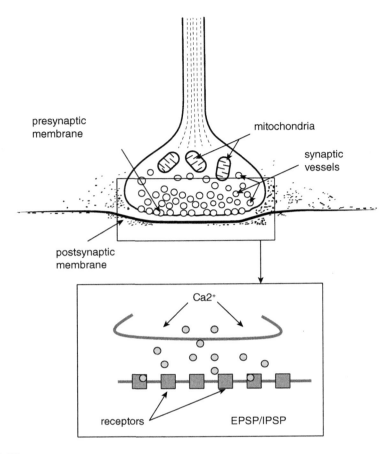

FIGURE 2.16
Synapse and released neurotransmitter. The opening of presynaptic calcium ion channels stimulates synaptic vesicles, which in turn release their neurotransmitters across the synaptic cleft, binding to receptors in the postsynaptic membrane (below). This process subsequently generates excitatory or inhibitory postsynaptic potentials (EPSPs or IPSPs).

superfluous neurons and their respective connections. The rule underlying this selection process is believed to be the degree of temporal correlation of firing patterns of input and output neurons. This illustrates that Hebb's rule, the principle earlier referred to as a mechanism for learning, also determines which neurons will 'win or lose' in the neural competition between neurons during early development (Deacon, 1997).

Axons grow relatively fast, and often reach their target cells before the growth of dendrites is completed. Myelination of the axons is a process that progresses to early adolescence, with neural connections of the prefrontal cortex only completed in late adolescence. Changes in the architecture of functional networks in the developing brain

INTRODUCING THE BRAIN

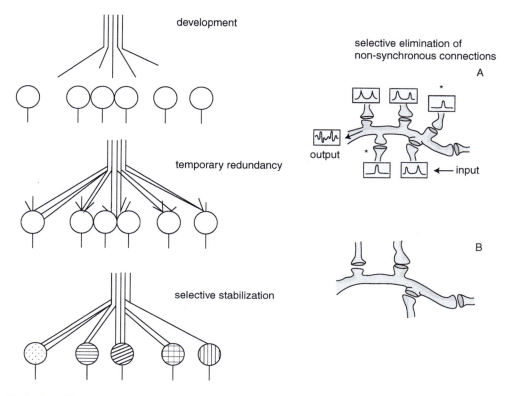

FIGURE 2.17
Left: three stages in brain cell development: primary growth, temporary redundancy and selective stabilization. Dotted lines: gradually disappearing connections. Right: lack of synchronicity as a possible mechanism that causes the selective elimination of neurons. A: original, B: the final state.

Source: Adapted from Changeux (1985) and Deacon (1997).

also become manifest in the increase in functional connectivity between frontal and posterior areas (Langeslag et al., 2013; Jolles, 2011; Sherman, 2014). Neurogenesis, i.e. the generation of new neurons in adult humans, remains a controversial issue. However there is evidence suggesting that neurogenesis of nerve cells takes place in the dental gyrus of the hippocampus in adults, and is a potential relevant mechanism underlying intact and disturbed memory functions in adults (Kempermann, et al., 2018).

Topographic, horizontal and vertical organization

An essential function of nerve cells is to encode information. A neural code is the property of a neuron or a cluster of neurons that will make it respond to specific physical characteristics of a stimulus, also referred to as its receptive field (see Box 2.8). For example, the organization of the visual system is *retinotopic*: specific locations of ganglion cells in the retina (their receptive fields) are mapped to specific geometrical positions (left/right, top/bottom) in the visual cortex. The retinal fields, in turn, correspond to different regions of the visual field. Not only does the retinotopic organization apply to the visual cerebral cortex, but also to intermediary structures as the thalamus and lateral geniculate nucleus that relay visual information from the retina to the primary visual cortex, Receptive fields can vary from 1.2° in V1 (primary visual cortex) to as large as 40° in TE (inferior temporal cortex), an area in the secondary visual cortex downstream in the visual pathway. Location mapping is also characteristic for the somatic-sensory and motor areas of the brain, that have a *somatotopic* organization, with maps of the cortex providing a point-to-point representation of the body's surface. The higher the resolution (accuracy) of the body area, like in the fingertips, the more neurons represent that area. In the motor cortex, this somatotopy is particularly evident. For example, a stimulus applied to the medial wall of the precentral gyrus (just in front of the central sulcus, see also Figure 2.3) will create a movement of the foot. Applied to the lateral wall it will lead to movement of the tongue.

Spatial coding in auditory perception is called *tonotopy* or cochleotopy. But here the receptive fields of the hair cells within the cochlea do not respond to spatial location, but to specific frequencies of sound. The same principle holds for the receptive field of taste receptors, where chemoreceptors in one place on the tongue are sensitive to salt, in another place for the sweet property.

Cells in the cortex and their respective branches differ in form and function depending on their cortical region. Detailed knowledge of their anatomy and location resulted from microscopic histological techniques (e.g. Golgi staining) to classify neurons according to their morphology (also called cytoarchitecture). The resulting brain maps allowed to partition neurons of different regions of the cerebral cortex, according to reproducible differences in cell and fiber layering and packing (Figure 2.18).

Cortical layers and columns

The cortex forms a folded thin sheet of gray matter around 3 millimeters thick that has become highly convoluted in the course of evolution. Anatomists call each cortical fold a sulcus, and the smooth area between folds a gyrus. Histological techniques also led to precise sectioning of the thin layer of the cortex that contains unmyelinated cell bodies arranged in six horizontal layers (Figure 2.19). Cells in different layers not only differ in form but also in functional characteristics, dependent on the cortical region (e.g. visual,

INTRODUCING THE BRAIN

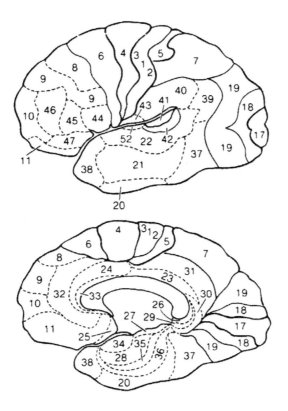

FIGURE 2.18
Classification and numbering of cortical regions according to Brodmann, by the form (cytoarchitecture) of cortical neurons. Other names are often used for the numbered regions (such as V1 for area 17) or their subdivisions (like V2, V3 and V4 for area 18). Brodmann regions have also been useful to classify large-scale functional networks of the brain.

motor) and depth of the cortical layer. Layer 1, the molecular layer, contains mainly glial cells assumed to support nerve cells; the deeper layers 2–6 contain nerve cells including pyramidal cells and granular cells. For example, in the somatosensory region, the cortex has a thick layer 4 with many small stellate (or granule) cells that accumulate in a dense layer, and receive primarily afferent axons from the thalamus. The motor region, in contrast, has a thick layer 5 with many large pyramidal cells sending out efferent axons. Underneath the sixth layer, the efferent and afferent axons together form fiber bundles or 'fasciculi'. They connect regions in the posterior and anterior regions of the cortex within the same hemisphere, called association fibers (Figure 2.14) or the opposite hemisphere called commissures, the largest central part being the corpus callosum. Afferent axons enter the cortex, coming from

INTRODUCING THE BRAIN

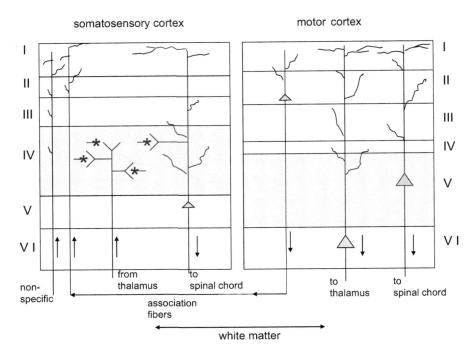

FIGURE 2.19
Schematic view of six cortical layers. I = molecular layer with glial cells. Left, somatosensory cortex with thick layer IV and stellate cells. Right, motor cortex with thick layer V and pyramidal cells.

nuclei in the thalamus, or other cortical areas within the same or within the opposite hemisphere. Many of the thalamocortical pathways function as 'feedback loops' with re-entries to the same neurons that sent out signals to the cortex. Similarly, efferent axons (or 'tracts') leaving the cortex connect to targets in other parts of the cortex at the same side, to the other hemisphere, or to subcortical nuclei of the thalamus (called projection tracts). Axons of pyramidal cells leaving the cortex are involved in the control of motor neurons that control our muscles, for example to the colliculi superior that control eye movements or to motor neurons in the brainstem that control movements of our limbs.

The layered structure of the brain applies not only to the neocortex but also to the cerebellum, superior colliculi and the lateral geniculate nucleus in the thalamus. Only in the nuclei of the basal ganglia, the cortex does not show a layered, but more a 'patchwork' arrangement of neurons.

In addition to horizontal layers, the primary sensory regions and motor regions in the cortex also show a distinct columnar organization. A cortical column is a group of neurons in the cortex perpendicular to the cortical surface of around 2 mm deep that have nearly identical receptive fields. Their isolated function also follows from their anatomy: neurons have many more vertical and reciprocal connections within a column than horizontal connections with cells in adjacent columns.

Following Mountcastle's pioneering work on the architecture of the somatic-sensory cortex (Figure 2.20), Hubel and Wiesel (1959) were the two pioneers that started exploring the structure of the primary visual cortex. They discovered orientation sensitivity as one of the hallmarks of neurons in the primary visual cortex. Across a 2 × 2 mm chunk of space – also referred to as a cortical module – the neurons have similar location sensitivity, with different columns corresponding to different orientations, input from the left and right eye, color sensitivity and size sensitivity. The same modular organization is repeated for each location in the primary visual cortex. A series of these chunks thus allows for the full representation of the external visual space.

Local networks in the cortex

Neurons at the cortical level also tend to cluster in small densely connected communities of cells that talk only to cells not too far away. The intrinsic arrangement of these smaller local circuits was primarily identified on the basis of microscopic studies that

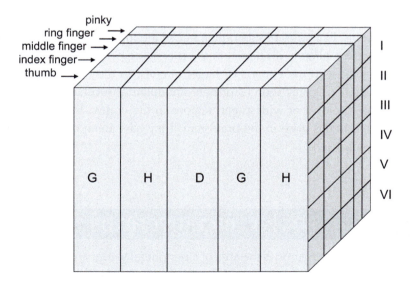

FIGURE 2.20
Idealized example of vertical columns and horizontal layers of the somatosensory cortex. Each 'slice' (from front to back) corresponds to a different finger. Different letters (columns from left to right) correspond to different somatosensory features: G = joint, D = pressure and H = hair. In the visual cortex, we find another type of organization. Here separate columns are specialized for line orientation, the left and right eye and the shape of visual objects.

subsequently categorized neurons according to the shape of cell bodies (as represented, for example, in the Brodmann map of Figure 2.18). In other cases, the extrinsic innervations of the cortex from the thalamus determined their organization. These could take shape as cortical 'slabs' placed side by side like books on a library shelf, or as 3D 'chunks' or 'mini-modules' in subsections of the cortex, comprising combinations of horizontal layers and vertical columns (as shown in Figure 2.19). Finally, neurons are also categorized according to the type of neurotransmitter that modulated their activity, or the reaction of the cell bodies to specific antibodies.

In the primary cortical regions, the function of local networks is to provide 'percepts'. That is, copies of the features of the perceptual environment. In the secondary association areas, receptive fields will gradually increase in size, relative to those of the primary sensory cortex. For example, in neurons of the extrastriate visual cortex, local networks already encode for combinations of features, rather than separate features. Further upstream in the visual pathway, neurons in the inferior temporal cortex still form columns, but these occupy a much larger area. These neurons fire not to specific features, but to full objects: hands, faces or various geometric shapes.

Subcortical nuclei

At the subcortical level local circuits also take shape as anatomically distinct clusters or 'nuclei'. Here the cell bodies do not always form horizontal layers, but more circular patchwork patterns. Examples of subcortical nuclei are the basal ganglia, thalamus and amygdala, structures already discussed in the preceding paragraphs. The role of these nuclei becomes clear in the context of larger circuits. In these circuits they function either as relay stations or as sources of neuromodulatory substances that project via various pathways to local or widespread regions in the cortex. Most of the dedicated neurotransmitter circuits arise in the brainstem. They have been described in detail in the preceding paragraphs.

BOX 2.8   RECEPTIVE FIELDS

A receptive field of a neuron is the area of a peripheral sensory receptor (a specific section of the skin or the retina), within which stimulation will cause the neuron to fire. It may also be defined in terms of the stimulus, that is as the section of the physical dimension of a stimulus (the size of visual field, range of line orientation, the segment of a color spectrum of a visual object, or the segment of frequency spectrum of an auditory stimulus), within which the stimulus will make

continued

the neuron fire. In the primary visual cortex, sensory cells are arranged in different geometrical columns that code for location, orientation or color and movement.

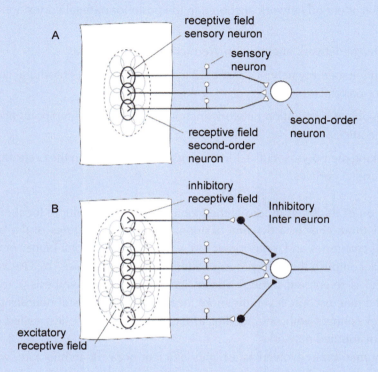

The receptive field is larger for a second-order neuron than for sensory neurons (see insert, A, dashed larger ellipse and small solid ellipses, respectively). The receptive fields of higher-order neurons commonly have a central excitatory region, surrounded by a region controlled by an inhibitory interneuron (figure B). This arrangement will increase the spatial resolution of the sensory system (see insert B). Adapted from Kandel et al. (1991).

Large-scale networks

Functional segregation methods have gradually receded in favor of functional integration methods, presenting images of much larger functional networks (Koch & Davis, 1994). The billions of neurons in our brain connect with one another in circuits, via an astonishing number of 10 trillion synapses. The numerous smaller cell assemblies cluster in a smaller amount of large-scale functional or 'core networks', a term that was first used by Mesulam (1990). In his view, the human brain contains at least five major core functional networks:

- a spatial attention network anchored in the posterior parietal cortex and frontal eye fields,
- a language network anchored in Wernicke and Boca's areas,
- an explicit memory network anchored in the hippocampal-entorhinal complex and inferior parietal cortex,
- a face-object recognition network anchored in the middle-temporal and temporo-polar cortices,
- a working memory-executive function network anchored in the prefrontal and inferior parietal cortices.

The function of the brain in toto is the global mapping of multiple local maps, which connect with another in a dynamic fashion. Correlated structures of the brain create perceptual categories and motor programs, without the need of a higher order supervisor. They accomplish this by a process called 'recursive synthesis' by Gerard Edelman: information is re-entered through successive and recursive synthesis across maps in time. At the macroscopic level, the more local cortical clusters of neurons and subcortical nuclei connect with one another in larger neural assemblies, called systems, or global or distributed networks.

The human brain evolved as a highly efficient network architecture, whose structural connectivity is capable of generating a vast repertoire of functional states. Understanding how these functional states emerged from patterns of communication between large numbers of neuronal elements, is one of the enduring challenges of modern neuroscience. So far, few studies have attempted to describe the functional properties of the brain in an integrated fashion, using the complex architecture of structural connections to elucidate its functional properties. But new techniques and insights developed in the last two decades now offer a glimpse into the complicated way various structures of the brain work together as an integrated whole.

Imaging techniques

The advent of techniques for measuring in vivo brain activity in humans with imaging techniques like MRI and fMRI supplemented and sometimes even converged with findings derived from basic neurobiology and neuroanatomy. Although anatomical studies provided an abundance of valuable information on specific regions and its smaller circuits and nuclei, it remained mostly unknown how regions communicated with another. It also became increasingly clear that it was difficult to attribute a specific function to a cortical area, given the dependence of cerebral activity on the anatomical connections between distant brain regions. Box 2.9 presents a summary of some large-scale networks identified with fMRI in conditions of rest or during active task performance.

Neuroimaging has become a predominant method in 'systems neuroscience' over the past twenty years, establishing functional segregation as a principle of brain organization in humans. Imaging studies further supported the view that cognitive functions are represented as large-scale networks extending over widely separated regions of the brain, often encapsulating more local segregated networks. The question of how these segregated activities are integrated proves much more difficult to answer.

BOX 2.9 SUMMARY OF LARGE-SCALE NETWORKS IDENTIFIED WITH FUNCTIONAL IMAGING (SEE ALSO FIGURE 4.23)

- Large-scale network: a term referring to neural systems that are distributed across the entire extent of the brain, in particular the cortex.

- Default-mode network (DMN, sometimes referred to as a 'resting state' or 'task-negative' network): includes the posterior cingulate cortex, the medial prefrontal cortex and the lateral parietal cortex, showing increased activity during a 'baseline' condition, or when an individual is at rest. Presumed to form an integrated system for self-related cognitive activity, including autobiographical, self-monitoring and social functions.

- Intrinsic connectivity network (ICN): a large-scale network of interdependent brain areas. It includes brain networks captured in either the resting state (like the DMN), as well as in task-based neuroimaging data. The term ICN was proposed by Seeley et al. (2007) as an alternative for 'resting-state network', since the brain is never completely at rest.

- Central-executive network (CEN): brain network responsible for high-level cognitive functions, notably the control of attention and working memory, linking the dorsolateral frontal and parietal cortices, particularly the intraparietal sulcus.

- Frontal-parietal attention (FPA) network: a network in the dorsal convexity of the human frontal and parietal lobes, presumed to be crucially involved in the selection of sensory contents by attention. It comprises the intraparietal sulcus, the inferior parietal lobe and the dorsal premotor cortex, including the frontal eye field. The FPA can be seen as a specific form of the CEN.

continued

> ▶ Saliency network (SN): a network consisting of three main cortical areas: the dorsal anterior cingulate cortex, the left and anterior right insula and the adjacent inferior frontal gyri. The SN presumably represents a collection of regions of the brain that select which stimuli deserve our attention.

Development of techniques was needed to assess the temporal and even causal relationship between areas in the working or resting brain. A promising step in that direction is made by network neuroscience that conceptualizes brain function as emerging from the collective action of numerous system elements and their mutual interconnections. Although it also incorporates a field like neural genetics, mapping the functions of the brain with greater precision has been one of its primary targets. Network neuroscience represents brain networks as sets of neural elements and their pair-wise connections, often summarized in the mathematical form of an adjacency matrix (also known as a connection matrix). The next section briefly considers some of the techniques that are used to assess patterns of connectivity in the human cortex, and briefly introduces some large-scale cortical-subcortical circuits that are of particular importance in understanding how memory functions are implemented in the brain.

Linking structural to functional networks

Structural connectivity (also called *connectome*) reflects the anatomical (physical) relationships between neural elements; that is, their synaptic connections or inter-regional projections (the 'wiring diagram'). Imaging techniques like MRI enabled mapping the brain's structural architecture in much more detail than in the earlier years of Brodmann (1909). This held for the neural connections (white matter tracts) as well as for distinct regions (grey matter) in the brain. Tractography, an MRI technique based on diffusion of water molecules, enabled to produce detailed 3D maps of the long- and short-distance fibers that provided the necessary structural framework for functional MRI studies. Another MRI–based contribution made it possible to parcellate human cortical areas on a more detailed scale than with the older cytoarchitectonic maps of Brodmann (see Box 2.10 and Figure 2.21).

Functional connectivity describes the set of pairwise statistical dependencies between the neurophysiologic signals (time courses) recorded from individual neural elements (already introduced in the methods section of Chapter 1). Of particular importance were low-frequency oscillations (0 01–0.1 Hz) of BOLD fMRI time series that occur in resting state networks. This research suggested that in the brain the shortest paths are indeed utilized to ensure reliable and efficient communication and hence stronger functional connectivity. Conversely, a longer path length between two neural elements could be

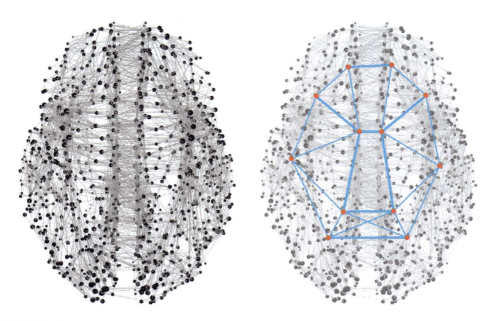

FIGURE 2.21
Linking structural connectivity and functional connectivity. Left: a network of structural connections (grey lines) that link distinct neural elements (brain regions; black dots). Right: The resulting statistical dependencies (in blue) among regional time series are expressed in functional connectivity.

Source: Adapted from Koenigsberger et al. (2017).

associated with less direct signaling, yielding weaker functional interactions. Indeed, several studies have shown that the magnitude of functional interactions shows a negative correlation with path length.

To explore the functional significance of specific regions in the resting-state fMRI, it is necessary to compare it with a conventional task-dependent fMRI. It starts with selecting a brain region (called a 'seed' region, e.g. the motor cortex) that shows a high level of activation in the task of interest (e.g. a finger tapping task). After correlating the seed voxel with the time series of the resting state voxels, and subsequently with all other voxels in the brain, one obtains a functional connectivity map reflecting all voxels that are functionally related to the voxels in the seeded area.

Modeling functional networks

Functional network modeling revealed interesting functional characteristics of larger assemblies of neurons measured at the voxel level. The increased blood flow in activated areas in fMRI scans also appeared to correlate with the electrical activity of cell

> **BOX 2.10 CONNECTOMY: A NEW APPROACH IN BRAIN RESEARCH**
>
> There are globally two ways to study the complex structure of the brain. The first is *cartography*; the second is *connectomy* (van Essen, 2013). Cartography implies the mapping of specific brain areas based on the structure of grey matter (cytoarchitecture) or white matter (myelin architecture). Much has been achieved in this field through in vitro microscopic analysis of slices of brain tissue of deceased animals or humans. Connectomy, in turn, is based on in vivo imaging of the structure and function of the brain with MRI and fMRI. It also aims at analyzing properties of the total brain (called connectome), rather than those of isolated areas (Sporns et al., 2005). Much of the research in this field has been bundled in the Human Connectome Project, which aims to design a complete and precise map of human brain connections (van Essen et al., 2012). Connectomy has made it possible to draw cortical maps with much greater precision and based on more neural information, than the older cartographic maps based on the anatomy of cell bodies. For example, Martin Glasser and colleagues, using MRI and fMRI, succeeded in constructing a detailed 3D map containing 180 different areas, based on multimodal cortical parcellations of group averaged imaging data. Parcellations were based on information that included measurements of cortical thickness, brain function, connectivity between regions, the topographic organization of cells in brain tissue, and the levels of myelin. Each discrete area on the map contains cells with similar structure, function and connectivity. Another improvement was a new technique for fiber tracking called *tractography*. Tractography is an MRI-based 3D modeling technique used to represent neural tracts using data collected by diffusion-weighted images visually. These structural MRI maps are far more accurate than the older myelinographic maps, and often provide the 'skeleton' for computing functional imaging maps (Figure 2.21).

assembles firing synchronously. An exciting new avenue is studies of connectivity in large-scale networks of the brain in a resting state (see Box 2.9), shedding more light on the overall structure of the brain. This finding suggested that a high level of global efficiency of the brain might originate from the small-world organization of modular networks, which combined highly dense local connections with more sparse long-range connections. In particular, the fibers of the white-matter cingulum tract seemed to provide the connections between more widely separated activated local networks. Interestingly, activated areas in a resting state condition often resemble patterns of activity found in the task-related fMRI conditions, suggesting that it reflects some 'default' condition of the brain, keeping its systems running to meet demands of the environment that may turn up.

Communication efficiency

Defining criteria for communication efficiency of brain-based networks has been one of the challenging problems raised in neural network modeling (Koenigsberger et al., 2017). Understanding the relationship between structure and functionality from a natural selection perspective is particularly challenging in the case of biological networks. Biological systems are not engineered from a preconceived concept, but have evolved from 'tinkering' of already existing structures. Experimental and computational studies suggested that a hierarchical modular organization emerges as an optimal cost-efficient solution to diverse problems. Examples are facilitating the coexistence of functional integration and segregation, and enabling evolvability and adaptability while minimizing wiring and energetic costs.

So far, the new imaging methods do not tell much about what the active brain is doing. Although there still is a gap separating cognitive and network functionality, links are beginning to emerge between empirical studies of brain networks and formal models of cognition. For example, local networks now are also implicated in theories of learning, allowing to link features of network topology to the cost of cognitive control. Thus, studies of the functional architecture and dynamics of networks in the brain have increasingly begun to illuminate formal accounts of human cognition and behavior.

Cortical-subcortical networks

With networks becoming more complex, it is likely that already existing simpler networks (operating at lower levels of the brains hierarchy) are extended and combined, while it is less likely that complex structures are generated entirely de novo. When these networks evolve, they will maximize the overall processing power of the neural architecture, including the evolutionary older structures. Nonetheless, modeling of functional networks as introduced earlier has focused almost exclusively on large-scale networks in the cortex, without considering its connections with the subcortical areas.

Almost every region in the cerebral cortex connects via long reciprocal pathways with subcortical structures. As described earlier, this includes connections with the amygdala, hippocampus, basal ganglia and cerebellum but also with nuclei responsible for the production of the neurotransmitters dopamine, acetylcholine and noradrenaline. Their collaboration mainly takes place through cortical-subcortical processing loops, whose primary function is the modulation (enhancement or attenuation) of neocortical activity. Due to their connectivity to the cortical regions, these structures have a significant 'pivotal function' within the large-scale networks (called 'appendages' by Gerald Edelman).

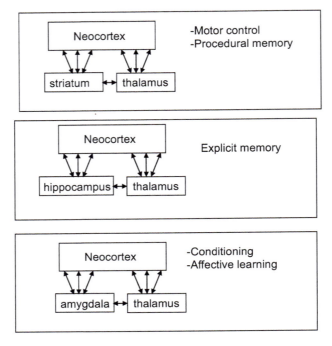

FIGURE 2.22
Some highly schematical circuits, connecting neocortex with subcortical structures, and their functions.

Figure 2.22 presents some (highly simplified) examples of such circuits. Control of motor and motor learning processes, for example, takes place through a circuit that includes areas in the frontal cortex and structures in the thalamus and basal ganglia (upper panel). A network consisting of the hippocampus, thalamus and the posterior and prefrontal cortex is involved in storing information in explicit (conscious) memory (middle panel). Associative and affective learning are regulated by a network of areas like the thalamus, the amygdala and the medial-ventral regions in the frontal cortex.

Laterality and the brain

Introduction

Most studies of the functional properties of the brain have highlighted regions of the frontal, posterior and temporal cortex, associated with perception, action and storage of information. The clear functional differentiation between the regions along the anterior-posterior axis of the brain contrasts with that of the two cerebral hemispheres. This creates the impression that hemispheric functions underlying cognition are globally similar. Contrasting to this view, cognitive researchers have discovered that the two halves of the brain do differ in their functional properties.

Since cerebral lateralization and language are both uniquely tied to humans, it is not surprising that evolution has approached the two issues as two sides of the same coin. Lateralization is, therefore, an essential vehicle in an evolutionary scenario of language development. The left hemisphere supposedly evolved gradually from tool handling to a more extended system of communication, while the right hemisphere probably evolved as a system with extended representations of the perceptual environment (Donald, 1991).

The functions of the left and right cortical hemispheres are not only a subject of science but have also received a tremendous public interest. But public interest often led to simple left/right dichotomies, with rational, linguistic and analytical versus intuitive, spatial and holistic as the most common classifications. In this paragraph, we argue that the complex structure of the brain and its related cognitive functions do not always justify their absolute functional separation and that hemispheric specializations are rather relative than absolute. The following section addresses two aspects of cerebral organization and lateralization, the anatomical characteristics of the left and right hemispheres and their connections, and their functional evolutionary characteristics.

Anatomy and functions of the cerebral hemispheres

The strong symmetries of the human body are manifested most clearly in the pairwise organization of body limbs like arms, legs and the senses. Less conspicuously it is also manifested in the topography of the primary sensory and motor areas in the brain to where our body parts and senses project.

Symmetries

The 'homunculi' of the somatosensory and motor cortex are a well-known example of body-to-brain mapping is (Figure 2.23). The primary visual and auditory cortical areas show the same strict symmetry: areas for analysis of color, shape and motion, but also analysis of sound characteristics are structurally similar in the left and right hemisphere. It also occurs in the secondary areas, considered to be the site of higher mental functions, memory, attention and awareness and lower structures of the brain like the amygdala, basal ganglia, thalamus and hippocampus. The overall structural similarity of the two halves of the brain gives rise to the suggestion that they also function as equivalent and autonomous systems of information processing.

Behavioral studies, however, have presented a different picture, suggesting that there are marked differences in the functioning of the two halves of the brain, in particular the capacity of the left cortical hemisphere for language and speech. Motor skills

INTRODUCING THE BRAIN

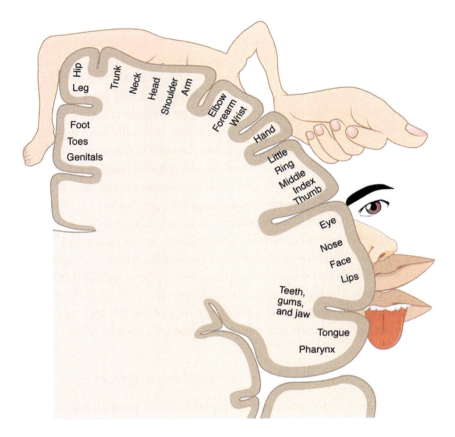

FIGURE 2.23
The symmetrical topographic organization of the primary somatosensory cortex (Penfields 'cortical homunculus'). The same symmetry is found in the primary motor cortex and the auditory and visual projection areas of the left and right cerebral hemispheres.

Source: Wikipedia. Creative Commons Attribution 3.0, Unported license. Author: Open Stax college.

performed by the right hand and controlled by the left cortical hemisphere are generally better developed than those of the left hand in most right-handers, forming 90% of the population. Visual-spatial attention functions, however, are better developed in the right posterior half of he cortex. For example, attention neglect occurs more often after lesions in the right than in the left parietal cortex.

Early research conducted by Norman Geschwind suggested that these functional differences could arise from anatomical differences in the temporal lobe of right-handers. In 65% of these right-handers, the planum temporale appeared to be stronger developed in the left than right temporal lobe; 24% showed no difference, and 11% showed a larger area in the right hemisphere (Geschwind, 1979). But more recent studies using

MRI techniques presented a less clear picture of the difference in the anatomy of the temporal plane (Beaton, 1997). Later, Geschwind and Galaburda hypothesized that production of the male sex hormone testosterone could be a significant causal factor in the development of left/right handedness, implying that testosterone production in prenatal development caused the left hemisphere to lag. This development could have led to a predisposition of two symptoms in left-handers: dyslexic disorders and disorders of the autoimmune system, leading to higher sensitivity to allergic conditions. This theory also accounts for the fact that left-handedness occurs more often in men than in women, in particular in male twins (Galaburda, 1990).

Microanatomic research has also revealed differences in structure and organization of cell groups between the left and right posterior temporal hemispheres. For example, neurons in the left temporal cortex appear to exhibit a more explicit column structure than neurons in the right temporal cortex. The precise relationship between the microstructure of brain regions and lateralization of cognitive functions, however, still remains an open question.

Connections of the corpus callosum

The corpus callosum is a massive bundle of white matter that connects areas in the frontal, central and posterior cortex. The frontal part is called genu ('knee') and has a pointed end called rostrum (see Figure 2.24, left). The middle part is called truncus

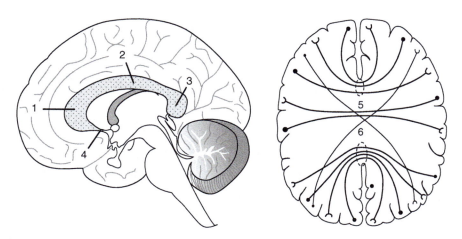

FIGURE 2.24
Left: Medial view of the corpus callosum with main connections. 1 = genu, 2 = truncus, 3 = splenium and 4 = rostrum. Right: Horizontal view of the two callosal 'radiations': forceps minor (5) and major (6).

Source: From Kahle (1986).

('trunk'), and the thickened back end is the splenium. The U-shaped callosum fibers (also known as radiations) connect the anterior and posterior hemispheres of the brain. The front part is called forceps minor, the rear part forceps major (Figure 2.24, right).

The secondary visual areas (area 18) contain very dense interhemispheric connections, while the primary visual areas (area 17), and the hand and foot regions of the somatosensory projection area (areas 1, 2 and 3) are not interconnected at all. The anterior part of the corpus callosum is involved in higher order transfer of semantic formation, while in the more posterior regions the transfer concerns perceptual (visual, tactile and auditory) information.

The corpus callosum is not the only connection between both hemispheres. There are links between hemispheres at lower levels of the brain as well, in the hippocampus, the thalamus, the anterior commissure (anterior to the thalamus) and posterior commissure (posterior to the thalamus).

Finally, two types of tracts can be distinguished in the corpus callosum. Fibers projecting to the same regions in both hemispheres (called homotopic or symmetric fibers) and fibers projecting to different regions in both hemispheres (heterotopic fibers, see Figure 2.25). Heterotopic fibers too have collaterals that project to the area in the same (ipsilateral) hemisphere from where they originate. An example is a nerve fiber originating in the left prefrontal cortex projecting to the premotor areas of the right and left

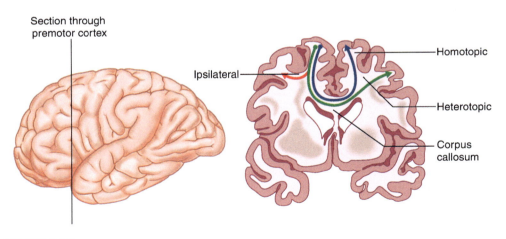

FIGURE 2.25
Coronal section of the premotor cortex (left) with three types of callosal fibers (right): homotopic, heterotopic and ipsilateral fibers.

Source: From Gazzaniga et al. (2002).

hemisphere. These ipsilateral fibers and projections are developed more strongly than the contralateral fibers.

Function of callosal connections

The corpus callosum provides primary means of communication between the cerebral hemispheres, thus forming the basis of concerted cortical action (Gazzaniga & Sperry, 1967). Hemispheric specialization must also have been constrained by callosal evolution. Although the corpus callosum promotes communication between both hemispheres, there is still no agreement on its precise role in mediating human behavior. The primary motor and visual areas contain relatively few hemispheric connections that suggest a relative autonomy of the pathways and local networks within each hemisphere, which process visual input and motor output.

The secondary or association areas that form the site of higher cognitive functions are located in large-scale networks, distributed over a relatively wide part of the brain. In these networks, the denser callosal connections between the two hemispheres suggest intensive two-way patterns of communication between the cortical regions at the levels of anterior, posterior and temporal cortices. Such patterns might ensure a high level of processing as well as redundancy of perceptual, memory and action related regions in the brain.

In specific cognitive tasks sensory projections to the cortical hemispheres become activated in a differential fashion. A suitable example are visual-spatial attention tasks that require focusing on positions in the right and left visual fields (see also Chapter 4). Indeed, attention research using measures like event-related potentials and functional imaging did show differential activation of the extrastriate regions to input from the contralateral positions in the visual field. Also, inhibitory connections can help to suppress movements of limbs that are driven by the other ('wrong') hemisphere, thus playing a more competitive role. An example is grabbing or catching a ball with the right hand rather than the left.

An often-used tool in experimental research, focusing on the specific functional quality of the hemispheres, is the divided visual field paradigm. This paradigm takes advantage of the anatomically crossed (contralateral and more direct) projections of information presented in the right and left halves of the visual field to the opposite hemisphere (Figure 2.26).

The corpus callosum develops as part of the myelination process in the first years of our lives. This development is not only characterized by dendritic arborizations and growth of synaptic connections but also by the increased selectivity of connections with target neurons to which the axons project. In the early years after birth, the interhemispheric connections, collateral fibers and their projections develop into stable patterns of selective connections. Presumably most of the denser connections between

INTRODUCING THE BRAIN

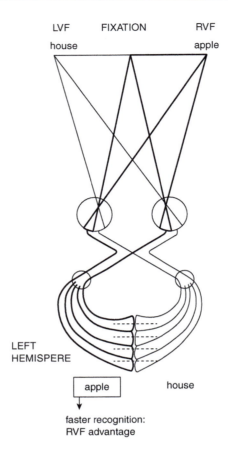

FIGURE 2.26
The divided visual field (DVF) paradigm. Words presented tachistoscopically in the left and right visual fields (LVF, RVF) project via opposite halves of the retina, the optic chiasm and thalamus to the opposite (contralateral) visual cortices. Notice that this set-up does not ensure complete functional separation between the hemispheres. That is because information to the specialized hemisphere (e.g. via the solid lines from the RVF to left hemisphere) can still 'cross over' to the other (ipsilateral) hemisphere through the corpus callosum (e.g. via the stippled lines to the right hemisphere).

homotopic (symmetrically located) regions with identical functions in the right and left hemisphere will survive this selection process, in contrast to the less dense connections between the heterotopic (asymmetrically located) regions.

Evolutionary perspectives

From an evolutionary perspective, both symmetry and asymmetry of the brain may have contributed to adaptations to the environment.

Symmetry

According to Corballis, the symmetrical organization of our brain resulted from gradual and successive adaptations, which took place during the process of evolution and increased the chances of survival (Corballis, 1989). Land animals, for instance, learn to run in straight lines because a linear motion is the most efficient connection between two points in space. In addition, they also have to learn to respond rapidly to obstacles, such as predators showing up unexpectedly at the left and right sides of the body. The resulting symmetry of brain functions not only applied to perceptual and motor functions, but probably also expanded to a cognitive function like procedural memory. As a result memory representations for movement patterns to the left and right also became symmetrically organized.

Another evolutionary advantage of a 'dual brain' could be the greater redundancy and processing capacity (compared to the capacity of our lungs, which indeed is larger with two lungs than with one). In case of damage to one hemisphere, the other hemisphere can also function as a backup system and take over the functions of the damaged hemisphere.

Asymmetry

Interhemispheric communication does not always imply that the hemispheres cooperate with another. Hemispheres also become engaged in some form of competition, in which case the callosal fibers that form their connection would be inhibitory rather than excitatory. So, as activation builds up in one hemisphere, the homologous areas in the opposite hemisphere are being inhibited. This development would favor an asymmetric, rather than a symmetric pattern of functioning of the cerebral hemispheres.

BOX 2.11 ASYMMETRY OF THE BRAIN, NOT UNIQUE FOR HUMANS

One generally assumes that right-handedness is a typically human property, created during evolution through the use of tools. Old rock drawings suggest, for example, that prehistoric man used tools preferably with the right hand. The shape of tools of prehistoric man also points in the same direction. Although non-human primates appear to have a particular preference for the right-hand side, development of related parts of their brain could have lagged as compared with human beings. This development possibly resulted in non-lateralization of animal speech. However, a study by Cantalupo and Hopkins (2001) has cast new light

continued

> on these findings. With MRI images of primates' brains, they found an asymmetry in area 44 (Broca area) in non-human beings like chimpanzees and gorillas. According to the researchers, this area is also involved in gestures that, when made to the right, are often associated with production of sounds and rudimentary voicings. This development may have continued and ultimately led to real speech in humans.

Under the forces of evolution, some functions in the brain could also have become gradually segregated, along with the growing demands for limited cortical space. These functions then become modified in one hemisphere, but not in the other. Such a development could have stimulated a pattern of relative, rather than absolute, specialization of the cerebral hemispheres. When one function in the brain becomes more strongly lateralized, other regions in the cortex become co-opted by the same function. Such a process reduces cortical redundancy, but also guarantees a more efficient and flexible division of cortical space than with functions laid out across the hemispheres in a strictly symmetrical and parallel fashion. Another interesting feature of this functional architecture is that in complex tasks, subcomponents assigned to dedicated structures in the two halves of the brain are activated in concert, although their contributions might vary (see also Figures 2.27 and 2.30).

Control functions

Even within an architecture subserving relative hemispheric specialization, symmetry would remain useful for externally controlled perceptual functions, because external incentives can arise from anywhere in the surrounding space. However, internally generated functions (e.g. complex motion or speech, and coordination of movement sequences), would be driven more efficiently by one than by two hemispheres, from a computational point of view. Involvement of two control centers would end up in conflicts in the coordination of these functions. In terms of the economical use of neural space, it is more advantageous for top-down control of cognitive functions to be driven by mechanisms located in a single hemisphere.

Handedness and language development

Left-right handedness can be the platform where genetic and hormonal factors play an essential role in early development. The initial thought was that a single gene controlled handedness. However, more recent studies suggest that multiple genes contribute to this trait. Each of these genes has a weak effect by itself, but together they play a significant

INTRODUCING THE BRAIN

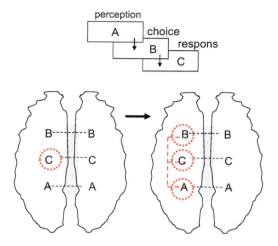

FIGURE 2.27
The 'snowball effect'. Hypothetical pathways connecting the left and right hemispheres (dashed lines). Left: a subcomponent of a cognitive task (e.g. the response stage) is biased to activate a part of the left hemisphere network (red circle). Right: eventually, the entire task will become co-localized in the left hemisphere (red dashed lines and circles representing the perception and choice stages). The reason is that connections within a hemisphere are more efficient (i.e. shorter and less subject to neural noise) than connections between the hemispheres.

role in establishing hand preference. Studies suggest that at least some of these genes help to determine the overall right-left asymmetry of the body starting in the earliest stages of development. Some parts of the brain are precisely programmed by the genes, other parts (perhaps the majority) are programmed more loosely, and shaped in interactions with the environment. Genetic and non-genetic factors can also affect different parts of laterality.

Within the course of evolution, a characteristic such as left- or right-handedness could have formed the basis for developing unilateral control of complex cognitive behavior. Accordingly, the left-brain linkage to 'dexterous' tools could have paved the way for language evolution and laterality. In a similar fashion right-handedness could have created a platform in the left hemisphere for other generative capabilities than language. Kosslyn described this pattern of development as the 'snowball effect', according to the metaphor of a rolling snowball, growing larger by collecting snow particles on its way down the hill. If a subcomponent of a complex cognitive task is biased to activate a neural substrate in one hemisphere (e.g. the left hemisphere), other subcomponents recruited by the same task are likely to activate compatible substrates in the same hemisphere (see Figure 2.27). The two preconditions for the snowball effect are that a) the structural anatomy of the left and right hemispheres is bilaterally neutral, and b) connections *within* a hemisphere are more effective than connections *between* hemispheres, since they have to bridge a much smaller distance, and are less subject to neural noise than the long-ranging corpus callosum fibers.

In other cases, however, the developing brain may select a trajectory leading to hemispheric differentiation of task components. This could occur when a heterogeneous task, or a subtle intrinsic bias in developing brains, leads to a break-up and subsequent 'assigning' of specific cognitive subcomponents to different halves of the brain (Deacon, 1997). For example, although the bias towards the left hemisphere is more pronounced for the production of language, the perception of language may have become less strictly lateralized or even lateralized to the right hemisphere.

Language functions in humans might have evolved from an earlier cultural stage, with emphasis on 'mimetic' skills. Mimetic skills rest on mimesis: the 'ability to produce conscious self-initiated representational acts as intentional but not linguistic' (Greenfield, 1991; Donald, 1991). Mimesis is different from imitation, because it involves invention, or generative capacity, to produce new body movements and expressions, still found in dance rituals of Australian aborigines (see also further ahead).

In addition to language functions, cognitive tasks that compete for attentional resources might also be prone to the snowball effect. Split-brain research (see following) has shown that for some tasks attentional resources are represented bilaterally in the two hemispheres. In healthy (intact) subjects, however, these resources are more likely to be assigned to one hemisphere, to avoid competition between the hemispheres. Such a mechanism counteracts parallel processing of information in both hemispheres, and causes the hemisphere that subserves one crucial element of the task to handle other elements of the same task as well.

Split-brain studies

Hemispheric specialization has been the subject of numerous studies on patients as well as on healthy subjects, using the divided visual field paradigm as an experimental tool. Because in healthy subjects the corpus callosum is still intact, it is often hard to determine if the behavioral effects obtained in these tasks reflected the unique quality of information processing within each hemisphere. Communication between the hemispheres could still have biased the behavioral results through the intact corpus callosum. In split-brain patients, this problem does not occur because of the cut callosum fiber connections.

This surgical operation is used on patients who have severe epilepsy, when even heavy medication does not suppress the seizures. The cutting of the corpus callosum prevents local seizures that originate in one hemisphere to spread to the other hemisphere. The operation leaves the (crossed) sensory and motor pathways intact that send information from senses to the brain, and from the brain to the muscle, which makes the divided visual field task a suitable tool to stimulate one hemisphere independently from the other (Box 2.12). In general, split-brain patients cannot integrate visual information between the two visual fields. In some rare cases, however, they may also benefit from the functional separation of their hemispheres. A classical finding in visual search tasks with normal subjects is the linear increase in response time to target stimuli, with the

INTRODUCING THE BRAIN

BOX 2.12 SPLIT-BRAIN RESEARCH

The divided visual field paradigm, used to study brain functioning in split-brain patients, is based on the anatomical arrangement of the afferent visual pathways in which the left and rights halves of the visual field project to the opposite visual areas of the brain, while subjects fixate a cross in the center of the screen.

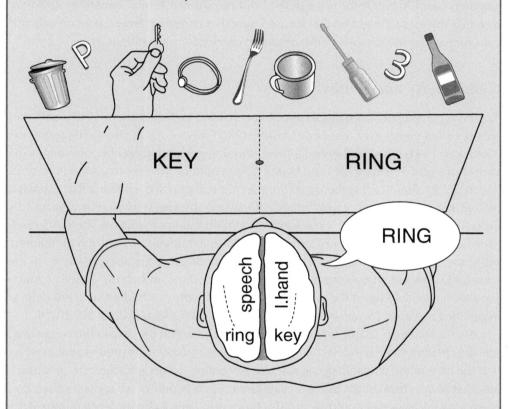

Insert: set up of the visual half-field task to study information processing in split-brain patients. Source: Gazzaniga, M. (1998). The split-brain revisited. *Scientific American* 297: 51–55.

Two words or pictures of objects (such key or apple) are presented briefly (e.g. 200 ms) and simultaneously in the left and right visual fields. When asked to repeat what they see, the patient's verbal left hemisphere will respond with 'ring'. But when asked to pick up the object presented on the screen, he will use his left hand that is controlled by the right hemisphere, to pick up the key. Even though their hemispheres function independently, split-brain patients do not perceive themselves as a 'double' person.

number of non-target stimuli. A split-brain study using a visual search task demonstrated a benefit of response times in patients relative to normal controls, on trials when target and non-target stimuli appeared in different fields (Luck & Hillyard, 1994). This was about 50% relative to the condition in which targets and non-targets appeared in the same field. This suggested that in visual search, the hemispheres of patients functioned as independent and parallel processing resources. Remarkably, visual-spatial focused attention (see Chapter 4 for more details) did not show a similar benefit in split-brain patients. The reason might be that focused attention relies to a large extent on subcortical structures, of which the interhemispheric connections are still intact.

Generativity and syntax

According to Michael Corballis a specific mechanism in the left lateral prefrontal hemisphere called Generative Assembly Device (GAD) specializes in generating sequences (Corballis, 1991). This mechanism allows combining a limited number of symbols in a variety of ways. The symbols used by the GAD could be words but also 'action units' (Figure 2.28). Proof of this theory is found in clinical practice, showing that lesions of the left hemisphere often cause aphasia (language disorders) as well as apraxia (disorders in performing complex movements). Within human evolution, the GAD could even have been the precursor of language facilities in humans, in the form of 'mimetic' skills, the ability to generate a great repertory of bodily and facial expressions. In line with GAD a recent study suggested that pointing gestures in babies, started as touch. They then probably layed the ground for their 'first words'. Children who are delayed in pointing are also slower to develop language skills (O'Madagain et al., 2019).

Angela Friederici (2018) recently confirmed the view that the human brain contains a specific circuitry that has evolved to subserve the human capacity to process syntax, which is at the core of the human language faculty. According to Friederici the core structure in the adult human brain might be the arcuate fasciculus, a bundle of white matter fibers connecting Wernicke (area 22) and the anterior Broca area (area 44) in the left hemisphere. It is much less conspicuous in young children and absent in great apes. The arcuate fasciculus is also a core element in the speech production model proposed by Norman Geschwind in 1965. This model accounts for the ability to transfer word representations in the superior temporal cortex to Broca area in the left frontal cortex. Although the wiring of a rudimentary 'grammar circuitry' is possibly already present in early childhood, stimulation in a subsequent sensitive phase is necessary for its full development in early adulthood. In Friederici's model area 44 is responsible for the 'merging': binding together words to form phrases and sentences. In this model the language circuits consist of two pathways, an ascending dorsal pathway (consisting of the arcuate fasciculus fibers) from area STG to areas 44, and a ventral pathway looping back from area 44 to STG (Figure 2.29). The location of area 44 seems to match well with the GAD device as proposed by Corballis.

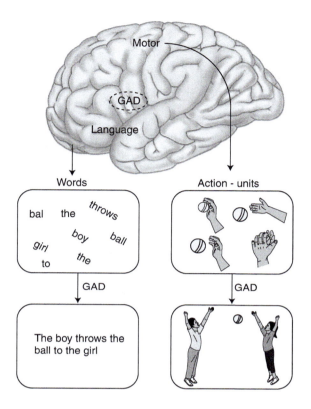

FIGURE 2.28
The Generative Assembly Device (GAD), a hypothetical mechanism in the left prefrontal cortex, that according to Corballis controls both the motor as well as the language area. It may be involved in generating verbal sentences as well as action sequences.

Source: Adapted from Gazzaniga et al. (2002).

Varieties of laterality

The study of cerebral lateralization has always attracted much attention from popular psychology, where unfortunately it has created a source for speculations about the laterality of almost every aspect of the mind. As a result, the two halves of the brain became a favorite target for practically everyone's favorite dichotomy of mental functions (Deacon, 1997). The common belief that cerebral lateralization caused the human mind to split up in two major complementary cognitive systems could have even created a bias among editors of scientific journals to accept articles reporting differences between hemispheres, rather than equally qualified articles reporting no differences.

The functional specialization of higher mental functions has developed from a fundamental anatomical symmetry of the cerebral hemispheres. Such a development favors relative and not absolute hemispheric differences, perhaps even in right-handers.

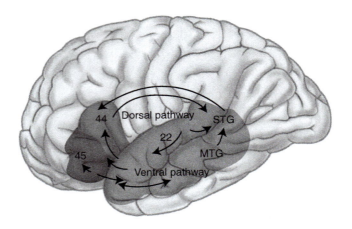

FIGURE 2.29
Simplified map of pathways and co-activated areas in the left hemisphere presumed to underlie the language circuit. The dorsal pathway runs from area 22 (Wernicke area) and STG (superior temporal gyrus) to area 44 (the arcuate fasciculus). The ventral pathway runs from area 22 to areas 44 and 45. It then loops back from area 45 to MTG (medial temporal gyrus) to STG. Area 44 is presumed to 'merge' words into phrases and sentences in syntactic working memory. The ventral route is presumed to be involved in feedback to support grammatical processes and linking semantics to grammar.

Source: Adapted from Friederici (2012).

Right-handed persons are often capable of performing complex motor actions like writing with the left hand after some practice. In most right-handers, language functions link to the left hemisphere, but also partly depend on the right hemisphere. The latter explains why patients with severe brain injury in the left hemisphere sometimes show a remarkable recovery of language functions in due course. Probably because homologous areas in the right hemisphere are capable of compensating for the deficit in the left hemisphere.

What is lateralized?

The dichotomies used to characterize functions of the left and right hemispheres can globally be divided in two categories (see also Allen, 1994 for an early systematic overview). One category emphasizes the specific content of tasks or stimuli. Examples are the most common verbal, versus spatial dichotomy, retrieval of semantic knowledge versus retrieval of episodic knowledge (Tulving), and a bias to express positive emotions (approach behavior) versus negative emotions (avoidance behavior, Davidson) to the left and right hemispheres, respectively. The second category relates to differences in processing style or strategy of the left and right hemispheres. Examples are a serial-analytical versus a holistic strategy (Gazzaniga) and a focal versus a distributed processing strategy (Semmes, 1968).

> ### BOX 2.13 NEUROMYTHS
>
> The popularity of brain research in the media also leads to simplifications of the role of our brain and the way it affects human behavior. Incorrect or profound statements about human behavior are usually taken more seriously with the predicate 'neuroscience' or 'brain' (or: Neurorealism')*. Often too far-reaching interpretations of scientific data are cast in the form of objective truths. For example, educators and mental coaches are often tempted to modern pseudo 'brainwashing.' Even scientists may come close to 'neuromything' in their eagerness to emphasize the relevance of their research to media or funding agencies. Some examples of neuromyths:
>
> ▶ We usually only use 10% of our brain.
> ▶ Children in their first three years experience a sensitive period in which brain development benefits from much stimulation (for example toys or an enriched play environment).
> ▶ A brain scan can read the mind.
> ▶ Brain training programs may create new neurons with age.
> ▶ A stimulating learning environment with many new incentives releases dopamine in the brain, which improves learning performance.
> ▶ Mirror neurons form the neural basis of human empathy and social cognition.
> ▶ Not drinking enough water (less than six glasses a day) causes the brain to shrink.
> ▶ Adolescents display impulsive and unrestrained behavior because they have a not yet fully developed prefrontal lobe (dubbed 'immature teenage brains').
> ▶ Differences in individual learning performance mostly arise because of differences in left or right hemisphere dominance.
> ▶ General intelligence (IQ) as such has little meaning, neuroscience teaches us that there are several forms of intelligence (for example: musical, social, emotional and cognitive).
>
> *Sources: O'Connor et al. (2012), Howard-Jones (2014), Bruer (1999), Fernandez-Duque (2015), Owen et al. (2010), Altikulac et al. (2018).

Often, hemispheric specialization is not expressed in what we referred to earlier as unitary or 'global' conceptualizations of cognitive functions, e.g. attention, memory, emotion and even language, but in its subcomponents. At the molar levels, cognitive functions are a too-complex process to be split up in cerebral dichotomies, but rather represent a mosaic of smaller entities and local networks.

By contrast, episodic and semantic memory, retrieval and encoding seem to correspond to different brain structures, and sometimes to different hemispheres. Content-based accounts of functional specialization further pointed to the two subcomponents of working memory, the phonological loop and visuospatial sketchpad, corresponding with left and right hemispheres respectively. Comprehending and producing language, for example, not only cover the classical language areas posterior and anterior to the Sylvian fissure of the left hemisphere, but also recruit areas in the right hemisphere. Concerning speech, lesions of the right hemisphere disrupt prosody (the way we vary articulation to express emotions or intonation) much stronger in the right than in than in the left hemisphere.

In many individuals, the left hemisphere is dominant for language. Split-brain patients comprehend a simple grammatical sentence like: 'the boy catches the ball' with their right hemisphere, but not a more complex version like 'the boy catches the ball, thrown to him by the girl'. But on a more elementary level, studies of recognition of visually presented words revealed that different words activated different neural assemblies in the left and right hemispheres. Function words like adjectives, prepositions and auxiliaries that are important for the grammatical structure of a sentence activated neural assemblies in the left hemisphere. Content words, like adjectives and verbs that depend on perceptual elements and are essential for meaning, activated areas in both hemispheres (Pulvermüller, 1999), suggesting that content words will thus show relatively weak, and function words relatively strong, lateralization (see Figure 2.30).

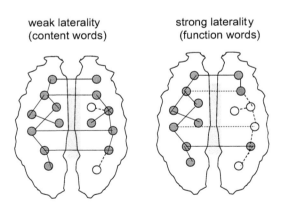

FIGURE 2.30
Hypothetical picture of the distributed representations of single word activations in the brain. Left: weak laterality (content words). Right: strong laterality (function words). Processing of words utilizes neural assemblies in both the right and left hemispheres. Function words make a stronger appeal to verbal modules in the left hemisphere than content words, which have a more perceptual character and a more even distribution across the hemispheres.

3 | Representation, computing and control

CONTENTS

- Introduction
- A catalog of representations
- Computations in the brain
- Control functions of the brain

'Men judge things according to the organization of their brain' Benedict de Spinoza *Ethics*

Introduction

In a strictly operational sense the principal function of our brain's cognitive system is to represent, store and retrieve information. Representations include our 'knowledge of the outside world' but also 'knowledge of the inner world' and 'knowledge of actions'. They are our 'mental objects', if you will. When activated in the brain (in our short-term memory) they are highly transient events. When not active, representations slumber in our long-term memory, where they are written in the wiring of nerve cells and the synaptic weights of the brain's networks. Pinning down mental representations is the 'route to rigor' in psychology (Pinker, 1997), since they allow to isolate the essential components or building blocks of more 'molar' entities of cognition, often referred to as tasks or functions like reading, memory, emotion and actions. Moreover, these representations have also opened new ways to link mental operations to underlying neural structures. The brain's networks are biological systems, not artificial networks or computers, although there is an intriguing analogy between the on-off state of neurons and the 1/0 state of core elements of the digital computer. However, it is clear that the brain is an analog organism that a) is much slower than a computer, b) does not have rigid chips but neurons and synapses that prune or die, and c) evolved not to 'crunch numbers but to adapt to conditions of the environment' (Smith Churchland, 2002). Nevertheless, computers and their AI implementations can be helpful as models to solve some big questions of cognitive neuroscientists, who often seek refuge to neural measures in defining the brain's functionality but unfortunately don't find their questions answered by merely looking at functional images.

How fundamental operations like the encoding of information, pattern recognition and learning take place in biologically plausible networks is one of the unresolved questions. In an organism like the brain, representations reside in patterns of neural assemblies, that is, in connectivity patterns formed in local, or more distributed networks of the brain. From an evolutionary perspective, it helps to have a brain with the capacity to prepare or anticipate events that might happen but are not happening now. The ability to form representations has its roots in internal genetic mechanisms, stemming from a chain of adaptations during their evolution, and built on the genomes of our fossil ancestors. This process has created restraints, for example on the maximum number of nerve cells in our brain, but also on the development and configuration of the wiring diagrams of its networks.

Most of the time representations become activated due to interactions with the environment. But they also arise spontaneously, or are recruited intentionally by our imagery and working memory systems. They may vary from simple 'percepts', mental images of the outside world, to more complex 'ideas' or 'concepts' or even action programs. For example, looking at a tiger at the zoo and then closing your eyes will probably activate an animal which is almost a copy of the animal you just saw (probably 'read out' directly from your primary visual areas). The brain represents information according to the coding principles embedded in neurons and their connections. Which in turn are 'nothing else' than configurations of synaptic weights, to be discussed in greater detail further in this chapter.

Computations are – broadly defined – the active elements that serve to process information and translate input to output. They could imply the consolidation of new elements in, or retrieval of old elements from, neural networks that form the basis of our memory. In the motor systems of the brain, computations involve mobilization of 'plans of actions' (like a program for the execution of skilled movements) stored in our motor memories. Together with representations, they form the building blocks of complex neural networks and associated cognitive processes. In the cortex, in particular the visual and the motor cortices, computations can be intertwined with memory representations. Thus, computations either originate from the same neural structures that store representations, but ignited into an active state, or represent processes generated in different dedicated networks (possibly located higher in the neural hierarchy) recruiting representations stored in long-term memory.

Particular types of computations, briefly considered in this chapter, are control mechanisms. Although one may argue that control is a 'special case' of neural computation, it also differs from other forms of computation systems. Computations work on the specific content of data stored in representations. By contrast, control systems have a non-specific regulatory and modulatory function. Control may include inhibition or excitation of input (sensory) or output (motor) channels of the central nervous system. In the final section, the focus will be on more integrative functional models of the brain's organization, in particular on distributed hierarchical systems that incorporate the other more local elementary mechanisms related to representations and computations.

A catalog of representations

Representations play a role in various processes, such as perceptual observation, memory, awareness and attention, but also in motor processes. They are the knowledge elements of our brain's network created by learning, on which our memory system depends. In visual search, for example, they guide our perception, when we scan a full table looking for a specific object. Representations of motor processes consist of specific coordinates of the successive body parts like hand and fingers, from the start to the end of a motion range. This 'action knowledge' must be available in our motor subsystems prior to execution of skilled movements, often without any conscious awareness.

Representations take different guises that globally depend on two factors, the state of a neural assembly and its location in functional cerebral space, i.e. the cortical regions where specific cognitive operations take place.

State of the brain

Representations vary according to the active or passive state of their related neural assemblies: active representations represent elements of short-term memory, passive representations the dormant versions of the same elements in long-term memory. Stated differently: active representations are patterns of activity in networks of the brain that 'happen now' (like in visual perception). Passive representations refer to the dormant capacity of a network residing in configurations of connection weights (Smith Churchland, 2002, see also Figure 3.1). Notice, however, that the distinction between active and passive representations reflects different positions on a brain-state continuum, rather than a distinct dichotomy. During learning, for example, representations of visual

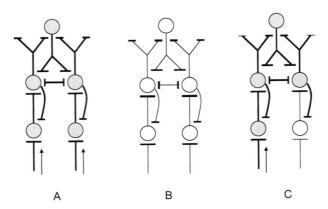

FIGURE 3.1
Hypothetical states of a network with various types of connections (efferent, afferent, recurrent, diverging and converging). Grey: active, white: inactive connections and neurons. A: network activated via two input channels. B: After stimulation, only synaptic connections remain active. C: One channel input suffices to reactivate the greater part of the dormant network.
Source: Adapted from Fuster (1995).

objects in networks of the brain may gradually show a transition from a highly active, to moderately active, to dormant state.

Passive representations always are implicitly present as connection weights, implying that they are not directly accessible for conscious exploration. Note however, that although the active brain is usually seen as the site of consciousness, the active state of a representation does not always lead to conscious awareness. For example, briefly presented visual patterns may prime neural circuits in the sensory cortex without any conscious awareness (Schacter, 1995). In a similar fashion, representations of skilled and highly practiced movement in the motor cortices are often not associated with any conscious experience when utilized.

Functional cerebral space

Functional cerebral space follows two gross divisions in the anatomy of the cerebral cortex, the anterior/posterior division and the division in left and right hemispheres. The resulting four subdivisions traditionally link to four major types of cognitive operations: perceptual, motor, verbal and non-verbal, in respective order.[1] A general assumption from memory research is that cortical areas that process certain types of information are also the repositories where that information is stored. Accordingly, memory representations may vary following the four different subdivisions of the cerebral cortex. Pairing the four anatomical subdivisions with the two possible states of representations

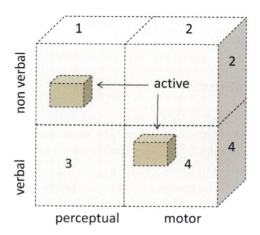

FIGURE 3.2
Simplified model of functional cerebral space with three major divisions: verbal-nonverbal, perceptual-motor and active-passive, resulting in eight subdivisions. Light areas represent dormant (non-active) neural assemblies constituting long-term memory. Dark boxes represent active neural assemblies associated with short-term memory. For example, the dark upper-left box represents an active non-verbal perceptual representation of an object in the environment (e.g., subserving visual mental imagery). The dark lower-right box represents an active verbal motor representation (e.g., subserving speech).

(active/passive) results in eight subdivisions of representational space (see Figure 3.2). The notion of functional cerebral space is thus based on the idea that different parts of the brain do different things. This might relate to different *contents* of memory, as well as to various aspects of its *context*, for example, its spatial (*where*), temporal (*when*) and source (*how*) characteristics (see Chapter 6 for a further elaboration).

Textbooks of cognitive psychology traditionally divide human memory in long-term memory and short-term memory, with long-term memory split-up in explict and implicit subforms. The model presented in Figure 3.2, however, rests on the assumption that short-term and long-term memories are not qualitatively different structures or regions, but refer to two different states, active versus dormant, of the same neural assemblies in the cortex (following Fuster, 1995).

The model is also neutral as to the explicit implicit dichotomy. Its only restriction is that passive representations are – by definition – not accessible for conscious exploration. For example, non-verbal perceptual knowledge (represented in subdivisions 1 and 5) as such does not yield access to consciousness, but only its short-term activated subset of neural elements (the dark box in subdivision 1).[2]

What different forms of implicit memory have in common is that they do not rely on the hippocampus and adjacent medial-temporal structures (see Chapter 6 for further details). Which is one reason why they refer to knowledge we have no conscious access to, even when the underlying neural assemblies are in an active state (e.g. in conditions like priming or conditioning).

Complex representations

Complex representations have the polymodal cortex as their home base, which together with their large receptive fields makes them less dependent on the sensory quality of perceptual input. The complexity of representations is not only manifested in verbal-semantic concepts, but also in forms of action, varying between complex perceptual-motor skills (the repertoire of a professional tennis player, for instance) to skills used in speech or musical performance (the concert pianist who translates musical concepts into movements of hand and fingers). Motor representations do not function in isolation, but depend on networks that link perceptual-spatial functions of the posterior-parietal cortex and motor structures in the anterior cortex. Two other related forms of complex representations considered in this paragraph are 'dispositional representations', a concept developed by Anton Damasio and 'meta-representations', which both relate to internally generated perceptual images including the notion of the 'self'.

Conceptual knowledge

Are concepts relating to the meaning of a word represented at an abstract level, irrespective of the modality of the senses, or whether a word is spoken, heard or written? More likely is that concepts are represented in distributed networks of the temporal cortex, containing various specific perceptual elements like form, color or sound or even action elements like grasping and reaching (Allport, 1985). The word 'telephone' for example could activate networks with elements like form, ringing and grasping (Figure 3.3). Activation of an individual element of the network would then suffice to ignite the entire network. Common manufactured objects like hammers or scissors are often manipulated, and therefore associated with kinesthetic or motoric representations. Farah and McClelland (1991) went one step further and proposed that semantic memory consists of separate visual and functional subsystems, and that living things must be primarily based on visual, and non-living objects on functional, attributes. They based their model on simulated neural networks with artificial 'lesions'. These models, stating that basic perceptual and action elements in fact constitute the building blocks of semantic memory, clearly contrast with the view that semantic memory is represented in some abstract, modality-independent, 'conceptual' domain, remote from the mechanisms of perception and motor organization.

These examples further suggest that distributed networks in the brain underlying conceptual knowledge must have strong associative relations (Collins & Loftus, 1975). Neural elements or 'nodes' in such networks would spread out to adjacent or even

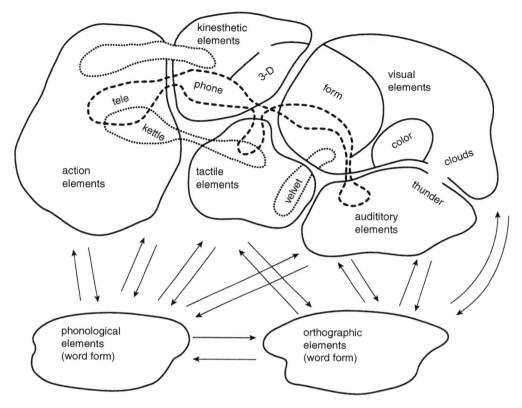

FIGURE 3.3
Allport's model of conceptual space representing concepts as a collection of perceptual elements distributed over many different domains of knowledge.
Source: Adapted from Allport (1985).

more remote local networks, constituting a much larger neural assembly than in local networks representing less meaningful concepts. Depending on the site of lesions in areas where knowledge resides, patients would either have problems with naming objects (e.g. the inferior temporal gyrus, Damasio et al., 1996) or would show 'neglect' of objects in the visual field (e.g. the posterior parietal cortex).

Conceptual knowledge stored in the temporal association cortices sometimes exhibits a specific category hierarchy. Patients may recognize a face as belonging to a male or a female, but not its unique quality (the face of a specific member of their family). Studies of lesions of patients by Hannah Damasio (see Tranel et al., 1997) have shown that brain lesions in different parts of the left temporal lobe related to specific deficits in naming persons, animals or tools (Figure 3.4). This suggests that these networks contain specialized word knowledge at the conceptual level, rather than at the word (lexical) level.

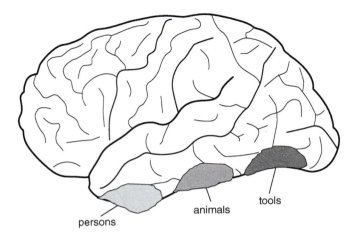

FIGURE 3.4
PET activations in the left inferior temporal lobe during the naming of persons, animals and tools. Naming persons mostly activated the temporal pole, naming animals the middle portion and naming tools the posterior portion, overlapping with the occipital area.

Source: Adapted from Damasio et al. (1996).

Action representations

Action representations are associated with neural circuits in the motor regions of the anterior cortex. Depending on the complexity of an action or movement, different hierarchical levels of representations can be distinguished. The supplementary motor area (SMA) in the anterior cortex, for example, is dedicated to complex action programs, while more elementary representations depend on the premotor and motor areas, involved in the execution of movement. It remains an open question how representations of movements are coded, stored and retrieved in performing skilled or novel movements. Control of movement depends on various trajectories, involving sequences of coordinates of body segments, muscle coordinates or joint angles stored in the motor cortices. When necessary, these motor programmes will be converted to specific motor instructions. Neural network models have been successfully applied to mimic human motor performance, using computations carried out on stored 'models' of simulated movement trajectories (Jeannerod, 1994; Bullock & Grossberg, 1988; Jordan, 1996).

Movements are guided by perceptual-spatial coordinates residing in areas of the posterior-parietal and somatosensory cortex. This is accomplished mainly by reciprocal connections between the parietal and prefrontal cortex that create a direct link between spatial perception and action. These circuits might also underlie the 'mirror neurons' identified by Rizzolatti et al. (1996) in the premotor cortex of monkeys. Mirror neurons do not only fire during actual movements, but also in detecting movements, such as gripping or mouth movements made by others. In line with this reasoning, lesion studies suggested that concepts relating to actions and tool comprehension involve overlapping parietal-frontal regions (Tranel et al., 2003).

Dispositional representations

How does the brain use topographically organized representations to experience recalled images? The solution suggested by Anton Damasio lies in 'convergence zones'. A convergence zone is a small assembly of neurons that keep 'dispositional representations', a latent firing potentiality that triggers activity in neural assemblies with which they have strong interneural connections. Dispositional representations reside in an encrypted and dormant form in the higher-order association cortex. They do not represent a picture per se but reconstitute images from the primary sensory areas. The contents exhibited in image space are in explicit form.

Convergence zones bear some resemblance to 'gnostic cells' (a single cell that stores a complex visual representation) with one difference: they only contain the binding code, not the compact representation of the individual perceptual features themselves. An alternative for convergence zones is 'ensemble coding', discussed in the next paragraph.

Self-representations

Self-representations or meta-representations bind other lower order representations together. One role of self-representation is to produce a model of the body or parts of the body as belonging to 'myself'. Self-representational capacities could reside in circuits in the human brain that have developed during evolution, perhaps enabling a versatile capacity to project oneself into various conditions as options for alternative actions. Or to block impulsive and potentially harmful actions. Self-representations also vary in quality and degree depending on certain drugs, or states of high or low arousal, like drowsiness.

Self representations assumedly involve regions in the somatosensory cortex representing a map of the body, as well as autobiographical memories. They might also involve regions in the language areas in the left anterior and posterior cortices. Test of self-awareness in animals and young children have often relied on the mirror recognition test (Gallup, 1970). For example, chimpanzees, when placed before a mirror, may first react as if they see another animal, but then gradually get involved in self-exploratory activities, suggesting that they indeed are recognizing themselves. Children develop self recognition in the mirror test around the age of four. Note however that the mirror test mainly captures the part of self-awareness that depends on awareness of the body. They do not necessarily reflect a more abstract 'theory of mind', or 'shared intentionality', such as knowing or feeling the intentions, beliefs or desires of others (Call & Tomasello, 2008; Gazzaniga et al., 2014).

Codes in the brain

Representations are chunks of knowledge. Knowledge is information stored in neural structures in higher association cortices. The process of capturing information is called (en)coding. The question now arises whether the perception of a particular object depends on the firing of one or a few 'smart' cells, or a group or ensemble of cells each with a somewhat different responsiveness. These two views are discussed next.

Local coding

In primitive organisms, codes may already be present in a single nerve cell, a principle known as local encoding. A classical example applied to human perception is that of the 'grandmother cell', a single gnostic cell that stores a visual representation of Grandmother's face. A gnostic cell is thus supposed to carry much information, which will make it fire rather infrequently to complex features or events in its sensory input. The grandmother cell concept is a metaphor often used to clarify why local coding cannot account for storage of complex representations in the brain of highly developed mammals like humans. A problem with local coding is that it demands excessive brain space, since a separate cell in the brain is occupied by every unique event, ranging from simple features to complex visual patterns that turn up in our life. An argument against this principle is that the human brain does not contain sufficient nerve cells to store the multitude of billions of impressions a person experiences during his life.

Vector coding

A neurally more plausible solution lies in distributed coding, also referred to as 'coarse', ensemble or vector coding (a vector is a row or matrix with the elements represented as numbers). Vector coding implies that information is stored in an array of elements (e.g. <2,1,4,5>) with each element representing a specific feature of a perceptional image, for example, the color, orientation and form of a specific object. Vector coding does not require neurons to be finely tuned to specific features in perceptual space. Fine or precise tuning is more compatible with the local coding principle, which holds, for example, for neurons in the central area of the primary visual cortex, called the calcarine fissure. Vector coding, in contrast, implies coarse coding, a property of secondary neurons in the association cortices of the brain, that have a relatively wide tuning curve.

Although the individual cell is highly sensitive to a particular feature of a stimulus dimension, for example a 90-degree line orientation, it also fires at a broader range of orientations (for 50 and 120 degrees see Figure 3.5). Coarse coding has the advantage of redundancy. For example, when a cell is damaged, neighboring cells that are set to the same attribute can take over the task so the overall function will not be compromised.

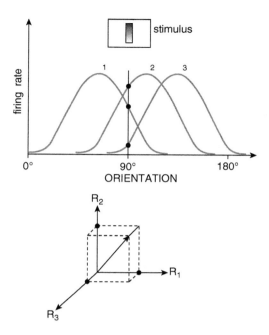

FIGURE 3.5
Example of coarse coding. Top: three cells and corresponding overlapping tuning curves. Three cells are needed to detect the orientation of the vertical line. For example, cell 3 will display the same fire pattern at 180 and 90 degrees. Bottom: three vectors in line orientation state space associated with the three cells. Coarse coding implies that nerve cells may participate in different neural representations, and provides redundancy to 'back up' defective neurons in a cortical network.

Sources: Adapted from Churchland & Sejnowski, (1992).

Also, with low quality of input – for example with a weak visual stimulus – multiple cell contributions can increase network output for specific characteristics of this stimulus.

Vector or coarse coding is seen as a general strategy the brain exploits to create representations. As such it applies not only to orientation, but also to color space and even the motor system. Motor regions are organized somatotopically, in primary as well as secondary motor areas. Movements may vary in force, velocity and direction. Research on the motor system in monkeys by Georgopoulos (1995) sheds new light on the way the motor cortex represents the direction of movements. The monkey was trained to move a joystick in eight different directions, while electrical activity of the brain was measured with an array of microelectrodes, placed in its motor cortex (Figure 3.6).

Each movement activated around 242 motor neurons, indicating a broad tuning to the direction of a movement. The average of the population vector (representing the overlap of the output of different neurons coding for each specific direction) appeared

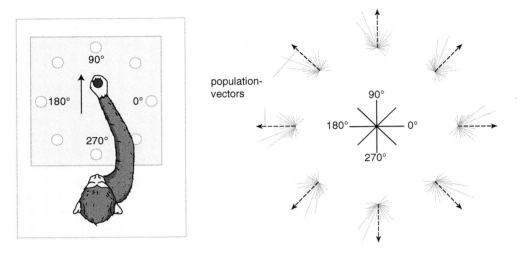

FIGURE 3.6
Experimental setting for measuring cortical representations of the direction of movement in the monkey. Right: population vectors for each of eight different directions of movement. The dashed arrow is the average of all reacting neurons.

Source: Adapted from Georgopoulos (1995).

to correspond accurately with the actual direction of each movement. Moreover, the population vector also predicted the direction of the intended movement in the period before onset of the movement by the joystick. In summary, vector or ensemble coding ensures efficient use of neural space, since a relatively small number of overlapping groups of neurons are needed for carrying out neural computations, identifying different objects or making different movements in space.

The ensemble coding principle is displayed in Figure 3.7 (middle and lower panels). In an ensemble any part or 'node' (also called a feature detector) has multiple functions. For example, a particular node can be used to recognize a giraffe or a tree. Ensemble coding also explains how our brain separates new (unfamiliar) and old (familiar) objects. In order to identify an object as new, it is also necessary to activate some old nodes in the network. The same principle explains why we sometimes make mistakes in recognition of this object, for example when object 1 not only activates elements of this object 1, but also elements of object 2.

Ensemble coding seems to be the central principle of neurons keeping representations of objects in the temporal lobe, where selectivity of cells is always relative not absolute. The finding that a single neuron in the monkey's temporal lobe fires when presented with an object like a hand is no proof of a gnostic cell, but rather that the cell is part of an aggregate of broadly tuned neurons in the temporal lobe. Similarly,

REPRESENTATION, COMPUTING AND CONTROL

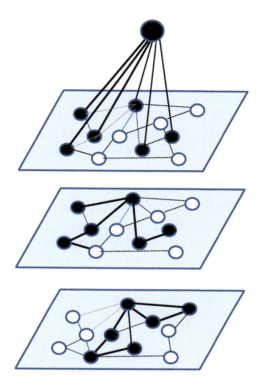

FIGURE 3.7
Schematic illustration of two principles of coding in a network. Upper panel, a separate binding unit links elements in a network. Middle and lower panels illustrate ensemble coding with neural elements forming alliances in different, but partly overlapping configurations in the same structural network. Black lines and circles represent active connections; dashed lines and white circles, inactive connections.

face cells in the human fusiform gyrus (FG) are not necessarily gnostic but most likely belong to a larger functional aggregate of cells. The FG topographically connects the striate cortex to the inferior temporal lobe via the ventral visual pathway, and plays a pivotal role in high-level vision. The encoding scheme used for faces may also apply to other classes with similar properties. In primates as well as men faces might not be 'special' but rather represent a 'default special' class in the primate recognition system (Gauthier & Logothetis, 2000).

How does the brain solve the binding problem?

An essential role of association areas in the brain is to integrate and 'bind' information from different areas.

Binding was the term used by von der Malsburg (1996) to name a process that combines simple visual stimulus characteristics (color, location and form) into complete perceptual images. In the visual system, information flows from the primary visual cortex via two pathways – called the dorsal and ventral stream – to the parietal and temporal cortices respectively. Neurons in both areas have large receptive fields, with parietal neurons being more sensitive to eccentric locations and temporal cortex neurons more sensitive to central locations of stimuli in the visual field. The ventral pathway is globally involved in object recognition ('what'), the dorsal pathway in identifying its location ('where'). Despite the separation of the two visual areas, we still see a red square at the top of the computer screen and a blue triangle on the lower part of the screen. To put it differently, information from distant areas in our brain must flow together to create a conscious perception of the complete perceptual object.

In a more general sense, the term 'binding' is often used to account for the ability of the brain to integrate perceptual information separated in space and time. It implies integration between different modalities (visual, auditory), between features of the same modality (pitch, timbre, loudness) and in time (understanding a sentence or conversation). This raises the question of how the brain solves the binding problem.

Binding units

One possibility already considered earlier is that the brain contains special binding units in higher-order areas where information from different lower order areas converges. For example, to connect color and form there should be a unit (in the temporal lobes) that receives input from areas in the cerebral cortex (like the visual area in the occipital lobe) where these stimulus features are analyzed. When the combination of triangle and red is common, it is conceivable that it will be represented in a separate neuron that only responds to input from neurons that encode red and triangle properties.

Convergence could also play a part in our memory systems, either in their explicit or implicit forms. Subcortical binding structures come into play here also, like for example the hippocampus consolidating new impressions in episodic memory. A likely scenario is as follows. Cells in the hippocampus contact distant cortical areas via reciprocal pathways. During learning, hippocampus cells start binding information coming from various sources: temporal information from the frontal cortex, spatial information from the parietal cortex and object information from the temporal cortex (Cabeza et al., 2008). Shortly after consolidation, information stored in cortical representations is still in a labile state, which makes it easier to retrieve or to reactivate its content from the codes that still reside in hippocampal representations. On the longer term, the hippocampus-cortical connections will gradually give way to horizontal corticocortical circuits, in order to further strengthen the cortical representations into a more stable state (upper and middle panels of Figure 3.7 may serve to illustrate these two consecutive phases of consolidation).[3]

Notice that a similar scenario could also extend to other forms of learning, for example associative and motor learning, where subcortical structures like the basal ganglia or the cerebellum could play a role similar to that of the hippocampus in consolidating implicit forms of memory in the respective cortical areas (Ashby et al., 2010).

Interaction

Alternatively, binding can be achieved through a dynamic process of interaction between neurons or cortical areas themselves, without the intervention of a separate area or binding unit where the information from these areas converges. This principle, referred to earlier as ensemble coding, involves interactive binding, a property of temporarily interconnected neuronal pools. The question then arises as to how the individual cells 'know' to which networks they belong. What specific features, for example, has a cell belonging to a 'grandmother network' to distinguish itself from its role in another network? This probably requires relation-codes that specify functional links established with other cells in the network. Clustering of cells in local networks with short neural connections could create favorable conditions to establish stronger coherence and efficiency of the ensemble. Such modular networks would indeed function relatively autonomously and 'encapsulated', to use Fodor's terminology.

Synchronicity

Information is encoded not only by spatial properties of neurons, but also by the relative time of firing of different neurons. Especially binding cells or cell assemblies separated by longer distances could be problematical. Here, a temporal coding mechanism might be required, ensuring that the right population of nerve cells fires at the right time. For example, when we observe or recognize objects, spatially distributed cells exhibit synchronous activity based on their specific features in the order of milliseconds. Such a mechanism does not necessarily require a separate binding unit, but could result from the interactive self-organizing process of reciprocal and parallel interactions in the network itself (see Figure 3.8).

In their perception model, Engel and Singer (2001) have described how synchronicity might aid in detecting figure-background relationships, like a stimulus pattern that automatically 'pops out' of a visual field (the proverbial black sheep in a flock of white sheep). In this case, only populations of cells that correspond to features of the target will show synchronous activity, while populations of cells corresponding to the features of the background don't.

Synchronicity could also underlie the formation of memory representations via subcortical-cortical circuits as discussed previously, with structures like the hippocampus

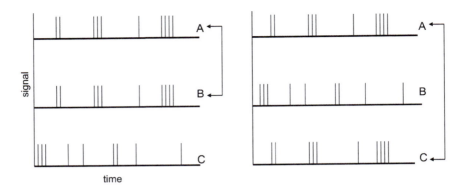

FIGURE 3.8
Example of temporal binding. Individual neurons in a network form functional groups based on synchronous activity. Cell A connects with a particular color, and cells B and C with individual objects. In the example left, A (color) will be associated with object B, in the example right, with object C.

and basal ganglia functioning as binding sites of information stored in cortical networks (Figure 3.6).

Top-down influences

Selective attention, a typical example of a top-down process, is assumed to play an important role in binding perceptual features (Niebur et al., 2002). In particular, 40Hz (40 cycles per second) fluctuations in the electroencephalogram, are taken to reflect synchronicity in the firing of neurons created by the focusing of attention. Visual spatial attention in particular is seen as a powerful top-down mechanism for binding of elementary information entering the visual pathways. Treisman and Bundesen have formulated two influential theories of binding of information in the visual domain. Treisman emphasized visual-spatial attention as a mechanism of binding of simple features in her feature integration theory (FIT), while Bundesen developed a more general model in his theory of visual attention (TVA), based on biased competition in visual short-term memory (Kastner & Ungerleider, 2001, see also Chapter 4 for more details). In conjunction search of stimulus characteristics, like searching for a black sheep in a flock of white sheep and black goats, this more active form of binding is more likely to occur. Attention to a target that contains the relevant combination (a black sheep), may cause neuronal populations that correspond with this combination of features to become more synchronized than populations of neurons that correspond with irrelevant combinations. Attentional control could even trigger synchronous activity in more heterogeneous cell populations, e.g. in combining stimuli of different modalities (for example sound combined with color). A consequence of synchronous or coherent activity would be strengthening of synaptic connections between neurons, which in turn could contribute to even stronger synchronicity.

Event-related potential as well as imaging studies have supported the notion that the posterior parietal region of the cortex plays an essential role in establishing conjunctions between neural representations. This process takes place during visual search of conjunction targets, as well as during switching of attention between locations in space. In sum, these studies have suggested that synchronized firing of neurons could indeed be a necessary code that the brain uses to link neural representations of features in conditions of involuntary, as well as voluntary selective attention.

Broca area (area 44) serves as a final example of a top-down binding site for language. Area 44 and the left inferior frontal gyrus of the frontal brain is of particular importance for unification operations required for binding single-word information, which becomes available sequentially and spread out in time into larger structures (Hagoort, 2005). Its function has been described as binding words into sentences and phrases, using the long-range connection of white matter, like the arcuate fasciculus (Friederici, 2017).

Synchronicity in imaging networks

Synchronicity is a central principle too in interpreting functional relations between cortical areas as reflected in BOLD signals that form the basis of fcMRI. The power of fcMRI lies in detecting synchronicity within local clusters of neurons as well as between more distant regions connected via long-range connections of white matter tracts. BOLD signals are manifested as relatively slow oscillations (0.1 Hz, 1 per 10 seconds) in the hemodynamic activity that could, at least in part, originate from intrinsic neural activity (Greicius et al., 2009). Their coherence, either in a resting state or during performance of a task, is seen as a reflection of their functional relationship. While the precise origin of these fluctuations is still unknown, they could reflect concurrent energetical costs of a global neural network that links different regions in the brain. In the resting state they could, for example, reflect a 'dynamic repertoire' that is recycled or rehearsed (Sporns, 2014).

Computations in the brain

Computing in the brain means a change in the pattern of activation of a network and its associated representations. Computations thus involve the formation of associations between input and output, constrained by specific rules. It is not easy to draw a sharp conceptual line between representations as discussed in the previous section. For example, in vision and motor functions computations could be intertwined with memory storage (Eichenbaum, 2012). In some cases, computations might mirror the active state, i.e. the firing patterns of the same networks that form the basis of representations. One could further argue that principles like encoding and binding, that underlie formation and retrieval of representations, must also involve neural computations since they depend on the transformation of information residing in neural assemblies.

The blurring of the distinction between various forms of computations and their related disciplines has also led to some confusion concerning its precise meaning (Friston & Dolan, 2010). The term computation has different connotations in cognitive psychology, and in 'connectionism', where it has appeared in two guises: the modeling of artificial networks as well as real, biologically plausible networks. The following section highlights and discusses some of the standard computational approaches, used in cognitive psychology and computational neuroscience.

Information processing models

A favorite type of computational model is the information processing model, as designed by cognitive psychologists, utilizing specific task manipulations to infer properties of the mind's machinery from the speed of reactions. Of particular importance was the selective attention model, proposed by Donald Broadbent at Cambridge University. Broadbent conceptualized information processing in a model that encompassed sensory input passing a limited-capacity system, controlled by higher levels of the brain responsible for filtering out – or 'gating' – relevant information (see Chapter 4). Another popular model developed by experimental psychologists examined chronometrical characteristics of successive 'stages' of information processing, in the domain of memory recognition. The memory search task invented by Saul Sternberg, for instance, was designed to measure the efficiency of human recognition memory, assuming that after sensory analysis, input was compared with items held in short term memory (the memory set) and then was sent to the output (motor) system.

In information processing systems it's essential to distinguish between the inputs of a system and its internal computations. Both will constrain the outputs of the system, which it only can carry out by using computations implemented in its internal architecture. A number of these studies have described separate components or 'stages' of processing, relating to input (perceptual), central (memory related) or output (response or motor related). Information processing paradigms have also proven to be a powerful empirical tool in cognitive neuroscience, where they provide an objective framework and explicit task manipulations to study brain activity. Performance measures, supplemented with measures of brain activity like ERP and fMRI, appeared to be a fruitful approach to examine information processes from the perspective of the brain as well as of cognition. Moreover, processing components as derived from behavioral paradigms were relatively easy to reconcile with functions of the brain. Similar to behavioral models, perception, central and motor processes in the brain have traditionally been linked to specific anatomical regions in primary and secondary association areas of the cortex (Figure 3.9). The following sections focus on each of these components from a brain-computational perspective.

Input functions

The retina's computational function is to convert physical energy (light) into electrical information, which then passes through the thalamus to the primary visual cortex. In the visual cortex computational structures are involved in the analysis of various types of elementary information. For example, when watching a moving red ball, the raw image from the primary visual areas must first be 'disassembled' into some simple features like shape, color and motion. This analysis takes place in specific structures in the surrounding 'extrastriate' areas. Subsequently, a synthesis of these separate features leads to the identification of the observed object. This process involves association areas further upstream, like the parietal and temporal as well as the frontal cortical areas.

Central functions

Central functions include processes that have an intermediary function between purely perceptual and motor processes. Some of these central processes are: a) comparing incoming information with current memory representations, b) searching for existing memory elements in long-term memory, c) storing new memory elements, and d) translating stimuli to responses. Functions a–c mainly apply to the recognition and storage of new information in memory. Cognitive psychologists, in particular, have attempted to identify mental operations using specific paradigms to test hypotheses relating to processes underlying recognition memory (Sternberg, 1969; Shiffrin & Schneider, 1977). These studies provided valuable insights into the serial and the parallel character of memory search.

A popular conception developed in memory research was that recognition is the output of a comparator mechanism (Just et al., 1996; Barlow, 1994). Comparator mechanisms have a basic and universal function in the brain. For example, perception of an object like an apple is not a passive process that produces a copy of the object, but is based on comparing incoming information with an existing 'model' or memory representation of its features. This involves knowledge of different apples, their color, flavor, and 'affordance', that is the implicit invitation to manipulate or grasp the apple (Gibson, 1979).

Comparator mechanisms also played a role in theories postulating a mnemonic filter, a mechanism that serves to distinguish relevant from irrelevant information or actions. Models of selective attention in particular assumed that selective facilitation or

Input (perception)	Analysis and synthesis of stimulus characteristics	Posterior cortex
Central (memory)	Storage, comparison, retrieval, response translation, decision	Posterior and anterior cortices
Output (motor system)	Action programming, instruction generation, motor execution	Anterior cortex

FIGURE 3.9
Three major processing components, their involved computations and related brain regions, as a general framework in studies of information processing.

inhibition results from matching incoming stimuli with a representation held in working memory. An example is the attentional trace theory proposed by Risto Näätänen (1992). The attentional trace is a voluntarily maintained representation of the physical characteristics of a relevant stimulus that separates it from the irrelevant stimulus. This in turn is presumed to reflect a matching process that becomes more sharply tuned as a function of time. Another version of a mnemonic filter is found in the neuronal model theory, as initially conceived by the Russian psychologist Evgnewy Sokolov (1963). Sokolov assumed that new stimuli are initially stored as internal 'models' (Figure 3.10). A neuronal model starts as a raw internal representation of a novel stimulus. With the repeated presentation, the representation becomes gradually stronger rooted by a process called habituation. Habituation implies a gradual consolidation of the representation in long-term memory, in synchrony with a build-up of inhibition of afferent input. A 'mismatch' to a novel or unexpected stimulus occurring in the stream of habitual stimuli will then elicit the orienting response (OR), which removes the inhibitory blockade of afferent input and facilitates learning of new stimuli.

Later studies have suggested that neurons in the hippocampus could function as familiarity-novelty detectors, similar to comparator mechanisms. This would also fit with the alleged role of the hippocampus and the adjacent rhinal cortex, as a temporary buffer of unstructured storage of information, to complement long-term storage of information in the neocortex (Kumaran & Maguire, 2005, 2007). Novelty detection may not be restricted to the hippocampus, but implemented in a larger network containing sections of the anterior hippocampus, the thalamus (the mediodorsal nuclei) and the prefrontal cortex (Løvstad et al., 2012).

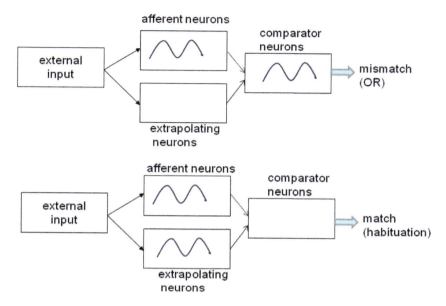

FIGURE 3.10
OR (orienting response) model as proposed by Sokolov. Afferent neurons (upper middle boxes) receive external input from new as well as repeated stimuli. Extrapolation neurons (lower middle boxes) only react to repeated stimuli, where they gradually build up stronger internal representations. Comparator neurons (at the right) only 'fire' to a mismatch between afferent and extrapolation neurons.

Source: Adapted from van Olst (1971).

Spontaneous firing of the hippocampus neurons could also contribute to the phenomenon of 'déjà vu', the sense of familiarity that sometimes occurs spontaneously in patients as well as healthy persons. Research with epileptic patients found that synchronized neural firing between the entorhinal cortex (an area in the medial temporal lobe) and the hippocampus, increased during electrical stimulations that induced déjà vu. This finding suggests that some sort of coincident occurrence in the medial temporal lobe structures could trigger activation of the familiarity system (Bartolomei et al., 2004).

Input-output translation

A much-debated question is how the brain manages to translate input to output, that is, perception to action. Information processing models either postulated a specific 'discrete' response-selection mechanism, or a 'continuous flow' mechanism to account for input-output translations (Eriksen & Schultz, 1979; Miller, 1988). In contrast, brain studies did not support a modular discrete view of S-R translations. Instead, they suggested that the link between perception and action is implemented in the connectivity of networks of the brain that allowed a continuous interchange between the perceptual and motor regions. Especially the posterior-parietal region seemed to play a crucial role in establishing this interchange in what became known as the 'perception-action cycle' (Fuster 1990; see also Chapter 5). Neurons in areas 5 and 7 of the parietal cortex connect via reciprocal pathways with areas 6 and 8 in the frontal cortex, which respectively control movements of body limbs and the eyes (Goldman-Rakic, 1995; see also Figure 3.11).

During learning of S-R associations, synapses of axons of parietal neurons strengthen their connections with cells in the frontal cortex, thus establishing circuits that control voluntary as well as automatic movements. These circuits probably also explain the existence of 'mirror-neurons', discovered by Rizzolatti (Rizzolatti & Craighero, 2004) in the monkey motor cortex. Mirror neurons appear to be active not only during execution of movements, but also in observing movements of others. In a similar vein, Mesulam (1981) found that lesions in areas of the right parietal cortex were associated with motor neglect of the left body parts, providing additional support for the notion that connections between parietal and motor cortices are crucial for motor control.

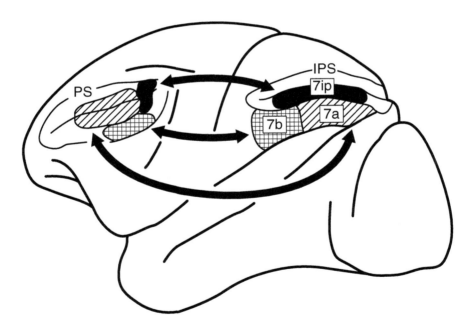

FIGURE 3.11
Lateral view of the rhesus monkey brain with connections between the intra-parietal sulcus (IPS) and principal sulcus (PS) in the frontal cortex. Similar connections exist in the human brain between parietal and prefrontal cortices.

Source: Adapted from Cavada & Goldman-Rakic (1989).

Output functions

At the output side, neural computations play a role in the form of action programs. There is sound evidence that actions are composed hierarchically and contain a sequence of significant segments, each of which translates into more simple movements. Picking up a glass means extending our arm, spreading our fingers and then grasping it. Parts of the movement program are carried out in advance. When we reach out for the glass, our brain already begins to grasp the object, before our hand reaches it.

Control of movements globally comprises three levels of computation of increasing specificity: action programming, instruction generation and movement execution (Kosslyn & Koenig, 1992). These three processes globally correspond to three regions in the motor hierarchy of the anterior cortex: the supplementary motor area (SMA), the premotor area (area 6) and the motor area (M1). The premotor cortex in particular receives massive input from the posterior parietal lobe, an area presumed to provide the spatial coordinates of movement trajectories. The motor structures in the anterior cortex are also linked with parts of the basal ganglia in planning and coordinating movements. A specific contribution of the basal ganglia might be to provide an 'urgency signal' that adjusts the weighting of speed versus accuracy during decision making (Thura & Cisek, 2017).

The line dividing computations and representations is especially hard to draw in the motor systems of the brain. Motor memories are assumed to reside in cortical as well as in subcortical areas, like the basal ganglia and the cerebellum, from where they are recruited either directly by the frontal cortex or triggered indirectly by input from the posterior parietal cortex to the frontal cortex.

Connectionist models

Computation involves a transformation of information from input to output, like in computers. Networks in the brain differ in several respects from those in computers, as well as from 'connectionist' networks that use computer algorithms to simulate 'brain-like' activity. Nevertheless, computer simulations have proven to be useful to investigate alternative theories about the way mental processes are represented in the brain, or manifested in human behavior (Feldman & Ballard, 1982).

Connectionist models are not intended to model neurons or synapses of real brain networks. They simulate learning rules in which strengthening of a synapse is not local or 'Hebbian' (i.e. dependent of simultaneous firing of pre- and postsynaptic neurons), but created by backward propagation from the output of the network, to affect neurons more buried in it. A simple example of a connectionist-type computation is presented in Figure 3.12. Two input neurons (input unit) connect to two neurons (the hidden unit), that converge with a third neuron (the output unit). The output threshold of the output unit is set to value 10.

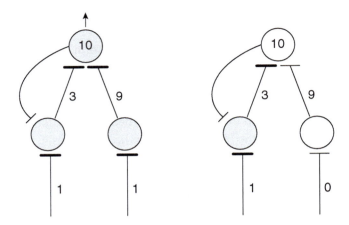

FIGURE 3.12
A simple computational ('connectionist') model with two input neurons, a hidden unit with two neurons, and one output neuron with its firing threshold set at 10. Dark areas indicate active neurons and synapses. Numbers indicate the strength of input and output. The output neuron has a recurrent connection to the hidden unit. Only the output neuron of the left network produces output.

Numbers indicate the strength of the (excitatory) connections between the different units. For example, if the input of both input neurons is 1 (1/1), total activation of the output of the hidden unit (9+3) will produce a value that is strong enough to cause the output unit to fire. However, if the input is 1/0 or 0/1, the total activation (3 or 9) will not reach the output threshold. Networks often receive feedback from recurring connections. Recurrent connections are excitatory or inhibitory and exert a modulating influence on the input or the hidden units. If the input device is insufficiently activated (for example, not having value 1, but 0.5), this value can be increased utilizing feedback of the output (or higher order) unit to boost activation of the hidden unit. Although connectionism also stresses the distributed and delocalized character of neural computation, it remains mostly silent on the potential roles of network topology and emergent dynamics in the functioning of large-scale neuronal systems.

Pattern-association networks

Applied to the brain the term computation has a more specific meaning, namely: 'establishing a functional state of a neural structure in which characteristics of the outside world or actions in the form of code are recorded'. It relates to processes underlying perception, memory or motor functions, and even components of cognitive processes like memory search, mental imagery and pattern recognition. Such networks allow a precise,

REPRESENTATION, COMPUTING AND CONTROL

even mathematical quantification of neurons at the local synaptic level. Figure 3.13 presents an example that illustrates the principle of pattern association in memory, used to specify simple learning and retrieval operations. The computational network shown here is an example of a specific building block for neural architectures, repeated in many parts of the brain. In this network a vector containing the unconditioned stimulus (ei = dendrite receiving neuron) is paired with a vector of the conditioned stimulus ($r'j$ = axon sending neuron) through a synaptic matrix with modifiable synaptic weights (wi,j) that follows a simple Hebbian learning rule (Rolls & Treves, 1998).

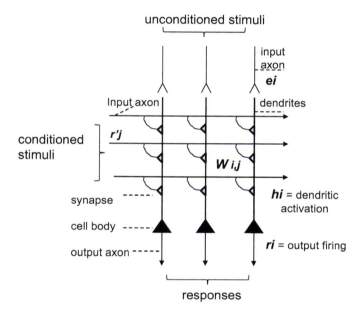

FIGURE 3.13
A prototypical modular network with a vector of unconditioned stimuli (ei) and a vector of conditioned stimuli ($r'j$) and responses. Unconditioned stimuli fire output neurons (ri). Conditioned stimuli have horizontal axons with modifiable synapses (wij) to the dendrites of the output neurons. Learning occurs via a simple Hebbian rule; see the box below for clarification of terms.

Source: (adapted from Rolls & Treves, 1998).

Firing rate output neuron: $r_i = f(e_i)$, determined by the unconditioned stimuli

Learning: $\delta w_{i,j} = k\, r_i r'_j$, Hebbs rule: representing conjunctive firing of presynaptic neuron $r'j$ and postsynaptic neuron ri

Recall: $h_i = \Sigma_j r'_j\, w_{i,j}$, with h_i representing the sum of all activations produced by neuron i through each strengthened synapse w_{ij} by each active neuron r'_j.

REPRESENTATION, COMPUTING AND CONTROL

The network allows specifying its various operations, such as firing rate, learning and recall, as illustrated in Figure 3.13.

Analyzing the functional properties of networks

In order to understand the working of these pattern-associate modules in the context of large-scale brain networks, it is important to have an idea of the brain's system-level organization and its overall connectivity.[4] Computational modeling, based on functional imaging of the brain in particular, has provided an integrated quantitative framework. Network models applied to real brain data need criteria to partition the brain into regions or areas that are internally coherent, according to anatomical or functional criteria. Using a branch of mathematics called graph theory, network models represent complex systems as sets of separate elements (nodes) and connections (edges) between these elements (Sporns et al., 2007).

A graph expresses a complex network as a function g = (v,e), with v the collection of nodes and e the collection of connections in the network. The three critical properties of the graph are cluster coefficient (local connectivity of a graph), path length (average distance between two nodes, which provides global connection information) and node degree (number of connections of a node). Also, hubs represent nodes that have a high level of overall connectivity (van de Heuvel & Sporns, 2013, see Figure 3.14 for an example).

Examples of 'hublike' structures with many short- and long-ranging connections are the amygdala, hippocampus, thalamus and the posterior parietal cortex. Another feature is modularity: the extent to which a group of nodes forms a separate community or subnetwork in the overall network. A modular network contains several isolated

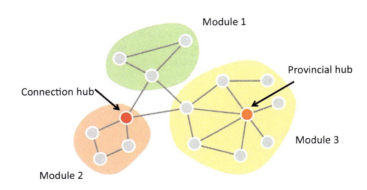

FIGURE 3.14
Building blocks of large-scale networks: nodes (light gray), modules and different types of hubs are part of larger subsets of neural elements.

Source: From van den Heuvel & Sporns, (2013).

subnetworks with strong internal connections between the nodes. The network view implies that functional specialization arises in large part from connectivity and interactions, rather than from specialized circuitry within isolated processing units.

It is worth emphasizing that functional connectivity in the brain expresses statistical dependencies among time courses (correlations) that do not generally represent direct neuronal signaling (Koenigsberger, 2017). Thus, large-scale network analysis of structural and functional connectivity offers only limited insight into the mechanisms by which neuronal systems compute – that is, the rules underlying the transformation and encoding of neural response patterns in both local and distributed circuits. This limitation partially reflects the focus of many network studies on task-free or resting brain functional connectivity. However, the strong point of network models is that they allow a view of the whole architecture of the brain networks. Thus, the building blocks integrated into the whole brain network, but now with greater emphasis on the connectivity between its constituent parts.

Computational modeling

A new and promising perspective in cognitive neuroscience involves the combination of computational modeling and imaging. It involves the application of computational and mathematical methods to formalize theories about the relationship between brain and cognitive functions, with the limitation that the temporal resolution of fMRI signals is too crude to test predictions about processes that transpire over relatively brief timescales. Computational models have proven to be a useful tool in functional imaging, for example in testing certain assumptions regarding the efficiency of empirically derived structural or functional MRI networks. In such an approach fMRI is preferably used as a tool for confirmatory research aiming to answer questions like, does a model or theory correctly predict the results of an fMRI experiment? Alternatively, which of two competing models gives the best account of fMRI data? (Ashby & Waldschmidt, 2008). Others have attempted to explain fMRI data as quantities the brain must encode, under-simplifying assumptions about the brain's workings.

Control functions of the brain

Information processes at the neural level indeed bear a certain resemblance to the operations of a computer. This applies not only to basic processing mechanisms associated with representations and computations, but also to control processes. In addition to in- and output systems and a memory system, computers have a central processor, a set of operations that control in- and output and the transfer of information to and from their memory. At the brain level, the distinction between control and computational systems implies a difference in specificity: computational systems usually have a specific task in processing 'data' – information coming from sensory or motor systems or stored in memory. The role of control systems is less specific. Their principal task is not to process specific information but rather to adjust, regulate or modulate input from the sensory system and output to the motor system. Control systems fall in two different categories, automatic and attentive (or executive) control.

Automatic control

Automatic control systems regulate processes in the autonomic nervous system. These maintain a state of balance or 'homeostasis' through circuits initiated and fed back to the hypothalamus. The hypothalamus regulates basic drives like hunger and thirst, and the production of the stress hormones cortisol, adrenaline and noradrenaline, secreted by the adrenal glands. Automatic control also plays a role in the motor system. The cerebellum seems to be particularly involved in the fine-grained adjustment of the initiation, direction and timing of voluntary movements, and in correcting small 'errors' (deviations between intended and performed movements) in feedback from the muscles and the body (somatosensory) system. Dopaminergic circuits originating in the basal ganglia and projecting to different areas of the motor cortex have an essential function in modulating the coordination and planning of movements.

Attentional and executive control

Attentional systems, associated with networks in the posterior and anterior cortices, are another example of control. They are responsible for the selection of information and action, and operate via reflexive ('bottom-up') and voluntary ('top-down') modulation of the output of sensory and motor structures via excitatory and inhibitory circuits. Visual-spatial attention, for example, is considered to increase the 'gain' of sensory input channels, when attention is directed to the location of objects in the visual environment. Gain – or enhanced output – could result from selective facilitation, which on the level of individual neurons is manifested in an increased firing frequency or stronger synchronous activity. It could also result from selective inhibition (or 'gate' function), in order to suppress irrelevant information or irrelevant actions (Figure 3.15, see also Aron, 2007). Further in this book several examples are given of the inhibitory role of pathways linking prefrontal structures with nuclei in the thalamus (Chapter 4), and in the basal ganglia (Chapter 5), involved in inhibiting distractive stimuli, or initiated responses, respectively. Baddeley's working memory model is a second example of a higher-order

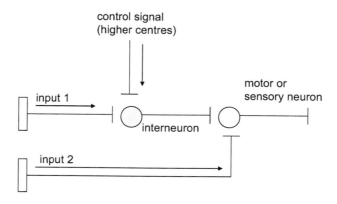

FIGURE 3.15
Example of modulation by a 'gate' function involving inhibition of a sensory neuron output by a control neuron. Input 1 will be blocked by inhibition from an interneuron (in black), allowing input 2 to flow to the motor or higher order sensory neuron.

control system (Baddeley & Hitch, 1994). This system postulates a central executive system in the frontal cortex, which recruits visual-spatial or acoustic representations ('slave systems') in the posterior cortices.

A similar system might be involved in mental imagery, where higher cortical areas are assumed to generate images by activating visual areas in the posterior cortex (Farah 1984; Kosslyn & Sussman, 1995; Kosslyn et al., 1995; Pearson et al., 2015), even using the same processes or representations critical in visual perception.

Studies of functional connectivity in the brain made it possible to map the networks involved in executive control, while subjects performed various cognitive tasks. These studies globally confirmed the findings of earlier work that relied on invasive measures of the brain activity of the monkey (Goldman-Rakic 1995; Desimone & Ungerleiter, 1989; LaBerge, 1995). A recent example is the central executive network (CEN) described by Seeley et al. (2007), a network activated in a variety of cognitive tasks that make demands on working memory, attention and response selection.

To conclude, one may assume that long-range connectivity between higher and lower structures is an essential structural condition for brain networks to exert control. Frontal brain areas that connect via the posterior-parietal cortex and parietal-thalamic circuits to primary sensory areas are a suitable example. Representations in the prefrontal cortex of tasks and goals exert control over behavior by providing top-down biases that guide the flow of activity along processing pathways, in posterior structures responsible for task execution as described by Miller & Cohen (2001) and Botvinick & Cohen (2014). Subcortical-cortical loops subserving modulation of motor areas through neurotransmitters are a third example.

Putting it together: hierarchical distributed networks

The brain is a macro system where large-scale networks, each consisting of local networks, cooperate with another in an integrated fashion (Bressler & Menon, 2010). A simple example of the distributed character of these networks is presented in Figure 3.16, which seems to be globally supported by studies using functional connectivity MRI (fcMRI).

The general pattern emerging from these studies is that of distributed networks that function on the basis of coherent activity of local areas. These networks incorporate both modularity and connectivity as the two fundamental principles of the organization of the brain. Modularity describes the specific local activity, connectivity the information exchange between these areas in a large-scale network (Mountcastle, 1978; Meunier et al., 2009).

Coherent activity of specialized areas within the networks is the basic principle underlying cognitive functions. However, the functional architecture of cognitive systems, traditionally associated with the cerebral cortex, emerge from a hierarchy where cortical areas also interact with subcortical structures.

Hierarchical principles have gradually pervaded modern theories of complex biological systems in general, and of the brain's functional architecture in particular. The idea of distributed hierarchical networks, already emphasized in early theories (see Simon, 1962; Luria, 1973; Felleman & van Essen, 1991) fits in with notions derived from evolution theory, and also with modern views on the efficient organization of biological systems. Complex systems are organized in a hierarchical manner, which implicates that they can also be partitioned or decomposed in more local systems or modules, a principle already introduced in earlier chapters of this book (but see also Figure 3.16). Insights derived from biological hierarchies approximate the principle of topological modularity: implying that nodes or nuclei in local networks have dense connections

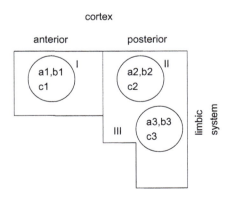

FIGURE 3.16
Schematic presentation of modules and networks in a distributed network covering cortical (anterior I, posterior II) and subcortical (e.g. limbic, III) areas. Each global function (e.g. A) is partitioned in local functions (e.g. a1,a2,a3) distributed over a large area of the brain (I,II,III).

with nuclei in the same module, and more sparse connections with nuclei belonging to other local networks or modules (Newman, 2006).

Hierarchies can be interpreted in various ways. One interpretation is that of a processing sequence. For example, the well-known organizational scheme of the primate visual system (Felleman and Van Essen, 1991) implies a sequential ordering of visual cortical areas from the visual sensory periphery to 'higher-level' areas involved in more abstract aspects of vision. Another widely used definition of hierarchy is that of a repeated encapsulation of smaller elements in larger ones (Kaiser et al., 2010; Robinson et al., 2009). Encapsulation on an extended spatial scale of the brain may vary from the lobes of the brain to cortical mini-columns. On a smaller topological scale they refer to areas containing small functional elements called 'canonical circuits' (Douglas & Martin, 2004) within regions like the visual cortex. Hierarchies also occur in temporal aspects of brain activity. Learning processes may vary from activities that take days and longer, to neuronal firing at the millisecond scale. Body movements and speech possess features at different temporal scales, implying that slowly changing neuronal states associated with more global aspects of speech and movements, also encode (or embed) trajectories of faster signals. Quantitative modeling of networks has also confirmed the crucial role of the hierarchical organization of large-scale functional networks. The principle, in this case, is called hierarchical modularity (see Kaiser et al., 2010): neural elements (or nuclei) of a specific (lower-order) module are not only connected with another, but also with elements of other modules which together form a higher-order module.

The flexibility of neurocognitive networks

Structural connectivity of a network concerns the framework or 'skeleton' of areas and their interconnections. Functional connectivity, in contrast, involves functions or processes that take place within the structural network. Which trajectories are chosen by the brain depends on the type of cognitive operation, and the cognitive load imposed on these operations. For example, elementary processes such as observation and recognition of objects are likely to run via both parallel and serial circuits. These circuits will be activated essentially bottom-up, meaning that information will flow automatically from the senses via intermediate structures to the higher levels (Figure 3.17, F1).

Bottom-up processes will usually run fast, because they use circuits with synapses that already formed synchronous connections. Processes under voluntary control will have a preference for top-down circuits in the brain. Examples are conscious retrieval (search in memory), focused attention, error-correction, and processing of new or unexpected information. Mental imagery might even be implemented in higher-order structures directly recruiting sensory regions (circuit F3 in Figure 3.17). Extended practice or cognitive training may increase speed and efficiency of information processes in the brain, resulting in selection of more direct trajectories and bypassing structures involved in early learning (Box 3.1).

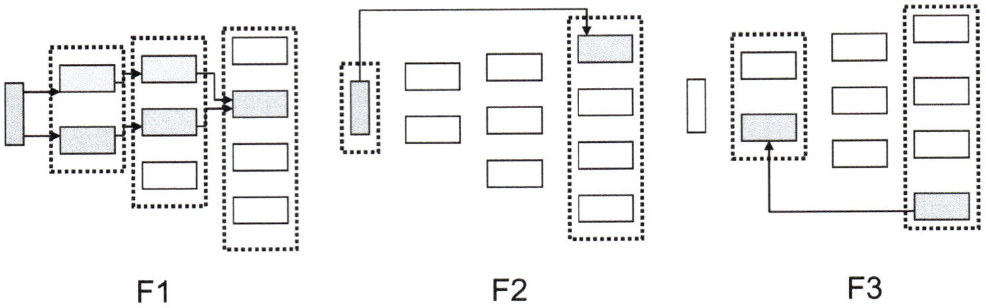

REPRESENTATION, COMPUTING AND CONTROL

F1   F2   F3

FIGURE 3.17
Hypothetical functional circuits (F1, F2 and F3) implemented within the same structural network. Dark areas are active. F1: Serial and bottom-up. F2: Bottom-up: the lower level directly affects the higher level bypassing the middle levels. F3: Top-down: the higher level directly affects the lower level.

BOX 3.1   FUNCTIONAL PLASTICITY

Functional plasticity relates to changes in the effectiveness of functional networks in the brain, as a result of learning. Despite the great public interest in commercial 'brain training' programs claiming to improve cognitive abilities, research so far has not confirmed that these programs have a transfer of effects to tasks beyond the specific tasks involved (Owen et al., 2010). During cognitive training of certain motor and cognitive tasks, the specifically involved neural connections are strengthened, which leads to increased efficiency of synapses and the flow of information in their networks. Cognitive training may counteract cognitive decline, for example in mental performance and cognitive slowing of the elderly (Mayr, 2008). It is also unlikely that this is a consequence of neurogenesis: the growth of new neural connections. Instead, its role seems to be to reactivate existing connections in neurocognitive networks, which prevents them from losing their functionality: also known as the 'use it or lose it' principle.

At the performance level, mental training in matched controlled settings has shown to be effective in improving cognitive activity directly related to the training tasks, with some generalization to measures of memory (e.g., Mahncke et al., 2006). At the neural level, positive effects of mental practice have been attributed to neurotransmitters such as glutamate and calcium. These substances play a role at the cellular level, in the formation of associations between nerve cells, and as such on memory and learning processes. Results of studies investigating the effects of cognitive training on brain activity using PET and fMRI measures are ambiguous. In motor tasks, studies reported a short-term effect of increased blood

continued

> flow in the motor areas. In demanding cognitive tasks, a gradual decrease of cerebral blood flow was found in frontal areas as a function of prolonged practice. This effect could be a clue that with practice these tasks need progressively less effort and make fewer demands on executive functions in areas such as the prefrontal cortex (see also: Kelly & Garavan, 2005, and pages 272–275).

Notes

1. Verbal–non-verbal is used here as a short-hand for different encoding systems assigned to the left and right hemispheres that do not overlap with the (much less disputed) perceptual-motor functions assigned to the anterior and posterior divisions of the cortex. Other suitable dichotomies that may serve to categorize functions of the left and right hemispheres are non-spatial versus spatial or analytic versus holistic.

2. Access to consciousness per se does not necessarily imply conscious awareness. Strength of activation is a second factor. Stimuli that have access to consciousness always activate some elements in long-term memory, but do not cause sufficient activation to reach the threshold necessary for conscious awareness (Cowan, 1995).

3. An example of a computational model based on binding elements of memory in a separate binding unit is the TraceLink model proposed by Jaap Murre (1997). TraceLink is inspired by the hippocampus temporarily activating cortical networks during consolidation. Data simulated with TraceLink successfully predicted certain memory deficits.

4. Chapters 4–7 of this book will globally follow such a systems approach by dealing with gross functional pathways and regions that form the basis of neurocognitive systems like attention, memory and emotions.

4 | Activation, attention and awareness

CONTENTS

- ▶ Introduction: the hierarchy of activation, attention and awareness
- ▶ Neurobiology of activation
- ▶ Attention: manifestations, varieties and methods
- ▶ Neurobiology of attention
- ▶ Awareness and consciousness

Introduction: the hierarchy of activation, attention and awareness

The state of activation of the brain is closely related to the processes of attention and awareness. Their close relationship is manifested at various temporal scales of cortical activation running from global ('tonic') to more local or specific ('phasic') fluctuations.[1] The most global state is characterized by the transition between waking and sleeping, regulated by structures in the brainstem. In the 1970s, researchers discovered a structure in the hypothalamus, the suprachiasmatic nucleus (SCN). This 'biological clock' regulates the 24-hour rhythm, also called 'circadian' (circa = about, dies = day) rhythm. They also found that lesions of the SCN in the rat abolished the circadian pattern, but not the total amount of sleep. Light serves as the 'zeitgeber', the signal that 'sets' the clock. In humans, shift work and jet lag disturb the circadian rhythm.

During wakefulness and sleep, consciousness is not constant, but subject to spontaneous fluctuations that vary between highly alert, alert, relaxed wakefulness to drowsiness (think of the familiar 'post-lunch dip'). Likewise, sleep is not a homogeneous condition, but varies along different sleep stages. Most familiar are the dream or REM (rapid eye movement) stage, and deep (slow wave) sleep. REM sleep is seen as a condition that promotes storage or consolidation of new impressions in memory. Not all memories profit from sleep (see Diekelmann et al, 2009, for a review). Deep sleep is often associated with a recovery period of the brain.

The transition between different sleep stages is influenced by subcortical areas. Deep sleep is primarily regulated by structures in the basal forebrain (anterior and dorsal of the hypothalamus), REM sleep by structures in the pons. In the laboratory, REM sleep of animals includes PGO waves (pons, geniculate, occipital), brief bursts of electrical activity that originate in the pons, which then propagate to the lateral geniculate nucleus and the primary visual cortex. Activation of the same circuit during REM sleep in humans is responsible for the rapid eye movements and vivid visual images that are often experienced during the dream state. The major goal of resting sleep appears to be the blocking of transfer of sensory information through the thalamus, achieved by bursts of spikes or 'spindles' generated in the thalamus.

Wakefulness and sleep also include highly specific activational states (Figure 4.1). During wakefulness, selective attention is accompanied by a state of differential activation, implying selective facilitation of relevant and concomitant inhibition of irrelevant events. A famous example is the 'cocktail party' effect discovered by the British psychologist Colin Cherry in 1953: in a noisy environment, we are still able to focus our attention on a single conversation. During sleep, specific activational states occur during REM sleep when we experience a kaleidoscope of specific experiences and images.

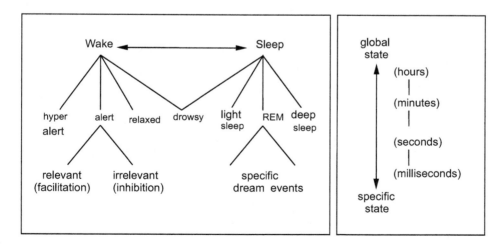

FIGURE 4.1
Left panel: hierarchy of three levels of cortical activation. Sleep-wake cycle incorporating gradually more specific levels. Right panel: the temporal scale for each level. Global states show slow ('tonic'), and specific states relatively fast ('phasic') fluctuations.

ACTIVATION, ATTENTION AND AWARENESS

An interesting finding from fMRI studies is that of a default or resting state network. This shows that the activity pattern of the brain in rest is not so different from the brain while performing a cognitive task, reflecting that even in rest our brain is occupied with spontaneous associations, thoughts, images and memory processes.

BOX 4.1   AROUSAL, ACTIVATION AND ALERTNESS

The 19th-century prevailing theory of waking and sleep rested on the simple principle that the waking state depended on sensory input and produced conscious awareness, while sleep lacked these qualities. The discovery of brainstem networks, such as the reticular activating system (RAS) by Moruzzi and Magoun, was an important step toward a more refined theory of consciousness. Activation circuits with diffuse projections to the cortex provided the neural substrate responsible for graded changes in excitability of cortical neurons and the state of consciousness (see Figure 4.2). Research into the activity of the intact brain became a reality after the discovery of the electroencephalogram (EEG) by Hans Berger in 1929. Similar to the waking state, electrical activity of the sleeping brain was manifested in various EEG rhythms competing for dominance. However, the specific patterns elicited in various sleep stages also suggested that the sleeping brain has its own and unique neural dynamics.

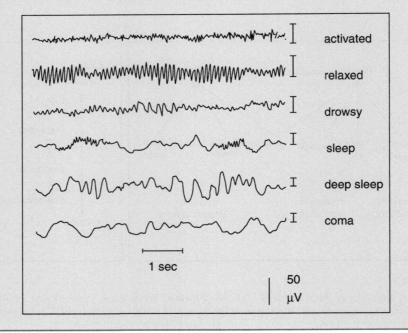

continued

> So far, these developments took place under the umbrella of neuroscience. Donald Lindsley made a crucial step towards integration of neuroscience and cognitive psychology in the early 1960s. Influenced by the writings of William James, Lindsley proposed the framework of a Behavioral-Cognitive continuum, reflected in parallel changes in the EEG, alertness, and attention (see insert). The theory of a behavioral-cognitive continuum driven by a single mechanism in the brainstem may now seem a bit outdated. However, activation as a nonspecific modulating force remains an important principle in modern cognitive neuroscience, in interpreting patterns of functional brain activity in rest and in cognitive performances.

The right part of Figure 4.1 indicates the time course of the different activation levels. Global levels, associated with the transition between waking and sleeping, occur with a relatively long-lasting cycle representing the circadian rhythm. Fluctuations of activation at more specific levels are manifested on gradually faster time-scales. At the most specific level, phenomena of selective attention can occur within a fraction of a second. The hierarchy of mental states as depicted in Figure 4.1 seems to run largely parallel with the structural organization of the brain. Global states fluctuating at a slow time scale are regulated by structures in the brainstem, specific and faster-fluctuating states by higher structures at the level of diencephalon, limbic system and cortex.

The following sections focus in more detail on the neural as well as functional aspects of activation, attention and awareness.

BOX 4.2 THE FUNCTION OF DREAMS: SCRAMBLER OR SYNTHESIZER?

The theory of dreams is one of Sigmund Freud's genial inventions (Freud, 1939). During sleep, a 'censor' protects man from the 'latent' or 'true' dream content. The censor takes care to hide – or disguise – the true content of the dream, by transforming it into another more symbolic form. According to psychoanalyst theory, the (often traumatic) content is too painful to be consciously experienced. The censor thus provides a distorted ('scrambled') but acceptable version for the conscious mind.

From a different angle, Allan Hobson (1988) suggested that, although the content and images of dreams may often appear strange and even weird, they are still a product of the rational brain. It tries to create order in the chaos of images that

continued

> spontaneously invade the dream. These images are often accompanied by rapid eye movements, elicited during sleep (REM sleep), using the PGO (Pons Geniculate Occipital) pathway. During the waking state, eye movements usually occur in synchrony with visual observations of objects in the outside world. During our dreams, similar images may 'pop up' in the occipital areas of the brain, but deprived of 'input' from the outside world. The rational brain then tries to 'glue together', or synthesize, these spontaneously activated images into a somewhat coherent, albeit sometimes also bizarre, story. According to Hobson the dream content is not a distortion, but an attempt at synthesis. Put in mechanical terms, the device used by the dream machine has more in common with a 'synthesizer" than with a 'scrambler' (Hobson & McCarley, 1977).

Neurobiology of activation

The terms activation and arousal are often used indiscriminately. Activation, however, has a somewhat broader coverage because it refers not only to the state of the cerebral cortex but also to that of the autonomous nervous system and of behavior. In contrast, arousal is often used in a more restricted sense to designate the excitatory state of the cerebral cortex (see also footnote 1).

Introduction

The information processing revolution in neurobiology, with its stronger emphasis on specific computational processes in the brain, has also transformed activation theories. This has led to the insight that activation is not merely the diffuse condition regulated by a labyrinth of structures collectively called the reticular activating system (Moruzzi & Magoun, 1949; Lindsley, 1961, Steriade, 1996). Instead, activation represents a mix of processes regulated at the level of the brain-system in different groups of neurons with specific effects on processes at the level of the cortex. New insights concerning large-scale networks connecting structures in the brainstem and the limbic system with regions in the cerebral cortex were a related development.

Structures in the brainstem, collectively known as the mesencephalic reticular activating system (RAS), are connected via ascending pathways to the hypothalamus, nonspecific thalamic nuclei, limbic system and cerebral cortex. The RAS regulates not only cortical activation but also causes excitation and inhibition of autonomic functions and muscle activity through descending nerve fibers that lead to the medulla and spinal motor units. The ascending reticular system (ARAS) receives input from three different sources, lower metabolic processes regulated by the hypothalamus, external stimuli, and input from higher cortical processes. Figure 4.2 depicts the two ascending activation circuits from brainstem to cortex, an indirect route (a) that runs via nonspecific nuclei of the thalamus, and a direct 'extrathalamic' route (b) that bypasses the thalamus. There also is a feedback loop (route c) from cortex to the thalamus and the brain stem. The function of these circuits is briefly discussed next.

Thalamic nuclei

The thalamus contains three groups of nuclei that are involved in the activation of the cortex (see also Chapter 2, Figure 2.9 for a more detailed view). The first group consists of specific relay nuclei of the lateral dorsal and lateral ventral thalamus. The ventral portion contains the medial and lateral geniculate nuclei at the posterior part of the thalamus. These nuclei link input from the auditory and visual sensory organs to specific projection areas in the cortex. The second group is formed by nuclei of the pulvinar that connect to the temporal, posterior and frontal association areas of the cortex. The third group consists of nonspecific nuclei, or diffuse projection nuclei, located in the midline and intralaminar portions, and the reticular nucleus of the thalamus (Kandel et al., 1991). Of particular importance are the pathways a and b (Figure 4.2) discussed next, that receive their primary input from structures in the RAS and activate broad areas of the cortex.

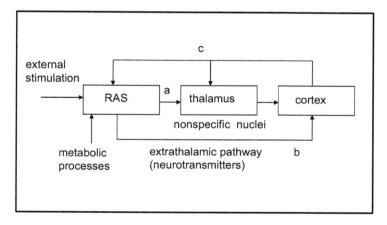

FIGURE 4.2
Three circuits involved in the regulation of the activation state of the cerebral cortex by the RAS. The indirect route (a) runs via the thalamus. The direct route (b) runs directly from the RAS to the cortex. Route (c) transmits input from the cortex to thalamus and RAS.

Thalamocortical circuits (gate system)

Nonspecific nuclei in the thalamus project via ascending excitatory pathways to areas in the cortex. Here, a thin layer of inhibitory cells encapsulating the thalamus, called the reticular nucleus (abbreviated: RN) plays an important role. RN is the only nucleus in the thalamus with inhibitory connections that project back to the relay neurons, making it function as a 'gate' (Skinner & Yingling, 1977; Steriade & McCarley, 1990).

All thalamocortical (upstream) and corticothalamic (downstream) nerve pathways pass the RN. Other excitatory relay cells of the thalamus transmit information from the senses (visual, auditory and touch) to the sensory areas in the brain (see Figure 4.3). Cells in the lateral geniculate nucleus (LGN) for the visual sensory modality are an example. The primary function of the RN is to keep the LGN gates to the visual cortex closed. This function is accomplished by inhibitory (Gaba-ergic) synapses of RN axons with LGN relay cells. Afferent nervous pathways from the reticular formation have inhibitory synapses with the RN. These pathways diffusely project to neurons in RN. Consequently, activation of the reticular system (for instance, by a sudden loud noise) will lead to global disinhibition of the RN. As a result, the thalamic gates in LGN will open massively, allowing sensory input to flow freely to the cortex. Thalamic gating also serves as a specific mechanism regulating top-down effects of selective visual-spatial attention on sensory input, described in the attention section of this chapter.

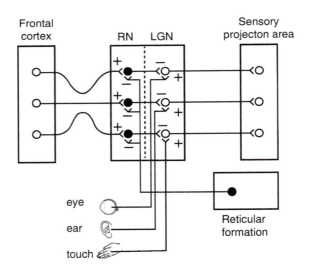

FIGURE 4.3
Thalamic 'gate-model' of cortical arousal as proposed by Skinner & Yingling (1977). Neurons in RN (reticular nucleus) inhibit gates in the LGN (lateral geniculate nucleus) to sensory projection areas. The joint effect of facilitatory axons from the frontal cortex and inhibitory axons from the reticular formation controls the inhibitory neurons in RN.

Extrathalamic pathways (gain system)

A second afferent circuit activates the cortical state in an even more diffuse manner. In contrast to the thalamocortical system with axons arranged in a vertical (radial or columnar) fashion, axons of the extrathalamic system intersect in a horizontal (tangential) way, crossing diffusely multiple columns in the cortex (Foote & Morrison, 1987). This system projects directly without (or with only sparse) relays in the thalamus to targets in the forebrain. Its function is increasing the 'gain', via four aminergic circuits originating in the brainstem, producing acetylcholine, noradrenaline, serotonin and dopamine. All four neurotransmitters are responsible for modulation of neural input to the higher cortical areas.

At least three different neurotransmitter systems in the brainstem control the state of cortical arousal. One is the locus coeruleus with its widespread noradrenergic projections to the cortex, the hippocampus and the thalamus. The two other neurotransmitters are acetylcholine, produced by nuclei in the pons and basal forebrain, and serotonin produced in the raphe nuclei in the medulla and pons. Noradrenaline is released when novel or unexpected stimuli elicit the orienting response, thereby improving the signal to noise ratio in sensory neurons (Gabay et al., 2011). It has numerous projections to the parietal cortex, superior colliculi and the pulvinar of the thalamus. The impact of acetylcholine on the brain is more complicated, involving projections to the motor pathways, in particular those that originate in the basal ganglia where acetylcholine interacts with dopamine. Consolidating sensory impressions in the hippocampus is the second role of acetylcholine. Serotonin (5-HT) also projects diffusely to the cortex where it regulates the sleep-wake cycle as well as mood states.

Dopamine circuits (discussed in Chapter 2) are not exclusively connected with cortical arousal, but influence the brain more specifically. Dopamine has massive projections to the neostriatum of the basal ganglia and the motor cortices, where it is involved in motor control. The mesolimbic dopamine pathway, with its projections to the ventral striatum and anterior cingulate, participates in networks that control the motivational and emotional states.

Activation and stress

Stress is commonly defined as a reaction of the nervous system to a threatening event or condition. It involves mobilization of additional energy for adaptation or 'coping' with the eliciting event (called 'stressor'). The resulting activation pattern is manifested not only at the level of the brain, but also at that of the autonomic nervous system (Frankenhaeuser,1981). Figure 4.4 highlights the stages of the standard physiological response that accompanies stress. The hypothalamus acts as the main initiator of the stress response. It is preceded and controlled by an (implicit) evaluation in higher centers of

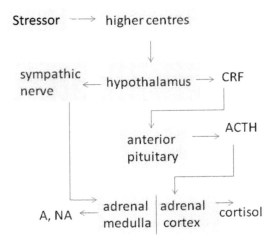

FIGURE 4.4
Two circuits mediating the stress reaction. Left, the fast route via the sympathetic nerve to the adrenal medulla, producing adrenaline (A) and noradrenaline (NA). Right, the slow route via anterior pituitary and adrenal cortex producing cortisol. CRF = corticotropin release factor; ACTH = adrenocorticotropic hormone. See text for clarification.

the limbic system, with the amygdala and ventromedial prefrontal cortex as most likely candidates. This process, also known as cognitive appraisal, sends a 'red flag' signal to the hypothalamus when it detects a threatening event. Local networks in the amygdala may learn and 'remember' specific stress-related information. Once stimulated by an individual stressful event, the circuit will modify the influence of future incentives on the response system, in the form of a bias of its synapses for future stress stimuli. Studies of rodents revealed that early postnatal experience altered the hypothalamic stress and induced release of stress hormones in adult rats (Plotsky and Meaney, 1993). In the hypothalamus, several core nuclei subsequently react to the acute stressor. Some nuclei receive concurrent input from the RAS, and others react to the stressor by producing specific hormones (neuromodulators) transmitted to stations further downstream. The hypothalamus has two output routes: a slow pathway through the anterior pituitary gland and the adrenal cortex and a fast pathway.

In the slow pathway, neurons in the paraventricular nucleus of the hypothalamus secrete the hormone CRF (corticotropin release factor) which stimulates the anterior pituitary gland to secrete ACTH (adrenocorticotropic hormone). ACTH, in turn, stimulates the adrenal cortex to secrete glucocorticoids (cortisol) in the bloodstream. CRF is also secreted in the brain where it acts as a neuromodulator/neurotransmitter in regions of the limbic system.

The fast route runs from the sympathetic part of the autonomic nervous system to the adrenal medulla that produces adrenaline (A) and noradrenaline (NA). Cortisol promotes the production of glucose from fats and proteins. It is an essential fuel of the metabolic system, which can also pass the blood-brain barrier. Cortisol reconnects to the hypothalamus, where it inhibits the production of CRF.

Under conditions of chronic stress cortisol has a detrimental effect on the hippocampus memory system, mediated by cortisol affecting the glucocortcoid receptors in the CA1 area of the hippocampus (Sapolsky, 1992). Adrenaline and noradrenaline secreted by the adrenal gland in the bloodstream also contribute to energy mobilization. After some time metabolites will pass into the blood, where they can be detected in urine samples. Threatening situations associated with feelings of fear and panic are not the sole cause of stress reactions. These may also occur after a prolonged or strenuous mental activity. Stress hormones are even released in stimulating situations that are experienced as pleasant. Parachuting, skiing, and mountain climbing, producing the much coveted 'noradrenaline rush', are some examples. Studies of freely behaving mice revealed that neurons of the hypothalamic–pituitary–adrenal axis show increased activity to aversive stimuli, as well as decreased activity to repeated appetitive stimuli, suggesting that CRF neurons encode the positive and negative valences of stimuli (Kim et al., 2019).

Attention: manifestations, varieties and methods

Many a chapter dealing with attention has started with William James' famous quote 'everyone knows what attention is'. Indeed, everyone seems to intuitively know what attention is, in particular the way it manifests itself in our daily subjective experience. Still, it has been difficult to give a precise definition of attention. The main reason being that attention has several varieties and meanings, such as alertness, concentration, awareness and consciousness.

Much of attentional knowledge was based on intuition and introspection at the end of the 19th century, and was reexamined, corrected and sometimes confirmed by the scientific approach of the late 20th and early 21st century. Neuroscientists investigating effects of auditory selective attention using single cell brain recording in the cat (Hernandez-Péon, 1966), came close to identifying the underlying selective mechanism in the brain. In addition, early theories and paradigms of selective attention developed by cognitive psychologists became a fruitful source of inspiration for cognitive neuroscientists looking for the sources of attention in the human brain.

Selection as the core element of attention

One of the intuitive notions is that attention 'fills the mind', if only for a brief moment of time, like a momentary thought or experience. Attention seems to 'lift out' or magnify perceptual images and ideas that otherwise would have passed unnoticed in the stream of events that temporarily activate our brain, implying that the computational process of neural selection also depends on the energy level of the signal event. One of the major goals of attention is to enhance the efficiency of mental processing, in terms of its accuracy and speed. Increased accuracy is accomplished by selecting relevant events and concurrently suppressing irrelevant events at the input side as well as the output side of processing. At the brain level such an operation requires mechanisms of information selection, as well as mechanisms that modulate (e.g. enhance or suppress) elements in the information flow. More specifically, it requires a difference between the modulatory processing of target subset elements and its surrounding distractive elements (LaBerge, 1995). This might be achieved by increasing the output of the target subset more than that of the surrounding subset. Distraction can make it harder to accurately identify targets when other objects are in its direct vicinity, especially when they share features with the targets. In search tasks, serial search is an effective strategy for the brain to restrict interference with competing distracters, by comparing stimuli in the display 'one by one' with a memory representation of the target.

Attention may also be used to coordinate several action elements, like performing two tasks or actions simultaneously or intermittently, or coordinating a sequence of words into an effective sentence. Such activities would intuitively be guided by selection of a goal or image functioning as an 'anchor' around which coordinated actions are organized. This would rely to a large extent on our working memory that provides access to the involved cognitive or action elements.

The manifestations of selective attention

According to LaBerge (1995) selective attention manifests itself in three ways; *preparation, selection and maintenance*. It is important to notice that all three involve the selective operation of attention, but on different time scales and with different functions. Preparatory attention is a sustained version of selective attention operating on a scale of seconds prior to an expected stimulus event (like preparing for a red traffic light to turn green). The speed of perceptual decisions or planning of actions benefits from preparing or anticipating certain events. An important role of anticipation is that it activates or 'presets' neural assemblies prior to the actual stimulus and associated response, thus ensuring fast reactions when the stimulus arrives. Preparation can be driven by an image or 'template' of the stimulus or action held and memorized in working memory. William James considered it as an imaginary duplicate, functioning as a 'pre-perception' of the stimulus. This 'prior image' of the location or attributes of the stimulus was supposed to do a part of the 'job' of the sensory processing a perceptual event triggered by the actual stimulus. After the stimulus event has occurred, selection involves a 'snapshot' operation involving the selective identification of the event which may only take 200–500 milliseconds. This function of preparation nicely illustrates how the selection and enhancement properties of selective attention work together to speed up processing of a target event. The difference between the two fundamental functions of selection, presetting neural assemblies during internal mental preparation and the actual sensory processing of the stimulus, comes close to the distinction between the 'control' and 'expression' mechanisms of attention in the cortex, to be described in more detail further ahead.

Finally, preparatory attention may also be interpreted in terms of some attentional capacity or 'resource', or 'continuous quantity' allocated across tasks (LaBerge, 1995).

The maintenance part of attention is often described as a long duration free-floating state of vigilance or sustained attention, possibly only restrained by a mental set to 'be aware of anything relevant that might happen'. Examples are watching the birds in the sky and listening to music. Vigilance tasks may serve as another example of the maintenance part of selective attention, guided by particular low probability attributes or spatial locations of objects. Think of the air-traffic controller scanning a computer screen. Here perceptions correspond to stored mental representations of rare deviations that occur in regular aircraft flight patterns. Errors may slip into vigilance performance due to fluctuations in a performance bias or perceptual sensitivity of the observer.

Reflexive and voluntary attention

In general, we can break down selective attention in two categories, reflexive attention (externally driven by objects in the sensory world) and voluntary attention (internally driven by mental events) (Figure 4.5). A related terminology is *exogenous and endogenous orienting*, which is based on the metaphor of a mental spotlight in Posner's theory of visual spatial orienting. Orienting involves 'aligning attention with a source of sensory input or internal semantic structure stored in memory' (Posner & Cohen, 1984). These two forms of attention recruit different neural pathways controlling attention respectively in a bottom up or top down fashion, with selection manifested globally at the sensory or the preparatory levels, as clarified in the earlier paragraph. Figure 4.5 also illustrates that the selective attention process is composed of intensive and selective operations, associated respectively with the modulation and informational content of the information flow. Modulation is achieved by selectively enhancing (or suppressing) activity in the cortical circuits regulating the information flow in the perceptual and action systems of the brain.

Despite the interconnection between intensive and selective aspects of attention at the neural level, they may receive differential emphasis in subcategories of reflexive and focused attention (such as arousal and orienting, divided and focused attention), to be described in greater detail in the following sections.

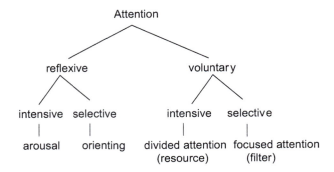

FIGURE 4.5
A simple hierarchical classification of various forms of attention and their expressions. See text for clarification.

Reflexive attention

Reflexive attention ('exogenous orienting') is a form of attention that is automatically evoked or 'captured' by external events, sounds or images in the environment (Yantis & Jonides, 1984). Sudden or intensive stimuli usually interrupt ongoing processes because they are important to the survival of the individual, who must respond to potential threatening events in its neighborhood. Young babies, for example, often appear to react with movements of their eyes or head to sounds, objects or persons appearing in their field of vision. One might also say that babies are highly distractible to stimuli from the environment.

Reflexive attention comes close to the concept of the orienting response, originally described as a mismatch between an external and an internal representation (Sokolov 1963) and related concepts like automatic orienting and exogenous cueing. What all these concepts have in common is the notion that presentation of novel or unexpected stimuli leads to a temporarily increase of arousal, followed by orienting to the source of the stimuli with the increased arousal reflecting the intensive aspect and orienting the selective, or cue function, of the stimulus (Figure 4.5 lower left). The eliciting event is considered as the 'call' or precursor, and reflexive attention (or orienting) is the answer to the call (Öhman, 1979; Näätänen, 1992).

Voluntary attention

In contrast, voluntary attention ('endogenous orienting') is intentionally directed to certain events from a source *within* the perceiver. It only develops during late childhood. Similar to reflexive attention, voluntary attention has two components, intensive and selective, that blend with another in their neural expression.

Divided attention The intensive aspect of voluntary attention is synonymous with the 'amount of attention' or 'mental effort' allocated to a difficult task. It is also labeled as divided attention because in contrast with focused attention subjects have to deal with several stimuli on a display, or perform several tasks at the same time. Divided attention has been examined in two basic paradigms: visual search and dual tasks. What both tasks have in common is that they require a division of attention across multiple sources of information rather than a single source. The processes involved in divided attention tasks have often been interpreted as 'demanding' or 'effortful', rather than in terms of selection.

Visual search tasks In normal daily conditions, we constantly move our eyes to search for objects in the environment. When driving on the freeway our eyes automatically scan the traffic stream, jumping to unexpected visual events. When searching for a lost object, our eyes search for a specific object among other objects that matches with the familiar representation stored in long-term memory. In a crowd of people, it's easier to find a friend with a red hat (which she promised to wear) than searching for her familiar face.

The time needed to locate the target on the screen is plotted in a search function, which displays the time needed to find the target as a function of the number of distracters in the array. In conditions when a distinctive physical feature of the target – like a red T – 'pops out' from the blue Ts as distracters, the search function remains flat. This is because the search process was triggered by exogenous processes that Anne Treisman called 'pre-attentive' (Treisman & Gelade, 1980). In contrast, when the target is defined by a conjunction of two features (for example a red T among blue and red Ts and Ls, Figure 4.6), the search function has a positive slope. Treisman took this as evidence that search occurs in a serial self-terminating fashion. These results were found independently of eye movements, suggesting that similar to spatial cueing, visual search is also based on covert attention (see the paragraphs further ahead for a discussion of more theoretical implications of spatial attention and visual search).

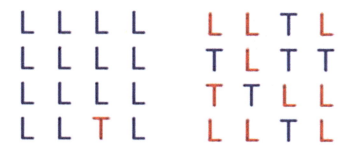

FIGURE 4.6
Two versions of the visual search tasks (find the red T): feature search (left) and conjunction search (right).

Visual search tasks have frequently been used in experimental settings when subjects searched for targets in displays with varying numbers of distracters ('display set') as well as with a varying number of targets belonging to a pre-memorized 'memory set' (Sternberg 1969; Shiffrin & Schneider, 1977). These studies specifically served to unravel the characteristics of controlled versus automatic modes of information processing. Search for targets in conditions that incorporated variable memory sets ('varied mapping') induced controlled search, contrasting with fixed set ('consistent mapping') conditions where search functions gradually flattened out, as the search became more automatic. With extended practice, initially demanding controlled search gradually changes into an automatic mode of information processing, designated as automatic detection (Shiffrin et al., 1981). The latter paradigms placed greater emphasis on mechanisms of control and allocated capacity than on selective mechanisms. Some studies used the same paradigms with electrocortical measures of the brain (ERPs) as converging measures. These confirmed the notion of enhanced energetically costs, as reflected in sustained negative potentials increasing in amplitude with a greater load of the search task (Okita et al., 1985; Wijers et al., 1989; Rösler et al., 1995).

Dual tasks In the dual task paradigm, also referred to as 'multitasking', subjects have to perform two tasks simultaneously. The tasks will interfere with each other if their joint appeal to a common resource exceeds the available capacity. If more capacity is allocated to task A (driving a car in heavy city traffic) less will be available for performing task B (having a conversation with the person in the seat next to you). In conditions that involve systematic manipulation of the priority of two tasks (e.g. 90/10, 50/50 and 10/90 differential emphasis), performance shows a linear trade-off suggesting that the tasks draw on the same pool of resources (see Figure 4.7). A difficult task would also show less interference when shared with an easy or highly practiced task (Strayer & Kramer 1990).

The theoretical basis of divided attention as briefly introduced earlier has been the subject of some controversy. Some have argued that divided attention is merely an instruction given to subjects, and not an actual sharing of an attentional quantity. The real way people deal with dual tasks might not be sharing but a fast shifting or switching of focused attention between tasks (Pashler, 1994). This suggests that the boundaries separating the intensive (or preparatory) and selective manifestations of voluntary attention may not be as distinct as suggested in our earlier classification. An argument in support of the view that some divided attention conditions favor the allocation of attention in a graded way, is that selective (focused) attention mostly becomes manifest in short lasting differential activation of attended versus unattended features of a stimulus. Divided attention, in contrast, extends over a more extensive period, may vary in intensity and spread to a broader area in space and of stimulus attributes. Subjectively, the mental set in the related tasks also seems to more strongly reflect the energy than does the selective aspect of attention (see also Wickens, 1986).[2]

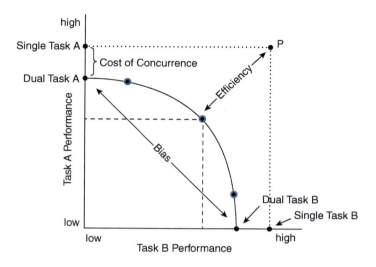

FIGURE 4.7
Hypothetical example of a performance trade-off function between the performances of two tasks of equal difficulty (A and B). P = optimal performance in single-task conditions. Costs of concurrence: constant 'overhead' costs in dual relative to single-task conditions. The left diagonal (Bias) represents the effects of relative emphasis of tasks A and B respectively (black dots on the curved line corresponding with 80/20%, 50/50% or 20/80%, respectively). Efficiency: variations in the quality of dual-task performance along the right diagonal. For example, performance may gradually become faster and more accurate after extensive practice (with the trade-off moving towards the upper right corner).

Source: Adapted from Johnson & Proctor (2004).

This is clearly manifested in the intuitively appealing concept of mental effort, as introduced by Daniel Kahneman in the 1970s. Effort is manifested in the activity of the sympathetic branch of the autonomic nervous system, for example in a dilation of the pupils (Kahneman, 1973). Its neural underpinning is the arousal system in the brain, responsible for the modulation of the intensive aspect of attention (Robbins & Everitt, 1994). With the advent of neuroimaging methods, mentally demanding activities that relied on working memory were also reflected in the increased activity of brain areas involving the dorsolateral prefrontal cortex. This confirmed the intuitive notion that 'brain work', similar to effortful physical activity, demands energy and is therefore reflected in an increased blood flow transporting oxygen and glucose to the involved areas. The concept of mental effort became affiliated with the theory that activity of the brain depended on a 'reservoir' of limited resources allocated to cognitively demanding tasks (see also Figure 4.9).

Focused attention can be defined as the function by which certain information is selected for further processing. It is usually considered to be a mechanism protecting the brain from an informational overload. Experimental studies of visual spatial

ACTIVATION, ATTENTION AND AWARENESS

attention have often used visual-spatial cueing tasks in which subjects attend to briefly presented stimuli on a display, while fixating on a point in the middle of the screen. This set-up is typical to elicit covert attention, a condition when attention is directed to a position in space, without moving the eyes to the cued location. This would otherwise have confounded the mental aspect of the attention spotlight with the greater perceptual acuity of the fixated target (Posner & Cohen, 1984).

Two different types of cueing, direct and symbolic, have been applied in spatial cueing tasks. In direct cueing, a bright flash is briefly presented at the location of the subsequent target, while symbolic cueing uses a central arrow pointing to the most likely location of the target (Figure 4.8). Direct cueing elicits an automatic form of reflexive attention that is characterized by 'inhibition of return'. When the target appears in the range of 50–200 ms after the cue, the reaction time is considerably faster than in a non-cued condition. At longer intervals subjects start to react slower, which is taken as a sign that attention to the cued location becomes inhibited. Apparently, automatic orienting evolved as a short-lasting phenomenon, which could be a sign of adaptation to visual environments, where many things happen at short intervals. It would then be a better strategy for the visual system to focus on new locations, instead of returning to the same location. In case the target at the attended location is of interest, the brain might decide to focus on it longer, to extract more information from the meaningful event. In this case the initial reflexive mode of attention is followed by the voluntary mode of attention.

Symbolic cueing is used to manipulate voluntary selective attention. It also involves covert attention since the subject has to suppress the natural tendency to make a saccade

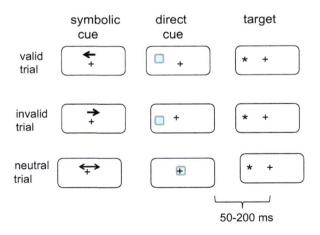

FIGURE 4.8
Spatial cueing task with two types of cueing (symbolic and direct) associated with voluntary and reflexive attention. Arrows indicate the direction of covert attention. The facilitatory effect of direct cueing on performance only occurs in a critical cue-target interval between 50–200 ms.

to the target appearing at peripheral positions on the computer screen. The symbolic cue can be an arrow indicating the correct (valid) position of the target or the incorrect (invalid) position.

When valid trials occur frequently (for instance, 80% of the time) subjects will react much faster to expected than to neutral (50%) targets. They react much slower to unexpected targets (20%) trials. On valid trials, faster reactions are taken to reflect the 'benefits' of the mental spotlight that enhances efficiency in processing sensory stimuli. Slower reactions to invalid trials, in contrast, are ascribed to the 'costs' associated with the extra time needed to 'disengage' the mental spotlight from the incorrect location and subsequently move it to the correct position. Further in this chapter we shall see that electrocortical, as well as neuroimaging indices taken from the brain in spatial cueing tasks, confirmed the suggestion from performance studies that spatial attention might indeed enhance early perceptual processes.

Bottleneck versus resource theories

The concept of limited capacity lies at the heart of attention theories. It implies that human information processing capacity cannot simultaneously process all stimuli from the environment. The solution proposed in theories of attention is that of selecting or limiting the flow of information that reaches the senses.

Filter models

Stage models of selective attention as developed by Donald Broadbent (1958) proposed the idea of an informational bottleneck; a filter, gate or structural limitation in a critical stage of processing where irrelevant (or unattended) information is denied access to further processing (Figure 4.9 left). Broadbent's model was based on early auditory studies showing that in situations of a high sensory load (the classical 'cocktail party') persons can block out irrelevant stimuli that fall outside the focus of their attention.[3] Later, a milder form of bottleneck was proposed where a strict gating mechanism was replaced by the notion of an 'attenuation' filter, allowing significant unattended information to 'slip through' the filter and intrude our mind. For example, a voice in the crowd mentioning your name would likely attract your attention, despite your involvement in a conversation with a friend. Such intrusions can be seen as a clever adaption of the brain allowing to treat signals that carry highly relevant information with priority. Its ecological value becomes apparent in the more exotic example of a wild animal in the African steppe. Despite its involvement in devouring its prey, it still needs to keep a sharp eye and ear for signals of potential danger coming from intruders of its territory. Finally, some have argued that the concept of a selective filter is intrinsic to differential activation (enhancement) of elements in long-term memory (Cowan, 1995). From this

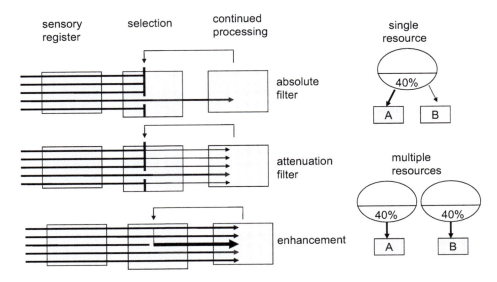

FIGURE 4.9
Simplified view of two types of theories of attention. Left: three versions of structural bottleneck theories: absolute and attenuation filtering and differential enhancement. Right: resource theory with single and multiple versions. See text for clarification.

point of view, all stimuli initially activate elements in long-term memory, with focused attention differentially activating (or enhancing) significant features or features of stimuli already residing in long-term memory (see Figure 4.9 bottom panel, and Figure 4.18).

Resource models

The second type of a limited capacity theory was proposed in resource models. Resources were originally defined in terms of an attention system that voluntarily allocates capacity in response to the demands imposed by a cognitive task (Kahneman, 1973; Wickens, 2008; Gopher, 1986; Norman & Bobrow, 1975). The increased load was assumed to lead to greater mental effort to meet the demands of the task, which in turn was reflected in increased arousal. Capacity or resource models of attention were often based on tasks that manipulated the load on working memory, like for instance the complexity of mental arithmetic operations or the number of elements held in memory in a memory search task. In the same tasks, time pressure could also play a role as far as it was inherent in the structure of the task, that is, to the extent that it contributed to the difficulty of the mental operation (Kahneman, 1973). Resource models were tested more specifically in the setting of dual-task conditions that required subjects to perform two tasks simultaneously, as discussed earlier. Subsequent studies also demonstrated that the amount of interference between tasks performed simultaneously depended on its specific cognitive operations. For example, when a verbal task is shared with a spatial-motor task interference is much less than between two verbal tasks or two spatial tasks. Taken together, this suggested that capacity allocated to a task might not only depend on a single global resource, but also on the structure of the tasks and their respective demands on specific capacities or resources. It was also suggested that separate processing resources have their anchor in the functional architecture of the brain. This concerned divisions between regions associated with specific in- or output functions (visual versus auditory modalities, manual versus vocal modes of responding) or more central functions (spatial versus verbal, perceptual-central versus response-related processes (Wickens, 2008; Kinsbourne & Hicks, 1978).

In later studies the metaphorical concept of resources gradually gave way to concepts based on the functions of the brain, in particular functions controlling human working memory, also referred to as executive functions (Bunge et al., 2000). An influential model by Cohen (Braver & Cohen, 2000) proposed that the dorsolateral prefrontal cortex (DLPFC) plays a critical role in executive attentional control, suggesting that separate areas would be suitable candidates for control of resources, the concept that guided earlier studies of dual-task performance. In particular, they suggested the DLPFC to be a key element for the deployment of attention to different processing streams (Miller & Cohen, 2001). It was specifically proposed that different processing streams are represented in different processing units within DLPFC, with attention control being implemented through the differential activation of the units associated with each processing stream (Low et al., 2009).

Early versus late selection

At the end of the 20th century, the 'early versus late selection' debate became a central issue in studies of selective attention. This was centered around the question at which stage the attention bottleneck should be located: early or late in the processing stream. Early selection processes assumedly have an early onset and run off automatically without any expression of unattended stimuli in consciousness. Late selection, in contrast, implies that attended and unattended inputs are processed equivalently by the perceptual system, until reaching the stage of semantic encoding. Thus, late selection may also depend on the meaning and not only on perceptual features like in early selection. It could also involve conscious awareness of unattended stimuli.

Task conditions that favor early selection are instructions to select events using simple features like position, color and orientation. A high perceptual load is also crucial, like the presence of many elements in a visual display during visual search, or high speed of presentation of auditory and visual stimuli (Lavie, 1995). At lower presentation rates, or with fewer elements in the display subjects will have sufficient time to pay attention to significant aspects of stimuli. In addition, pictures of familiar meaningful objects are hard to ignore, because they automatically activate representations in long-term memory. A typical demonstration of a late selection is the 'negative priming' effect, as described by Tipper in 1985. In his experiment, subjects must name line drawings of familiar objects printed in red (a table), superimposed on an ignored familiar object printed in green (a dog). Subjects received two pairs of superimposed objects, the prime and the probe. If the previously ignored object became the attended object on the subsequent probe trial, the subjects were slower at naming the object, indicating that they must have processed the ignored object on the basis of its meaning, and not its color.

It may not be too farfetched to suggest that knowledge of brain systems and their global and local networks contributed to bridge the artificial gap, created between the two contrasting theories. As shall be elaborated in the following sections of this chapter, it became increasingly evident that early and later selection processes are both implemented in the brain's functional architecture. In the hierarchy of processing, this would include early filter-like mechanisms to modulate sensory input (referred to as the *expression or site* of attention), as well as general-purpose networks involved in cognitive control that comprise the *source* (or cause) of attention and are flexibly allocated to various external as well as internal processes. Such a flexible mechanism could also move the locus of selection to a late stage of processing, depending on the task demands (Yantis & Johnson, 1990). It also became clear that identification of objects (instead of isolated features) is possible without early selective enhancements or modulations in structures like the thalamus. These 'late selection' processes are achieved by information flowing from the sensory to associations areas like IT (inferotemporal cortex). These objects are correctly identified without attentional modulation or 'filtering', since sensory information entering the visual systems directly activates existing memory representations in networks of the temporal cortex, via the ventral pathway.

Is spatial attention special?

Theories of visual attention have often emphasized the unique role of spatial attention, suggesting that spatial processing mechanisms in the brain are activated, even if the position of the stimulus is not a relevant feature. Selection of positions in space also occurs earlier in the flow of information than attention for nonspatial features, taking shape as modulations of the same areas in the primary auditory cortex and extrastriate visual areas that are involved in sensory perception.

The specific role of spatial attention was verified in studies using electrocortical measures (ERPs). Attention focused on the position of targets in the visual field was reflected in enhanced amplitudes of the P1 component at the occipital scalp, which topography followed the retinotopic mapping of the visual field into the cortex (Mangun & Hillyard, 1995, see also Figure 4.16 further ahead). Attention to nonspatial features of stimuli like color and shape were also reflected in ERP components over the extrastriate visual cortex, but without the typical enhancement of sensory ERP components found in spatial attention tasks. Animal studies and studies of cortical lesions in humans further suggested that the parietal cortex is a key region in controlling spatial attention modulations in the sensory regions (Desimone & Duncan,1995; La Berge, 1995; Hopfinger et al., 2001).

Feature integration

The Feature Integration Theory (FIT) of Treisman (Figure 4.10) is another example of a position-specific theory. This theory states that simple features like color, orientation and shape are always detected automatically at relatively early 'pre-attentive' stages of processing. Voluntary spatial attention to the target stimulus is then needed to merge the features into complete objects in a 'location map'. FIT targets are often letters that 'pop out' against grouped letters different in color (e.g. a green T against a background of blue Ts), or different in form (a black T against a background of black L's). Duncan and Humphreys (1989) therefore suggested that the FIT paradigm may also be seen as a test of perceptual grouping, instead of parallel versus serial search.

Bundesen proposed an alternative theory of visual binding in his theory of visual attention (TVA, Bundesen et al., 2005). TVA builds on the theory of biased competition as developed by Desimone and Duncan (1995), which means that it could also serve as a general theory of visual attention. In short, TVA proposes that the brain detects an object in the visual field to have a particular characteristic, which enables the brain to store it

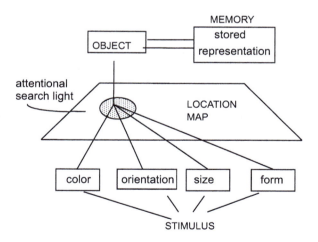

FIGURE 4.10
Treisman's 'feature integration' model as an example of a position-specific theory of selective attention. Attention functions as a search light directed to a position on a location map. The location map binds different features of the stimulus into a perception of the complete object, matching with a predefined representation in memory.

in a category as a red letter, which may or may not be relevant to focus on. According to this theory attention is not allocated to separate features, but to characteristics that together form a 'perceptual unit'. A number of visual categorizations that ascribe features to objects compete ('race') to become encoded into visual short-term memory, before a specific category is selected. Each of the possible categorizations is supported by sensory evidence, but the competition is biased by multiplication with attentional weights (high weights on important objects). At the neural level, this takes place in reciprocal circuits, between the pulvinar of the thalamus and the extrastriate cortex.[4]

Similar to object-based models of attention, as formulated by Duncan (1984) and Kahneman et al. (1992), TVA puts little emphasis on spatial location as a binding site. In these models, attention is not primarily directed on positions in space, but on objects. Studies showing that ratings of certain features are usually more accurate if they belong to the same object than when they belong to different objects support this view. TVA may also be seen as a theory that integrates the two selection principles that were originally formulated by Broadbent: selection of the basis of a physical characteristic (stimulus set or filtering) or the category of a stimulus (response set or pigeonholing). The filtering part of the model selects inputs by criteria specified by one control parameter (e. g. a front-end visual system), while the pigeonholing part classifies the selected inputs with respect to categories specified by another parameter (e.g. a high-level executive system, Bundesen et al., 2005).

Attentional neglect

Attentional neglect implies that patients fail to attend to stimuli opposite (contralateral) to the side of the lesion in the brain. This confirms the importance of spatial selection mechanisms to direct attention to positions in the outside world. Usually, a lesion in the right inferior parietal area of the brain causes the deficit. Patients are not aware of – or neglect – objects at locations in the space opposite the site of the lesion. A particular variety of neglect is extinction. Extinction is demonstrated in a task that requires patients to fixate on a central spot on a screen, while two objects are briefly displayed, simultaneously to the left and right of the fixation point (see Figure 4.11, bottom). In this condition, patients fail to report the left-hand figure (and will report 'horse'). But when presented successively, they will accurately report each figure. So neglect could reflect a deficit in spatial attention or spatiotopic mapping manifested in selectively 'truncating' the mental spotlight when multiple stimuli appear in the visual field.

Another task in which unilateral neglect has been investigated is the spatial-cueing task. Response times are typically longer for invalid than valid trials, presumably because attention has first to 'disengage' from the incorrect cued position, and then move to the correct position. Neglect patients are slower still for contralesional than ipsilesional targets on invalid trials (Figure 4.12), suggesting that these patients might have a particular problem with disengaging attention and remain 'stuck' to the incorrect cued position.

ACTIVATION, ATTENTION AND AWARENESS

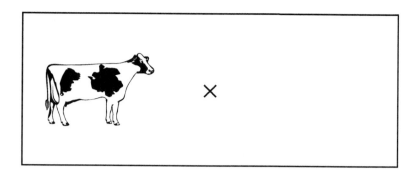

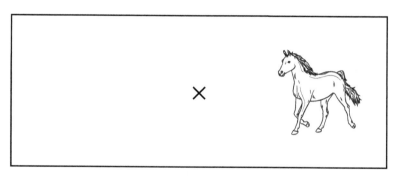

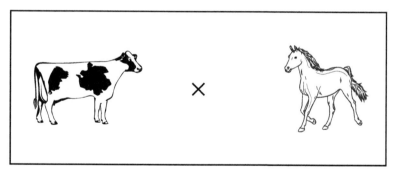

FIGURE 4.11
The extinction effect. Neglect patients do not notice the left figure if two figures are presented briefly and simultaneously (bottom panel). When presented briefly and successively (top and middle panel), each figure is reported normally, probably indicating a limited capacity of spatial attention, due to a lesion in the parietal region of the hemisphere.

Lesions often cause attentional neglect in pathways linking the parietal cortex to other regions in the cortex. Depending on the location of the lesion in the network, neglect becomes manifest as a sensory, motivational, spatial or motor deficit (Mesulam, 1981). In particular connections between area 8 of the parietal cortex with the colliculi superior and the frontal eye fields (area 9) could play a role in mediating visuospatial neglect.

ACTIVATION, ATTENTION AND AWARENESS

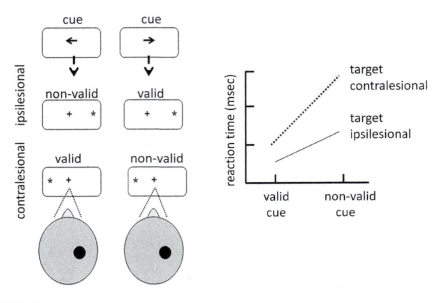

FIGURE 4.12
Spatial cuing task (left) and reaction times (right) of patients with unilateral neglect (caused by lesions in the parietal area of the right hemisphere). On valid and non-valid trials the target appears respectively at the expected (validly cued) and unexpected (invalidly cued) position. Patients show a drastic increase in reaction time as compared to normal subjects to non-valid contralesional targets.

Source: Adapted from Posner & Cohen (1984).

These lesions would specifically impair the movements of the attentional spotlight, as well as limit the extent of the area of the visual field, contralateral to the side of the lesions. This could lead to certain forms of dyslexia (for example, when seeing the word human, the patient says man). There have even been cases suggesting that unilateral neglect extends to a person's visual imagery of the environment (see Box 4.3). Neglect is not necessarily limited to visual stimuli, but occurs to the location of sound stimuli, and in the perception of one's body image (not feeling the left half of the body).

Memory and attention

Attention is manifested in the modulation of perceptual functions, but is also intertwined with memory functions (Desimone et al., 1994). For example, the notion of an attentional spotlight is not so different from that of activated elements in short-term memory, taking form as involuntary orienting to novel events, or a voluntary focus controlled by working memory. Models of reflexive attention have often postulated a

ACTIVATION, ATTENTION AND AWARENESS

mechanism that compares sensory input with an internal memory representation or neuronal 'model'. In addition, the notion of limited capacity, another central element in attention theories, is also compatible with that of short-term memory as a limited capacity processor.

The relationship between attention and memory works in two directions. First, attention may facilitate consolidation, i.e. the storage of new information in long-term memory. Second, the memory process may also assist attention: directing attention or detecting a target in visual search is often guided by an internal representation of the object serving as a target. The central role of memory in regulating attention is a central element in Cowan's theory of attention, depicted in Figure 4.13. His model rests on the assumption that short-term memory (STM) is an activated subset of long-term memory (LTM). A stimulus activating STM will not automatically trigger consciousness, but only when it activates a sufficient number of neural elements (displayed as the 'focus' of attention). Stimuli associated with automatic and over-learned responses will bypass the focus of attention in STM and automatically link structures in the motor cortex to the response. Novel stimuli, in contrast, produce a mismatch with the neuronal model stored in LTM and elicit an orientation reaction which also reaches the focus of attention (arrow 2). With repeated representations of the same stimulus, initially novel stimuli will lead to habituation of the orienting response and block access to consciousness (arrow 3).[5]

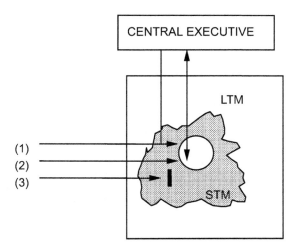

FIGURE 4.13
Simplified view of Cowan's model of memory-attention interaction. Short-term memory (STM: shaded area) is depicted as an activated subset of long-term memory (LTM). Conscious focal attention (white circle) is a subset of elements in STM that can be activated in two ways, by orientation to novel or unexpected stimuli (arrow 2) or by voluntary attention (arrow 1). Voluntary attention is directed and controlled by a 'central executive'. Arrow 3 indicates habituation (inhibition) of repeated stimuli, thus prohibiting access to focal attention.

A central executive mechanism, located in the anterior cortex, controls voluntary attention. Via top-down corticothalamic circuits this mechanism activates elements in working memory, which could contain a representation of the target (or the 'to be attended' feature). In contrast with orienting triggered by mismatch, voluntary attention depends on a match between the target and the memory representation. A match will activate focal attention and trigger the associated overt response. Partial matches, or stimuli associated with automatized skills, will activate fewer elements in STM, and will thus make fewer demands on the central executive, even bypassing the focus of attention.

Neurobiology of attention

The strength and promise of cognitive neuroscience lie in the possibility to link and integrate theories on human performance and its cognitive determinants with structures and networks in the brain. The previous sections have provided an overview of some metaphors: filter, resource, effort, spotlight, and a central executive to describe various components of attention. The variety of views on attention developed in cognitive research are difficult to integrate into a single comprehensive framework.

Nevertheless, the various models and paradigms from which they emerged have considerably contributed to describe attention in more operational terms than the introspective notions introduced by William James some 125 years ago. With the advent of cognitive neuroscience, cognitive psychologists as well as neuroscientists became gradually interested in solving the problem of how attention processes could be expressed in the biological hardware of the brain. Models of attention and related paradigms of cognitive research were now implemented in animal research, as well as in research of patients and non-patients using performance measures concurrently with measures like event-related potentials, lesions of the brain and functional imaging.

BOX 4.3   NEGLECT AND MENTAL IMAGERY

Various studies have suggested that neglect is not a purely sensory disorder. Patients with neglect have been reported to forget shaving the left part of the face, or to panic when they awake in the night, feeling a part of the body as not belonging to itself (see Sacks, 1985). Neglect may even extend to mental imagery. Two patients with a right lesion in the brain were asked to describe a well-known square in their hometown Milan, the Piazza del Duomo that they had visited regularly.

continued

They first asked the patients to describe the square, imagining it from the northern side, standing on the church steps. They gave an accurate description of the buildings at the western side (right from the perspective of the imagined position), but a distorted description of the building at the eastern side, contralateral to the site of the lesion. Then the same question was asked, now with the patients imagining standing from the perspective at the southern side of the piazza, facing the church. This time only buildings at the eastern side were described accurately (again at their right), while neglecting those at the left. The piazza was of course well known to the patients, meaning that they could accurately describe from their memory all the buildings at the left as well as at the right sides. When they relied on the images produced by mental imagery, they only failed to report the objects contralateral to their lesion.

Source: Bisiach & Luzzatti, (1978).

An essential function of attention lies in magnifying the content of information transmitted in perceptual and action systems (Kok et al., 2006). This fits in with the discovery in neuroscience that information transmission within the sensory and/or motor pathways of the brain is modulated and selectively enhanced by cortical-thalamic circuits. Attentional control (either by exogenous or endogenous sources) is essential for the efficiency of neural computations involved in the transfer of perceptual information to and from memory networks. These functions of attention are also in agreement with the principles of evolution, in particular the notion that attention assists perception, memory and action systems, thus flexibly adapting and tuning these systems to the varying demands of the environment.

Mechanisms of expression and control

William James already was aware of two forms of attention, which he described as 'accommodation of sensory organs', and 'anticipatory preparation from within the ideational centers, concerned with the object to which attention has been paid'. That is to say, attention in the role of modulating sensory perception, and attention manifested as expectation and anticipation.

More recently, researchers Corbett, Posner and LaBerge made a similar distinction when they distinguished between 'performing' or 'expressive' mechanisms (James' accommodation of sensory organs) and mechanisms with a controlling or executive role (James' ideational centers). Figure 4.14 presents an outline of the network of the brain associated with these two forms of attention, to be discussed in more detail in the following sections.

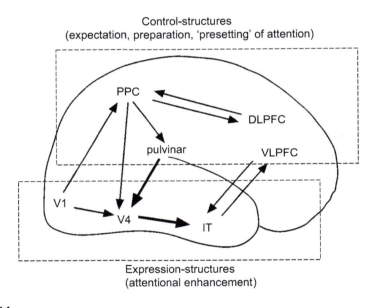

FIGURE 4.14
Network model of selective attention with higher centers in the cortex (PPC, DLPFC and VLPFC) regulating preparation, presetting and expectation in expression structures (V1, V4, IT) via the pulvinar nucleus of the thalamus. See text for clarification.
Source: Adapted from LaBerge (1995).

Expression mechanisms

Effective selection implies that information in relevant neural pathways is amplified relative to that in non-relevant pathways. These pathways are situated in the primary and secondary areas of the neocortex. In action selection, it would concern processing of 'action-relevant information' in structures of the motor system, in perceptual selection processing of sensory information in structures of the sensory systems. In the visual system, it involves the extrastriate cortical regions (V2, V3, V4), but also extends to the inferotemporal cortex (IT), when it concerns the identification of more complex and complete configurations like familiar objects and human faces.

The strong link between attention and perception had already been demonstrated in early electrophysiological studies, confirming that visual-spatial attention enhances the excitability of neurons in the visual cortex. Studies with macaque monkeys, using microelectrodes, made it possible to map the receptive field of individual neurons, as well as to separate effective from non-effective stimuli. They showed that focusing of visual attention on objects in the visual field is accompanied by modulation of the activity of cells in area V4 of the visual cortex, but not of cells in 'earlier' areas (V1, V2 and V3).

In a seminal study by Moran and Desimone it was found that activity in V4 to an attended (effective) stimulus (red bar upper left in Figure 4.15) was attenuated, relative to the condition of attention being directed to the other (not effective) stimulus, in the same receptive field (the blue bar). After training the monkey to attend to a stimulus outside the receptive field, no modulation (i.e. attenuation) of the response to the red bar was present. Only when two stimuli were presented close to another within the same receptive field of V4, spatial competition inhibited the area around the unattended stimulus.

In humans, attention selection in the brain was first demonstrated electrophysiologically for stimuli in the auditory modality. Hillyard discovered that attention to sounds presented rapidly to both ears became manifest in an enlarged N1 component to stimuli in the attended ear. These seminal findings, supporting early selection models of attention, were replicated in a later study by Woldorff and Hillyard. The latter study found an even earlier effect of attention called the P20–50 component (Woldorff & Hillyard, 1991). This early attentional modulation was identified by using magnetic recordings and MRI that allowed to locate the source of the P20–50 effect in the primary auditory cortex with greater precision.

Visual selective attention was investigated in studies that used two different methods to present stimuli, sustained cuing and trial-by-trial (or transient) cuing. In the first case, subjects are instructed to focus on the same stimulus attribute over a block of trials. The stimuli could be presented in random order in the left and right fields (spatial attention), or at central positions in the colors red and green (nonspatial attention). In the

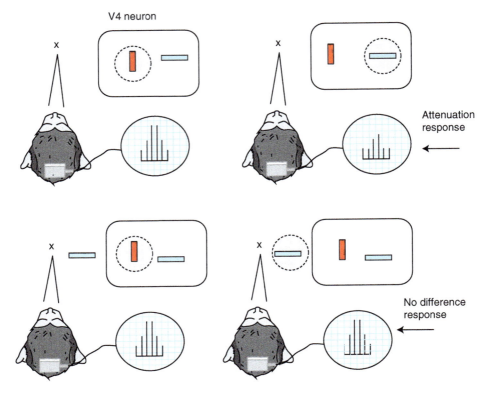

FIGURE 4.15
Selective inhibition in the macaque monkey. Left column: attention directed on the red bar. Right column: attention directed on the blue bar. Attenuation of V4 response to the unattended red bar in the same receptive field. However, no attenuation of the response to the red bar when attention is directed to the blue bar location outside the receptive field.

Source: Adapted from Moran & Desimone (1985).

trial-by-trial approach, each trial starts with a cue indicating the position or color that has to be attended to. Relevant and non-relevant stimuli are always presented unpredictably within a block of stimuli. Subjects are instructed to press a button only when a target (a slightly deviant stimulus occurring less frequently) appears among the stimuli with the attended feature. In these studies, the primary focus is on the effects of attended versus unattended stimuli, not on the effects of the cue on the activity of the brain.

Figure 4.16 (left) illustrates the global layout of a spatial visual selection task, with the subject fixating a central cross on the screen and attending to locations in the left or right field dependent on the cue. In this task-setting, visual-spatial attention became manifest in an enhancement of the early ERP components P1 and N1. P1 and N1 components are designated as sensory or 'exogenous' components because unattended visual stimuli also

ACTIVATION, ATTENTION AND AWARENESS

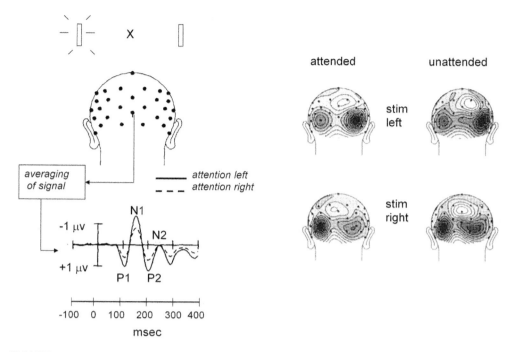

FIGURE 4.16
Left: averaged ERP signal (P1/N1) recorded at the occipital scalp to stimuli presented at attended and unattended locations in the visual field. Right: topographical mapping of P1 for attended as well as unattended location (black = positive polarity).

Source: Adapted from Mangun & Hillyard (1995).

elicit them. Interestingly, the enhancement of P1 and N1 components showed a retinotopic topographical distribution over the occipital scalp, implying that the attention effect (that is: the difference between attended and unattended maps) was always largest at the location contralateral to the field of stimulation. These enhancements of the P1 component were found in tasks using symbolic as well as direct cuing, suggesting that the same type of process underlies reflexive and voluntary spatial attention (Hopfinger & Mangun, 1998).

In sum, these results indicated that visual-spatial attention follows the principle of sensory-gain: it enhances information of the afferent sensory path. Attention to nonspatial stimulus features like color, form and orientation appears to elicit a different pattern of ERP components. The sensory-gain principle that held for effects of visual-spatial attention on components like P1 and N1 was not replicated for nonspatial attention. In contrast with the P1 and N1 components, the components affected by nonspatial attention were designated as 'endogenous', because they typically only occur to attended stimuli. Attention to nonspatial characteristics elicited a 'selective negativity' over posterior scalp sites in the range 150–350 msec, with a somewhat earlier onset of 'selection positivity' over the frontal-central scalp (Kenemans et al., 1993).

ACTIVATION, ATTENTION AND AWARENESS

Source localization studies as well as PET and fMRI studies (see Figure 4.17) further suggested that these nonspatial ERP components were also generated in the extrastriate (ventral) regions of the visual cortex (Hillyard & Anllo-Vento, 1998; Kastner et al., 1998; Kanwisher & Wojciulik, 2000; Corbetta et al., 2000).

Control mechanisms

The cause of attention are not the mechanisms for expression of attention. Expression is primarily manifested in modulations of information in the sensory cortical pathways (Jonides, 1981; LaBerge, 1995). At the level of neural discharge, this could imply the frequency, phase and intensity of the firing of neurons. The cause of attention refers to the external or internal sources controlling attention that differ for reflexive and voluntary attention.

Reflexive attention is initiated by exogenous sources of stimulation, such as a sudden onset of sound capturing attention automatically and modulating the content of

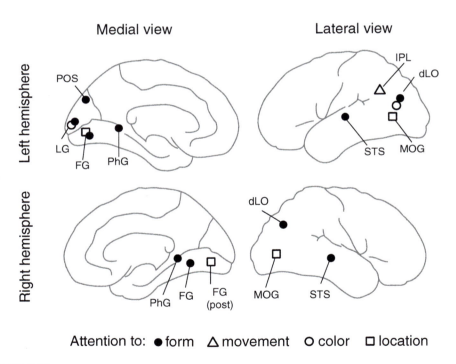

FIGURE 4.17
Results of PET studies showing expression of visual attention to features like form, movement and color and location. Symbols: FG = fusiform gyrus; PhG = parahippocampal gyrus; POS = parieto-occipital sulcus; STS = supra temporal sulcus; MOG = middle occipital gyrus; IPL = inferior parietal lobe; dLO = dorsolateral occipital cortex; LG = lingual gyrus.

Source: Adapted from Gazzaniga et al. (2002).

154

information. Mechanisms of reflexive orienting are rooted in the oculomotor system and may even control attention in conditions of covert attention, through structures as the superior colliculi (see ahead). Their primary task is not selection but shifting of attention to the source of stimulation (Colby & Goldberg, 1999). After the source of information is detected, it is followed by subsequent activity serving to establish its identity by selective enhancement of its features, e.g. its velocity, color, form and direction.

In contrast, voluntary attention is triggered by an internal event that causes attention to be directed to a particular stimulus or action before it actually occurs. If the activity of cortical modules responsible for perception and action is already elevated when these stimuli or actions occur, its processes will run more efficiently and will require little additional processing. Often an informative cue is presented before the target stimulus, to elicit processes like expectation or preparation. Preparation may be driven by an image of a perceptual feature or a specific action held in working memory, based on information delivered by the cue. Processes that control preparation probably recruit top-down pathways in the brain. These pathways originate in the posterior parietal cortex (PPC), dorsolateral and ventrolateral prefrontal cortices (DLPFC and VLPFC), respectively. In these areas neurons typically show enhanced firing during the delay between a cue and subsequent target stimulus. In summary, the attention system of the brain allows a functional separation in two subsystems, the 'source' of attention and the 'site' of its expression, that is, the mechanism involved in the actual selection of information. Similarly, the lungs and air passages are the sites of breathing, whereas brainstem nuclei control the breathing muscles (LaBerge, 1995).

Attentional control takes place in a network centered on the corticothalamic pathways, connecting areas in the prefrontal cortex and posterior parietal cortex with expression structures in the perceptual pathways (see Figure 4.14). The following sections consider the anatomy of some of these structures and related mechanisms in more detail, and then illustrate their manifestations in the active brain.

BOX 4.4 THE FATE OF STIMULI THAT DO NOT RECEIVE ATTENTION

What happens to unattended stimuli or events, often referred to as the 'dark side of attention'? One possibility is that these stimuli will not be processed at all. This may occur when the underlying neuron populations are insufficiently activated, or actively inhibited. The fate of non-attended stimuli has been a topic of investigation in various types of tasks. Examples are the dichotic listening paradigm, the inattentional blindness paradigm, and the attentional blink paradigm.

continued

ACTIVATION, ATTENTION AND AWARENESS

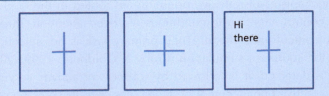

In the dichotic listening or shadowing task, different trains of speech are being offered at the same speed to both ears of a subject, while the subject is asked to only pay attention and repeat each word presented at one ear. Subjects then usually cannot recall any detail of words presented to the unattended ear. Inattentional blindness (or change blindness) is the phenomenon that subjects observing certain complex visual scenes are often not aware of unexpected and irrelevant events happening in a visual scene. An example is a briefly presented word or sentence, like 'Hi there', when looking at line figures at the same time, and asked to react whenever the horizontal line is longer than the vertical line (see left side of insert).

Attentional blink means that subjects do not notice the presentation of a second visual target stimulus, if it follows the first stimulus in less than half a second. It's like attention has 'blinked' for a short moment, or was still in its 'refractory' period like a muscle reaction. Apparently, in this case, the visual system is not yet ready to process the second stimulus.

Interestingly, what the three cases have in common is that the unattended or 'missed' stimuli are sometimes still processed implicitly. This was inferred from the finding that these stimuli still elicited a response at the brain level (in the form of an ERP or fMRI response). Possibly, in situations where the information processing system is heavily loaded, unattended stimuli that reach the brain activate insufficient neurons to reach the level that is required to trigger conscious awareness. These findings may also serve to illustrate the principle that the activation of representations in memory is a necessary, but not sufficient condition to elicit conscious awareness (Chapter 3).

Role of the thalamus

The inhibitory role of the reticular nucleus (RN) of the thalamus in controlling sensory input to the lateral geniculate area (LGN) was already emphasized in the 1977 model of Skinner and Yingling. Central in their model was the reticular formation regulating the state of arousal through disinhibition of RN neurons (see Figure 4.3). The thalamus with the RN also plays a pivotal role in LaBerge's model of selective attention. Similar to the model of Skinner and Yingling, LaBerge's model incorporates inhibitory neurons. However, in his model, the net effect of the RN is a selective enhancement and not inhibition of afferent input to the cortex. The reason for this is that attended input from the thalamocortical afferents concurrently suppresses activity in the parallel afferents associated with the unattended input. This principle, also referred to as *lateral inhibition*, forms the basis of the thalamic filtering in LaBerge's model.

Of particular importance to visual attentional processing in the posterior cortex, are the connections between the pulvinar and the occipital, temporal and parietal lobes. In LaBerge's model, the pulvinar is a key player, ideally suited to afford the parietal cortex a way to influence extrastriate cortical processing (Figure 4.18). The second largest thalamic nucleus is the mediodorsal nucleus with extensive reciprocal connections to prefrontal areas like the dorsolateral and ventrolateral cortices. In contrast to the thalamocortical connections between the pulvinar and posterior cortex, the reciprocal connections between the frontal cortex and the mediodorsal thalamus are under control of tonic inhibitory input from the basal ganglia. This seems to make the latter circuitry particularly suited for selection of actions initiated from the frontal cortex (see further Chapter 5).

Using PET scans from healthy subjects, LaBerge discovered that activation of the pulvinar is stronger in tasks that rely on 'filter functions' than in tasks that do not. For example, if the subject needs to detect a letter in the middle of the other letters, like an O in the middle of letters Q and G, the pulvinar shows a stronger activation than with the target appearing in an empty display. The enhanced activation (glucose uptake) was most conspicuous in the portion of the pulvinar contralateral to the field of presentation of the stimulus pattern. The role of the pulvinar in visual attention processes was also emphasized in animal studies carried out by Desimone, Petersen and Robinson. In these studies microinjections with the substance muscimol (a GABA agonist potentiating inhibitory effects at its synapses), were applied to the left part of the monkey's pulvinar. Petersen found that this greatly increased the reaction time in switching of attention from the ipsilesional field, to the contralesional field relative to non-injected monkeys (Petersen et al., 1985; Robinson & Petersen, 1992; Robinson, 1993). Desimone further demonstrated that deactivation of the pulvinar by injecting muscimol into more lateral parts of the pulvinar, which has many links with V4 and IT, caused greater disruption of monkeys behavior when a distracter was simultaneously present in the 'good' (ipsilesional) field (Desimone et al., 1990).

Role of the superior colliculus

The superior colliculus is responsible for the control of eye movements, especially saccades. It is part of the tectopulvinary pathway, considered as an evolutionary older visual route. Lesions of its nuclei impair the ability to make eye saccades, as well as covert visuospatial attention. The colliculus not only assists the attentional spotlight to move to relevant positions in the visual field, but also ensures that attention does not return to the same position, the phenomenon of inhibition of return.

Animal research by Desimone has shown that deactivation of nuclei of the superior colliculus impairs the performance of monkeys in a color discrimination task, with colored bar patterns presented at different locations in the visual field. The monkeys were not allowed to make eye movements. It turned out that deactivation of the superior colliculus only affected the performance of the monkey if a distracter was simultaneously present in the visual field. These findings are reminiscent of those obtained with deactivation of the pulvinar. Together they suggest that attentional modulation by these subcortical structures reflects some form of competition between stimuli, which is resolved in networks of the oculomotor system. According to LaBerge the specific role of the circuit between the posterior parietal cortex and superior colliculus in the attention network is to inhibit information in the area surrounding the target. This would support and strengthen the role of the thalamic circuit in enhancing the target information relative to its surrounding distracters.

Role of higher centers

Voluntary attention is expressed in the sensory pathways by enhancement of target information relative to distracter information. The mechanism that produces enhancement lies in higher cortical centers that include the posterior and anterior cortex. Both regions regulate cognitive processes such as expectation and preparation that are initiated in neural circuits of working memory, before the involvement of the subcortical structures. The dorsolateral prefrontal cortex (DLPFC) keeps the spatial location of the upcoming target in working memory (for example, the location of the letter O in the GOQ display). Furthermore, the ventrolateral prefrontal cortex (VLPFC), assumed to contain the representation of nonspatial attributes, controls the preparation of the shape of the letter O. Both frontal areas connect to the pulvinar through the mediodorsal nuclei of the thalamus. In LaBerge's model of attention (see Figure 4.18) preparatory attention is conceptualized as a 'peaked distribution' of activated representations in working memory.[6] This distribution is constructed by the pulvinar, and represents cortical cell activity that increases as the cells correspond more closely to the expected or selected characteristics. The strength of activation is highest for the attended feature and decreases monotonously with the divergence of features from this attribute. The shape and amplitude of the activity distributions are also stored in working memory.

A central element controlling spatial attention in this corticothalamic circuit is the posterior parietal area (PPC), designated by LaBerge as the 'position module'. The location of objects is encoded in the PPC map. It is then projected through the pulvinar, which further enhances the activity distribution at its highest point, while reducing its

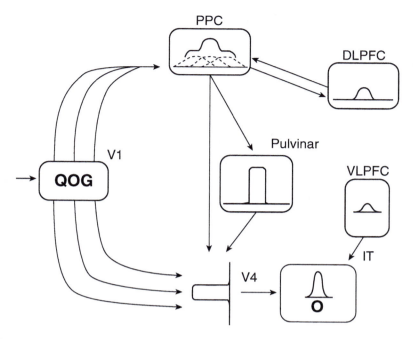

FIGURE 4.18
Schematic model of attentional control on activity distributions in the dorsal and ventral streams shortly after the onset of the target display. V1 sends output to PPC as well as V4. The subject prepares for the target (central letter O), flanked by distracters Q and G. In the dorsal stream spatial working memory (DLPFC) contributes to enhance activity at its highest point in the location map in PPC, which is further amplified in the pulvinar and projected to V4 in the ventral stream. Here, working memory for expected target shape (VLPFC) provides additional enhancement of the target represented in the inferotemporal cortex (IT).

Source: Adapted from LaBerge (1995).

surrounding locations (Figure 4.18). The resulting peaked activity distribution of the pulvinar is then transmitted to area V4 in the ventral stream, where it adds to the input flowing from V1. Preparatory attention to nonspatial features of the target like its shape (as controlled by VLPFC), then also adds to the final representation of the target in V4.

Empirical studies: ERP and fMRI

Earlier cued selective attention tasks using imaging measures were not concerned with the effects of the cue, but only with the effect of attended versus unattended stimuli on brain activity (Hillyard et al., 1994). Later, cued attention tasks also considered effects of preparation or expectation in the cue-target interval, requiring to keep instructions and cue information in working memory, before the presentation of the target. An ERP study performed by Slagter et al. (2005) verified that visual cues for locations and color selection elicited a late positivity starting at 260 ms post-cue. This positivity reached a maximal amplitude over the midline dorsal posterior scalp regions, and was not sensitive to the dimension of the cued feature (i.e. color vs. location). The cue effect could be dissociated from the effect of attention on P1/N1 components elicited by the subsequent target. The cue-related positivity was generic, that is, it coded for generating a global attentional set in spatial as well as nonspatial tasks.

fMRI studies where information delivered by the cue varied from trial to trial, reported similar but more detailed results. fMRI studies by Hopfinger et al. (2000, 2001), Corbetta and Shulman (2002), Corbetta et al. (2009) and Slagter et al. (2006, 2007) showed that effects of control of visual attention triggered by a cue signal were most conspicuous over the posterior parietal and frontal association areas (see Figure 4.19).

The effects of preparation in these studies reflected the activity of areas in the brain involved in executive control, and not so much expression of attention. These results seem to correspond well with the higher centres in LaBerge's theoretical model of visual attention, depicted in Figure 4.14. They also have much in common with the central executive network (CEN) and 'frontal-parietal attention network', assumed to reflect executive functions as identified in later fMRI studies, using working memory tasks (Seeley et al., 2007).

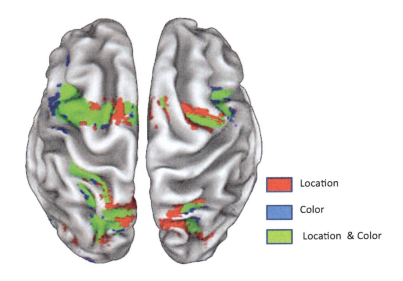

FIGURE 4.19
Fronto-parietal attention network in the brain showing significant activations in the interval between cue and target in a selective cueing task (fMRI data). Red, blue and green boxes indicate activations to symbolic cues for location, color or both location and color of the target in separate sessions of a mixed block paradigm. Overlay on an inflated 3D brain surface.

Source: Adapted from Slagter et al. (2007).

Determining the direction of visual-spatial attention

The notion of top-down control of perceptual systems by higher systems plays a central role in models of selective visual attention. These models were largely confirmed by some fMRI studies revealing not only the specific regions but also the patterns of connectivity involved in attentional control. An anatomically distinct frontal-parietal (or dorsal) network mediates voluntary orienting of attention to locations, where behaviorally relevant targets are expected (Bressler et al., 2008; Hopfinger et al., 2000; Corbetta et al., 2009). These studies strongly suggest that the dorsal network modulates visual processing in preparation for expected input via top-down connections to visual areas.

Relatively few studies have addressed the issue of the directionality of attentional control. One reason could be that the primary aim of methods to quantify BOLD signals was to assess unique patterns of connectivity, and not the direction or causal relations between various brain regions. Recent advances in fMRI analysis now allow measuring effective connectivity between brain regions, using dynamic causal modeling (DCM; Friston, 2011). DCM is a promising tool to critically test the hypothesis of top-down control in visual spatial attention tasks, executed by the frontal-parietal networks in the human brain.

A study by Vossel et al. may serve to illustrate the potential of this approach. The study examined the role of the dorsal and ventral network, comprising the intraparietal sulcus (IPS) and the frontal eye fields (FEF) in modulating the visual cortex, while subjects anticipated an upcoming stimulus. It used a modified version of the Posner location-cueing paradigm, with central predictive cueing. It also tested for direct modulatory effects of the FEF on the visual cortex (with or without indirect influences via the IPS). DCM of regional responses in the dorsal network, identified in a conventional (SPM) whole-brain analysis (Figure 4.20 upper panel), was used to compare the different functional architectures. Bayesian model selection showed that top-down connections from the left and right IPS to left and right visual cortex, respectively, were modulated by the direction of attention (Figure 4.20 lower panel).[7]

Complex cognitive tasks: ERP studies

In a second category of experiments, subjects had to perform complex tasks involving memory search, mental rotation or solving arithmetical problems. These tasks were thus more concerned with divided than with focused attentional operations, which allowed manipulating the load of cognitive operations. Their effects on neural activity stretched out over longer periods than the short-duration phasic ERP components, elicited by single stimuli.

Earlier ERP studies of working memory using long S1-S2 intervals had already identified slow electrical potentials, varying in amplitude with the difficulty of cognitive task operations. In verbal working memory tasks, these ERP effects are most

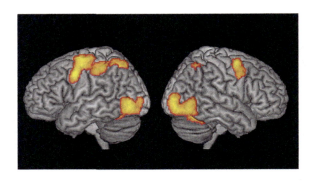
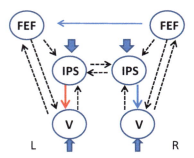

FIGURE 4.20
Upper panel: Whole-brain SPM analyses, contrasting invalidly with validly cued targets revealing significant activation of bilateral dorsal frontoparietal regions, visual areas and supplementary motor and left motor cortex. Lower panel: Winning model in DCM model space for connectivity between FEF, IPS and visual cortex (V), as to the direction of attentional orienting. Fixed connections and modulatory (bilinear) effects on connections are illustrated with dashed and solid arrows, respectively. Connections exhibiting significant (according to post hoc standard t-tests) bilinear or modulatory effects are highlighted in color (red indicating significant negative modulatory effects, and blue indicating significant positive modulatory effects).

Source: Adapted from Vossel et al. (2012).

conspicuous above the central scalp, and in visuospatial tasks above the parietal scalp (see Figure 4.21).

These effects, labeled as 'search negativities' (Ruchkin et al., 1988; Wijers et al., 1989; Rösler et al., 1995), probably reflected activation of the same frontal and parietal areas that were described in terms of a frontal parietal control network in later fMRI studies (Seeley et al., 2007).

Cognitive control: the role of frontal cortical areas

Cognitive control is not limited to the domain of selective attention, but is involved in a variety of functions involving working memory, language comprehension, inhibition and emotions. It is clearly an overarching concept, used whenever a cognitive task makes demands on working memory. Neural research investigating sources of control

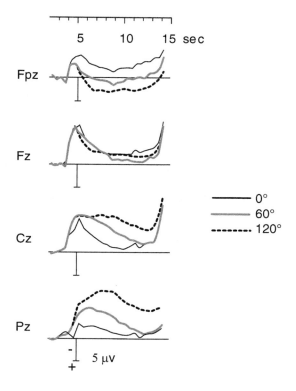

FIGURE 4.21
ERPs at four midline scalp locations in a mental rotation task requiring rotation of a geometrical pattern over 0, 60 and 120 degrees, respectively. Slow potentials show an enhanced negativity ('search negativity') with greater load of the task, with largest effect over the parietal (Pz) scalp site.

Source: Adapted from Rösler et al. (1995).

have assigned a pivotal role to the prefrontal cortex (PFC). Fuster (1995) and Goldman-Rakic (1995) demonstrated in their seminal animal studies that the PFC is active in a delayed reinforcement task, when the monkey must wait and remember the location of the reinforcing stimulus. Similarly, human research has shown that tasks requiring an internal plan or rules for future actions also rely on the PFC. In particular, the lateral prefrontal cortex plays a crucial role in establishing global functional connectivity in the brain, that forms the basis of cognitive control, as well as 'fluid' (creative problem solving) intelligence (Cole et al., 2012).

Miller and Cohen (2001) summarized the role of the prefrontal cortex in a critical review article in which they introduced their 'guided activation' model. In this model, programs stored in PFC control the premotor as well as the posterior areas. The ability to guide current behavior simultaneously with activation of abstract goals illustrates the hierarchical nature of these control processes and the associated prefrontal-cortical networks.

In their view, the appeal to the PFC is not so much determined by the difficulty of the cognitive task, but rather by the degree of abstractness of the plan, or the rules. The neural condition that facilitates control could be the degree of coherent activity between the PFC and more distant cortical areas. Recent research suggests that in particular, oscillations in the high-frequency gamma band (80–150 Hz) and theta band (4–8Hz) of the EEG might form the basis of these coherency patterns (Cavanagh & Frank, 2014; Voytek et al., 2015).

Another form of control is affective control, regulated by the anterior cingulate area, located near the ventromedial prefrontal cortex. The anterior cingulate has been associated with a 'reward-based decision-making and learning' system. The networks of the brain involved in affective control differ from those regulating cognitive control and will be considered in more detail in Chapter 7.

Awareness and consciousness

The homunculus is synonymous with the reflective, conscious mind, and somehow, somewhere in the protean parenchyma of the mind, it must reside.
Donald, 1991 p. 365

Consciousness remains a controversial subject in cognitive neuroscience, but is not an isolated theme. Indeed, the question of conscious versus unconscious processing of information has been a central element in virtually every sub-domain of cognitive psychology. In a strict sense, consciousness is not an independent function, but rather an activated state of functions like perception, memory, emotion or even the motor system. Each of these functions has implicit (unconscious) or explicit (conscious) manifestations, two terms coined by David Schacter.

Although consciousness is the most hotly debated topic in current psychology magazines, newspaper supplements, and best-selling books, it might not be the unitary function as often suggested in these media. When we break consciousness apart, we discover that it represents an amalgam of various 'sub-states'. Consciousness has also been a favorite target for philosophers, since ancient Greek philosophers first attacked the problem. Early philosophy often concerned the subjective aspect of consciousness and the experience of one's 'own self'. Ironically, cognitive psychologists have often shown more interest in the role of unconscious than of conscious processing, for example when it concerns processes underlying human decision making. Unconscious – or implicit – processes play a role in affective learning and conditioning, using evolutionarily old circuits in the limbic system of the brain that regulate primary and secondary drives and emotions. These limbic circuits also connect to networks underlying cognition and decision making, thus adding an affective element to rational processes (Damasio, 1994; Kahneman, 2011).

Manifestations of consciousness

Consciousness and awareness are the products of a hierarchical system, with various levels of organization differing in the degree of specificity of the related brain areas. Figure 4.22 depicts a simple model, with consciousness manifested at three different levels. Basic structures in the brainstem that evolved in earlier stages of evolution regulate lower levels of awareness. Higher levels are regulated by cortical structures that developed later in the course of evolution, with frontal and posterior association cortices controlling structures in the thalamus and sensory region via top-down circuits. The hierarchical structure of consciousness partly answers the question of if non-human mammals have access to consciousness too. An animal like a dog or monkey also has 'consciousness', but its manifestations would probably be limited to representations at the level of alertness and orientation to signals from the outside world, and from its body (see also: Premack & Woodruff, 1978 for an early discussion). The ability to generate internal forms of attention and awareness, serving self-reflection and language, is seen as a unique development of H. Sapiens with its large forebrain.

Alertness

Alertness or 'wakefulness' refers to the most basic level of consciousness, regulated by the brainstem structures. Alertness is a passive state of consciousness also known as 'wakefulness' that occasionally allows stimuli of the environment access to higher brain structures via thalamocortical and extrathalamic pathways.

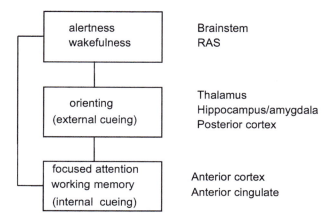

FIGURE 4.22
Schematic model of consciousness, manifested as alertness, orienting, focused attention and working memory. Related brain areas are shown at the right.

During sleep, information from the outside world does not penetrate into the brain. Not only are these events not consciously perceived, but they do not reach higher cortical centers at all. Here, the strong tonic inhibitory modulation from nonspecific thalamic nuclei (the reticular nucleus in particular) blocks sensory input to the brain. In the waking state, consciousness fluctuates globally between two states or modes: an active mode controlled by the demands imposed by the environment or by cognitive tasks, and a rest mode in which the environment more or less unconstrains the brain. Interestingly, neuroimaging research found brain activity in rest, involving both the medial anterior and posterior areas (see Figure 4.23). The amount of activity or 'default state' (Raichle et al., 2001) was even stronger than in active task conditions.

Orienting

Reflexive orienting to new or unexpected stimuli from the environment is manifested in an automatic short-lasting surge in brain activation, assumed to facilitate perception of sensory events, as well as the consolidation of new information in long-term memory. Although reflexive orienting is elicited automatically, it also involves the conscious perception of the eliciting event, when its relevance activates voluntary attention to explore its content further. Access to consciousness thus seems to be restricted to significant events, selected for further exploration. It is possible that all input initially activates elements in long-term memory, with novel or meaningful stimuli activating more elements. Frequently presented or repeated events will gradually lose access to consciousness through habituation, inhibiting neuronal elements in short-term memory (as clarified in Cowan's model in Figure 4.13).

The 'strength of activation' theory, although parsimonious, does not specify how the brain distinguishes between meaningful (or novel) and non-meaningful (familiar) information. Orienting response theory (introduced in Chapter 3) proposes that raw perceptual information passes a mechanism, also known as a mnemonic filter that compares input with existing representations in LTM. In this theory, the comparator mechanism 'decides' according to a match/mismatch process whether meaningful or novel stimuli are allowed further access to consciousness. It could be located in the hippocampus and medial temporal cortex, the same structures that are involved in the consolidation of new information in long-term memory.

Focused attention and working memory

In voluntary attention, consciousness is activated from an internal source, presumably controlled by representational systems in the dorsolateral prefrontal cortex. A second important source is the ventromedial prefrontal cortex, which has dense connections with the amygdala in the limbic system, and the ventral portion of the hippocampus.

This network seems to be primarily responsible for the regulation of conscious emotional experience of affective stimuli, which are 'pre-processed' in the amygdala at a more reflexive or preconscious level. PET studies, in particular, have suggested that areas in the prefrontal cortex are also under control of the anterior cingulate, an area considered to be crucial in regulating decision making and resolving a conflict.

Subjective experiences, and the sense of 'self' have created the suggestion that consciousness should reside somewhere in the brain, preferably at a strategic central position. Its function would be to integrate and even interpret information from the outside world, like a spectator in the theater. However, neuroscience so far has not been able to find such a local center of coordination or source of awareness. Instead, it has been suggested that consciousness arises from the coordinated activity of many different brain sites. In line with this view, Bernard Baars proposed that the overall function of consciousness is the availability of a global workspace. The primary functional role of consciousness is to allow a 'blackboard' architecture to operate in the brain, in order to integrate, provide access and coordinate the functioning of large numbers of specialized networks, that would otherwise operate autonomously. In tasks relying on automatic processing such as perceptual motor skills, the emphasis would shift to more localized and specialized modular structures (Baars, 1988, 1997, 2003).

The workspace model has been worked out in a simulated brain model by Dehaene and coworkers (Dehaene et al., 2017). In this model, salient sensory stimuli temporarily mobilize excitatory neurons with long-range axons, igniting a global activity pattern. The global brain state also links distant areas, including the prefrontal cortex, through reciprocal connections and inhibits surrounding workspace neurons, thus preventing the conscious processing of alternative stimuli. This process would include automatically activated processors that contribute to the processing by workspace neurons without entering consciousness.

Still open is the question of whether consciousness is a cause or a consequence. Does the conscious state per se facilitates coordination of extensive areas (as assumed in the global workspace model), or is it merely a byproduct of neurons in working space that together exceed a certain threshold of activation?

The self

Many researchers assume that the ability for self-reflection is uniquely human and linked to the brain's higher executive network. Damage in this network not only leads to loss of cognitive control but also to a reduced awareness of the own identity. An intriguing part of consciousness is the sense of 'me'. When something hurts my arm I do not only feel pain but also may think: 'this is me feeling pain'. Self-representational capacities could be related to circuits in the human brain that have developed during evolution, perhaps enabling a versatile capacity to project oneself into various conditions as options for alternative actions (Donald, 1995). The richer architecture that underlies these higher order ('meta-') representations enables second-order evaluative structures to carry out specific plans for future actions (Knight and Grabowecki, 1995; Smith Churchland, 2002). It is often difficult to distinguish between the self as a direct experience from the one reproduced from memory. Confusing the 'raw' experience with its reconstruction in memory is a 'compelling cognitive illusion' (Kahneman, 2011, see also Gillihan & Farah, 2005). The memory representation is nevertheless the one that we often use to make decisions, although it might be a distorted version of the 'real self' as experienced in the actual moment.

The sense of self could rely to a certain extent on autobiographical memory, although this would only reveal a part of the picture. It would also need more direct input from the bodily state. Lesions in the right parietal cortex can lead to a feeling of 'not belonging to me' of body parts, opposite to the site of the lesions. This suggests that awareness of the body might indeed be one of the factors that influence self-representation. Accordingly, Damasio speaks of our 'neural self', a representation of our body in the somatosensory regions of the brain receiving signals called 'somatic markers'. Somatic markers may come from the autonomous nervous system and its associated neurotransmitters, but also from the muscle system. The somatic signals converge in the ventromedial prefrontal cortex, an area involved in the regulation of higher emotions. Recent fMRI studies of brain activity in rest have isolated three areas in the default mode network (see further ahead) involved in self-referential activity; the posterior cingulate cortex, the medial prefrontal cortex and the inferior posterior lobe. Self-related processes were driven via the posterior cingulate cortex and moderated by the regulatory influences of the medial prefrontal cortex (Davey et al., 2016).

The unrestrained mind

The free running mind, unrestrained by a cognitive task, has recently received a renewed interest. This impulse came from the discovery in neuroscience that the brain in rest is not a passive organism, but an amalgam of active brain regions, some of which are also active when one feels emotions or is involved in cognitive activity. These findings would undoubtedly have pleased William James, who was primarily interested in the phenomenological side of attention: the wandering mind and 'stream of consciousness'. Two examples that have received broad interest are the default network and the salience network, identified in task-free settings by Seeley and colleagues.

Default network

The default network (DN) encompasses the posterior and anterior cortical midline structures, with major hubs being located in the posterior cingulate and the medial prefrontal cortex (called the core system), the precuneus and the angular gyrus of the lateral parietal lobe (Andrews-Hanna, 2010; Figure 4.23; see also Figure 7.10 for a more detailed view of these medial structures). DN is suppressed in some manner in task-controlled conditions. During rest, it assumedly represents spontaneous cognitive processes and serves to keep areas in the brain that are usually active during controlled task conditions in a state of preparedness or 'stand by'. In contrast to the attentional network that is preferentially recruited when we turn our attention towards the external world, the resting state network seems to be primarily involved in internally oriented mental processes, also described as *mentalizing*: the process of spontaneously or deliberately picturing and understanding one's own, or another person's mental states. Interestingly, findings suggest that brain activity in the resting state and in the absence of an explicit cognitive demand may be relevant to the differences in intelligence (Song et al., 2008).

Salience network

The salience network (SN) has its center in the paralimbic anterior cingulate and frontoinsular cortices, with extensive connectivity with subcortical and limbic areas (Figure 4.23). The SN consists of three main cortical areas: the dorsal anterior cingulate cortex, the insula and the adjacent inferior frontal gyri. In the network, the insula is sensitive to notable events, where its core function is to mark such events for additional processing and to initiate appropriate control signals. Meta-analytic neuroimaging studies point to at least two major functional-anatomic subdivisions within the anterior insula that contribute to the detection and processing of salient information: a dorsal region that is routinely active during attention tasks, and a ventral region that is routinely active during affective experience (Touroutoglou et al., 2012).

The anterior insula, in turn, has been described as an integral hub in mediating dynamic interactions between other large-scale brain networks, involved in externally oriented attention and internally oriented or self-related cognition (e.g. Menon & Uddin, 2010). Interestingly, the insula has also been implied in response inhibition in the stop-signal paradigm. In this task, trials with reaction signals are randomly interspersed with trials where stop signals after the reaction signals tell the subject to stop the intended response. Activation of the right anterior insula was most conspicuous on unsuccessful stopping trials (Ramautar et al., 2006; Bartoli et al., 2018). The findings suggest that the insula might not be related to response inhibition as such, but instead register the saliency of the stop signal, in particular on failed inhibition trials.

Validating the salience network

Similar to the DN, the SN also covers a large-scale functionally connected brain network that is active in the resting state. Both networks clearly exhibit deactivation during

ACTIVATION, ATTENTION AND AWARENESS

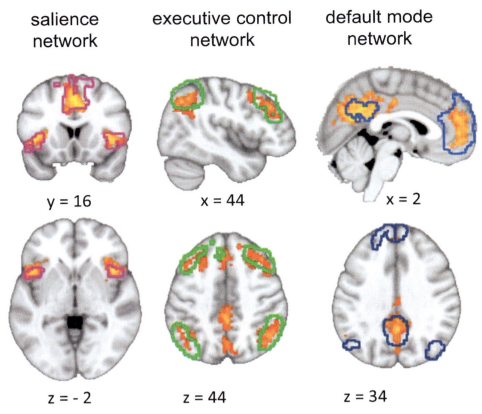

FIGURE 4.23
Salience, executive control and default mode networks. Colored areas highlight the specific areas within each network. Upper panel: coronal (left), lateral (middle) and medial (right) sections. Lower panel: horizontal sections.

Source: Adapted from Young et al. (2017).

the performance of an externally oriented attention-demanding task, and high cerebral blood flow and oxygen consumption during the resting state. Although its functional role is not uniformly defined, SN is often assumed to select stimuli that deserve our attention. A related function would be detecting and filtering information necessary to maintain goal-directed behavior by shifting attention between external and internal processes.

Since DN and SN networks are identified in conditions unrestrained by cognitive tasks, many studies, especially those from the applied clinical domain, have used external sources for validating their functional significance. Clinical researchers, for example, investigating the salience and default mode networks, have compared brain patterns of patients with healthy controls and found that decoupling of the two networks was characteristic for certain deviant mood states as occurring in severe forms of depression (see also Buckner et al., 2008 for a discussion of the clinical relevance of the DN's function). A balance between the two networks, on the other hand, has been associated with 'mindfulness', a state of mind characterized by attending to the moment and a 'flow' of consciousness (Bishop et al., 2004). Another method used to validate the content of these networks consists in correlating neural indices extracted from task-free fMRI with behavioral indices (like scores of attentivity or working memory) collected in a separate session in a large group of subjects.

To what extent does spontaneous activity of the brain in task-free settings correspond with affective and cognitive brain states elicited by external events or conditions? Seeley and colleagues hypothesized that the salience network, built around the paralimbic structure, would relate to processing of emotional events, while these effects would be less conspicuous in the central executive network. To test this hypothesis, Seeley and coworkers selected active regions (ROIs, regions of interest) in separate conditions, making demands on working memory and a task-free condition, respectively. They then correlated the regions of functional connectivity within each network, with subject pre-scan anxiety scores. They found that pre-scan anxiety ratings correlated significantly with functional connectivity in two nodes in the salience network: the dACC and the left DLPFC. Anxiety ratings showed no correlation with functional connectivity in the executive-control network.

A study by Young also compared the relationship between the three major networks, the SN, DN, and the executive control network in a group of 120 subjects in task free conditions. In these studies, the core salience, executive control and default mode networks were also selected by using templates (or seeds) extracted from a separate standard database (Young et al., 2017). This study further suggested that the state of arousal of the subjects (manipulated in a separate anxiety producing video clip) affected areas in the saliency but not in the executive network. Most notably, the results showed that cohesion (within) the salience network had a monotonically increasing association with arousal indices, while the cohesion of this network with the executive control network peaked at moderate arousal. These results suggested that the salience network is optimally able to engage the executive control network to coordinate cognitive activity, but is unable to do so at tonically elevated noradrenergic levels, like those that occur with acute stress.

Another approach followed by Ham and colleagues compared behavioral indices and neural signals from subregions in the SN network, derived from the same task condition. Their study used causal dynamic modeling and Bayesian statistics to disentangle regions of the SN and those from other networks in an active task setting. They found that the paralimbic areas and frontal anterior cingulate were more active during error than non-error trials in a Simon task, confirming the idea that error signals are a vital source of saliency (Ham et al., 2013).[8]

Constraints of task-free states of the brain

The content of the mind, unrelated to what a person does, has been the focus of a recent review of Christoff and colleagues. They presented a novel and challenging framework for understanding spontaneous thought and mind-wandering (see Figure 4.24). According to Christoff the terms 'task-unrelated', 'stimulus-independent' and 'spontaneous' are sometimes used interchangeably in the cognitive and neuroimaging literature. However, their usage can be problematic because they designate separable dimensions. One dimension is the *mode* of our thoughts or mental states. This may vary from the extent they are spontaneous, automatically constrained or deliberately constrained. A constraint is anything that 'limits the free flow of contents of thought, and how these contents change over time'. Spontaneous thoughts arise freely without strong constraints on their content, or the transitions from one thought to another. Dreaming is one example; creative thinking (demanding some deliberate constraints) another. The definition of automatic constraints is 'a family of mechanisms that operate outside of cognitive control to hold attention on a restricted set of information'. For example, both affective and sensory salience can act as sources of automatic constraints. Deliberate constraints refer to goal-directed mental states, equivalent with cognitive control. They refer to a flexible mechanism that can be freely allocated to various goals. For example, we can deliberately maintain our attention to a dry and boring lecture, bringing our thoughts back to the lecture whenever they begin to wander.

A second dimension in the model is the *orientation* of thoughts. Within each of the three modes of thoughts, orientation of thoughts can be either *internal* (stimulus independent) or *external* (stimulus dependent). For example, in the automatically

Mode	Orientation
Spontaneous (relatively unconstrained)	Internal
automatically constrained	Internal External
deliberately constrained	Internal External

FIGURE 4.24
Varieties of task-unrelated thought (adapted from Christoff et al., 2016). This involves three sub-varieties of thoughts (Mode), each of which may be internally or externally oriented (Orientation). See text for clarification.

constrained mode a student who is trying to fall asleep may find it hard not to ponder about an examination the next day. Alternatively, a person in a library may find it hard to ignore a buzzing fly. An example of an internally oriented deliberate constraint is the car driver who is already planning the multiple errands she wants to combine into a single car ride. Counting tiles in a waiting room to fight boredom exemplifies an externally oriented deliberate constraint. Anxious and obsessive disorders are further clinical examples of mental states with strong automatic constraints. Clinically significant deviations in spontaneous thought become manifest in either excessive variability (like in ADHD) or excessive stability (like in depression) of thought contents over time.

Christoff and colleagues also presented a neural model suggesting how large-scale networks, discussed earlier, relate to the dynamics of thought, and how they may interact in conditions of automatic and deliberate constraints (Figure 4.25). For example, during spontaneous, internally oriented thought, the default network (DN) subsystem centered around the medial temporal lobe exerts a relatively strong diversifying influence on the stream of thought, in the context of relatively low deliberate and automatic constraints exerted by the frontoparietal control network. In contrast, during deliberately constrained conditions, the frontal-parietal network dominates the default mode (core section) and salience networks. Its role might be that of 'top-level management' control, constraining thought in a relatively general, nonspecific manner. The salience network,

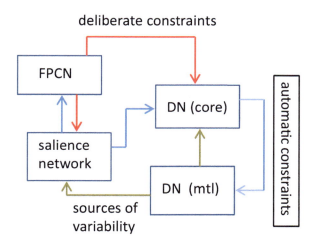

FIGURE 4.25
Large scale network involved in task irrelevant thoughts. DN (core): default core network; DN (mtl): medial temporal lobe region of the default network; FPCN: frontoparietal control network. Red arrows: subsection of the network dominated by deliberately constrained thoughts (in the context of relatively weak internal sources of variability, and relatively weak automatic constraints). Blue arrows: subsection of the network dominated by automatically constrained thought (in the context of relatively low deliberate constraints, and relatively weak internal sources of variability). Brown arrows: subsection of the network dominated by spontaneous, internally oriented thought, in the context of relatively low deliberate and automatic constraints.

Source: Adapted from Christoff et al. (2016).

in turn, exerts automatic constraints on the dorsal attention network and frontoparietal executive networks. It's role in 'igniting' the attentional systems in the brain would be in line with suggestions made by Seeley and Menon and colleagues, discussed earlier. In addition, a growing body of evidence suggests that the generation of spontaneous thought may be closely linked to the default mode section centered around the medial temporal lobe.

Christoff's model serves as an example of the flexibility of large-scale networks in recruiting different neural assemblies, dependent on the dynamics of processes in the brain, triggered by external or internal sources. Declaring the dynamics of the wandering mind as the principal goal of an investigation, is certainly a great challenge. It might, however, also present new methodological problems, if investigators leave the relatively safe path of task-induced constraints. Traditional experimental design at least allows focusing on predefined mental states, in more tightly controlled conditions, both with respect to what the subject 'is doing', and to the content and time flow of information in the brain. In contrast, Christoff and colleagues see promises in an approach that intends to combine 'online experience sampling or first-person measures of ongoing thought dynamics, with measures of neural activity'. A neurophenomenological approach, in order to illuminate the variability of brain dynamics, remains an outstanding challenge (Fazelpour & Thompson 2015). Such an approach, however, could also get stranded in case-studies, describing specific neurocognitive states of specific individuals. Its promise then would be to supplement experimental task-oriented studies in providing new and more detailed insights into the relationship between objective (task-restrained) and subjective (unrestrained) states of the brain.

Notes

1. The terms 'awareness' and 'consciousness' will be used indiscriminately in the present chapter to designate the waking state of the brain. The terms 'arousal' and 'activation' are used as synonyms whenever applied to the state of the brain.
2. According to LaBerge (1995), the preparation manifestation of attention would be capable of being modulated in intensity, and hence could also accommodate the resource metaphor, including feelings of effort associated with divided attention operations.
3. Later Broadbent distinguished between two models of selective attention, called stimulus set (*filtering*) and response set (*pigeonholing*). In response set, selection is not determined by the physical characteristics of a stimulus, but by its meaning or category. A simple example is an experiment employing mixed arrays of letters and digits in which only digits are relevant stimuli. Subjects would never be expected to respond with a letter, since letters, by definition, are not allowable responses.
4. Although Bundesen's model is neutral concerning particular anatomical localizations of its computations, it does mention the extrastriate cortex as a main binding site. Brain-based

models of selective attention, however, often also incorporate the posterior parietal cortex (PPC) as a major binding site. PPC is reciprocally connected with the visual cortex as well as the pulvinar of thalamus. It thus seems plausible that it is also implicated in a circuitry regulating neural computations as described in the TVA model.

5   Theories of WM that assume a focus of attention differ in what functions they ascribe to the focus and the assumed scope of the focus. Cowan (2005), for example, assumed that the focus of attention can hold up to about four independent chunks, while others assumed a focus of attention limited to a single chunk. Oberauer (2009) has proposed an integration of those two views into a framework that distinguishes three states of representations in WM: the activated part of LTM, the region of direct access (roughly corresponding to the broad focus in Cowan's theory) and the focus of attention.

6   Näätänen (1992) proposed a similar conceptualization of attention in his theory of the 'attentional trace', i.e. 'a voluntary maintained representation of the physical characteristics of a relevant stimulus' (Chapter 3, p. 14).

7   The strength as well as limitation of DCM depends on the regions selected in model space. In the present study, for example, the directed connections from FEF to IPS were selected on the basis of a prior report of Bressler et al., (2008). Most fMRI studies focusing on attentional control networks using the spatial cueing paradigm (e.g. Hopfinger et al., 2000), however, have emphasized the dorsolateral prefrontal areas instead of the FEF. In addition, the pulvinar of the thalamus, frequently implicated in the covert spatial attention process (LaBerge, 1995), has generally received much less emphasis in neuroimaging studies of attentional control than its cortical associate, the posterior parietal cortex.

8   The Simon task, originally used by J. R. Simon (1963), is a choice reaction task manipulating spatial compatibility by presenting incompatible trials (responding with the right and left hand to centrally presented words LEFT and RIGHT, respectively) with compatible trials (responding with the right hand to RIGHT and left hand to LEFT). The Simon effect will also show up for incompatible positions of colors (e.g. red and green) presented at left and right positions in the visual field (for example, when instructed to react to red with the right hand and green with the left hand).

5 Perception and action

> **CONTENTS**
> - Introduction
> - Visual perception
> - Action systems
> - From perception to action
> - Time perception

Introduction

Information processing models often treat perception and action as separate modules, representing the input and output sides of the information processing sequence. From the perspective of the brain, however, their separation is largely artificial because perceiving organisms perform in a dynamic environment. When we follow a bird with our eyes, rapidly changing coordinates of the target are sent to the frontal eye fields and oculomotor neurons, to guide pursuit movements of our eyes. The visual system interacts with its environment, with vision guiding the action system, and the action system controlled by constraints imposed by properties of a visual target.

Perceptual functions are overwhelmingly complex. Visual perception, for example, is not a single process but subdivided in primary and higher-level vision. The primary visual system translates the physical energy of the retina to electrical impulses, conveyed via electrochemical synapses to the primary visual cortex. Higher vision involves the pathways connecting the primary visual cortex to the posterior dorsal and temporal cortices. The same principle holds for the motor regions of anterior cortices, involving execution of movements and the preparation and planning of motor programs.

While information is transmitted from lower to higher centers in the brain, the receptive fields of the involved neurons increase drastically, and so does the complexity of neural representation of objects. Encoding transforms from precise coding in local networks, to coarse coding in larger ensembles of neural populations. In the visual cortex, for example, the receptive fields increase from 1.2° in V1 to 3° in V2, 8° in TEO (temporal-occipital junction) and 40° in IT (inferotemporal cortex). The inferotemporal cortex is of particular importance for higher visual functions (Tanaka, 1992).

The same principle applies (but in reversed order) to the motor system with information flowing downstream from supplementary motor cortex (SMA) to premotor and primary motor cortex to motor neurons in the spinal cord. The present chapter does not describe the various structures, pathways and relay stations of perception and motor systems in detail. After specifying the major components of the visual and the motor systems, later sections focus on interactive models linking perception to action, and the role of the posterior parietal cortex in dealing with different kinds of potential actions. Particular emphasis will be on the oculomotor system, as the pre-eminent system depending on the fusion of visual perception and action. The final section of the chapter deals with time-perception, a function incorporating the estimation of the duration of perceptual events, as well as the control of the timing of movements.

Visual perception

Projection of the visual environment to the brain largely determines the architecture of the visual system. The functional division between two cortical regions, often referred to as the dorsal ('where'), and ventral ('what') system, reflects the separation of the two parallel afferent visual pathways. When traced back in the visual hierarchy their separation already starts in the primary visual cortex (V1), from where they relay via different nuclei of the thalamus to their separate destinations in the posterior parietal cortex (PPC) and inferior temporal cortex (IT).

From eye to brain: geniculostriate and tectopulvinary routes

Visual information from the eye reaches the visual cortex via two separate parallel circuits: the geniculostriate pathway and the tectopulvinary pathway (see Figure 5.1). The majority (90%) of the optical nerve fibers form the first route, only 10% of the fibers the second. A more detailed description of both routes follows.

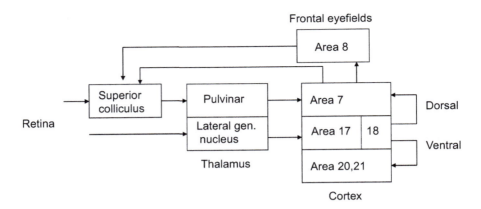

FIGURE 5.1
Two afferent visual sensory pathways: the tectopulvinary route (on top) running from superior colliculus via the pulvinar of the thalamus to area 7 in the parietal cortex, and the geniculostriate route (below) running via the lateral geniculate nucleus to area 17 in the primary visual cortex. In area 18 (extrastriate cortex) the geniculostriate pathway further splits into the dorsal route ('where' system) ending in parietal cortex area 7, and the ventral route ('what' system) ending in temporal cortex areas 20 and 21.

Geniculostriate route

The geniculostriate route, or primary projection system, runs from the retina through the lateral geniculate nuclei (LGN) of the thalamus to the visual projection area, also known as V1, area 17 or area striata. At a more detailed level, this route can be further differentiated into two specific pathways.

Ipsi- and contralateral pathways The first pathways contains nerve fibers coming from the lateral sides of the retina (the temporal retinae), and projecting to the visual cortex of the same (ipsilateral) hemisphere (Figure 5.2). The second pathway contains nerve fibers coming from the medial sides of the retina (the nasal retinae), that cross over to the (contralateral) visual cortex of the opposite hemisphere. Another way of putting it is that the right sides of space project to the left halves of the retina of both eyes, while the left sides of space project to the right side of the retina of both eyes. The same retinotopic projections are found in subsequent stations, the LGN and area V1. Here the right and left visual fields project to the contralateral (left) and ipsilateral (right) halves of the LGN and V1. In the LGN, ipsi- and contralateral pathways connect with alternating layers (Figure 5.2, lower part).

Magno- versus parvocellular routes A second differentiation within the geniculostriate pathways is that between the magnocellular and the parvocellular systems, which also relay in different layers of the LGN (Figure 5.2, magno: layers 1 and 2, parvo: layers 3, 4, 5 and 6). The terms parvo and magno relate to the specific properties of two

> ### BOX 5.1 BLINDSIGHT
>
> Neuropsychologist Larry Weiskrantz discovered that patients with damage to the primary visual cortex were still able to detect the location of an illuminated spot in the defective or blinded part of their visual field, called *scotoma* (Weiskrantz, 2000). In this experiment, the patient was asked to move the eyes after a tone towards an illuminated spot, presented in the defective visual field. It turned out that they performed significantly better than in a control condition, in which no stimuli were presented after the tone. The patient, however, was not aware of the stimuli that had elicited his eye movements, when presented in the defective field. Weiskrantz, therefore, called this phenomenon blindsight. The same phenomenon sometimes occurs in patients with lesions in one half of the primary visual cortex, for example, the left half. If the stimulus in the good visual field (left) was presented simultaneously with a stimulus in the bad visual field (right), the response was still delayed as compared with a condition when only one stimulus was presented in the good field. Blindsight findings are however still subject to controversy. This is because they do not rule out the possibility that patients had used residual functions of the visual cortex in the geniculostriate route, and not so much of the tectopulvinar route. There could still have been small intact islands, or 'peeping holes' in the lesioned area, leaking information from the bad visual field.

types of ganglion cells directly behind the retina and their associated clusters of neurons in the visual cortex. Parvocells are small and sensitive in detection of details, color, and slow movements; magnocells are large and sensitive to detect global contours and fast movements.

Tectopulvinary route

The second route runs from the retina via the tectum, and then proceeds through the thalamus pulvinar nucleus to the posterior parietal cortex (PPC area 7). The tectopulvinar pathway is considered to be an evolutionary old route, that mainly supports visual-spatial orientation. An essential link in this route is the superior colliculus in the tectum. The superior colliculus contains a visual representation of the environment, as well as spatial 'maps' of the body surface and positions of sound in space. In contrast to the somatosensory cortex, the representation of body space is not dependent on tactile but on visual stimuli.

The superior colliculus is also involved in the control of saccades. It does this in cooperation with the frontal eye fields (area 8) in the anterior cortex, and the posterior

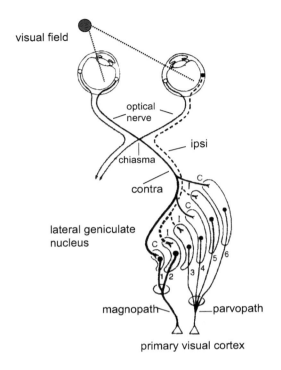

FIGURE 5.2
Inputs of both retinas to different layers in the lateral geniculate nucleus (LGN), and primary visual cortex. Shown are the projections from the left visual field to the right LGN and primary visual cortex. The dotted line is the ipsilateral pathway of the right eye, the solid line the contralateral pathways of the left eye. Ipsi and contra pathways connect with alternate layers in the LGN. Also shown are the magnocellular and parvocellular pathways. These connect respectively with layers 1 and 2, and layers 3, 4, 5 and 6 of the LGN. These pathways originate from ganglion cells behind the retina but are only shown from the LGN.
Source: From Kandel et al. (1991).

parietal cortex (see also Figure 5.16). The superior colliculus plays an important role in attention capture: the reflexive orienting toward a stimulus. Consequently, damage to the superior colliculus not only impairs saccades but also shifts of attention, that is covert attention, to different positions in space.

The role of the tectopulvinar pathway as a backup system (or secondary route) to support vision in the geniculostriate pathways, is suggested in studies of patients suffering from blindsight (see Box 5.1).

Blindsight results from damage of neurons in area V1 and possibly also from its surrounding visual areas. Although blindsight patients could not 'see' patterns of light presented to the blind part of the visual field, they did show a tendency to move their eyes to the source of stimulation. This could indicate that they still relied on the second tectopulvinar pathway to direct visual attention to stimuli in the blind field (Weiskrantz, 1986).

Further stations in the visual cortex, dorsal and ventral routes

The differentiation between magnocellular and parvocellular pathways in the LGN continues until their arrival in area V1. Cells in V1 are organized in cortical modules with six layers and columns tuned to various line orientations. Here the parvo and magno routes connect to different laminae (sublayers) of layer 4, where the parvo pathway splits into blob and interblob systems (globally specialized in form and color) and the magnosystem specialized in motion and spatial relationships (Deyoe & van Essen, 1988). The three routes (blob, interblob and magno) associated with these systems then further propagate to the higher visual areas V2, V3, V4 and V5 (Figure 5.3), also called extrastriate (outside striate) areas. In these areas the strict functional differentiation between earlier pathways gradually diminishes. For example, V4 and V5 are both sensitive to form and movements, while V5 (or MT) is more specifically linked to movement detection. Eventually, the parvopath ends in IT (inferotemporal cortex) and the magnopath in area PC (parietal cortex).

They then have changed names to 'ventral' and 'dorsal' pathways. The dorsal pathway ending in the parietal area is called the 'where' route, because of its specialization

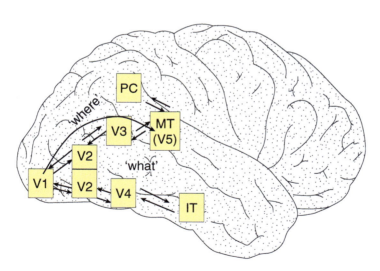

FIGURE 5.3
Different stations and pathways in the human visual cortex and their interconnections. Top: dorsal or 'where' route, below: ventral or 'what' route. IT: Inferior temporal cortex; PC: parietal cortex. See text for further clarification.

in analyzing spatial or position information. Most of the input to the dorsal path comes from the magnocellular system. The ventral path derives its input from both the magno- and parvocellular systems and is called the 'what' route, because of its specialization in analyzing nonspatial features. Neurons in the temporal cortex and the end of the ventral pathway also form columns, as in the primary visual cortex. But they have a much larger receptive field and are not specialized in the detection of elemental features – like in the primary cortex – but rather of full objects: hands, faces, various geometric shapes etc.

For example, monkey research has shown that neurons in its columns are particularly sensitive to specific combinations of elemental features. Thus, a nerve cell in its temporal area will only fire when presented with a face or hand, but not by a round shape or a vertical line.

The connections between the primary and higher secondary areas are both ascending (feedforward) and descending (feedback). This anatomical principle is also referred to as 're-entry', an important element in the hierarchical organization of networks of the visual system (Edelman & Gally, 2013). Ascending pathways are involved in bottom-up processes of perception, which are necessary for the proper functioning of the higher order areas. For example, the IT region cannot properly identify objects, when elementary stimulus features are missing. Conversely, the descending connections have a predominantly modulating (top-down) function. For example, they can strengthen or weaken the functioning of sensory areas – like in selective attention – but are not crucial for the functioning of perception at the primary levels.

Visual illusions

Visual illusions formed a popular subject in academic psychology of the late 20th century, probably because they provided the first evidence that the brain's perception of the external world differed from the physical reality. The list of perceptual illusions is still growing, but some famous examples still cited in the textbooks of psychology are the Müller-Lyer illusion, an optical illusion consisting of a stylized arrow, illusory motion (Zeki, 1993), the Rubin vase and, perhaps the most famous of all, the Ames illusion. Object constancy is a particular visual perceptual skill that requires recognizing items regardless of their change in size, shape, color, texture, context or orientation. For example, size constancy refers to the fact that our perception of the size of objects is relatively constant, despite the fact that their projections on the retina vary greatly with distance. But by using distance cues such as linear perspective, we see a car driving in front of us on the highway not as a smaller, but as a more distant vehicle.

A door or window frame is still seen as rectangular despite its different orientation. Visual illusions arise when we trick the senses by artificially changing the context, the figure-background relationship, or the perspective of objects. In the Ames room for example, the observer has the illusory impression that he looks into a normal boxlike rectangular room. The room is cleverly transformed into a trapezoidal room, with the left back corner further away from the observer than the right back corner. Because the observer is deprived from perspective cues he will see a subject in the left corner as much smaller than the same subject when standing in the right corner (Figure 5.4, shows the apparent and real size of the left subject).

Higher-order vision

Perception is the ability to identify perceptual objects in the environment. Typically, it is distinguished in lower-order and higher-order perception. Lower-order perception relates to identification of elementary stimulus characteristics. This is accomplished in the previously discussed perceptual modules V1, V2, V3, V4 and V5. In contrast, higher-order perception refers to the recognition of objects and their meaning. It depends on areas in the brain that participate in the conscious identification of objects, like the posterior parietal, temporal and frontal association areas.

An example of a disorder that affects higher-order perception is visual agnosia. Patients with damage in the temporal association areas are no longer able to recognize, for example, animals or objects, while their basic perceptual and attentional functions are still intact. These patients have problems with interpreting their visual input, often caused by damage to the temporal lobes or occipital-temporal areas. This prevents patients access to areas in the brain where the meaning of objects is stored. Such disorders may also be category-specific: for example, a patient cannot name living beings, but is still capable to name non-living objects.

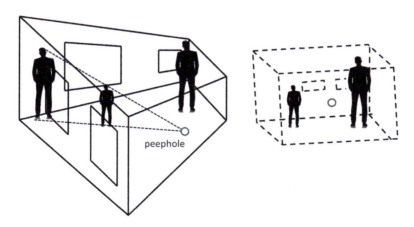

FIGURE 5.4
Reconstruction of the perception of objects in the Ames room. Left: the observer looks through a peephole in the front of a distorted trapezoidal room but, through the narrow angle of view, has the false impression of seeing a box-shaped room (drawn at the right). A person standing in the left (and more distant) back corner of the room will appear smaller to the observer than the same person standing in the right corner of the room.

PERCEPTION AND ACTION

Higher-order visual perception is an extremely complex process, implemented in a large-scale network encompassing posterior and temporal cortices (Churchland et al., 1995). The organization of the networks can be schematically represented as a flow diagram, with various subsystems carrying out specific computational operations (see Figure 5.5). Visual input to the eyes first passes a visual buffer, the striate and extrastriate areas of the occipital lobe discussed in the previous section. Relevant information in the buffer is selected and enhanced by the attentional system and transmitted to the brain systems responsible for encoding spatial and object properties, the 'where and what' systems (Mishkin et al., 1983). Attention can be triggered from exogenous or endogenous sources. In particular, cells in V4 of the visual buffer are particularly sensitive to attentional modulation further upstream. The output of dorsal (parietal) and ventral (temporal) regions in the posterior cortices converge in the associative memory system. This probably includes the same parietal and temporal cortices that are involved in encoding of location and object information.

As said before, a special property of neurons in the inferior temporal cortex is not 'firing' in response to elementary features, but only to complex characteristics of objects like faces, hand shapes and geometric patterns. The code of these objects is apparently not stored in single cells, but in larger neural ensembles.

In associative memory, information from the dorsal and ventral streams of the visual system is compared with information residing in long-term memory representations. This initially only concerns nonspatial input from the ventral stream. A familiar object

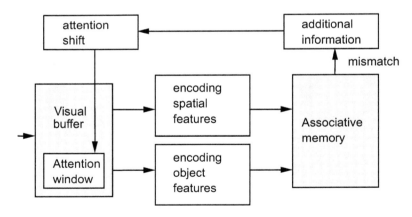

FIGURE 5.5
The visual system and subcomponents underlying higher vision.
Source: Adapted from Kosslyn & Koenig (1992).

will elicit a match, and thus a full identification, with the stored memory representation. Identification of objects that produce mismatches or partial matches can still be successfully identified by searching for additional information in long-term memory. The resulting visual search process will then also recruit visual-spatial attention, using input from the dorsal stream, to shift to new locations in the visual field.

This process continues until a satisfactory match with the internal representation is found, or in case of a relevant new object until the new representation is stored in memory. An important aspect of higher visual perception is the ability to recognize objects in space, despite their varying retinotopic image. If we move our eyes from the left to the right, all objects in a room will jump to different locations on the retina. Neurons in the posterior parietal area are able to solve this 'problem' by converting retinotopic coordinates into spatiotopic coordinates. The ability of the parietal cortex to determine the precise locations of objects in space is remarkable, given the fact that the receptive fields of its neurons are very large. Apparently, encoding in this area is not based on precise but on coarse coding as introduced in Chapter 3.

BOX 5.2   PROSOPAGNOSIA

Prosopagnosia patients do not recognize their own face in the mirror, or faces of famous movie stars and politicians. Some may even not recognize their own dog or car. When this occurs in combination with other recognition disorders, recognition of faces is more strongly affected than that of other objects. Prosopagnosia often occurs after damage of the area adjacent to the superior temporal sulcus. This sulcus is visible between the superior temporal gyrus and the middle temporal gyrus of the right hemisphere. Other areas like the medial fusiform gyrus, and the temporal pole (the foremost part of the temporal lobe) also appear to be important for recognizing unique facial characteristics of specific persons.

The more posterior parts of the temporal cortex, such as the temporal-occipital area adjacent to the extrastriate visual cortex, seem to be more specifically linked to recognition of facial features like hair and lips. The same area appears to be associated with gender recognition (does the face belongs to a man or a woman?). Prosopagnosia is a common disorder of higher perception, affecting mainly perceptual processes regulated by the end station of the ventral pathway. The disorder illustrates the close connection of memory and higher perceptual processes, especially when it concerns the involvement of the temporal cortex.

How the senses interact

Functions like seeing, hearing, smelling and tasting emerge from specific sense areas in our brain. They form the building blocks of our cognitive-perceptual interpretation of the outside world. But only by combining information of the senses, we obtain a complete impression of an object. Attention and memory systems help us to put individual perceptual characteristics together into a meaningful object. This holds for stimuli within the same modality (for example, the shape, color, movement of a ball) as well as to stimuli of different modalities (for example, the sound and images in a movie).

How exactly the brain manages to solve the 'binding problem' remains an open question, although some areas have been assigned a central role in merging or coordinating different senses. The posterior parietal cortex, for example, receives input from different sensory modalities, and combines information to form multimodal representations of extrapersonal space (Mountcastle et al., 1975). The superior colliculus is another structure, involved in coordinated orientation of various sensory organs as the ears, eyes, limbs, whiskers (in hamsters and rats) and the mouth. Both structures are involved in spatial orientation and integration, suggesting that spatial factors are particularly important for interaction between the senses. Since location itself is an amodal property it can be extracted by different senses (Spence & Driver, 2004). Evidence of the crossmodal links between vision and audition, created by spatial attention, stems from behavioral as well as from electrophysiological studies. For example, spatial attention directed toward a particular location in space has been shown to enhance brain responses to non-target visual stimuli at the occipital scalp. But it also enhanced brain responses to non-target auditory stimuli at the central scalp, presented at the same location (Eimer, 2004).

Crossmodal plasticity in sensory deprived subjects

Subjects deprived from input in one sensory system, often show an improvement in performance in other intact sensory systems. For example, early deafness may improve visual orienting to environmental stimuli. Congenitally deaf cats, compared with hearing cats, were shown to have superior localization in the peripheral visual fields and lower visual movement detection thresholds (Lomber et al., 2010). These behavioral effects may reflect compensations achieved by improvement of the intact perceptual abilities and related brain areas. Another possibility is that they result, at least in part, from channeling input from the intact sensory modalities to the brain area deprived of its natural input: the visual area for the blind and auditory area for the deaf subjects. Some evidence from neurophysiological and neuroimaging studies is presented in the following paragraphs.

Blind subjects Blind subjects have been reported to use striate and extrastriate areas in the occipital cortex, to assist their performance in tasks depending on other stimulus modalities. Transient magnetic stimulation (TMS) of the occipital visual cortex distorted the tactile perceptions of blind subjects, whereas this had no effect on tactile performance in normal-sighted subjects (Cohen et al., 1997). Blind subjects performing verbal memory tasks showed a greater activity in their visual occipital (striate and extrastriate) cortices than sighted subjects (Amedi et al., 2003). The same effect was also found for speech comprehension, with greater occipital activity varying as a function of syntactic difficulty and semantic content (Röder et al., 2002). Functional imaging studies of people who were blind from an early age further revealed that their primary visual cortex was consistently activated by Braille reading, auditory spatial processing and tactile discrimination tasks (Collignon et al., 2007, 2009).

Deaf subjects Crossmodal interactions could also explain why visual stimuli activate neurons in the auditory cortex in deaf humans. Although these effects are also found in normal hearing subjects in certain crossmodal tasks, there is growing evidence that in hearing impaired persons these responses might reflect specific 'rewiring' or cross-modal reorganization. A visual stimulus like a moving dot pattern, for example, was shown to activate the auditory projection area in deaf, but not in normal hearing control subjects (Finney et al., 2001). Another study found stronger recruitment of the superior temporal gyrus, and thus of a large part of the secondary auditory cortex, in deaf humans during sentence reading, as compared to matched hearing subjects (Hirshorn et al., 2014).

Together these findings may indicate that improved visual orienting in deafness, relative to normal hearing could have developed from additional activity in the auditory areas. The structural dominance of the visual system could be the reason why deaf subjects still recruit their auditory system.

The role of supramodal structures While the underlying mechanisms that support these complex patterns of cortical specialization after sensory deprivation are not yet entirely understood, an emerging view is that cross-modal reorganization is most likely to occur in areas that are involved in supramodal computations. Two possible systems responsible for intermodal integration were mentioned in an earlier paragraph, the superior colliculus and the posterior parietal cortex. Visual cues could be involved in aligning neural maps of auditory space via the superior colliculus, connecting with the inferior colliculus which in turn connects to the auditory nuclei. The same mechanism might operate in early blindness, which often leads to a superior performance in tasks depending on tactile or spatial auditory cues, relative to people with normal sight (King, 2004). In this case, auditory or tactile location cues might enhance already existing pathways between visual neurons in the SC and visual occipital cortex. This in turn may provide additional input to the processing in the other modalities.

Memory for faces

Young children already have an innate inclination to look at faces, which suggests that memory for faces must be linked to a hardwired bottom-up circuitry in the visual system, which also guides visual search for human faces. With respect to face recognition, there is evidence to suggest that the brain integrates information delivered from different sensory modalities by synchronizing movements of the face and sounds produced by a speaker. In remembering faces of familiar persons, we are often able to reproduce from memory not only their facial characteristics, but also the associated voice and manner of speech. Research suggests that when recognizing faces we use a network in the posterior temporal cortex in which the face and voice areas connect via direct structural connections. Functional neuroimaging consistently has shown that three bilateral regions in the occipital-temporal extrastriate visual cortex respond more strongly when viewing faces than when viewing other visual images (see also Haxby et al., 2000). These connections occur in particular between the gyrus fusiformis and the right superior temporal gyrus (Box 5.3). Lesions in the superior temporal gyrus area may lead to problems with voice recognition (*voice agnosia*), just as lesions in the fusiform gyrus lead to problems with recognizing familiar faces (*prosopagnosia*).

BOX 5.3 TALKING HEADS: HOW OUR PERCEPTIONS OF FACE AND VOICE MELT TOGETHER

Experts seem to agree that the ability to recognize faces is rooted deeply in the genes. Our genes not only contain information about the identity of other familiar humans, but also include facial cues such as attractiveness, sex, emotional expression and, last but not least, the human voice. The ability to recognize these features could have been an essential condition in the survival of humans in the course of evolution. Magnetic resonance studies and studies of neurological patients have represented further evidence that the fusiform face area (FFA) could be a domain-specific 'hot spot' in our brain, specialized in recognition of faces. Also, twin studies have shown that competence in face recognition is an individual heritable trait, comparable to that of general intelligence.

How about voices? In naturalistic conditions, the muscles of our head that control the mouth, eye movements, and eyebrows are continually moving and, more importantly, producing articulated sounds. The human head is typically a dynamic 'talking' head, and because movements of the face and articulated speech always occur in temporal alignment, they provide a powerful interactive cue that they belong to the same person.

continued

> Belin and colleagues further suggested that in line with face recognition, voice recognition also depends on a specific area or network in our brain. This network is called the temporal voice area (TVA) in the right superior temporal sulcus. Similar to prosopagnosia after damage of the FFA, phonoagnosia is found after damage of the TVA. Another exciting feature is that these areas or networks seem to be tightly coupled. This implies that when we recognize a familiar face, we activate in synchrony the unique vocal signature of the person behind that face. Recognizing a voice would then also have an evolutionary benefit, in helping us to identify a person in suboptimal visual viewing conditions, or when visual acuity declines in old age. Strong face-voice coupling could also explain why our memory of faces often corresponds with a clear representation of the associated voice. Even when we think of a familiar person we have not seen for many years, we often are still able to reproduce in our mind the typical face and voice.
>
> Source: Belin et al. (2004), Von Kriegstein & Giraud (2006), Schweinberger et al. (2011).

Senses mislead

In other cases the same synthetic power of the brain may also mislead us in interpreting the visual environment. Some examples follow.

- ▶ Synesthesia is a name for a deviation in perception where stimulation of the sense in one modality concurrently elicits a sensory experience in another. For example, a sound can be associated with an experience of a color, or even more strange, a color is being tasted. Sometimes a color or sound may evoke a certain feeling. Most common forms are the associations between letters and color and sound and color. Synesthesia is believed to result to from 'leakage' or cross-talk between areas in the secondary visual cortex that are normally shielded from each other by inhibitory neurons (Ramachandran & Hubbard, 2001).
- ▶ In some 'synesthetics' the experience could also have been caused by top-down influences that follow an indirect route in the brain, with the resulting synesthetic experience having a different character than that caused by a crossover in the visual areas (see Figure 5.6 for an example).
- ▶ The ventriloquist effect is an illusion created by visual spatial attention dominating nonspatial vision. If visual attention is focused on a certain location in space, a sound produced elsewhere may seem to come from the target that is seen. In case

PERCEPTION AND ACTION

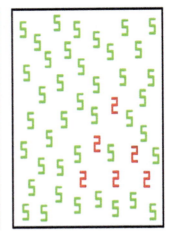

FIGURE 5.6
People with a tendency for grapheme color synesthesia may see letters or numbers printed in black in a specific color. The numbers in the left panel are then perceived as shown in the panel on the right with the numbers 2 (perceived as green) 'popping out' from the background of the numbers 5 (perceived as red).

of conflict between a visual spatial observation and another sense, the visual spatial system always wins.

▶ The rubber-hand-effect is based on the same mechanism, but now visual spatial attention misleads the touch sense. With simultaneous tactile stimulation of an artificial rubber hand (on the table in front of the subject) and the own hand (hidden under the table), it seems like the feeling comes from the rubber hand (Pavani et al., 2000).

Action systems

How does the brain control the immense array of muscle cells so that the whole body moves in the right way? This problem is probably the most basic one a nervous system evolved to solve.

Churchland & Sejnowski, 1988

Introduction: the hierarchical structure of the motor system

Like the visual system, the action system that controls movements is hierarchically organized. Higher, more anteriorly located regions in our association cortex generate an action plan, which is then sent downstream to lower regions in the premotor and motor cortex. The lower levels are responsible for translating the plan into specific movement parameters, like the location of the target and the movement trajectory, and then ultimately drive specific body parts and muscles involved in the actual execution of movement. When we reach out to grasp an apple, the motor plan 'grab apple' is converted to a right arm movement followed by a grasping movement of the fingers. Since action plans are partially activated in parallel with motor structures, the reaching movement could concurrently activate areas in the primary motor cortex controlling the fingers, in anticipation of the final act.

When translating action programs into specific movements, cortical structures are assisted by the basal ganglia and the cerebellum. The complete motor hierarchy consists of two parallel circuits, one running from higher to lower motor centers to structures in the spinal cord, and a second circuit that connects the supplementary motor area (SMA) to the basal ganglia and cerebellum (see Figure 5.7). The first circuit is sometimes called 'pyramidal tract', the second 'extrapyramidal tract'.

The right-hand part of Figure 5.7 globally indicates which control processes are associated with successive neural implementations. The conceptual level (the action plan) is followed by selection of the response system and its subsequent motor implementation. The response system is conceived as the repertoire of action representations stored in motor memory, from which a particular response is selected. For example, when meeting a familiar person, the concept 'greeting' is activated. This leads to a choice from the repertoire: 'smile, 'extending the hand', 'exclamation'. When a choice

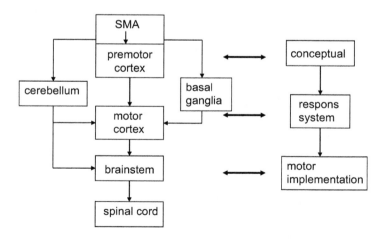

FIGURE 5.7
Left: global organization of the motor system. Higher levels control the lower levels, via cortical and subcortical circuits. Right: corresponding levels of motor control. The choice of a response system follows an action plan or concept and leads to the choice of specific motor action. See text for clarification.

is made ('smile') it is followed by its specific motor actions (activation of specific facial muscles).

The next section focuses in more detail on the different levels of motor control, dealing in succession with subcortical and cortical systems.

Subcortical organization and circuits

The subcortical structures that form part of the motor system constitute a complex circuitry of neural connections, of which the present chapter discusses only the most important elements. Figure 5.8 (upper section) shows two reciprocal pathways connecting the neostriatum (nucleus caudatus and putamen) with cortical areas. The major subcortical structures from these circuits, the basal ganglia and the cerebellum have already been described extensively in Chapter 2 and will not further be considered here.

Complex and motor loops

Both looping pathways receive input from the posterior and motor areas of the cortex. The first loop, also referred to as complex loop, passes the caudate nucleus and thalamus on its way to the prefrontal cortex. The second loop, called the motor loop, relays its output to the premotor cortex via putamen and thalamus. Between these two circuits of the basal ganglia there is a certain hierarchy in the level of motor control, with the complex and motor loops regulating respectively the planning and execution of movements. Both loops receive similar input from the cortex.

The lower section of Figure 5.8 shows a third circuit, formally not part of the basal ganglia, that links the cerebellum to the motor cortex, via the thalamus. The cerebellum receives input from the same cortical areas as do the complex and motor loops, but receives additional afferent inputs from the brainstem, and from visual, tactile and vestibular sensory organs. It also functions as motor memory for automatic and skilled behavior, varying from simple conditioned forms of behavior like the eye-blink reflex, to more complex sensorimotor skills. For example, when playing the piano, the cerebellum is crucial for the temporal coordination of movements. Finally, the cerebellum also receives input from the motor neurons in the spinal cord, which means that it participates in 'online' control of movements, allowing fast corrections of errors in movements.

Cerebellar lesions often impair the ability of patients to predict sensory experiences on the basis of current movement, like for example knowing where to put your feet when walking down a long staircase. These patients often not only have problems with the timing of movements, but also with judging the duration of a sound. The specific role of the cerebellum in precise timing and time estimation also explains why effects of lesions are most disruptive in performing highly practiced skills that often critically depend on precise timing.

PERCEPTION AND ACTION

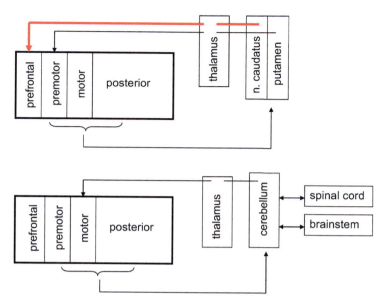

FIGURE 5.8
Upper section: Two cortical-subcortical loops linking basal ganglia and cortex: the complex loop (in red) and the motor loop (in black). Lower section: cerebellar-cortical loop between the cerebellum and the posterior and motor cortices. See text for further clarification.

Inhibitory circuits between basal ganglia and cortex

The neuroscientists Alexander and Delong (Alexander et al., 1986) described two important inhibitory pathways that connect structures within the basal ganglia, which they called the direct and indirect pathways (Figure 5.9). Both pathways receive their input from the cortex via corticostriatal projections (like in the complex loop shown in Figure 5.8) and then project back to the cortex via GPi/SNr (the internal section of the globus pallidus, together with substantia nigra pars reticulata).

Central to the network is GPi/SNr which has a strong inhibitory output to the thalamus and motor cortex as a baseline. This prevents competing motor plans, initiated at higher conceptual levels of the cortex, (prematurely) producing overt movements. GPi/SNr receives pulses from two major inhibitory trajectories, the direct and indirect path. The direct path goes straight from the striatum to GPi/SNr and is facilitated by substantia nigra (SNc) output via D1 receptors. The indirect path leads from the striatum, first to GPe and hence via the STN to GPi/SNr, but this pathway is inhibited by substantia nigra (SNc) output to D2 receptors. Notice that the net effect of the direct pathway implies more inhibition of GPi/SNr, thus leading to a decrease of its inhibitory output to the motor cortex and to *more movement*. The net effect of the indirect pathway (via D2

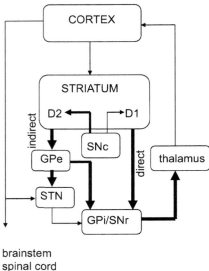

FIGURE 5.9
The two inhibitory circuits of the basal ganglia to cortex: the direct and indirect pathways. The central element is the GPi/SNr that tonically inhibits the cortex. GPi/SNr receives inhibitory input (thick solid lines) from both the direct and the indirect pathways. Dopaminergic projections of the substantia nigra (SNc) to striatum enhance the inhibitory effect of the direct path through D1 receptors and reduces the inhibitory effect on the indirect path via D2 receptors.

Source: Adapted from Wichman& DeLong (1996). Gpi=Globus pallidus interna; GPe=globus pallidus externa; SNc= substantia nigra pars compacta; SNr= substantia nigra pars reticulata; STN=subthalamic nucleus; D1, D2= dopamine receptors.

receptors) implies excitation of GPi/SNr, leading to an increase of its inhibitory output to the motor cortex and to *less movement* (Figure 5.10).

The effect of the basal ganglia on the cortex will thus reflect the balance of the two pathways. This is achieved in the looping circuit between the direct and indirect pathways. For example, less inhibition by the fast, direct pathway is followed by stronger inhibition by the slower indirect pathway.

Microstimulation studies have shown that the striatal motor territory contains somatotopic maps with separate parallel channels for arm, leg and face representations that are maintained throughout the basal ganglia's intrinsic circuitry. Moreover, within these limb representations, there possibly are additional discrete channels corresponding to particular movements (Alexander & Delong, 1985). Such an architecture enables a refined control of specific actions and movements. Action plans initiated in the prefrontal cortex (for example, a tennis player anticipating several options to return the ball from his opponent) would feed via Gabaergic projection neurons into the striatum where specific actions compete with

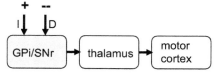

net effect: stronger inhibition via D causes less inhibition of motor cortex and more movement

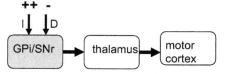

net effect: increased excitation via I causes more inhibition of motor cortex and less movement

FIGURE 5.10
Simplified view of the net effect of direct (D) and indirect (I) pathways on the inhibitory output of GPi/SNr (grey box) to the motor cortex. Thicker black arrows indicate stronger inhibitory output to the motor cortex. Upper panel: stronger inhibition of Gpi/SNr by D leads to *less inhibition* (more movement) of the motor cortex. Lower panel: stronger excitation of GPi/SNr by I leads to *more inhibition* (less movement) of the motor cortex.

other action presentations. Action selection (e.g. a backhand volley) would then result from the D1-dominant direct pathway selecting the most salient action. This is accomplished by 'breaking through' (disinhibiting) the barrier of tonic inhibition on the motor cortex exerted by GPi/SNr, and subsequently activating motor execution in the cortex.

The direct pathway, with two successive inhibitory links, is assumed to be particularly effective in producing rapid sequences of activity, by inhibiting in GPi only one pool of neurons at a time described as 'loser takes all' (Berns & Sejnowski, 1998). A possible scenario is that phasic dopamine release by neurons of the substantia nigra (SNc) in the striatum then serves as the triggering signal supporting selection of a single salient action among competing motor actions.[1]

The discovery of the differential inhibitory effect of direct and indirect pathways in motor control was also crucial for understanding the cause of Parkinson's and Huntington's diseases. In Parkinson's patients a drastic reduction of dopamine projections from SNc to D1 receptors reduces the inhibitory activity of the direct pathway, leading to a net reduction of cortical excitability and movement. In contrast, Huntington's disease is characterized by a degeneration of structures in the striatum, especially of Gabaergic and cholinergic neurons in the nucleus caudatus and putamen. This leads to an increased effect of inhibitory input along the indirect pathway to GPe/STN, with as net effect an increase of cortical excitability and movements.

Cortical organization: three systems of motor control

The principal task of the motor system of the brain is to transform plans of action in movements. There is good evidence that this process is carried out hierarchically: plans are translated in coarse actions, followed by more precise movements. The individual components of action do not have to 'roll off' in a strict serial sequence, but may also be carried out in overlapping segments of time. Three areas in the anterior cortex are involved in the preparation and execution of motor actions (see Figure 5.11).

These are in respective order the supplementary motor region (SMA), the premotor cortex and the motor cortex (M1, precentral gyrus or area 4). Area 8, located in front of the premotor cortex, is called the frontal eye fields (FEF) and is specifically important for regulation of eye-movements. More anteriorly located areas are responsible for programming of actions, while more posterior areas are involved in execution of actions. The posterior-parietal cortex (areas 5 and 7) also contributes to the preparation

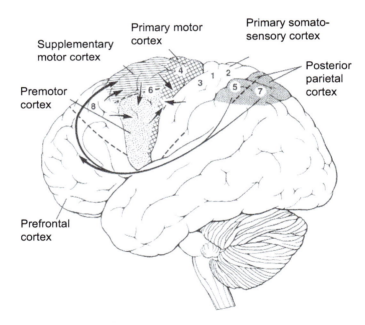

FIGURE 5.11
The main cortical areas (in dark boxes) involved in motor control in humans: the motor cortex (area 4 or M1), area 6 with SMA (medial part) and premotor cortex (lateral part). Area 8 represents the frontal eye fields (FEF). Posterior parietal regions (5 and 7 have many projections to the SMA.

Source: From Kandel et al. (1991).

and execution of motor actions. Not motor control is its principal role, but rather the translation of perception to action programs, and to provide the spatial coordinates of movement.

Kosslyn and Koenig have characterized the SMA, the premotor and motor cortex respectively, as the action programming, the instructions-generating and the movement execution subsystem. These three subsystems, to be described in greater detail, have a hierarchical relationship, with the higher systems sending output to the lower systems (see Figure 5.12). It is important to note that during the learning of motor skills, the three subsystems as depicted in Figure 5.12 will become differentially engaged, depending on the stage of learning. Early learning, for example, will make stronger demands on attentional and execution processes underlying the planning of actions. During more advanced stages of skill leaning, emphasis will shift to instruction generating and execution of movements, with cognitive demands gradually playing a more subordinate role.

SMA: the action programming system

The action programming system is located in the SMA, in the medial premotor cortex. The basal ganglia also participate in the control functions of the SMA via the 'complex loop', mentioned earlier. Their primary function is to support action programming, as well as the subsequent stage, instructions generation. According to Kosslyn and Koenig, the task of SMA is to provide higher order planning of movement or a 'set of goals or subgoals' to the instructions generating system.

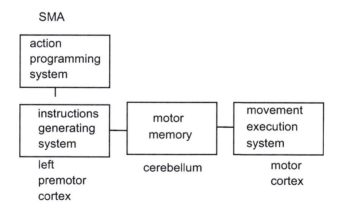

FIGURE 5.12
Three major motor subsystems, according to Kosslyn and Koenig: the action programming system, instructions generating system and movement execution system. The cerebellum is assumed to play a role in motor memory.

Human as well as animal research has shown that the SMA is involved in the timing of complex movements, internally as well as externally generated. A compelling case that demonstrates the involvement of SMA in high-level planning is a PET-scan study in which subjects were asked to move their fingers in a specific sequence, or to imagine making the same movement. The first condition activated M1 as well as SMA; the second condition only the SMA, suggesting a higher, more abstract function of SMA in motor control (Goldberg, 1985; Requin et al., 1992).

A number of studies using functional imaging of the brain have also focused on the differential role of the SMA and premotor cortex in motor learning. The general trend of these data is that initial learning, when the brain still relies on guidance by external input, is controlled by a circuit involving the SMA and dorsolateral prefrontal cortex. In this stage, motor learning occurs primarily at the level of action plans (and the formation of associated representations in motor memory) and not on the level of movement execution. At more advanced levels of learning, the activation pattern of the brain gradually becomes more dependent on the premotor and posterior parietal cortex and, at the subcortical level, on the striatum and the cerebellum, to guide motor behavior (see chapter 6). The final output of both circuits is the motor cortex, responsible for the execution of movement.

Premotor cortex: the instructions-generating system

The instruction-generatings system's task is to unravel the abstract action plan into several operational components, serving to instruct the motor system. One assumes that it is located in the premotor cortex, with the basal ganglia also contributing to this system via the complex loop. The premotor cortex receives massive input from the posterior parietal region, which provides the spatial coordinates of movement paths. For example, in the event of damage to this area, monkeys can no longer grasp an object if the immediate path is blocked by a transparent object. In that case they are unable to make a move 'around the object'. The premotor cortex could also play a critical role in learning novel movement trajectories. This seems to mainly involve the larger muscles of the trunk and arms, and not the smaller ones. Some areas in the premotor cortex might even possess qualities of movement execution, although this would represent the principle of 'weak modularity'. The left premotor cortex is presumed to have a special role in language production (Figure 5.12).

Motor cortex: the movement execution system

The motor cortex serves to perform more refined movements, like grabbing an object with the fingers of the hand. In particular it controls movements of the contralateral parts of the body. Although the basal ganglia also form part of this system via the 'motor loop', the cerebellum seems to be the primary subcortical structure to assist the control of movement execution. An additional role assigned to the cerebellum is that of motor memory. But this would mainly concern fully automatized actions, where the movement execution system provides the correct movement coordinates, without the intervention of the premotor cortex or SMA. The fact that many neurons in the motor area connect directly with motor neurons in the spinal cord, is consistent with its direct involvement in movement executions.

Finally, links between the primary motor cortex and the premotor cortex may also be critical in assisting the system that generates instructions, for example by providing feedback or correction of small deviations in the computation of the movement trajectories, (an additional possibility is that parts of the instruction system are embodied in the cerebellum). The motor cortex is organized somatotopically, meaning that each part of the body is represented in a separate part of the cortex. Especially the hands, the face and the vocal apparatus are projected to relatively large areas in the primary motor cortex. Neurons in the motor cortex are also involved in coding of the direction of movement. This was confirmed by Georgopoulus, who found that the direction of specific reach movements in the monkey corresponded with the firing of specific groups of cells in its motor cortex. The broadness of the firing pattern indicated that movement trajectories in the primary motor cortex are represented according to the principle of vector or coarse coding, and not according to precise coding (similar to coding for orientation of lines in the primary visual cortex).

BOX 5.4   THE GRASPING BRAIN

Grasping of objects is controlled by spatial as well as motor areas in the brain, in which spatial movements are prepared and executed. Figure 5.12 sketches the involved successive phases of the motor program followed in the brain. Grasping involves the intraparietal and supplementary motor areas (SMA), but the cerebellum as well. These areas represent the plan of action, independent of the actual involvement of the muscles or limbs. An interesting finding is that the same areas in the brain were activated during artificial grasping movements, when subjects were trained to control a robot's arm by pushing buttons on a panel. This finding was verified in a fMRI study showing that artificial grasping activated almost the same motor areas that were active during natural grasping movements. This effect did not occur when pressing of the same buttons was not related to movements of the robot arm.

Source: Umilta et al. (2008), Frey et al. (2014), Scott et al. (2015).

From perception to action

Introduction

For many years it was commonly assumed that by the time motor processing begins, cognitive processes have already decided what to do, and that only a single motor program is prepared before the initiation of movement. However, the neural system does not appear to support this assumption. Control of actions is a process that can only be fully understood by considering its interactions with perceptual processes. Our daily communication with the outside world is based on the continuous flow of information from the perceptual to the motor systems and vice versa. Interaction with the environment involves continuous and simultaneous processes of sensorimotor control and action selection, from the distributed representations of a limited number of response options.

A central role in controlling the link between perception and action is played by the posterior parietal cortex (PPC), lying at the cross-point of sensory areas and the motor areas in the frontal cortex. Its target areas (or 'effectors') in the anterior cortex involve the lateral premotor cortex and frontal eye fields. The dual role of various regions in the PPC network is to provide the spatial coordinates of the intended action, and to preset the effectors that – on the basis of available information – are part of the planned movement. In such a distributed system, several actions can be specified simultaneously. In particular, when a reach direction is initially specified ambiguously by sensory information, neural activity arises in the motor and premotor cortex that spans the entire angular range of potential directions. Later, when the direction is specified more precisely, the directional spread of the neural population activity narrows to reflect this choice. The following sections consider some models of interaction between the perception and action systems, and the neural systems in which they are implemented.

BOX 5.5 VOLUNTARY MOVEMENTS AND FREE WILL

Are voluntary actions produced by a previous subjective intention a reflection of 'free will'? One way to find out is to measure the electrical activity of the brain (the EEG) before and during a voluntary movement. In the EEG a slow negative wave, known as the 'readiness potential' (RP), shows up before overt movements, like a voluntary button press. The RP is manifested most clearly when recorded from the scalp over the central scalp site (Cz), just above the motor cortex. Usually, the RP its more substantial on the scalp site contralateral to the side of the overt motor activity.

continued

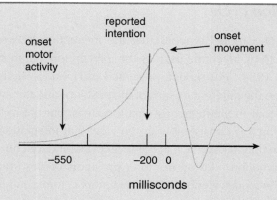

Libet et al. recorded the RP while asking subjects to press a button at voluntarily chosen moments. They were instructed to report the earliest moment that they became aware of the intention to press the button, by remembering the position of a rotating pointer on a clock as a time marker (Libet et al., 1982). It turned out that the onset of the RP occurred already 350 milliseconds earlier than the reported time (see insert).[2] The implications of Libet's study stirred many discussions, because they were taken as brain-based evidence that 'free will' rests on an illusion. We think to be the initiator of our actions, but the actual initiator is the brain, which is one step ahead of our subjective conscious experience. Later, Haggard and Eimer used a slightly modified version of the Libet task, in which the subject had to make a voluntary choice between a left and right button presses. In this case, the reported moment of conscious intention appeared to occur more in synchrony with the onset of the RP. The authors concluded that conscious intention is a phenomenon associated with response selection when it involves a choice from a repertoire of actions programs.

Models of social behavior of free will (see Lim et al., 2007), often use the predictability of behavior as the crucial defining criterion. Free will could be that two people, under the same circumstances, would choose to do different things. It could also imply that one person, under the same conditions, might do any of several things. But often one these conditions is not met. For example, on the basis of past behavior of individual persons, their future behavior may be highly predictable. Human behavior often follows predictable and automatic patterns, and is certainly not random in a statistical sense. Indeed, if free will is understood as either a predictable or consciously planned act, many forms of human behavior are not free, because they are triggered automatically with no conscious experience. Consciousness perhaps only applies to those cases when a new behavioral routine has to be learned, an old routine to be interrupted, or when an error needs to be corrected.

Source: Libet (1985), Haggard & Eimer (1999), Haggard et al. (2002), Lim et al. (2007), Soon et al. (2008).

Perception-action cycle

An early example of a model emphasizing the interaction between perception and action was referred to by Joachim Fuster as the 'perception action cycle' (Fuster, 1990; Quintana & Fuster, 1999). His model, presented in Figure 5.13 shows the reciprocal connections between the different regions of the posterior and the anterior cortex. These connections only occur in the higher association areas, but not in the primary sensory and motor areas, which is consistent with the view that integration of perceptual and action knowledge mainly takes place at the level of secondary cortical areas.

Perceptual information relevant to motor programs comes from different sources. One source is proprioceptive feedback from receptors in joints and muscles of the limbs that perform movements. Another important source of information is the location system in the posterior parietal cortex, situated at the interface between perception and action (Spence & Driver, 2004). It informs the higher motor areas responsible for preparing action plans, about the location of the target stimulus. In particular, the lateral intraparietal sulcus (LIP) in the parietal cortex might be an important site for perceptual decision-making. Neurons in the LIP of macaques trained to make saccades to visual target locations, exhibit firing rates that ramp upward during decision-making, assumedly reflecting the gradual accumulation of evidence toward a decision threshold. (Churchland et al., 2008). The process of evidence accumulation has been theorized to arise from the integration of noisy sensory signals by a bounded neural integrator, whose crossing of the activation threshold triggers a perceptual decision leading to motor action (Murakami et al., 2014).

In the model shown in Figure 5.13 various sensory and motor regions in the cortex are connected through vertical as well as horizontal reciprocal pathways. The vertical arrows indicate that cortical regions communicate in a top-down as well as in a bottom-up fashion *within* the sensory and motor hierarchies. The horizontal arrows indicate that beyond the primary sensory regions perceptual information also flows *between* the sensory and motor regions. The functional architecture of such a network accommodates serial processing within, as well as parallel processing between perception and action levels.

Given these conditions, the translation between perception and action can be expressed in a mix of serial, as well as in more continuous modes, of processing. In a strictly serial S-R model perceptual information would flow from primary to secondary areas, upstream in the sensory hierarchy, and then flow back via the secondary motor areas to motor units in the spinal cord. An alternative being that information delivered by the perceptual pathways to the secondary sensory cortices builds up gradually, and starts activating the secondary motor areas in a relatively early phase of processing. In this regard, it is important to note that the 'boxes' representing the various cortical areas in Figure 5.13 should not be interpreted as serial stages of processing. They rather

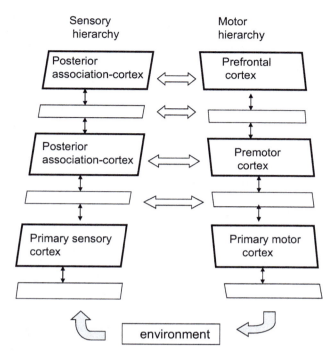

FIGURE 5.13
The perception-action cycle as depicted by Fuster (1990). Sensory and motor hierarchies in the posterior and anterior association cortices communicate with another via reciprocal pathways.

represent distributed networks, encapsulating smaller local networks, each representing smaller units of processing. This allows a mode of processing in which partial information from smaller units could already start to activate the motor system. For example, a young man may assume that the red hat in the crowd belongs to his fiancée, and starts waving his hand. Seconds later he discovers to his dismay that the hat belongs to someone else. On the brain level, this would probably have been reflected in activation of a neural assembly in the young man's premotor cortex, by the combined input from the color module in V4, and the supplementary motor cortex where the action plan is stored. Such a scenario would be compatible with the 'relatively continuous flow' model of information processing, with perceptual stages activating response channels on the basis of incomplete information.[3]

Response competition and affordance

Translating plans of action into movements is an extremely complex process, when all the participating structures in the brain are taken into account. In this process different motor plans will presumably compete with another. Importantly, the more recent studies clarify that it is hard to locate a specific 'locus' of decision making in the brain. More likely the decision to respond is made in distributed networks connecting posterior and anterior areas, possibly where there is a functional overlap in perception and motor functions. Here the process of deliberating between different options to act, is manifested in a competition within the sensorimotor system (premotor and primary motor cortex), combining information about potential actions (from the visual and parietal cortex) and evidence in favor of one action versus another (from the prefrontal cortex).

Mathematical modeling of simulated data shows that multiple potential actions within populations of cells in the frontal parietal cortex engage in a competition for overt execution (Cisek, 2006, 2007). This competition is influenced by a variety of biases, such as reward value or a sense of urgency. A bias could originate in prefrontal and supplementary motor areas (e.g. action selection, presetting the motor system) or in the basal ganglia (the urge to respond fast and even prematurely, see also Forstmann et al., 2010). On the basis of animal studies, Paul Cisek and David Thura suggested that activation of the basal ganglia reflects a 'commitment to a cortically determined choice', but not necessarily a selection of the target of movements. Their studies followed an 'ethological' approach, followed in models of decision making processes, that are inspired by the natural way animals interact with their environment. Central in this research framework are concepts like 'embodied cognition' and 'affordance' introduced by the American psychologist James Gibson.

Embodied cognition, in animal as well as in man, implies features of cognition that are already present in the body system. For example, the intelligent behavior of an octopus depends largely on the enormous amount of nerve chords in its eight arms, which makes these function as an extended brain. Affordances are implicit cues, delivered by perceptual objects, for possible action like the handle on a tea pot providing an obvious cue for holding.[4] Planning to grasp an object may also affect visual processing of task-relevant information in a search task.

The model that guided this research (Figure 5.14) illustrates the various circuits involved in motor control at the cortical and subcortical level. The reciprocal pathways between the posterior and anterior cortices regulate specification (movement planning) of actions. These cortical regions contain the representations of potential actions that compete with one another. If decisions depend on bottom-up visual features, like the salience of a visual object, the decision will initiate in the posterior cortex and move on to the anterior regions. The involved circuit then follows serial models, describing the flow of information through a number of intermediate stations or processing stages.

In contrast, if the parameters of potential actions using visual information are more complex, the decision should emerge from neurons in the prefrontal cortex before propagating back to the parietal cortex. The cortical regions are amplified by signals from the

PERCEPTION AND ACTION

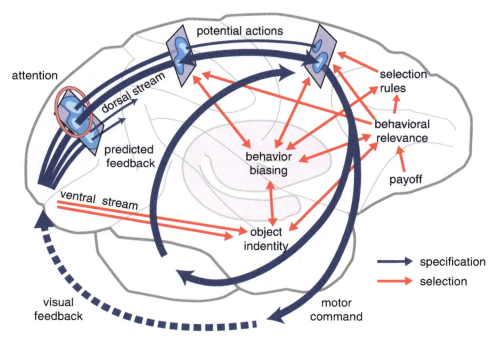

FIGURE 5.14
Affordance competition model of visually guided movement in the primate brain. Blue arrows: competing action selection in the dorsal stream. Red arrow below: ventral stream. Response competition is biased by input from the basal ganglia and prefrontal cortex that collect information for action selection (red arrows in the upper-right corner).

Source: From Cisek & Kalaska (2010). See text for further clarification.

basal ganglia and the prefrontal cortex, which bias the gain and the selection (decision and execution of actions). The basal ganglia modulate the competition taking place at several cortical loci. Because of reciprocal connectivity, their effect is reflected over a large portion of the cerebral cortex.

Cisek's model shares some interesting characteristics with Foster's earlier representation of the perception-action cycle. Both models are based on the functional architecture of the monkey brain, and present a distributed hierarchical system of neural processing. Hierarchies may embrace spatial, temporal as well as functional properties of neural networks (see also Felleman & Van Essen, 1991). Interestingly, a distributed hierarchical system accommodates several modes of processing of information, depending on the demands of or interactions with the environment. They allow: a) serial as well as parallel processing, b) top-down as well as bottom-up pathways, and c) modular as well as distributed processing. In line with option c, Kaiser et al. (2010) describe how distributed networks in the brain may function on the basis of a hierarchy of modules where higher order modules form 'hubs' that incorporate lower order sub modules by a process called 'repeated encapsulation'. Their role would be to form a 'super module' for multisensory integration (see also Zamora-López, 2010).

Modules show functional overlap, instead of being strictly delineated. Regions with many interregional connections, like the amygdala, the hippocampus, the lateral intraparietal area (LIP), and area 7, and perhaps also the basal ganglia, could function as hubs. Modules on top of the hierarchy may even expand to larger networks in the parietal and somatosensory areas of the cortex. The action plans themselves probably reside in the same areas of the frontal cortex that are responsible for the control of actions. Selecting the plan requires coordination between the SMA region relying on internal sources, and the premotor area relying on external sources needed to guide action (Rosenbaum, 1991). External sources to the premotor cortex are the posterior parietal and temporal cortices, the end stations of dorsal and ventral streams containing respectively spatial and object related representations.

Taken together, models of action selection seem compatible with the principle of biased competition, which also provides a framework for theories of visual attention. The most likely arena for competition between action plans would be the network connecting anterior and posterior cortices. Another area in the brain often related to response competition is the anterior cingulate, buried in the depth of the frontal lobe. This area seems to specifically engage the evaluation or monitoring of responses in reaction tasks, specifically designed to induce high response conflict. An example is pressing a right button on a response panel to a central arrow pointing to the right, flanked by arrows pointing to the left (e.g. < < < > < < <). Several studies using electrophysiological as well as fMRI measures found stronger neural activity in the anterior cingulate area in incompatible, compared to compatible, trials.

The role of the parietal cortex revisited

The numerous functions of the parietal cortex can be globally divided in a 'sensory' and a 'motor' network. The sensory network receives input from the extrastriate regions via the dorsal route. The stream is not unified, but progressively diverges into parallel subsystems, each specialized toward the demands of different sensorimotor functions and effectors, each of which specifies the spatial parameters of different kinds of potential actions. In such a distributed system, several actions can be specified simultaneously in advance. For example, when a reach direction is initially specified ambiguously by sensory information, neural activity arises in the motor and premotor cortex that spans the entire angular range of potential directions. Later, when the direction is specified, activity narrows to reflect this choice (Crammond & Kalaska, 1996). Studies of rodents and primates have suggested that the posterior parietal cortex (PPC) is also implicated in perceptual decision-making, with PPC circuits even playing a causal role (Zhong et al., 2019).

PERCEPTION AND ACTION

The motor network has mainly efferent connections with anterior areas (e.g. the premotor cortex and frontal eye fields), involved in the regulation of motor programs and ocular-motor processes. It is assisted by regions 5 and 7a of the parietal cortex, which have many output connections with the premotor region in the anterior cortex.[5] The motor network in PPC also involves a parallel distributed circuitry that, analogous to the sensory network, subserves various effectors like arm reaching, grasping, gaze and eye-movements (see Box 5.6 for the respective areas involved in the monkey brain). This is consistent with the idea that before the selection of the effectors, reach and saccade plans already begin to be specified simultaneously by different parts of the PPC. Indeed, during natural activity, eye and hand movements are usually executed in unison.

BOX 5.6 AREAS IN THE POSTERIOR PARIETAL CORTEX OF THE MONKEY WITH EQUIVALENT FUNCTION IN HUMANS

The intraparietal sulcus (IPS) of the supra-parietal lobe contains four major regions:

1. The lateral intraparietal (LIP) contains a map of neurons, representing the saliency of and attention to spatial locations. The oculomotor system uses it for targeting eye movements, when appropriate.

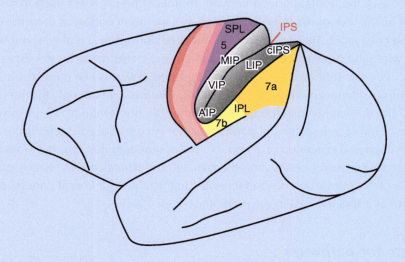

2. The ventral intraparietal (VIP) area receives input from various senses (visual, somatosensory, auditory and vestibular). Neurons with tactile receptive fields

continued

> represent space in a head-centered reference frame. The cells with visual receptive fields also fire with head-centered reference frames, but possibly also with eye-centered coordinates.
>
> 3   The medial intraparietal (MIP) area neurons encode the location of a reach target in nose-centered coordinates.
>
> 4   The anterior intraparietal (AIP) area contains neurons that are responsible for grasping and manipulating objects through the motor and visual inputs. They are responsive to shape, size and orientation of these objects The AIP and ventral premotor cortex working together, are responsible for visuomotor transformations for actions of the hand.
>
> Source: Insert adapted from Grefkes & Fink (2005).

Areas 7 and 5 also are of special importance for controlling processes like reaching and grasping objects. Damage to the motor network in the left hemisphere leads to apraxia, a motor disorder that is based upon a deficiency in the central programming of complex movements. A finer mapping of regions that function as interfaces between the perceptive and motor systems is found in the intraparietal sulcus (IPS). The IPS in humans lies at the base of the supra-parietal lobule (see Box 5.6 for details).

The role of the frontal-parietal network in linking perception to action also sheds new light on the 'mirror neurons' in the monkey's premotor cortex, as described by Rizzollati and colleagues. These neurons not only fired during the actual grasp movements, but also when the monkey observed the same movements made by the experimenter (Box 5.7). Human studies using fMRI also reported activation of cortical areas when subjects observed movements made by humans. This involved not only the inferior frontal gyrus, but the inferior parietal lobule and the superior temporal sulcus as well. No proof was found of a single neural population that encodes specific actions during both the observation and execution of action. Note that similar to humans, the monkey brain has numerous pathways connecting the parietal and frontal cortex, which opens the possibility of the mirror neurons in fact reflecting activity of a frontal parietal network, rather than of a specific area in the premotor cortex.

Oculomotor pathways

The oculomotor system is the system *par excellence* linking perception to action. Seeing and looking are strongly interactive processes during which the eyes, controlled by the brain, continuously scan and explore the visual environment. More complex objects,

BOX 5.7 MIRROR NEURONS: FACT AND MYTH

Mirror neurons were discovered in 1990 by Rizzolatti who placed depth electrodes in the premotor cortex (F1) of the monkey. To his surprise, the monkey not only showed activity in the premotor area when it grasped the food, but also when it watched the experimenter grasping it. The finding of Rizzolatti had a significant impact on the scientific world as well as on the general public, considering it as a discovery of the neural basis of social cognition, empathy and possibly even of a 'theory of mind'. The latter term introduced by David Premack implies the ability to assign feelings, thoughts and intentions to oneself and to others. Applied to humans, a popular behavioral example often quoted in this context is a baby copying someone's smile. These reactions would not only activate the brain areas associated with the mouth and facial muscles, but also reflect the baby's rudimentary understanding of the feeling or intentions of the other person.

Later fMRI studies with human subject discovered mirror-like neurons in other areas of the brain such as the parietal cortex, suggesting the involvement of a parietal-frontal circuit, rather than an isolated area in the premotor cortex. Questions were also raised about the functional meaning of mirror neurons and its associated cognitive functions. Perhaps the 'link' between perception and action is built into the human and animal biological system, activating neurons or networks in the brain associated with both 'seeing' and 'action'. It is well known that posterior and anterior brain areas in monkeys as well as in humans are linked to each other in a perception-action cycle. This could have been a benefit in the course of evolution. If action programmes in the brain are automatically set up when observing biologically relevant events, they are also better prepared for quick and efficient actions.

Sources: Kilner & Lemon (2013), Hickok (2009).

or conspicuous points in the visual field are examined more thoroughly than simple objects or less interesting points. Measurement of the eye-movements often reveal interesting 'scan-paths', i.e. mappings of the trajectory of the eye (Figure 5.15).

The main components and circuits of the oculomotor system are captured in Figure 5.16. A central player is area 7 in the *parietal cortex*, receiving input from the visual areas (17, 18, and 19). Area 7 controls both saccades and the slow pursuit movements of the eye, using circuits to the *superior colliculus* and *frontal eye fields* (FEF, area 8). The FEF controls voluntary eye movements as well as saccades, the superior colliculus mainly the involuntary or reflexive saccades.

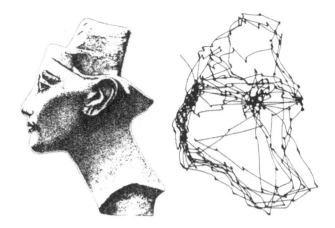

FIGURE 5.15
A 'scan-path' of eye-movements and saccades when viewing a complex figure. Significant points such as ear, nose, and eye are more frequently looked at and fixated than less significant points.

Source: Adapted from Yarbus, (1967). Springer Nature, permission nr 4553571269415.

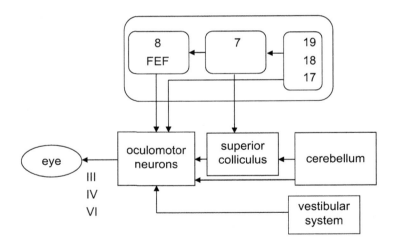

FIGURE 5.16
Diagram showing afferent and efferent connections of the oculomotor system. The FEF (frontal eye fields) and superior colliculus control saccades and movements of the eye. They both receive input from area 7 that is involved in the selection of locations in space. This area, in turn, receives input from the occipital cortex (areas 17, 18 and 19). Area 19 controls the depth of view and vergence of the eyes. The vestibular system regulates stabilization of the eyes during head movements. Cerebellum and superior colliculus are more specifically involved in automatic control of saccades and eye movements. III, IV and VI: optic nerves.

Source: Adapted from Kandel et al. (1991).

> **BOX 5.8 EYE CONTACT AND DETECTION OF THE DIRECTION OF GAZE**
>
> In both animals and humans, detection of the direction of eye gaze of others, such as looking away, direct eye contact, knowing what someone else is watching, plays an essential role in social contact. Dominance conflicts in animals often begin with looking at each other and ends when one of the animals turns its eyes away. Babies are capable of making eye-contact shortly after birth, suggesting that looking and detection of gaze is an innate trait, not developed by learning processes. Adults are often surprisingly aware if others look at them or do not, even when a person is in the periphery of their eye field. In particular, cells in the superior sulcus of the temporal lobe seem to respond to being fixated by the eyes of other persons. Autistic children can detect the direction of gaze and make eye contact, but seem to have difficulty understanding the implicated intent or emotion. For example when they are asked the question, 'which girl does Jimmy like most?', in a comic book showing Jimmy looking at Suzy but not to Anny. It is also interesting that babies from two blind parents, despite normal social development, tend to make less frequent eye contacts with other adults.
>
> Source: Baron-Cohen et al. (1995), Farroni et al. (2002), Senju et al. (2015).

Although both systems can function independently, their efferent pathways converge in common oculomotor nuclei of the brain stem. Voluntary and involuntary oculomotor pathways can also become engaged in a kind of competition. An automatic saccade, for example, triggered by a significant or sudden-onset stimulus, can be suppressed or even disrupted by the voluntary (FEF) system, in the early phase of the saccade (van Zoest et al., 2004).

Oculomotor neurons control the eye muscles through the cranial nerves and carry both a velocity and a position signal. If after a movement of the head the head stops, a neural integration mechanism will hold the eyes locked to the new position. This requires a mechanism at the cerebellar level. Oculomotor neurons therefore not only depend on the colliculi superior and FEF that control the eye movements, but also receive input from two reflexive mechanisms at the level of the brainstem. The first is the *vestibular system* initiated within the inner ear (the semicircular channels). It is driven by brainstem nuclei that correct the eye positions regulated by the oculomotor neurons for brief head movements. The second is the optokinetic system, which also depends on areas in the brain stem and regulates fixation of the eyes during slow and sustained head rotations.

BOX 5.9   EYE-TRACKERS ARE THERE TO HELP THE DISABLED

An eye tracker is a device for measuring positions of the of eye, most often by estimating gaze direction. The tracking device uses an infrared light source to illuminate the eye, in order to produce reflections that are captured by a camera. The images are then analyzed to identify the angle of the reflections, to calculate the direction of the gaze. Eye-tracking technology is used for many different purposes, but one of is most exciting applications has been to help patients with a neuromuscular disease called amyotrophic lateral sclerosis, also known as ALS, to communicate with the outside world. In people with ALS, the eyes are often the only part of the body that isn't paralyzed, making most products that require hand handling unusable for them. Wheelchair patients, not being able to even handle a joystick to steer their vehicle, can after some training learn to use movements of their eyes to control directional signs projected to a small TV screen attached to the wheel chair, interfaced to the electric steering system.

Most notably perhaps is that eye-tracking systems enable cursor control on a projected computer keyboard. Modern eye tracking systems, connected with a computer interface and special software, allow patients to control their computer, similar to the way a mouse lets you control it with your hand, or let you type letters using a word-processor. Since the eye muscles generally do not fatigue with use, the current devices can be used for an extended period of time.

The late Stephen Hawking, perhaps the most famous ALS patient ever, used a specially designed system attached to his wheelchair to control the mouse in Windows, allowing him to check his email, surf the internet, and to write lectures or an article. The software included a word prediction algorithm, using his former writings and vocabulary as a database that only needed to type the first couple of characters to select the whole word. After losing his voice, Stephen was even able to present lectures, by sending his created manuscripts to a speech synthesizer, and playing the speech file back to an audience.

Sources: Ball et al. (2007), Spataro et al. (2014).

Finally, two other cortical areas are involved in adaptive control of eye movements. These are the *occipital visual cortex* – also called the occipital eye field – and the *cerebellum*. Occipital eye fields are not only important for the control of pursuit movements of the eye and saccades, but also in regulating of the vergence of the eyes (eyes moving in different direction to keep the image positioned on both fovea), and the optokinetic nystagmus. Finally, this system also depends on adaptive control by the cerebellum, modulating the synaptic sensitivity of oculomotor neurons. The precise workings and locations of these feedback and modulating mechanisms however are not known.

Time perception

Time as such is not perceived, only the temporal relationship between certain events: after lightning we expect thunder, for example. Time perception is a multifaceted process involving perception, memory, awareness and the motor system, and so is a good example for the close connection between perception and action. Temporal coding also forms an essential aspect of episodic memory, which implies memory of people and events in a spatial temporal context. Taking account of the role of hippocampus in episodic memory (further elaborated in Chapter 6), it is likely that its cells also play a role in encoding of the sequence of events and laying down a temporal context that bind elements of an episodes together. The following paragraphs, however, will highlight aspects of temporal processing within the context of perception and action in perceptual-motor tasks.

Playing an instrument or a computer game requires accurate perceptual, as well as motor, timing. Time perception also plays a part in our daily subjective experience: sometimes time seems to be running fast, on other occasions very slow. Anticipation and preparation of predictable events lead to more efficient and faster motor reactions. The time interval between the unconditional (UCS) and conditional stimulus (CS) plays a critical role in conditioning. Events that took place recently are estimated to have happened further back in time, and events that occurred a long time ago, are estimated to have happened closer in time.

A common element in theories regarding time perception is the notion of an internal clock or oscillatory mechanism that counts pulses, but different from the circadian clock that controls daily cycles of activity. Another important element is the assumption of an interval timing mechanism, in which current time is compared with some expected or reference time in long-term memory. This suggests an emphasis shift from a perception-driven to a memory-driven mechanism as the core element of time perception.

The major challenge of time-perception theories concerns the question of how timing is represented in the neural system (Oprisan & Buhusi, 2014). The currently accepted view is that perception of time depends on multiple areas such as the cerebellum, thalamus, basal ganglia, as well as on the higher cortical structures. The neurotransmitter dopamine also appears to affect the perception of time. In the quest of neural analogs of an internal clock or oscillatory mechanism, patterns of synchronously firing neurons have become a central element in cognitive neuroscience theories of time perception.

Two varieties of the clock models are discussed next. Scalar expectance theory focuses primarily on identification of information processing components or 'stages' of time estimation. The striatal beat frequency model is a neural model of time perception, with neuromodulatory dynamics of the thalamocortical-striatal loops as central elements. The latter model can be seen as a neural implementation of some important components of the scalar expectancy theory.

Scalar expectancy theory (SET)

The scalar expectancy model is an influential information processing model of time estimation, initially developed by Michel Treisman in 1963 and further elaborated by John Gibbon (Gibbon et al., 1984; Gibbon & Church, 1984). Gibbon developed the set model to account for the pattern of behavior seen in animals, being reinforced to respond at fixed intervals. It divides the temporal processing system into three stages: a clock, memory and decision stage (Figure 5.17). The steps of the model are briefly summarized below.

▶ A stimulus that signals the start of a timed interval activates a switch, allowing pulses from a pacemaker to enter an accumulator. The resulting accumulation of pulses represents the elapsed time, which value is continuously sent to the working memory.

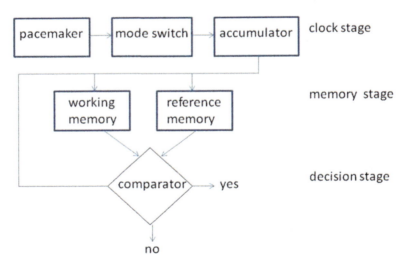

FIGURE 5.17
Scalar expectancy model of time estimation containing a clock stage, memory stage and decision stage.

Source: After Gibbon & Church (1984). See text for clarification.

- When reinforcement happens at the end of the timed interval, the time value is stored in a long-term memory (reference memory) as the expected time to reinforcement.
- During timing of the interval, the animal is continually comparing the current time (stored in working memory) to the expected time (stored in reference memory). More specifically, the animal continually samples from its long-term memory values of past trials, at which reinforcement occurred and compares these memory samples with the current values on its clock (comparator mechanism in Figure 5.17).
- The comparison mechanism calculates the ratio of current to expected time. When this is less than a criterion value it responds (yes), when the ratio is larger it does not respond. The set model accounts for a key observation in psychophysics called the Weber-Fechner law, implying that timing accuracy is relative to the size of the interval being timed. This is the 'scalar' property that gives the model its name. For example, when timing a 10 sec interval an animal might be accurate to within 1 sec, and when timing a 100 sec interval the animal would be accurate to only about 10 sec.

Neural models of timing

Perception of time is strongly tied to attention biases and expectations with regard to spatial, feature-based and action-related properties. Accordingly, temporal expectations may contribute to preset the neural mechanisms involved in the processing of forthcoming perceptual events or selection of actions (Nobre & van Eede, 2018). The ability to time intervals in the milliseconds range relies on different neural systems, associated with two forms of timing: explicit and implicit (e.g. Rao et al., 2007).

Explicit timing is used in estimating the duration of stimuli. Implicit timing refers to predicting or expecting the occurrence of an event in the near future, for example in conditioning or in practiced skills. These two forms of time-estimation do not involve the same neuroanatomical areas. Implicit timing often occurs in highly practiced motor tasks, involving the cerebellum, basal ganglia and primary motor cortex (see for example the motor loop in Figure 5.8). Explicit timing involves the supplementary motor area, the right prefrontal cortex and the basal ganglia (more in line with the complex loop of Figure 5.8).

Striatal Beat Frequency Model (SBF)

Current timing models have emphasized the role of neural oscillations in providing the 'raw material' analogous to the pulses or ticking of a clock. Ensembles of cortical glutamatergic pyramidal neurons (recall that glutamate is the major excitatory neurotransmitter in the nervous system) oscillate with varying intrinsic frequencies. Notably, some of these models suggested the involvement of the striatofrontal dopaminergic system, with the striatum functioning as the core timing system. The striatal spiny neurons integrate an astonishingly large number of afferents. Moreover, their oscillatory firing patterns occur in synchrony with conditioned time estimation, suggesting a mechanism involved in the detection of coincidence. Coincidence refers to a process by which a neural network encodes information by detecting the occurrence of temporally close, but spatially distributed input signals. These findings are of particular importance, because they might represent the neural analog of the internal clock, postulated in earlier information processing models of timing. Lesions of the striatum result in deficiencies in both temporal-production and temporal-discrimination procedures.

In their SBF model, Meck and colleagues proposed that timing is coded in the striatum by the coincidental activation of neurons, which produces firing bursts with periods spanning a much wider range of duration than single neurons (Meck et al., 2008). Populations of cortical (and thalamic) neurons phase reset (synchronize), and begin oscillating at their endogenous periodicities (the clock stage onset see also the left upper panel of Figure 5.18). After the cortical oscillators are synchronized at the onset of a trial, they will start to oscillate at a fixed frequency throughout the criterion interval. This property accounts for the close correspondence between aspects of interval timing and working memory performance, which are supposed to depend on the same neural representation of a specific stimulus.

According to the SBF model, the dopaminergic burst released from VTA (ventral tegmental area) serves three purposes. First, it triggers the synchronization of the cortical oscillators. Second, the sustained oscillatory activity reflects attentional activation of the thalamocortical-striatal circuits. Third, the burst at the expected time of reward reflects the updating and encoding of corticostriatal transmission.

Dopamine release from the substantia nigra pars compacta (SNc) at signal onset works in a similar fashion to reset the weights of the synaptic connections in the dorsal striatum (right panel of Figure 5.18). Learning-dependent changes in corticostriatal transmission are assumed to occur through corticostriatal long-term potentiation (LTP, see Chapter 6 for details). These changes make the striatal neurons more likely to detect the specific pattern of activation of cortical oscillators, at the time of reward delivery and/or feedback. The adjustment of corticostriatal synaptic weights (similar to the memory stage in the scalar expectancy theory) allows the striatal spiny neurons to discriminate and become 'tuned' to specific patterns of coincident oscillatory activity, increasing the likelihood of firing upon similar patterns of cortical activation in the future.

In sum, the role of cortical oscillation patterns in the striatum is to detect coincident activation between two successive events (i.e. patterns in those oscillations that mark relevant durations). The median spiny neurons in the striatum are able to detect these patterns, like recognizing musical chords, by acting as coincidence detectors or

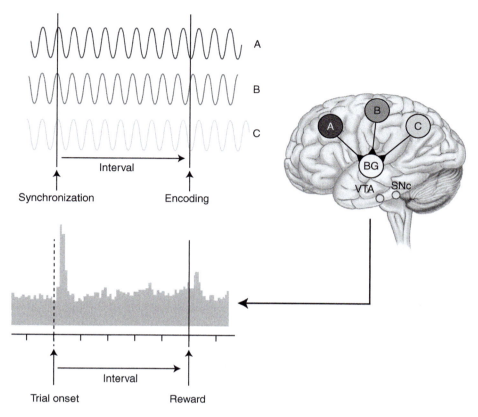

FIGURE 5.18
Striatal beat frequency model with three hypothetical oscillatory thalamic-cortical neurons (A, B and C) projecting to spiny neurons in the dorsal striatum of the basal ganglia (BG). Neurons in striatum continuously compare the current pattern of activation of cortical cells with the pattern detected at the time of the reward (coincidence detection). Dopaminergic projections from the substantia nigra pars compacta (SNc) and ventral tegmental area (VTA) are active at trial onset, functioning as a 'start-gun' that synchronizes the cortical oscillators (black arrow) throughout the interval, possibly modulating corticostriatal transmission, and at the expected time of reward coding for an error in reward prediction. Lower left panel: firing striatal neurons detecting the coincidence of the three cortical oscillators at the criterion duration.

Source: Adapted from Buhusi & Meck (2005).

comparators. In this respect they function much like the decision stage in the scalar expectancy theory.[6]

Aging and time perception

With advanced age, time seems to run slower than at a younger age. One possible explanation is that the perceived passage of time is related to the amount of new perceptual information one absorbs. When you're young everything is new, which means your brain has more to process and the perceived passage of time seems longer. This notion fits with neurochemical research showing that the release of dopamine when perceiving novel stimuli starts to drop past the age of 20, which makes time appear to go by more quickly. In addition, age-related gradual loss of novelty detectors in the hippocampus could also be a factor (see also Eagleman, 2008).

Others have pointed to neural changes which take place with advancing age at a more basic level, and affect altered time perception more directly than via the compromised novelty detectors in the hippocampus. The slowing of the internal clock might also be responsible for the subjective impression that the pace of life appears to speed up. The slower one's internal clock runs relative to the passage of physical time, the stronger the subjective *under-estimation* of the duration of intervals relative to objective time. For example, a 5-s stimulus seems to last only 4 s. But when asked to spontaneously produce finger taps at a 3-s intervals, a slower clock leads to an *over-estimation* of the interval duration, as manifested in longer and more variable intertap-intervals of 4 s duration. In an information-processing framework like the set model, time perception depends on the counting of pulses that accumulate while marking the passage of time. The counted pulses are simultaneously passed on to working memory, where they are compared with standard values drawn from reference memory. When people get older, there is a gradual depletion of dopamine in the basal ganglia and substantia nigra (Cabeza et al., 2005), the same brain regions known to affect corticostriatal circuits that drive the internal clock. The effects of a decline of tonic and phasic dopamine release in these pathways on time perception, fit with the SBF model discussed previously: a slower clock with increased variability in clock speed. Thus, altered time perception with aging might be associated with fundamental changes in the functioning of the cortico-thalamic-basal ganglia circuits that implement timing in the hundredths of milliseconds-to-minutes range (Turgeon et al, 2016)

Notes

1   A problem with the basal ganglia functioning as an independent fast action selection filter is that the relatively slow conduction along the indirect pathway, as compared to that along the direct pathway, would result in premature activation of the 'focus', compared to the inhibition of competing movements (Nambu, 2008). More likely then is that action selection takes place in the cortex with the role of the basal ganglia more compatible with processes as learning, habit formation or response bias than on-line motor control (see Delong & Wichman, 2017, for a recent update of their 1985 parallel model). The prefrontal cortex, in particular, could be a key player in selecting actions from multiple alternatives, preferentially activating competing D1 and D2 pathways in basal ganglia.

2   Matsuhashi & Hallett (2008) presented auditory probes during preparation of spontaneous button presses, telling the subject to abort the intended response. Comparing the timing of probes and consequent actions allows to determine during which time period the participant was aware of their intention to act. The advantage of this method is that timing of an intention to act is measured in real-time rather than introspective after-action performance.

3   This relates to the problem of 'grain size' of information processing units as introduced by Jeff Miller (1988): a variable is more continuous to the extent that it has a small grain size, and more discrete to the extent that it has a large one. At the continuous extreme is a minimum unit of zero; at the discrete extreme is a minimum unit that covers the entire range of variation, so that no value lies between two other values. In summary, it makes sense to apply the terms discrete and continuous to variables with very large or small grain sizes.

4   Would indeed the handle of the teapot automatically emit a 'grasp' signal to the motor system of the tea-loving citizens of Great Britain?

5   Anatomical studies in the macaque cortex, and functional imaging studies in humans have demonstrated the existence of different cortical areas within the intraparietal sulcus (IPS). Such functional segregation, however, does not correlate with presently available architectonic maps of the human brain. This is particularly true for the classical Brodmann map, which is still widely used as an anatomical reference in functional imaging studies.

6   According to Meck et al., (2008): 'striatal output travels to the thalamus along two pathways: the direct (dopamine D1 receptor mediated) and indirect (dopamine D2 receptor mediated), then loops back to the cortex and striatum, influencing the rate of oscillatory activity and permitting alterations in clock speed by changing the input to striatal spiny neurons (and producing a response).' Notice that the direct and indirect pathways of the basal ganglia presumed to control timing in the SBF model (as quoted between the parentheses above) are largely identical to the direct and indirect pathways described earlier in this chapter (Figure 5.9).

6 Memory systems

CONTENTS

- ▶ Introduction: the multiple manifestations of memory
- ▶ Memory and the brain: varieties of memory
- ▶ Encoding and retrieval in explicit memory
- ▶ Explicit memory: circuits, deficits and mechanisms
- ▶ Implicit memory: priming, learning and mechanisms

Introduction: the multiple manifestations of memory

Memory, meaning the ability to learn, retain and retrieve information, is a critical element of cognition. It also constitutes its 'backbone': processes like selective attention, planning, execution of movements and consciousness all depend in various degrees on memory programs stored in brain networks. Human memory is localized in the sense that 'particular brain systems represent specific aspects of each event, and is distributed in the sense that many neural systems participate in representing the whole event' (Squire, 1992). The cortex is considered to be the primary site of our memories, in other words our knowledge of the world and ourselves. Its building blocks are representations; elementary networks where input is paired with output through patterns with excitatory and inhibitory weights. Representations can be copies of perceptual features that allow the brain to recognize objects or people, or segments of skilled movements that are part of a motor program. Memories are not stored in specific locations in the brain, but in populations of neurons assembled in distributed networks, according to the principles of coarse coding. In these networks, learning is accomplished via Hebbian principles, with synaptic connections between neurons changing their weight as learning progresses. Memory representations may also vary in the state of activation of their underlying neural assemblies, which may either be dormant or become temporarily activated by external or internal events.

The present chapter first focuses on some essential characteristics and definitions of memory mechanisms underlying the divisions in short- and long-term, implicit versus explicit memory, and memory operations involved in encoding and retrieval (see also Box 6.1. for a general orientation). The sections that follow focus on the neural basis of memories, in particular on neurochemical mechanisms involved in consolidation. Separate chapters are devoted to explicit and implicit forms of learning and consolidation, highlighting the involved cerebral structures and cellular mechanisms. Attention is paid to various types of amnesia and the insights these studies have provided to illuminate the neural structures and pathways underlying various types of memory. Other issues discussed are the causes of forgetting, the reminiscence 'bump', memory decline as an aspect of normal aging and childhood amnesia.

> ## BOX 6.1 FORMS AND DEFINITIONS OF MEMORY
>
> ▶ Large-scale network: a term referring to neural systems that are distributed across the entire extent of the brain, in particular, the cortex.
>
> ▶ Memory: the ability to learn, retain and retrieve information.
>
> ▶ Long-term memory: a long-lasting store of information residing in various cortical regions of the cortex.
>
> ▶ Short-term memory: a temporarily activated subset of long-term memory.
>
> ▶ Working memory: an active (internally controlled) subform of short-term memory.
>
> ▶ Declarative memory (alias: explicit memory): memory with conscious access.
>
> ▶ Episodic memory: a subform of declarative memory, related to specific events or episodes in one's life ('when' or 'what' something happened).
>
> ▶ Relational memory: memory for relations among the constituent elements of an experience, assumedly anchored in the hippocampus.
>
> ▶ Semantic memory: a subform of declarative memory, related to knowledge of the world and the meaning of words. Does not require knowledge of context, like episodic memory.
>
> ▶ Nondeclarative memory (alias: implicit memory): memory without conscious access.
>
> *continued*

> - Procedural memory: a subform of nondeclarative memory, acquired in sensorimotor learning and manifested in skills like typing, reading or riding a bike.
> - Perceptual priming: a subform of nondeclarative memory, manifested as the ability to identify or react to a stimulus from prior exposure to that stimulus.
> - Conditioning: a subform of nondeclarative memory, involved in the associative learning of skeletal muscle and emotional responses.
> - Non-associative memory, relates to the learning processes occurring with repeated stimulation, like sensitization and habituation.

Memory depends on functional cerebral space

Cortical areas that process a particular type of information often also function as the repositories of memories for that information. For example, neuroimaging studies have confirmed that identical patterns of activity in the brain are elicited during encoding and retrieval of various types of stimuli. Movements visualized in memory before action (for example, by a golf player or a short-distance runner), were shown to activate the same regions in the motor cortex as during actual execution of those movements. Implying that a map of the functional anatomy of the brain may also serve as a global guide to localize the sites where information is stored in our memory systems.[1] Figure 6.1 presents a simple model of a functional cerebral space, divided according to three neural dimensions that correspond with the anterior-posterior, left and right and cortical-subcortical neuroaxes.

This model, already introduced in Chapter 3 (Figure 3.2), is relevant for distinguishing between differences between regions in the brain that carry out different types of cognitive operations. Possibly the same regions also form the basis of our memory system. As clarified in Chapter 3, representations may vary according to the type of information, processed or stored in different regions in brain-space. This may roughly involve the following two categories: the stage (perception versus action) of processing, and the code (verbal versus spatial) of processing.

Anterior-posterior axis

The gross anatomical distinction between the anterior and posterior regions of the brain globally corresponds to the areas that control action and perception. The anterior cortex is the store of 'action knowledge': our memory for specific motor skills, residing in the

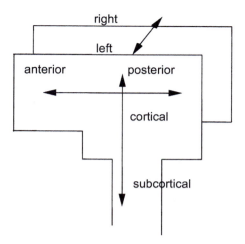

FIGURE 6.1
Three dimensions of 'functional cerebral space' relevant for classifications of various types of memory. The anterior versus posterior division is relevant for classifying action versus perception related knowledge. The left versus right hemispheric division is for classifying verbal versus spatial knowledge. The subcortical versus cortical dimension is particularly relevant for classifying structures involved in the consolidation of information (e.g. the hippocampus, and basal ganglia) versus subsequent storage of information in neocortical regions.

supplementary, premotor and motor areas. Action knowledge involves the formation of action plans, preparation or execution of actions. The posterior part of the brain contains the parietal and temporal lobes, separated from the frontal lobe by the central and lateral fissures. The parietal and temporal lobes respectively integrate spatial and object-oriented forms of information, received from the 'where' and 'what' pathways. The same areas also function as 'perceptual memories'. The primary and secondary areas of the visual cortex, for example, are involved in the processing as well as the storage of visual information. Sections of the temporal cortex are important for the processing and storage of object representations.

Left-right hemispheres

Hemispherical differences in information processing have often been associated with language, attention and emotion, but are also of importance for the code of the respective memories. In the model of Figure 6.1, the left and right cerebral hemispheres are taken to globally correspond with two different codes of processing: verbal processing associated with the left, and non-verbal spatial processing associated with the right hemisphere. The respective memories are thus stored in the same parts of the brain involved in the processing of information, i.e. verbal and semantic knowledge in the left, and spatial knowledge in the right hemisphere.[2]

Cortical-subcortical connections

The vertical axis sketched in Figure 6.1 refers to the distinction between phylogenetically new and old structures. Phylogenetically new structures include the neocortex, old structures include the brain stem, limbic system (including hippocampus and amygdala), cerebellum and basal ganglia. This classification is also of importance for the neurobiology of memory. While permanent memories are generally assumed to reside in neocortical structures, consolidation of new information recruits limbic circuits, connecting via subcortical-cortical pathways with regions in the neocortex. Declarative (explicit) learning might primarily potentiate synapses in the hippocampus, while procedural (implicit) learning presumably also potentiates synapses in the basal ganglia, connecting with motor regions (Box 6.1 contains a listing of different forms of memory).

Memory also depends on the state of the brain

Short-term and long-term memories do not refer to qualitatively different regions, but to different states of activation of neural assemblies in the cortex. The extent and strength of activation of memory representations determine largely their 'status' as short- versus long-term memories. Here follows a brief recapitulation of the major arguments.

Short-term versus long-term memories

The prevailing view of short-term memory is that it has a low capacity, and is more susceptible to decay (loss as a function of time) and interference than long-term memory. The capacity of long-term memory in contrast, is considered to be virtually unlimited. Short-term and long-term memories do not necessarily represent structurally differentiated neural systems. Researchers like Joachim Fuster and Nelson Cowan emphasized that the distinction between short- and long-term memories mainly refers to a difference in the functional *state* of memory structures, and not in a difference in structure or location of the brain regions involved. For example, meeting an old friend after a long period of separation will briefly activate a representation in your long-term memory, probably slumbering somewhere in the inferior temporal lobe. Most likely the encounter will also stir up a conscious recollection of your friend and some vivid details of your common past.

Note also that patients with amnesia often show a dissociation between maintaining more recent, and remote sections of long-term memory. This finding, however, would not necessarily justify a structural separation between short- and long-term memories. It rather implies that amnesic patients show a dissociation between two dynamic aspects of memory: a failure to consolidate new elements (like reporting what they had for breakfast), and the intact ability to reactivate old elements (like repeating seven digits) in memory. Referring to our earlier discussion of representations in Chapter 3, long-term memory refers to 'configurations of connection weights', while short-term memory refers to 'patterns of activity', when given specific inputs (Smith Churchland, 2002). Finally, the distinction active-passive must not be taken as absolute, but rather as representing the two poles of the state dimension. During learning for example, the connection weights of neural configurations will gradually transform from a predominantly active, or labile state, into a less active, or stable state.

Explicit versus implicit memory

The active state of short-term memory is a necessary but not sufficient condition to elicit a conscious experience. Information activating a memory representation will only become explicit (i.e. reach awareness) if the total amount of involved activated neural elements will reach a certain threshold. This principle seems to apply in particular to forms of declarative memory that depend on the medial temporal areas in the cortex. Forms of memory like priming and sensorimotor skills that depend on other cortical regions and pathways will often remain implicit, even with sufficient neural elements activated in their respective networks.[3]

The explicit-implicit distinction also depends on the way declarative memory is tested. For example, retrieval of the content of memory (e.g. a holiday scene) is often examined by referring to existing knowledge of events and episodes. However, the same memory representation may also be automatically 'primed' by external events without any conscious experience.

The 'ins' and 'outs' of memory: encoding and retrieval

Short-term memory is activated during retrieval, as well as during encoding of new information. The two hypothetical phases of learning, encoding and retrieval, are often depicted as two successive operations (Figure 6.2). A favorite metaphor that personifies these operations is that of the librarian. The task of the librarian is to register new book titles in a catalog, then store the books on a specific location in the library, and to recollect a particular volume when requested. Retrieval will be significantly faster if the

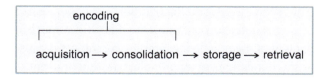

FIGURE 6.2
Processes that play a role in learning, remembering and retrieving information from memory. See text for clarification.

catalog is set up efficiently and provided with sufficient tags and entries.[4] Despite its simplicity, the metaphor has proven its practical utility, for example as a short-hand for classifying normal forgetting and memory disorders, and to deficits occurring in encoding, consolidation or retrieval.

Encoding

Encoding refers to the initial phase of learning, which includes two steps: a preliminary perceptual analysis of the physical or semantic characteristics of stimulus events, also called acquisition, and the subsequent consolidation in time. Acquisition is necessary to provide reliable input to the consolidation stage. A lack of attention, for example, or an insufficient perceptual quality of an object will often result in an incomplete acquisition, and less reliable input to the system responsible for consolidation of information in long-term memory. During consolidation new connections are formed in the brain, leading to permanent structural changes (designated 'storage' in Figure 6.2).

Clinical findings with amnesic patients have led to the supposition that acquisition and consolidation represent functionally separate processes, associated with different neural circuits. Patients suffering from amnesia are unable to remember new facts and events, often due to damage in the medial temporal region of the brain. A similar memory deficit is found in Korsakoff patients. These patients however, have lesions in the diencephalon, in particular the mediodorsal nuclei of the thalamus, an area with many projections to the prefrontal cortex (Mitchell, 2015). Thes lesions will thus likely affect the early sensory phase of encoding. On the basis of these findings, encoding may thus be conceived as a process that recruits anatomically and functionally separate circuits in the brain, associated with early acquisition and subsequent consolidation.

Forms of retrieval

Retrieval utilizes stored information to create a conscious representation, or to execute learned behavior like a motor act. It can become manifest in (or tested with) recognition or recall. These two forms of retrieval are examples of tests of declarative – or explicit – memories, that often correspond to consciously experienced events or episodes. In recognition, subjects will be presented with a picture of a face or an object and asked if they have or have not seen this before. Recognition is a rather coarse way to test memory, since it only requires detection of familiarity. Recall is a much more active way of reproducing the content of memory. For example, the subject is asked to summarize all the facts that he or she remembers of a particular meeting or event.

A method specifically used to investigate the content of biographical memories is cue-based retrieval, also called the Galton-Crovitz method. The method is a modification of Galton's technique whereby subjects are provided with a cue word and asked to retrieve an associated event name or episode. The cue words are meant to provide a neutral sample of the entire content of biographical memory (Crovitz & Schiffman, 1974). In another, less systematic, approach participants have to report important autobiographical memories, such as the most important events of their lives.

In priming, retrieval is manifested in the efficiency of overt behavior, like for example in faster or more accurate responses to a repeated stimulus. In other forms of nondeclarative memory, it could be manifested in the occurrence of a conditional response, or in an increase in the level of proficiency in skill learning. In sum, retrieval of nondeclarative forms of memory is chiefly due to reactivation of previously activated or formed neural routes, which enables quicker transmission of information.

BOX 6.2 PRIMING METHODS

Globally there are two distinct forms of priming, repetition priming and semantic priming. Repetition priming has often been investigated in lexical decision or word-fragment completion tasks. In a lexical decision task, the test stimuli are verbal stimuli, which consist of an existing or non-existent word. In the prior study phase, a number of words are presented for inspection. Notice that the instructions in the study phase merely serve to distract the subject from paying attention to the content or meaning of the word, for example, to name the color of words. In the subsequent test phase, the subject has to indicate with a button press response if the test word offered is a real word or a non-word (non-existent word), or to read the test word aloud. Responses appear faster for repeated words (house-house: the word house thus being part of the words from the previous study phase) than unrepeated known words (house-dog).

In the word-fragment completion task, the subject also sees a list of words. After a certain amount of time, fragments of the word are displayed, and the subject is asked to complete the words. Half of the test stimuli correspond to the study list, and the other half does not. Subjects benefit from having seen the words before, even when they do not recall having seen the words earlier. This form of repetition priming occurs independently from encoding the earlier presented words.

Priming effects are significantly smaller when study and test words are presented in different modalities, e.g. from auditory to visual words, confirming the notion that they depend on perceptual characteristics, and not on the meaning of stimulus material. This may also occur with non-verbal material such as faces, pictures of objects or abstract geometrical patterns. Initially, it was suspected that the effects of repetition priming were only short-lived, lasting for only a few hours.

continued

> Later, however, it became apparent that these effects may continue in periods of a few days or even weeks.
>
> Semantic priming occurs from the association between conceptual characteristics, like the meaning of words. For example, in a lexical decision task, the study word may be 'apple', after which the subject is offered a non-word or a real word. It appears that responses are faster for words that have a semantic relationship with the study word, like 'banana' than words that are not semantically related (like 'house'). Semantic priming of words possibly reflects automatic activation of nodes in a semantic network (implicit, or pre-lexical) or explicit (post-lexical) processes, for example when the interval between primes and targets is longer than 500 ms and subjects are allowed to encode the study word.

Tests of retrieval often show different results in patients with memory disorders. Some patients may recall an event by way of a recognition test, but not of a recall test. Amnesic patients performing poorly in tests of recognition and recall sometimes do show effects of priming. This finding suggests that behavioral tests based on reactivating implicit knowledge, rely on other neural circuits in the brain more than tests of explicit memory.

Retrieval and forgetting

A disorder in retrieval means that despite several attempts, one cannot gain access to stored knowledge. One possible cause – called the 'retrieval' or 'access' hypothesis of forgetting – is that the memory representation is still intact, but only its access is blocked. Problems with retrieval of episodic memory may occur after neurological damage to the prefrontal cortex, in particular the right prefrontal cortex (Henson et al., 1999). Assumedly, the role of prefrontal areas is to control the pathways, connecting to memories that are stored in other areas of the brain. A hypothetical scenario would be that specific 'binding units', located in the right prefrontal cortex, connect to memory networks in the temporal cortex via long-range ventrolateral pathways (see Figure 6.7 for some examples of involved circuits). These corticocortical pathways are not unique for retrieval of information from long-term memory, but are also be implemented in networks serving working memory. Problems with semantic retrieval (e.g. words and names) have been associated with the 'tip of the tongue' phenomenon, and attributed to the functioning of the medial temporal and left prefrontal cortical regions.

The loss of information stored in long-term memory, referred to as the 'storage' hypothesis, is seen as a second cause of forgetting. Loss of knowledge in long-term memory could result from active interference: for example, new information is 'pushed-out' or inhibited by existing knowledge or vice versa. A special case of forgetting is the suppression of unwanted memories, also known as 'motivated forgetting' (Anderson et al., 2004).

Forgetting could also result from merely structural processes. Examples are a decay or loss of memory traces, caused by weakening or loss of synaptic connections, loss of white matter of the nervous tracts or neurotransmitters during pathological or normal aging. The strength of encoding could play an important role in remembering and forgetting. Photographs of visual scenes that caused smaller activation of the right prefrontal cortex and parahippocampal cortex in the scanner when viewed for the first time were later remembered less well that those that evoked greater activations (Brewer et al., 1998). Loss of memory over time can follow two different and opposite temporal gradients. Forgetting implies that older memories are more strongly affected than more recent ones, which typically follows a 'forgetting curve'. The reversed pattern is called a 'Ribot gradient', implying that memories from early in life are better preserved than more recent memories. Retrograde amnesia is an example of a temporally graded memory loss that selectively spares more distant memories. Retrograde amnesia often results from a deficit in consolidating new memories, which in turn can be caused by lesions in the medial temporal cortex. For example, after electroconvulsive shock therapy, patients' memories formed at least 6 months before the treatment are relatively unaffected, while more recent ones are impaired (Meeter et al., 2011). Many neurological disorders, including Alzheimer's disease, are associated with a temporally graded retrograde amnesia, indicating that older memories are somehow protected against degeneration, while newer memories are not. Further in this chapter we shall discuss in more detail the various disorders of memory.

Memory and the brain: varieties of memory

One of the challenges in the cognitive neuroscience of memory is to map the traditional classifications between long- and short-term memories and their subdivisions, to networks of the brain. Converging evidence from animal studies, studies of patients with cerebral lesions, and experimental work using neuroimaging have created a new landscape that is still unfolding. The next paragraphs discuss different forms of long-term memory, and the neural circuitries involved in various forms of short-term memory and working memory.

Long-term memory

The notion that there are multiple memories, supported by specific brain systems, has been introduced and corroborated by research of Larry Squire and colleagues from UCLA, San Diego, California. His theory relates mainly to the structure of permanent or long-term memory. A core element of his model is the distinction between declarative and non-declarative memories (Figure 6.3). Daniel Schacter introduced the related distinction between explicit and implicit memories.

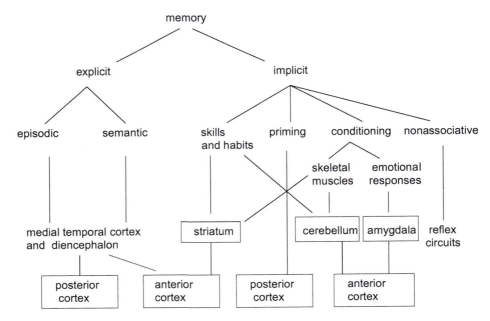

FIGURE 6.3
Layout of long-term memory and associated areas in the brain. Left: explicit (declarative) memory. Right: implicit (non-declarative) memory. Middle boxes show neural structures globally involved in consolidation processes. Lower boxes are presumed to be involved in permanent storage.

Declarative (explicit) memory

Explicit memory relates to knowledge to which we have conscious access, and in general depends on medial temporal structures in the brain. Traditionally, it is subdivided into two categories, episodic and semantic memory. Episodic memory is strongly autobiographical and refers to events that are time- and place-bound. Semantic memory refers to general knowledge of facts, language comprehension and knowledge of the world. It is often derived from episodic memories that gradually transform to semantic memory (become 'semantised'), while concurrently losing its sensitivity and association to particular events.

Studies of memory disorders in patients and lesioned animals have led to the insight that the medial temporal cortex including the hippocampus is essential in the formation of explicit memory. Other important sites are the diencephalon, with the dorsomedial nucleus of the thalamus, and the mammillary bodies as prime structures. They do not form the site of long-term memories, which is in the neocortex (but see Morris et al., 1990). As stated earlier, it seems plausible that declarative memories, with their predominantly perceptual character, are stored in the posterior and temporal cortical areas.[5] Studies of patients with brain lesions revealed that patients with lesions in the left inferotemporal lobe often have problems with naming objects like persons, animals or tools, suggesting that distinct areas in the left inferior temporal cortex are used for the storage and retrieval of conceptual knowledge in lexical and semantic networks (Damasio et al., 1996).

Non-declarative (implicit) memory

The term implicit memory is a descriptive label that refers to one way 'in which the influence of past experiences can be expressed in subsequent task performance – unintentionally and without conscious recollection of a learning' (Schacter et al., 1993; Moscovitch et al., 1994). Implicit memory thus refers to knowledge to which we do not have conscious access. It represents a more mixed category, including elements of perceptual as well as motor memories that correspond with different cortical regions and neural pathways (shown at the right of Figure 6.3). Explicit and implicit memories show a double dissociation, implying that they relate to specific brain systems, and behavioral deficits after lesions of these systems (Gabrieli et al., 1995).

What all forms of implicit memory have in common is that they do not make demands on the medial temporal regions. Some of its subforms like skills, habits and conditioning, summarized as 'procedural memory', are mediated by cortical as well as subcortical structures. The amygdala, basal ganglia (striatum) and cerebellum are involved either in consolidating implicit memories, or function as the structures where these memories are stored. An exception is priming, a subform of implicit memory where sensory pathways assumedly relay directly via thalamic nuclei to the posterior cortex. The various forms of implicit memory are briefly summarized as follows.

Priming refers to the faster recognition or identification of a stimulus based on an earlier exposure. This form of memory primarily relates to perceptual areas in the posterior cortex. Positive priming is often contrasted with negative priming. The term negative priming has its roots in studies of selective attention. The slow reaction due to the change of the distractor stimulus to the target stimulus is called the negative priming effect. When we pay attention to a particular stimulus, we perceive other stimuli surrounding the target as distracters, in order to help to focus attention. But when one of those distracters becomes the new target of attention, our response to the target is delayed, due to the residual inhibition effect.

Habituation is an elementary form of learning, where a physiological response to the stimulus shows a gradual decline in amplitude as the result of repeated presentations.

Sensitization, in contrast, reflects the increase of a response to a stimulus, due to the previous presentation of a high-intensity stimulus, like a loud tone.

Conditioning; in classical conditioning, an unconditional stimulus (UCS), often a noxious stimulus (e.g. a mild electrical shock), is paired with a subsequent conditional stimulus (CS), a neutral stimulus like a tone. Memory representations based on UCS-CS couplings are partly associated with motor functions, and partly with affective functions.

MEMORY SYSTEMS

Conditioned motor responses are mediated by cortical motor areas and motor units in the spinal cord. Limbic structures like the amygdala mediate conditioned affective responses (like startle) (see further Chapter 7). The cerebellum is also assumed to participate as a storage site of these associative forms of memory.

Sensorimotor learning relates to skills with common motor elements like riding a bike or learning to type on a keyboard. The storage of these forms of 'action knowledge' is likely to mainly occur in the more anteriorly located cortical areas. At the subcortical level, the striatum and cerebellum may also act as storage sites in the acquisition of motor skills. There are indications that this is mainly the case with highly practiced and automatic action sequences. The following paragraphs deal in more detail with the neural mechanisms controlling various forms of implicit and explicit memory.

Short-term memory as an activated subset of long-term memory

As clarified earlier, long-term and short-term memory can be seen as passive versus active *states* of memory. In contrast to long-term memory, conceived as an immense repository of dormant memory elements, short-term memory relates to networks with activated neural elements. Thus, short-term memory can be conceptualized as an activated subset of the same topographical region as long-term memory. Importantly, activation of a neural ensemble within the repository of long-term memory can take place via different circuits, depicted in the upper section of Figure 6.4. Globally these circuits follow the same pathways used for encoding, consolidation, and retrieval.[6] The three primary forms of short-term memory associated with these routes, are briefly described next.

BOX 6.3   CENTRAL EXECUTIVE HELPS GENERATING RANDOM NUMBERS

Randomness is the lack of predictability in a series of events. Throwing a dice, for example, will deliver a random number between 1 and 6. A statistical criterion of randomness is that in a long series there are an equal number of events, as well as sequences of events. But in a truly random sequence of events the probability is very high there are sequences that look like patterns. In a game of roulette, for instance, people tend to bet on red if the color red has turned up regularly in a row.

Human brains apparently have evolved to look for patterns, and to simplify the complex information reaching our senses. Human subjects were shown to be poor random generators. When asked to generate random numbers, subjects typically tend to avoid number repetitions and systematically deviate from mathemat-

continued

ical randomness. The number generation task is quite demanding, as it requires the subject to utilize a variety of criteria that constitute perceived randomness, and to memorize the current, the preceding and the future events. It relies heavily on working memory, and its capacity for 'looking back and looking forward'.

Allan Baddeley suggested that the capacity for generating sequences of random responses (or at least sequences that approximate the statistical criterion of randomness) relates to the central executive component of working memory. The finding that the degree of randomness systematically decreases as speed of generation is increased, or when the subject concurrently performs another task, suggests that the non-randomness (or greater redundancy) reflects some capacity limitation in information-processing. The random generation test also appeared to be sensitive to a range of neuropsychological conditions, assumed to affect executive processes, including frontal lobe injuries, Alzheimer's and Korsakoff's disease.

Sources: Baddeley et al. (1998), Baddeley (2003), Schulz et al. (2012).

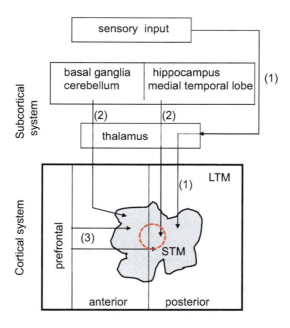

FIGURE 6.4
Schematic picture of short-term memory (shaded area: STM) as an activated part of long-term cortical memory (LTM). Activation of STM occurs in three different ways: 1) directly ('bottom-up') from sensory inputs and thalamus (priming), 2) mediated by consolidation from subcortical structures such as the hippocampus (declarative memory), or cerebellum and basal ganglia (procedural memory), and 3) mediated ('top-down') by the prefrontal cortex (working memory). See text for further clarification.

Sensory memory and priming (route 1)

In sensory memory as well as in priming, the cortical structures are directly activated by sensory input. This results in an early, short-lasting and 'bottom-up' form of short-term memory manifested in the neural elements of the primary and secondary areas. Its visual form is called *iconic*, and the auditory form *echoic* memory. Sensory memory has a high capacity but a critically short duration. George Sperling first tested its duration in his partial report task. When a square array of twelve letters was presented very briefly on a screen, subjects were able to recite a row of four letters, spatially cued by an arrow presented shortly after the array (Sperling, 1960).

These findings suggested that conscious access to visual sensory memory is only possible for a half-a-second period. Visual priming, a process that is elicited implicitly, is taken to reflect activation of visual word-forms in a perceptual-representation system (PRS), located in the extrastriate visual cortex. PRS is specifically sensitive to elementary features of the stimulus patterns (Schacter, 1992). Similar effects are obtained by priming in other sensory modalities, like audition and touch.

Short-term memory as a portal to long-term memory (route 2)

The notion that short-term memory functions as a 'portal' to long-term memory plays a role in theories of Hebb, Broadbent, Atkinson, and Shiffrin. Donald Hebb described short-term memory as a temporary 'reverberating' of activity of neural populations, which eventually transforms into a more stable pattern of neural connections. Short-term retention of meaningless verbal material like three consonants (XKR) is practically impossible if one prevents subjects from rehearsing the stimulus material, suggesting that activation of STM elements is very short-lived, due to the decay of memory elements (Peterson & Peterson, 1959). Consolidation of new material, therefore, seems to operate primarily on the basis of material presented with sufficient duration and that is not blocked from attention.

At the brain level, consolidation of new information is primarily mediated by structures outside the cortex. In explicit learning this concerns the hippocampus, in implicit (sensorimotor) learning the cerebellum and the striatum. Here, the term consolidation is used in a broader sense, as any process involved in storing information in the cortex via subcortical structures. During consolidation neural populations in the cortex are temporarily in a labile state, which lasts until sufficiently stable synaptic connections have been formed between these neurons.

Working memory (route 3)

Short-term memory can also be activated in a top-down manner, as a 'working memory', i.e. the consciously controlled temporary storage and manipulation of information.

Working memory is a limited-capacity but flexible form of memory, controlled by higher structures in the prefrontal cortex. It activates representations in the posterior as well as in the anterior cortex. Route 3 could also play a role in some forms of retrieval of knowledge. The importance of the concept of working memory for theories of higher control and executive functions, justifies further elaboration in the following section.

Working memory

The concept of working memory has its roots in cognitive psychology. In 1974 Alan Baddeley proposed that a working memory system consists of three main components, a central executive system that controls two subordinate (slave) systems, a visual coding system (visuospatial sketchpad) and an acoustic coding system (phonological loop). Working memory operations can easily switch between various sources of information and different sensory modalities, and their respective locations in the brain. Its functionality can, therefore, be defined in terms of a core mechanism that underlies networks of memory, selective attention and motor control. Working memory capacity is also seen as crucial element of general 'fluid' intelligence (Conway et al., 2002).

Although the central executive was initially meant as a concept, and not as a localized structure, later research enabled to link the concept to a network in the prefrontal cortex (Baddeley, 2003). The central executive is a modality nonspecific system of limited capacity, associated with structures in the prefrontal cortex (see Figure 6.5, left; note that the neural underpinnings were formulated later on the basis of neuropsychological patient studies). When imaging a favorite scene of your last holiday, for example, the central executive retrieves the images from your posterior cortex and then maintains the activated content in a buffer, using corticocortical loops. The choice of systems recruited by the central executive may vary according to the type of mental operation and the specific information highlighted by the internal 'spotlight'. The emphasis could be on semantic, visuospatial, or nonspatial features.

The phonological loop, for example, might be composed of three regions in the cortex: the lateral posterior cortex (Wernicke's area), the premotor cortex and the left prefrontal cortex (Broca's area, see also Paulesu et al., 1993). From the perspective of the brain, the only structural constraint for establishing connections between the central executive and its auxiliary systems would be the availability of long-ranging reciprocal connections. The candidate pathways would be the one connecting the dorsolateral prefrontal cortex to the posterior parietal cortex, and the other connecting the ventrolateral prefrontal cortex to the temporal cortical regions (Friedman & Goldman-Rakic, 1994).

Baddeley located his subordinate systems in the left and right hemispheres on the basis of neuropsychological findings, showing that lesions in the *right* parietooccipital regions often caused problems in visuospatial short-term memory. Deficits in the phonological working memory often occurred after damage of regions in a

> ## BOX 6.4 VERY LONG-LASTING MEMORIES, THE REMINISCENCE 'BUMP' AND 'PERMASTORE'
>
> Remembering new events becomes more difficult as we get older. Normal aging is accompanied by a decrease of connectivity in the networks of the brain, caused by loss of synaptic efficiency, loss of white matter and depletion of neurotransmitters. This, in turn, is responsible for a gradual decline in cognitive abilities including memory. It could also result in mild retrograde amnesia, described as the 'Ribot effect', caused by increasingly less effective consolidation of memory traces with advancing age. On the other hand, older people often have a surprisingly good memory for events and episodes from the distant past. Old episodic memories from periods over 50 years back in time, can often be retrieved without apparent effort.
>
> The long-term storage of ancient episodic memories in biographical memory (called the *'reminiscence bump'*) often includes times, places, associated emotions and other contextual knowledge. Vivid episodic memories often stem from late adolescence, the period between 15 and 25 years of age. One explanation of this phenomenon is the fact that adolescence was an important stage in their lives for many people. What was experienced then was also better retained in memory by its greater pregnancy or novelty. Another view, now seen as more plausible, is that neural memories (in particular the consolidation part) typically function better in early adolescence, resulting in more events remembered from that period than from subsequent periods in life.
>
> Biographical memory has a wider scope than episodic (time and place-bound) personal memories. It also includes semantic knowledge, like the name of teachers, famous politicians, or even highly practiced language skills obtained in early life, but never practiced in later years. Harry Bahrick introduced the term *'permastore'* for this kind of preserved old memories. Both types of long-lasting memories are probably based on the same mechanism, during the consolidation of declarative knowledge. The reasons why they remain uniquely preserved over long periods in life are still not fully understood.
>
> Sources: Bahrick (1984), Jansari & Parkin (1996), Janssen & Murre (2008), Meeter et al. (2008), Koppel & Rubin (2016), Rubin et al. (1998).

left hemisphere network, comprising lateral frontal and parietal regions. Human PET studies with normal subjects provided additional support for Baddeley's model. To name one, Jonides and Paulesu and colleagues found that performing a visuospatial memory task was accompanied by increased blood flow in the frontal and posterior areas of the right hemisphere. Performing a verbal phonological task produced a different pattern, showing up in the activation of the supramarginal frontal gyrus and Broca's area of the left hemisphere.

Another content-based working memory model, proposed by Goldman-Rakic, concerned the separation between spatial versus nonspatial subordinate systems (see right panel in Figure 6.5). In this model, the central executive does not function as a unitary system, but utilizes two specific control systems that extend the dorsal-ventral distinction of perceptual pathways to the prefrontal cortex. Goldman-Rakic's model was based on studies of working memory in rhesus monkeys in a memory delayed-reinforcement task (Goldman-Rakic, 1988). In these tasks, cells in the dorsolateral region of the prefrontal cortex (called principal sulcus), continued to fire in the interval when the monkey waited for the food to reappear at an expected location of the reinforcement platform.

The spatial versus the nonspatial character of working memory operations were also manifest in the specific cortical areas that became activated in neuroimaging studies of humans. Smith and Jonides (1995) were able to identify two neural circuits, possibly associated with identification of the spatial location and the category of an object, functioning as the subsidiary systems of working memory. The spatial task activated the prefrontal cortex and the posterior parietal cortex of the right hemisphere. In the object-identification task, the pattern shifted to the left hemisphere. Here the prefrontal cortex was activated concurrently with regions in the temporal cortex. These studies, therefore, seem to confirm Goldman-Rakics' dorsal-ventral model as well as Baddeley's left-right hemispheric model of subsidiary systems of working memory.

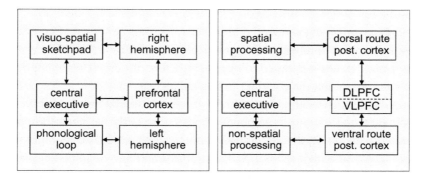

FIGURE 6.5
Left panel: Baddeley's model of working memory with corresponding anatomical areas in the left and right hemisphere. Right panel: Goldman-Rakic's animal model with corresponding areas in the frontal cortex.

Executive control

The previously mentioned studies confirmed the notion that working memory adapts flexibly to the cognitive demands of the tasks, with the site of activation of cortical regions reflecting the specific subsidiary systems involved. The role of the prefrontal cortex in these tasks could be that of a temporary repository of information, or 'buffer' for representations accessed from more distant areas by long-range corticocortical pathways (Goldman-Rakic, 2000). Later fMRI studies, using tasks designed to engage visuospatial focused attention and as well as working memory, also confirmed the involvement of dorsolateral prefrontal and posterior parietal cortical areas, identified as the frontoparietal network or central executive network (CEN; see Figures 4.19, 4.23 and 7.18 for examples).

The key players in this network are the dorsolateral prefrontal cortex (DLPFC) and the posterior parietal cortex (PPC), especially the intraparietal sulcus (or IPC). The hypothesis is that the network is a unified but internally differentiated system, connected via flexible 'hubs' in limbic and in visual and motor areas (Cole et al., 2014). CEN activity also appeared to be correlated with the performance in cognitive tests. For example, the strength of connectivity between areas in the frontoparietal network is reported to be related to the IQ of children (Langeslag et al., 2013) and adults (Cole et al., 2012).

Encoding and retrieval in explicit memory

Storage of information in the brain is the result of acquisition and consolidation, together also referred to as encoding (Figure 6.2). This terminology is particularly relevant within the domain of declarative or explicit memory. For non-declarative procedural memory, encoding-related activations occur in the motor as well as in non-motor brain areas during learning of motor skills (Grafton et al., 1995; Shadmehr & Holcomb, 1997). Note also that in tasks involving sequential and motor learning, retrieval effects are merged with encoding, and both reflected in a gradual increase of motor efficiency and related cortical activation patterns. These findings are therefore discussed in greater detail in the paragraph on implicit learning, further in this chapter.

In everyday life, encoding and retrieval of information takes place at widely separated time intervals. Trying to remember episodes from early life, therefore, not always yields a reliable picture of the actual events and of their spatial and temporal relationship. Most likely, our earlier memories have transformed into degraded copies, missing the lively character of the original impression. Experimental studies focusing on brain patterns associated with encoding and retrieval have therefore enacted both phases in the same paradigm, which made it possible to compare these functions more directly, and separated by much smaller intervals than in daily life.

An effective paradigm to study encoding is the *subsequent memory paradigm* in which brain activity is measured in the scanner while subjects are presented with items to remember. Later, their memory performance is tested outside the scanner, after which the original fMRI data are sorted as a function of whether these items were remembered correctly, incorrectly or forgotten. In a reversed order, neuroimaging data collected during retrieval can be sorted according to whether subjects recollected or did not recollect an item learned in an earlier session outside the scanner. Considering the short time interval between the encoding and retrieval phases in these experiments, the encoding process will reflect only the early phase of encoding, comprising acquisition and fast consolidation. This also entails a stronger involvement of the hippocampus in the retrieval phase. Slow consolidation (to be described in more detail further in this chapter) extends over a much longer time period and makes gradually increasing demands on cortical areas during the encoding as well as retrieval phase.

Prefrontal cortex

With respect to declarative memory, early PET and fMRI studies reviewed by Tulving and colleagues consistently reported differences between encoding and retrieval, referred to as the hemispheric encoding-retrieval asymmetry (HERA) model (Tulving, 1994; Nyberg et al., 1996, Nyberg, 1998). The model states that encoding involves the left hemisphere more than the right, while retrieval involves the right hemisphere more than the left. The reported asymmetries mostly concerned the dorsolateral prefrontal cortex (Figure 6.6). This general pattern was assumed to apply to different kinds of information: verbal materials, pictures, faces and a variety of conditions of encoding and retrieval. Another across-studies report (Cabeza & Nyberg, 2000) also incorporated differences between episodic and semantic retrieval conditions, showing that semantic retrieval (retrieval of semantic categories and not individual words) predominantly involved the left prefrontal cortex, which included Brodmann's 44, 45 and 46.

Later studies sketched a somewhat different picture of the neural substrates of encoding and retrieval. A meta-analysis by Spaniol et al. (2009) showed that encoding involved the left ventrolateral prefrontal cortex and the medial-temporal regions, whereas retrieval of episodic memories involved the left superior-parietal, but also the *left* prefrontal regions. The studies mentioned also concerned verbal material.

Some studies also pointed to material-specific effects. A study by Wagner and colleagues using event-related fMRI with words and pictures (visual textures), reported stronger activity in the prefrontal as well as the medial temporal cortex, during encoding for stimuli that were later remembered, relative to forgotten stimuli(Wagner et al., 1998). Later remembered words or pictures elicited stronger activity during encoding in the left parahippocampal region and left prefrontal cortex. Interestingly, pictures produced stronger activation in the *right* frontal cortex. Brewer and colleagues obtained a similar result using photographs, comparing later remembered pictures with forgotten ones (Brewer et al., 1998). Other event-related fMRI studies also reported left frontal activations, both during encoding and retrieval (Prince et al., 2005).

Taken together, the preceding studies suggest that prefrontal activations during encoding are probably not critical for the early consolidation of declarative memory, because lesions in these areas do not generally impair explicit memories. Instead, their role seems to lie in working memory, executive control or selection of relevant stimulus elements in the acquisition phase of encoding.[7] An influential theory of prefrontal cortex function, proposed by Miller and Cohen, is that prefrontal cortex–hippocampus interactions may be best understood by allusion to a railroad metaphor, in which the hippocampus is responsible for laying down new tracks, whereas the prefrontal cortex is responsible for flexibly switching between tracks. 'Schema modification', a term proposed by Frederic Bartlett, is another function assigned to the prefrontal cortex in supporting consolidation in the hippocampus (Bartlett, 1932). Schema modification is a long-duration incremental process involving the prefrontal cortices, and adding new associations to already learned associations. This theory will be discussed in more detail further in this chapter, in the context of the theory of Preston and Eichenbaum.

Concerning the prefrontal involvement of retrieval, the executive part of working memory may go a long way in accounting for its involvement of memory retrieval. Executive functions are generally not thought to be lateralized. However, a lateralized role of the prefrontal cortex in memory retrieval, does fit the idea that the prefrontal cortex is functionally partitioned according to the verbal-linguistic versus non-verbal spatial characteristics of the task. Such a differentiation is also in accordance with earlier findings of the material-specific role of the prefrontal cortex, with the left prefrontal cortex

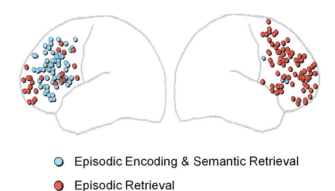

○ Episodic Encoding & Semantic Retrieval

● Episodic Retrieval

FIGURE 6.6
Global picture of results of imaging studies. Regions in prefrontal cortex showing effects of episodic encoding and retrieval, and semantic retrieval.
Source: Courtesy of Roberto Cabeza.

involved in semantic retrieval, and the right prefrontal hemisphere involved in episodic (pictorial) retrieval.

Complex processes, like semantic categorization and retrieval of word meaning in particular, have been linked consistently to the left prefrontal cortex. This included linguistic as well as 'generative' symbolic operations. For example, there is evidence to suggest that the left inferior frontal gyrus subserves selection of information among competing alternatives from semantic memory (Thompson-Schill et al., 1997). The same area could also play a crucial role in the unification of semantic, syntactic and phonological levels of processing (Hagoort, 2005). Specific left prefrontal regions recruited in complex semantic retrieval, would be Broca areas BA44 and BA45, traditionally considered as parts of a language circuit, connecting frontal and posterior language areas via bundles of long-distance nerve fibers (Friederici, 2017).

Although the role of the prefrontal cortex in episodic memory retrieval is less clear, there is evidence to suggest that episodic retrieval is intimately connected with top-down attentional functions (Nolde et al., 1998; Henson et al., 1999). This could specifically involve a circuit between dorsolateral prefrontal cortex and posterior parietal cortex (PPC), described earlier as the frontal-parietal attention network (see also Cabeza et al., 2008). In the light of findings supporting a specific role of the right PPC in spatial attentional control, and PPC deficits leading to attentional neglect, coactivation of the right prefrontal cortex and the posterior parietal cortex might also account for findings summarized in Figure 6.6.

Medial temporal regions

Both encoding and retrieval have been linked to regions in the medial temporal regions, including the hippocampus. Here follows a brief overview of some relevant studies. The differential role of the anterior and posterior sections of the hippocampus will be elaborated in greater detail in the section below on explicit memory and consolidation.

Encoding and the hippocampus

Using the subsequent memory paradigm, Ranganath (Ranganath et al., 2004) investigated brain activations during the encoding of words. In the encoding phase words printed in green had to be judged according to their size (small or big). Words printed in red had to be judged according to the object they represented (animate or inanimate). Only correctly recalled words (as verified in the subsequent testing period outside the scanner) activated regions of the posterior parahippocampal area as well as of the hippocampus proper. This significant role of the hippocampus in episodic encoding is in line with studies with amnesic patients and animal lesion studies, to be reported in greater detail further in this chapter.

Retrieval and the hippocampus

fMRI studies verified that the hippocampus is also involved in retrieval of information, such as words (Eldridge et al., 2000) or pictures of scenes (Montaldi et al., 2006). The study of Eldrige found that only words that were remembered correctly in the scanner (and were memorized in a previous encoding session outside the scanner) selectively activated the hippocampus. This study also allowed sorting word on the basis of their familiarity. Familiarity of the words however had no effect on the hippocampus.

In Montaldi's study, retrieval was tested with a mixed batch of old and new visual scenes. The old scenes corresponded with pictures the subject had studied in a separate encoding session, outside the scanner. In the encoding session subjects were asked to judge pictures according to their familiarity, or as recollected. fMRI results of the retrieval session showed that the hippocampus was only activated by recollected pictures of scenes. A different pattern emerged for items that were judged as familiar, with stronger activations found in the perirhinal cortex. The suggestion from this study is that activation of the perirhinal cortex alone is sufficient to evoke a sense of familiarity, while full recollection of the item in its context, requires the hippocampus (Eichenbaum et al., 2007). Squire et al. (2007) proposed an alternative perspective and suggested that the methods traditionally used to separate recollection from familiarity instead separate strong memories from weak memories.

Notice that the present studies were concerned with the early phase of encoding, comprising acquisition and fast consolidation. This implies that the involvement of the hippocampus in the formation of memories and subsequent retrieval is probably restricted to recent information and for a limited period. With other areas in the medial temporal cortex taking over retrieval in the subsequent slower phase of consolidation (see also Figure 6.8 further in this chapter). An exception could be the retrieval of contextual information, or learning conditions when new relational links are created with respect to already existing representations, which would lead to a much more extensive role of the hippocampus.

Reinstatement or transformation

Episodic memory enables humans to re-experience past events vividly, but how this is achieved at the neural level is not fully understood. One possibility being that the distinctive patterns found in imaging studies in the cortex during retrieval are the same as those recording during encoding. The general trend indeed shows that the same areas are activated during encoding and retrieval, supporting the 'reinstatement' hypothesis of episodic retrieval (Johnson & Rugg, 2007; Wheeler et al., 2000; Eichenbaum, 2012). This related to retrieval of visual stimuli and of sounds. The 'tranformation' hypothesis found an early expression in Frederic Bartlett's theory that remembering is a constructive process, 'an imaginative reconstruction or construction, built out of the relation of our attitude towards a whole active mass of organized past reactions or experience' (Bartlett, 1932, Wagoner, 2017). A more recent study further expanded the transformation view that memory retrieval is not a faithful replay of past events, but may also involve additional constructive processes to serve adaptive functions (Xiao et al., 2017, but see also Preston & Eichenbaum, 2013).

Explicit memory: circuits, deficits and mechanisms

What makes declarative knowledge so unique that it depends on the medial temporal areas in the brain? One answer to this question is that knowledge of events and episodes is often a composite of different types of information, stored in networks connecting different parts of the cortex. As discussed earlier, a particular function of the hippocampus and adjacent structures is to bind distinctive stimulus attributes or events that generally do not have a relationship. The latter function only becomes fully clear when it is considered in the context of the larger networks in the brain, or 'memory space', mediated by the hippocampus. The following sections will focus in more detail on the functional and time-related role of the medial temporal cortex and higher cortical areas in consolidation of declarative memories.

The binding role of the medial temporal region

Perceptual representations are the building blocks of declarative memory with spatial and object information respectively located in the posterior parietal and inferior temporal cortices. A generally accepted view is that the 'where' and 'what' perceptual streams from the cortex remain segregated until they reach the entorhinal region. They then flow together in the hippocampus, which stores the complex representations of the event-in-context, which is subsequently directed back to the parahippocampal area and the cortex (Eichenbaum, 2012). How the hippocampus and its surrounding regions 'manage' to bind the scattered neural elements of these areas remains a matter of speculation. In network conceptualizations, the role of the hippocampus is often described as a central node or 'hub', ideally located to establish connections via reciprocal pathways with cortical regions.

During learning, the hippocampus might build a short-term memory representation in the cortex, by activating its neurons via reverberating circuits. Long-term-potentiation of the synapses of hippocampal neurons, projecting to neurons in the cortical networks would then form the neural basis of consolidation. Additional input from neurotransmitters would assist in modulating or enhancing the consolidation process (see Figure 6.7). Adjacent to the hippocampus, the parahippocampal gyrus and entorhinal cortex possibly also play an important role in this process of cortical storage, especially when it concerns the binding of information derived from different sensory modalities.

MEMORY SYSTEMS

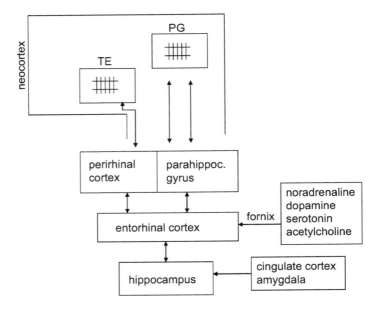

FIGURE 6.7
Connections between the medial temporal cortical areas (hippocampus and adjacent areas (bottom left) and two brain areas (top) that are important for the storage of information in long-term (explicit) memory. PG = posterior parietal gyrus; TE = temporal gyrus. Lower right; input from neurotransmitters and the limbic system.

BOX 6.5 MAJOR CIRCUITS IN THE HIPPOCAMPUS

The major circuit in the hippocampus starting from entorhinal cortex contains the following steps:

▶ Input from the entorhinal cortex goes to the dentate gyrus via axons of the perforant pathway, connecting with the dendrites of granular cells in the gyrus dentatus (see also Figure 6.11 for anatomical details of the hippocampus).

▶ The axons of the granular cells (called mossy fibers) in turn make synaptic connections with dendrites of pyramidal cells in CA3 (CA= Cornu Ammonis, or Ammons horn, consisting of three parts, CA1, CA2 and CA3).

▶ The axons of these pyramid cells then split in two bundles of axons (together called Schaffer's collaterals). One part of the collaterals contacts dendrites of the pyramid cells in the adjacent CA1. The other part leaves the hippocampus through the fimbria.

continued

> ▶ The fimbria consists of a bundle of axons that, when outside the hippocampus, is called fornix. The fornix has important input and output connections with other structures, including the diencephalon, brainstem, and limbic system.
>
> ▶ Axons of the pyramid cells of CA1 project to neurons in the subiculum, from where they leave the hippocampus either through the entorhinal cortex or via the fimbria.

Apart from its role in memory consolidation, sections of the hippocampus and other medial temporal regions are also involved in novelty detection and the orienting response (Sokolov & Vinagrada, 1975). Novelty detection represents a series of distinct processes, from the initial evaluation of a stimulus, the generation of mismatch signals, to the integration of novel stimuli and the creation of new representations. There is evidence to suggest that in humans these processes are implemented in a network including the mediodorsal thalamus and the medial temporal lobe cortex, with the output of its computations performed in other cortical structures, especially the prefrontal cortex (Kafkas & Montaldi, 2018). In the rhesus monkey, multiple channels of communication link the dorsolateral prefrontal cortex and the hippocampus via the parahippocampal gyrus, subiculum, presubiculum and adjacent transitional cortices (Goldman-Rakic et al., 1984). This circuitry would not only play a critical role in the detection of novel or significant events, but also in their subsequent consolidation, and even storage, in declarative memory.

The circuitry of consolidation and retrieval

Larry Squire proposed a model that further specifies the role of the hippocampus in the storage of information in the neocortex (see Figure 6.7). In this model, two major zones, the parietal and temporal cortex, are involved in the storage of explicit (mainly perceptual) knowledge. These are the regions where spatial and nonspatial information from the dorsal and ventral pathways reach their final destinations. Because the hippocampus creates the associative links in the network, it seems reasonable to assume that the same links also are involved in the retrieval of the information.

This assumption does not necessarily imply that retrieval is accomplished exclusively through the hippocampus. Indeed, there is evidence that in the event of damage or removal of the hippocampal areas, patients are often able to remember facts and events from the distant past. With the binding role of hippocampal structures gradually diminishing in time (see also Figure 6.8) the prefrontal and temporal cortex may possibly take over the role of the hippocampus. Neuroimaging research by Cabeza and Tulving, discussed earlier, made this a plausible scenario, with the right and left prefrontal regions becoming gradually more involved in the storage as well as in the retrieval of episodic (perceptual) and semantic (verbal) memories, respectively.

The time course of consolidation

Amnesia studies (to be discussed in more detail further on in this chapter) have shown that the extent of retrograde amnesia seems to increase, depending on the size of the damaged area of the consolidation network (Nadel & Moscovitch, 1997). This period is considerably longer if lesions not only affect the hippocampus but also the surrounding areas in the medial temporal cortex. In the *standard consolidation model*, as proposed by Squire and colleagues, the hierarchical structure of this network partly determines the consolidation process.[8] The hierarchy implies that when storing new information, the hippocampus and adjacent areas are the first to play an active role. This phase probably only extends over a few weeks (see Figure 6.8, event A is a hypothetical event

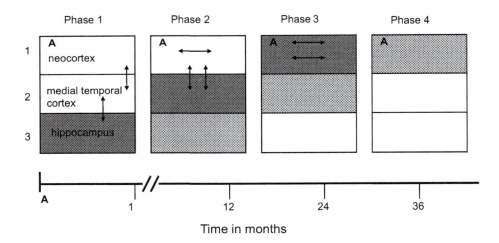

FIGURE 6.8
Hypothetical representation of the time-course of consolidation time (dark = active area, grey = less active areas). Phase 1 is when a sensory input (A) has reached the cortex via vertical reverberating circuits between the hippocampus, medial temporal cortex, and higher cortex. Phase 2: stronger vertical neural connections between medial temporal cortex and higher cortex, and horizontal (cortico-cortical) connections. Phase 3 and 4: further enhancement of cortical consolidation, in which the hippocampus and medial temporal areas no longer play an active role. Cortical lesions of hippocampus and medial temporal cortex in Phase 1 or 2 will complicate retrieval of event A but will have little impact in the following periods.

BOX 6.6 HIPPOCAMPUS BOOSTING PROSTHESIS NOW APPLIED IN HUMANS

Repairing memory deficiencies by implanting devices in the brain, has long been a dream for neurobiologic engineers. Recent developments however suggest that neural prosthetics, often considered as bordering science fiction, have a great potential value.

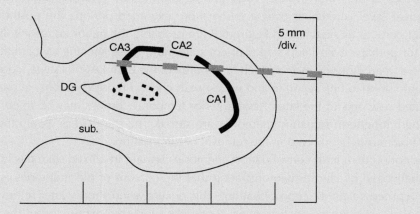

Researchers Theodore Berger, Dong Soon and Robert Hampson, neuroscientists from the Wake Forest Baptist Medical Center in the US, recently described a device, based on a 'macro-micro' depth electrode implanted in cells of the hippocampus. They utilized a combination of stereotaxic placement, imaging and neurons, recorded on each electrode to putative CA3 and CA1 neuroanatomical placements (see the insert of the recording sites interspersed with the 2 mm macro-electrode EEG). Subjects were epilepsy patients surgically implanted with intracranial electrodes to localize clinically based seizures.

Investigators tracked the firing patterns in the hippocampus, when the patients were performing an episodic memory task. From the recorded patterns, Berger, together with USC biomedical engineer Dong Song, created a mathematical model that *predicts* how neurons in each subject's hippocampus would fire during successful memory-formation. A major renovation of their approach was using the same individual firing patterns (assumed to contain the neural codes of memory consolidation), to stimulate the brain to mimic that memory formation. Follow up studies by Hampson verified that the stimulated trials exhibited significant improvement (35%) in both short-term and long-term retention of visual information.

Sources: Hampson et al. (2018), Song et al. (2018).

occurring at time zero). In particular, LTP could then be the crucial mechanism and driving force for the formation of synaptic connections in this learning phase. Later, (after a year or more) the role of the hippocampus is taken over by the adjacent parahippocampal region (phase 2). Eventual damage to the hippocampus would then have less severe consequences for remembering events (like event A, in Figure 6.8) that have already passed the initial phase.

How consolidation then proceeds in learning and consolidation is less clear. The general idea is that after the fast early phase, information is further consolidated at the cortical level, stretching over a much more extended period. The posterior and temporal cortices as sketched in Figure 6.8 are probably the major zones involved. At higher (or perhaps even later) stages of consolidation, these specific topographies get lost, and spread diffusely over a much larger area in the brain. At this stage, consolidation would serve to link separate and widespread cortical representations. In particular distributed networks in the lateral and anterior temporal cortices may be important as sites where long-term semantic memories are stored. The same areas would then also become increasingly involved in the retrieval of information.

The notion that, after consolidation, memories remain in a fixed state has however been challenged by studies demonstrating that the content of old memories is modified by a process called 'reconsolidation'. This occurs when shortly after retrieval or a retention test, substances or distracting conditions block the expression of the earlier memories (Walker et al., 2003), see Chapter 7 for more details).

fMRI studies suggest that an extensive network, called the *general recollection network*, is involved in the retrieval of ultimately formed episodic representations in the cortex, (see Rugg & Vilberg, 2013; Eichenbaum, 2012). Interestingly, this network has much in common with the earlier discussed default mode network, associated with spontaneous associative thinking in a state of rest.

The pattern of gradual consolidation as sketched in Figure 6.8 is consistent with forms of graded retrograde amnesia (the 'Ribot effect'), occurring in pathological states like Korsakoff's syndrome. However, it might also account for the decline of memory with normal advancing age, where recent memories appear to become gradually more vulnerable than old memories (see Box 6.4). Since medial-temporal patients, as well as normal elderly persons, often remain fully capable in retrieving more distant memories, the likely source of these forms of retrograde amnesia would lie in the encoding stage of memory, which depends on the integrity of subcortical and medial temporal areas.

Differential role of anterior and posterior zones of the hippocampal formation

Different regions of the medial temporal cortex presumably process different kinds of information. Anterior parts of the parahippocampal area (the perirhinal cortex) are involved in encoding of 'what' an item is, while the posterior parts of the parahippocampal area with 'where' it is located (Eichenbaum et al., 2007; Eichenbaum et al., 2012 see alo Figure 6.9). Even the hippocampus proper may not act as a unitary structure. The dominant view is that in the posterior hippocampus (called dorsal hippocampus in rodents) is implicated in memory and spatial navigation, and that the anterior hippocampus (ventral hippocampus in rodents: use D(orsal)P(osterior) and V(entral)A(nterior) as a memory aid, see also Figure 6.11) mediates stress and anxiety-related behavior (see Fanselow & Dong 2010; Strange et al., 2014 for a review). There are numerous reciprocal connections between the anterior hippocampus, the ventromedial prefrontal cortex and the orbitofrontal cortex. These connections allow modulation of the content of declarative memories, which includes adding context and affective value to declarative memories. Other notions postulate that anterior regions are more involved in encoding, and posterior regions in retrieval (Lepage et al., 1998; Dolan & Fletcher, 1999), or that anterior regions are more involved in relational memory and posterior regions are more involved in nonrelational memory (Schacter & Wagner, 1999). A complete review of the relevant theories is beyond the scope of this chapter. We here focus on two influential models focusing on the differential roles of posterior and anterior hippocampal sections, in particular with respect to the way they contribute to the gradually 'fanning' out of consolidation to larger memory networks. Both models share the emphasis of a small core in the medial-temporal cortex that gradually expands into a larger network, interleaving with more distant regions in an overall cortical network.

Schema updating

Based on the different functional anatomy of the dorsal and ventral hippocampus in rodents (called posterior and anterior in humans), Preston and Eichenbaum (2013) proposed an alternative model on the time course of consolidation. In the model, the dorsal and ventral streams of the perceptual system in the cortex converge in the hippocampus. There, in the posterior and anterior hippocampus, neural ensembles encode specific objects, and the context in which they occur, respectively (Figure 6.9).

Eichenbaum and colleagues have consistently emphasized the involvement of cells in the hippocampus in relation to the encoding of an episodic context, with time as well as space serving to define these contexts. Suggesting that crucial role of the hippocampus is the laying down of temporal context that binds elements of an episode (see Eichenbaum, 2014 for a review). The function of these 'time cells' might not be the perception of time intervals per se, but rather creating a temporal structure in spatial memory experiences. In particular entorhinal inputs to the hippocampus via the 'where' stream are essential for creating temporal links between associated events.

The consolidation process is not restricted to the hippocampus, but extends to an active dynamic interplay between the anterior hippocampus and the prefrontal cortex. According to the model, the ventral medial prefrontal cortex (VMPFC) accumulates

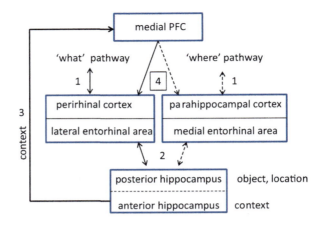

FIGURE 6.9
Model proposed by Preston & Eichenbaum (2013). Perceptual information from the 'where' and 'what' cortical pathways (solid and dashed lines, respectively) is sent to different sections of the medial temporal cortex (1), and is then transmitted to the hippocampus (2). In the posterior hippocampus, neural ensembles encode specific objects and the locations they occur within a context. Neural ensembles in the anterior hippocampus specifically link events within a context, and distinguish between different contexts. Contextual representations from the anterior hippocampus are then sent to the medial prefrontal cortex (3), which in turn influences the retrieval of specific object representations, via its projections to the medial temporal cortex (4).

Source: Adapted from Preston & Eichenbaum (2013).

information about the context of interrelated memories (see Figure 6.9). Outputs of the VMPFC are then sent back to the perirhinal and lateral entorhinal cortex, by which the VMPFC may bias or select the retrieval of event information in the 'what' stream (also including regions in the temporal cortex). The process of altering contextual knowledge is called *schema updating* by Eichenbaum, with the schema composing a 'context' of related memories, and the prefrontal cortex playing a key role in schema development and updating via a top-down pathway.[9] This pathway becomes active when new learning overlaps with pre-existing associations (for example, learning B – C having previously learned A – B). In this case the prefrontal cortex has to reconcile the conflicts in associations of the common elements (B is associated with C, and now also with A). As long as new information adds to existing representations (e.g. in regions like the temporal cortex), memory consolidation depends on an active interplay between prefrontal and hippocampal regions. Schema modification can thus be seen as a long-duration incremental process, with structures in the medial-temporal cortex gradually expanding and interleaving with more distant regions in an overall cortical network. It could also play a role in linking 'events' of episodic memory with 'facts' of semantic memory, thus interleaving episodic memories into a semantic structure. In closing, the present framework suggests that encoding and retrieval do not represent memory stages that are activated in succession, assigned respectively to the medial temporal and neocortical areas. It rather seems that they are processes that overlap in time, engaged in a continuous interplay, as long as new incoming information necessitates updating of existing memories.

Memory guided behavior

Building on the anatomy of the medial temporal cortex and its anatomical connections with the neocortex, Ranganath and Ritchey (2012) proposed a model of two neocortical systems for memory-guided behavior. Similar to the Preston/Eichenbaum model, it builds on two core elements of the medial-temporal cortex, the parahippocampal cortex and the perirhinal cortex, respectively receiving input via the 'where' and 'what' pathways of the visual system. A new element in their model however is the retrosplenial cortex in the parietal lobe.

The retrosplenial cortex connects extensively with the posterior parietal cortex, the parahippocampal cortex, the posterior hippocampus and posterior cingulate. The connectivity pattern of the perirhinal cortex, in contrast, shows multiple connections with the anterior hippocampus, the amygdala, the orbitofrontal cortex (OFC) and the ventral temporopolar cortex (VTPC, see also Figure 6.10). On the basis of these connectivity patterns, Ranganeth and Ritchey proposed two different memory-guided systems, with the hippocampal formation functioning as the central element. In their model, the anterior temporal system (AT) with the perirhinal cortex functioning as the core structure, supports

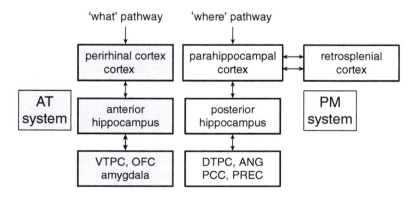

FIGURE 6.10
Model proposed by Ranganath & Ritchey (2012) of two medial-temporal neocortical systems. The anterior temporal system (AT) includes the perirhinal cortex and the anterior hippocampus. The posterior medial system (PM) includes the parahippocampal cortex, the retrosplenial cortex and posterior hippocampus. Funtional conctions with cortical areas of the AT system include the VTPC (ventral temporopolar cortex), the OFC (lateral orbitofrontal cortex) and the amygdala. For the PM system they include the DTPC (dorsal temporopolar cortex), the PCC (posterior cingulate cortex), the ANG (angular gyrus) and the PREC (precuneus) default network.

the 'significance of entities'. Its connections with limbic structures also suggest a role in the regulation of emotional memories. The posterior medial (PM) system in turn, with the parahippocampal and retrosplenial system as core structures, supports recollection-based memories and memory for scenes, with emphasis on spatial layouts, temporal relationship and contexts.

A new element in the model is the presence of parietal cortex, traditionally assumed to play a central in role in attention and multimodal integration. Although the role of the parietal cortex in memory is not yet clear, a distinct possibility is it's functioning as a buffer – or working memory – in a spatial memory system. This idea would correspond with the model of functional brain space introduced earlier in this chapter, suggesting that regions in the brain that carry out different types of cognitive operations might also form the basis of our memory system. The role of the posterior parietal cortex as a 'position module' in top down regulation of visual spatial spatial attention (emphasized in Chapter 4), would also justify its participation in a functional episodic memory network, in close cooperation with the parahippocampal cortex, perhaps with the retrosplenial cortex functioning as an interfacing zone within the PM system, as sketched in Figure 6.10. This supports the idea that the lateral parietal cortex functions as a spatial memory system, analogous to the inferior temporal cortex functioning as a non-spatial object-oriented memory system.

Although the posterior (parahippocampal) hippocampus might also participate in this interleaving process, its role is probably more strongly confined to learning new spatial relations between the location of objects, and the direction of movements. The overall function of the PM network could be to create cognitive maps expanding to the same cortical areas where spatial computations in routine actions and skills are performed, such as the parietal and temporal cortices (Rolls & Treves, 1998; Eichenbaum & Cohen, 2001).

Finally, the two previously sketched consolidation models may differ with respect to the anatomy and functional role of the involved networks, but they provide a clue to the potential diversity of hippocampal-cortical networks underlying declarative memory. Both models also underline the strategic role of higher cortical regions in schema updating, adding new elements and creating relational links with respect to already existing representations, resulting in networks with a much wider scope than the where and what systems from which they receive their input.

Relational memory

The theory of relational memory was developed by Neal Cohen and Howard Eichenbaum. It also forms an important element in the schema updating model of explicit memory introduced earlier. It defines relational memory as 'the memory for relations among the constituent elements of experience'. This might include the ability to remember names with faces, the locations of various objects or people, or the order in which various events occurred. Relational memories differ from episodic memories in that their content is not necessarily open for conscious exploration. Although the hippocampus system supports relational representations, these representations are built at the outset of encoding. Which implies that conscious awareness is an 'emergent phenomenon', but not the 'drive of relational processing' (Eichenbaum, 2012). Relational information refers, for example, to contextual information in visual scenes, like the presence of a certain object in a picture of a complex landscape. Human subjects are sensitive to changes in complex visual scenes (like when the object is missing in a manipulated version of the previously shown picture), without being aware of these changes. This was manifested in an increase of eye-fixations of the critical area in the manipulated picture (Ryan et al., 2000; Konkel & Cohen, 2009). In the same task, patients with damage of their hippocampus failed to show these eye fixations, while their performance in a single-item recollection task was normal. Which suggests that they had a specific deficit in their relational memory. These results confirm various neuroimaging studies showing that the hippocampus proper is essential for complex events, judged according to the relationship between items. Non-relational individually encoded items were shown to activate other areas in the medial-temporal cortex, such as the perirhinal cortex (Davachi & Wagner, 2002). The eye fixation study further illustrates that in certain situations relational memories are expressed as implicit memories. Explaining why it may show up in implicit eye movements in normal individuals, but not in patients with a damaged hippocampus.

False memories

False memories imply remembering events that never happened, or changing the details (Jacoby & Whitehouse, 1989). Cognitive psychology made clear that many instances of false memory can be attributed to semantic interference, using a test called the DRM (Deese, Roediger and McDermott) false-memory test (Roediger et al., 2001). Subjects are asked to memorize a set of words like 'snow,' 'winter,' 'ice,' and 'warm'. After a delay, subjects will typically falsely remember having seen the semantically related word 'cold'.

False memories arise from the same processes as do true memories, and hence their study reveals basic mechanisms of memory. Two theoretical principles underlying the organization of long-term memories are ensemble coding and spreading activation in semantic memories. What both principles have in common is the view that declarative memories can be conceptualized as a network where knowledge is described in terms of nodes and associative pathways between the nodes.

Ensemble coding implies that any part or 'node' in long-term memory has multiple functions. For example, a particular node can be used to recognize a giraffe or a tree (see Figure 3.7 for an example). This explains why we sometimes make mistakes in recognition of an object, for example when object 1 not only activates elements of object 1, but also elements of object 2 in the network.

A second theory, called spreading activation, refers more specifically to the organization of semantic memories. When part of the network is activated, activation spreads along the associative pathways to related areas in memory. Semantically related concepts (dog-bark) have stronger connections than semantically unrelated concepts (dog-tree).

fMRI studies have shed more light on the brain mechanisms involved in false memories, using the DRM paradigm. They have in particular revealed the underlying structure of neural representations of semantic knowledge, and how this semantic structure both enhances and distorts our memories. Martin Chadwick and colleagues found evidence that false memories emerge from a similarity-based neural code in the temporal pole, a region that has been called the 'semantic hub' of the brain (Chadwick et al., 2016). Using the DRM approach, they measured the degree of neural overlap between each set of DRM words and their related lure word. This result provided evidence that each individual has a partially unique set of semantic representations within the temporal pole, that have a direct impact on memory distortions.

The cellular basis of explicit learning

The left part of Figure 6.11 shows the major section of the hippocampus that has the shape of a curved tube, with the C-shaped cross section called 'ramshorn', derived from the Latin Cornu Ammonis. Its abbreviation CA is used for the hippocampal subfields, designated CA1, CA2 and CA3 that mainly consist of pyramid cells. CA4 is part of the dentate gyrus containing granular cells and 'mossy fibers'. Areas CA3 (with the adjacent dentate gyrus) and CA1 are of the most interest for establishing LTP. The dentate gyrus is almost completely fused with the lower part of the rolled horn shape part of the hippocampus (the ventral section), and mainly contains granular cells. The utmost lower part of the hippocampus, the entorhinal cortex, also consists of pyramid cells. It is the major input channel of the hippocampus, receiving input from the temporal association cortex and cingulate gyrus (see also Box 6.5).

Long-term potentiation

LTP was discovered by Bliss and Lømo in Oslo in 1973 in the rabbit hippocampus. LTP is a long-term change in the postsynaptic response of a neuron that results from prior stimulation with a high-frequency stimulus (called 'tetanic' stimulation). LTP is the most influential model of synaptic plasticity that might underlie our memory systems. It can be invoked in vivo, in live animals but also in vitro, i.e. in tissue preparations, that can stay alive for several days.

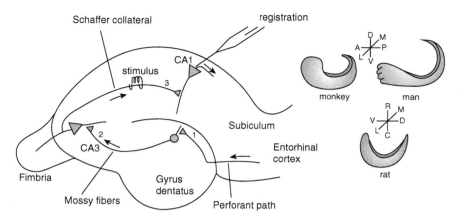

FIGURE 6.11
Left: major sections of the hippocampus (CA1, dentate gyrus, subiculum, entorhinal cortex, and CA3), and significant pathways (perforant path (1), mossy fibers (2) and Schaffer collaterals (3)). LTP is generated in area CA1, through stimulation of Schaffer's collateral. The fimbria (middle left), contains a bundle of axons called fornix, connecting with the septum and mammillary bodies. Adapted from Kandel et al. (1991). Right: anatomical sketch of the hippocampus in monkey and man (upper right) and in the rat (lower right). Notice that anterior-posterior division (A-P) axis in monkey and man is equivalent to the ventral-dorsal axis (V-D) in the rat. R and C in the rat refer to the rostral-caudal axis.

Source: Adapted from Strange et al. (2014).

LTP can last for hours in anesthetized laboratory animals, or for days in free-running experiment animals. The neurotransmitters noradrenaline and acetylcholine also provide input to the hippocampus via the fornix, modulating LTP. Nordadrenaline may thereby potentiate LTP in CA3 and the gyrus dentatus, while acetylcholine may potentiate LTP in the gyrys dentatus and CA1.

LTP is produced as follows. A weak electrical pulse is administered to the part of the Schaffer collateral that provides input to pyramidal cells in CA1. The resulting EPSP (excitatory postsynaptic potential) is then measured in the CA1 pyramid cells (see Figure 6.11). This response reflects the strength of the synaptic connection before LTP has taken place. Subsequently, Schaffer's collateral is stimulated for a second time with a high-frequency electrical pulse train (also called tetanic stimulation). When a weak pulse is administered after a short interval, the EPSP in CA1 has significantly increased relative to the baseline response. The reason being that the pulse train or 'burst' causes depolarization of the postsynaptic membrane. The LTP effect appears to be specific: only synapses within the postsynaptic neuron that were active during stimulation by the pulse train are potentiated. Other neighboring synapses on the same neuron have not changed. Long-Term Depression (LTD) in turn has the opposite effect, attenuation of the EPSPs. This occurs when pulses are presented at a slow rate, and not as a high-frequency burst. LTP has become the most prominent model of synaptic plasticity, underlying the acquisition of declarative memories, as well of nondeclarative subforms of memory, e.g. skill learning and conditioning, involving neural circuits in the striatum and amygdala.

Associative LTP

Associative LTP is an extension of Hebb's law. It can only be produced in the CA1 region, if two stimuli are presented simultaneously or shortly after another at different locations, i.e. different fascicles of the collateral of Schaffer (see Figure 6.12). When presented separately, the synapse stimulated by either the weak or the strong pulse, is not potentiated. Only when the weak and strong pulse occur together, they will produce LTP (in the form of an amplitude increase of the EPSP) in CA1. This because the strong pulse leads to depolarization of the postsynaptic neuron in CA1. If the strong pulse is simultaneously presented with the weak pulse, the synapse of the weak pulse is also potentiated (Figure 6.12, D).

This form of long-term potentiation (LTP), known as associative LTP, was shown in some cases to last for hours without decrement. Moreover, CA1's pyramid cells only respond to this specific input, not to input given to another dendrite, which is a sign of selective synaptic enhancement of the weak synapse.

BOX 6.7   A PILL TO ENHANCE MEMORY?

The discovery of the LTP mechanism also stimulated research to develop drugs to improve memory. This includes among other things Ampakinen™, enzymes that target non-NMDA receptors (such as AMPA receptors, receptors for glutamate that mediate fast synaptic transmission) and enhance the consolidation process. These agents have a modulating effect. They penetrate the brain where they stimulate glutamate production in synapses. Another category of substances with a similar effect are benzothiadizides. Different pharmaceutical companies are currently investigating these substances, in what appears as a 'race in developing memory-enhancing substances'*. Older adults with the diagnosis MCI (Mild Cognitive Impairment) are a suitable target group. This group has an increased risk of developing Alzheimer's disease. In view of the rapidly increasing elderly population, and an increasing risk of brain diseases such as dementia, there appears to be a major market for memory-enhancing drugs. Sometimes other clinical groups like schizophrenic patients and ADHD children also seem to benefit from AMPA receptor modulators.

* Lynch, (2002).

The role of NMDA receptors

The question arising is which molecular mechanism in cell and synapse now forms the base of these two forms of LTP. In neurons of the hippocampus, there are two different types of receptors, both of which are sensitive to the excitatory neurotransmitter glutamate, NMDA (n-methyl-d-aspartate) receptors and non-NMDA receptors. LTP relies on the action of NMDA receptors in the dendritic spines of the postsynaptic neurons in CA1, and the gyrus dentatus of the hippocampus. NMDA receptors control the calcium channels in the postsynaptic membrane. Magnesium ions normally block these channels. This blockade still exists when the NMDA receptor binds to glutamate, released from the terminal boutons of the presynaptic neurons (see Figure 6.12). Only after depolarization of the postsynaptic membrane, the blockade by magnesium is removed.

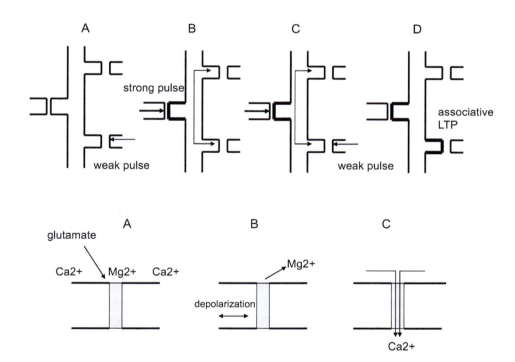

FIGURE 6.12
Top: an example of associative LTP. A: weak pulse administered on the dendrite of the postsynaptic neuron: no potentiation of synapse. B: strong pulse: depolarization and potentiation of postsynapse (in black). C: a weak and strong pulse occur simultaneously. D: now the postsynapse of the weak stimulus is also potentiated. Bottom: three corresponding states of the NMDA receptor (the shaded area) in the postsynaptic membrane. A: glutamate binds to the receptor. However, because it is blocked by magnesium ions (Mg2+), calcium (CA2+) ions cannot flow into the cell. B: depolarization occurs by an EPSP in the postsynaptic membrane which removes the magnesium blockade. C: Free flow of calcium is now possible for a period of 100–200 ms.

Calcium can then enter the cell, where it acts as an intracellular messenger that ultimately changes the strength of the synapse.[10]

Responding to the conjunction (simultaneous occurrence) of two factors, depolarization of the postsynaptic membrane, and release of glutamate in the presynaptic membrane, is the unique quality of NMDA receptors. This is why they are also referred to as 'double gated' channels, monitored by glutamate in the presynaptic membrane, and a voltage change in the postsynaptic membrane.

The production of both LTP and LTD can be blocked by AP5, a glutamate antagonist while AP5 has no effect on an already formed LTP. This is strong evidence that NMDA receptors are specifically involved in LTP formation, and that other (non-NMDA) receptors are involved in information transmission in an already potentiated synapse.

Amnesia and deficits in consolidation

Memory disorders form a very heterogeneous group, in which amnesia is considered to be the major disorder of declarative long-term memory. A wealth of information came from studies with patients with various forms of brain damage. Critical areas in the brain where damage led to memory disorders include the diencephalon (thalamus and the mammillary bodies), the hippocampus, the prefrontal cortex and the 'basal forebrain', a region in the brain that is responsible for the production of the neurotransmitter acetylcholine (Cohen & Eichenbaum, 1993). Taken together, the compromised regions could

---

BOX 6.8   PRIMING EFFECTS IN AMNESIA

Amnesia patients generally do not differ from normal subjects in certain forms of implicit memory, such as sensorimotor tasks or priming. The reversed pattern (called 'double dissociation'), namely an intact explicit memory but distorted priming, does also occur. Epileptic patient MS had a right occipital lesion described by Gabrieli et al. (1995), who compared his performance in a word priming task with that of amnesic patients. Test words presented with variable duration were primed by previously presented (masked) words. Amnesic patients benefited from the previous primes when the test words were presented very briefly, but showed less than normal performance in separate explicit recognition tasks when they were presented with old and new words and asked whether they had seen them before. MS, however, showed the reversed pattern: a normal performance in the explicit task but worse performance in the implicit reading task. These data emphasize that the right occipital cortex is important for sensory priming of visual forms, and also that declarative and nondeclarative memory can be doubly dissociated by brain lesions.

underlie problems in encoding as well as retrieval of memories, concerning events that happened either before or after the moment when brain damage occurred.

Earlier studies mainly depended on data from postmortem studies to detect the anatomical site of damage. Today, the location of brain lesions can be determined more directly with neuroimaging techniques. MRI, for example, is especially suitable for the precise determination of the lesion site, while fMRI and PET are more suitable for mapping the functioning of specific lesioned areas. Also critical were studies of memory performance in the rat and higher mammals like the monkey.

Patient studies

Studies of patients with brain damage made a substantial contribution in identifying structures underlying disorders in declarative memory. This mainly concerned subcortical structures, like the hippocampus and the thalamus.

Hippocampus and medial temporal cortex A classic case study in memory research was patient Henry Gustav Molaison (in short, HM) described in 1957 by Scoville and Milner. HM suffered from an incurable form of epilepsy, which was treated by surgical removal of the bilateral medial temporal cortex, including large parts of the hippocampus, the parahippocampal gyrus, and the amygdala. After surgery, HM showed a severe form of anterograde amnesia, a deficit that makes it impossible to store new information in declarative memory.

HM was no longer able to remember new facts, events, persons and objects with which he was confronted after surgery. Retrograde amnesia refers to the lack of ability to remember facts and events that occurred in the period before the moment of brain injury (see Figure 6.13).[11]

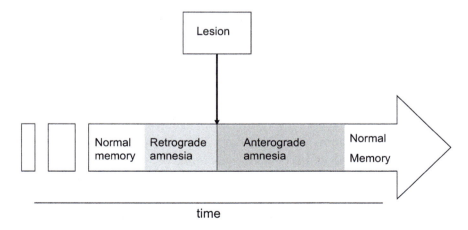

FIGURE 6.13
Schematic view of anterograde and retrograde amnesia. The lighter shade of retrograde amnesia indicates a lesser and more graded impairment than with anterograde amnesia.

HM's memory for events that had occurred before surgery was mostly intact, except for the last three years, with more severe impairment for the more recent years. This finding suggested that the consolidation of information in declarative long-term memory is a process that might even span several years. Remarkably HM's procedural memory, the ability to perform and learn new sensorimotor skills, remained largely intact. This was shown in a typical visuomotor test, the mirror drawing test (drawing a line between two lines that together form a five-pointed star, one sees only the mirror image of one's hand). HM's short-term (or rather working) memory, for example the ability to remember short digit sequences over a short period, appeared to be spared too. These findings gave a significant impulse to the development of the theory of multiple memory systems. The nature of HM's brain injury also indicated that the integrity of medial temporal areas is a critical condition for consolidating explicit, but not implicit (procedural) memories.

Later research by Squire confirmed the important role of the hippocampus in consolidating explicit memories. An example is patient RB, who suffered from brain damage caused by a restricted oxygen supply to the brain during a cardiovascular operation. RB also suffered from a mild form of anterograde memory with no sign of retrograde amnesia. After his death, a section of his brain revealed specific damage of the CA1 region in the hippocampus. Similar memory disorders were found by Squire using MRI in patients with specific hippocampal lesions. An advantage of these studies was that they allowed examining in detail the anatomy of the brain as well as the performance of patients when they were still alive.

Lesions of diencephalon Anterograde amnesia also occurs in Korsakoff's syndrome, often resulting from excessive alcohol consumption, and a lack of thiamine (vitamin B). It becomes manifest in graded anterograde amnesia, which increases as the disease progresses, implying that recent memories are much more affected than old memories. In Korsakoff patients, structures in the thalamus (especially the dorsomedial nuclei) are often damaged. There can also be damage to another area in the diencephalon, the mammillary bodies (Figure 6.14). The dorsomedial thalamic nuclei have many reciprocal connections with the prefrontal regions in the brain, which may explain why Korsakoff's syndrome often also affects higher functions like planning and coordination.

Amnesia resulting from damage in the diencephalon is presumably a deficit in acquisition of knowledge. Since this represents an early stage of encoding (see Figure 6.2), it is likely to affect subsequent consolidation of declarative memories. The diencephalon connects through many reciprocal pathways with areas in the hippocampus (Figure 6.14 presents a schematic view of the connections) important for both acquisition and retrieval of information in explicit memory. As a result, lesions in the diencephalon often lead to the same type of memory disorders, as lesions of the medial temporal area (see also Aggleton & Brown (1999) for a detailed anatomical account). Both Korsakoff patients and patients with hippocampal damage show a retrograde amnesia with a temporal (or Ribot) gradient. They have more problems remembering recent than old events and episodes.

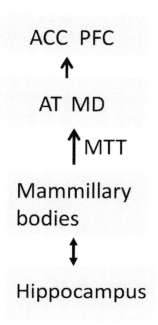

FIGURE 6.14
Schematic view of major sites of damage in Korsakoff patients. Mammillary bodies connecting with the hippocampus and via the MTT (mammillothalamic tract), with the anterior nuclei (AT) and mediodorsal nuclei (MD) nuclei of the thalamus. The ACC (anterior cingulate cortex and PFC (prefrontal cortex) are the cortical sites of projections from AT and MD, respectively.

They find it more difficult, for example, to recognize faces of public celebrities from the recent past than those from the more distant past. The temporal gradient in these patients may be an expression of a gradually increasing inability to store new knowledge in the brain, over a long period in life. When the disease started early in life, retrograde amnesia may extend to several decades. Thus, a problem with diagnosing disorders like Korsakoff's syndrome is that it is hard to locate the precise moment in time, when the damage to the brain has occurred (Albert et al., 1979). Consequently, it is often difficult to determine whether their amnesia reflects the inability to retrieve old knowledge (true retrograde amnesia) or the inability to store new knowledge (true anterograde amnesia).

Summing up, studies of patients with lesions in the medial temporal areas justify the following three conclusions.

▶ There seems to be a connection between the size of the lesion and the duration and severity of retrograde amnesia; with larger lesions, there is also a more extended period of retrograde amnesia.

▶ The finding that even in severe lesions of the medial temporal areas memories of past events and episodes remain intact means that these areas cannot be the site of long-term declarative memories.

▶ Hippocampal-cortical pathways have a temporary role in consolidating new memories in the cortex, which is gradually taken over by cortical networks.

Animal studies of amnesia

Animal research has supported the role of the hippocampus in consolidating explicit knowledge. In a seminal study by Squire and Zola-Morgan two groups of monkeys (a control and an experimental group) performed a discrimination learning task. The monkeys had to learn different lists of 20 pairs of objects at variable moments in time (16 to 2 weeks respectively) before surgery. The experimental group was then subjected to surgery, in which the hippocampus and surrounding area of the parahippocampal gyrus were lesioned. Two weeks after surgery, learning performance was again tested in the control and the experimental groups, with the previously learned lists being offered in random order.

The pattern of results of the experimental monkeys was very different from that of the control monkeys. They exhibited a temporal gradient, in which memory of recently learned material was worse than of material learned about two to three months before the operation (see Figure 6.15). The learning performance from the earliest period was approximately equal to that of the control group.

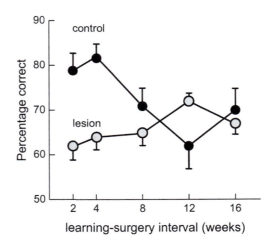

FIGURE 6.15
Retention curves of lesioned monkeys compared to normal monkeys as a function of the learning-surgery interval. The vertical axis shows performance in an object-discrimination learning task. Normal monkeys have a forgetting curve. Lesioned monkeys show a temporal (Ribot) gradient, with early learned lists being remembered better than recently learned lists.

Source: Adapted from Squire & Zola-Morgan (1991).

The control group showed a forgetting curve, with the recently learned material remembered better than the material learned earlier. These results were considered to support the hypothesis that consolidation is a process based on a gradual reorganization of acquired knowledge as a function of time, with the role of the hippocampus gradually decreasing.

Subsequent studies by Squire's group, using precise stereotactic surgery techniques, confirmed the role of the hippocampus and also its surrounding regions in a more refined test of declarative memory, the 'delayed non-matching-to-sample task' invented by Mishkin (Figure 6.16 left). In this task, animals have to choose between two objects, with only the choice of the new object being rewarded. The reward then serves as an 'incentive' rather than as 'reinforcement', i.e. a strengthening, of repeated behavior. Their study also showed that the amygdala played no direct role in consolidating declarative memory (compare N and A graphs in Figure 6.16 at the right).

Mishkin's previous work had revealed that the learning performance of monkeys in this type of task was mostly affected by damage to *both* the hippocampus and the amygdala, rather than only to the hippocampus (Mishkin, 1982, Mishkin & Appenzeller, 1987). Mishkin's study of removal of the amygdala also included the

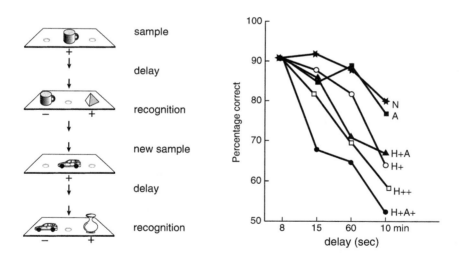

FIGURE 6.16
Left: delayed non-matching-to-sample task. The plus sign indicates the to-be-selected item. Each trial consists of a new combination of objects. Right: learning performance of monkeys with lesions in various areas of the medial temporal cortex). N = intact. H and A: Hippocampal and Amygdala lesions, respectively. H+ and A+: the surrounding cortical areas are also lesioned. H++: hippocampus and same cortical areas lesioned as with H+A+.

Sources: Adapted from Squire (1992).

surrounding perirhinal and parahippocampal areas. Later studies by Squires and Zola-Morgan made clear that lesions of the surrounding cortical area (denoted with ++ at the longest delay interval), and not the amygdala itself, were responsible for the memory decline of the monkey (H+A did not differ from H+, and H++ did not differ from H+A+, Figure 6.16 lower right).

Notice that these findings do not preclude that the amygdala can indirectly affect explicit memories in humans, by adding motivational or emotional valence of certain moving events. Such effects play a role in flashbulb memories, where the emotional context of events, like for example scenes of the collapsing Twin Tower, may provide an emotion 'tag' to these events. However, this does not necessarily imply that the involved memory representations are more accurate than non-emotional memories (Neisser & Harsch, 1992).

Cortical lesions

Most patient studies of amnesia concerned lesions of the hippocampus and diencephalon. Memory disorders caused by damage to the neocortical areas have a different character, often manifested in disorders in cognitive-semantic memory functions. These disorders include conceptual and lexical knowledge, and retrieving the name of objects.

Semantic dementia

Semantic dementia means a progressive loss of semantic memory. Lesion data suggest that the disorder is caused by a loss of white matter (myelin), or a loss of neurons in the inferior temporal gyrus, mostly so in the 'temporal pole', the most anterior part of the left anterior lobe (Mummery et al., 2000). Recall that the temporal lobe is also the end-station of the 'what' route of the visual system, crucial for the processing of the meaning of visual objects (see also Figure 6.17). These temporal regions are assumedly involved in the processing, as well as the storage of semantic knowledge. Which explains why patients often have difficulties in naming visually presented objects, like a picture of a house or dog. A patient may for example say: 'that animal barks' or 'I am afraid of that animal', which suggests that a picture of a visual object or animal may still activate correlated semantic, phonological or even affective features in the brain's conceptual network.

Agnosia

Agnosia is a collective name for disorders in recognizing objects that become manifest in a specific sensory modality. Examples are visual agnosia, auditory agnosia, tactile

> **BOX 6.9   CHILDHOOD AMNESIA**
>
> Childhood or infantile amnesia is the lack of memories from early childhood. This 'blank' period applies to both adults and older children, and includes approximately the first four years of life, with the sixth year of life as an upper limit. This is also the age at which children learn to speak, which suggests that childhood amnesia might be related to language development. Researchers like Patricia Bauer for example believe that infants have the ability to store early episodes and events in their memory, but are unable to consolidate or retrieve these memories due to their still insufficient verbal skills, in particular, those needed to talk about their experiences (Bauer, 2014). This could then, in turn, lead to a decay of their early memories. An alternative and perhaps more plausible explanation is that the infant brain still lacks the refined neural machinery and the diversity of synaptic connections needed to store memories in the networks of long-term memory. As a result, the impressions from the outside world are not yet fully consolidated in long-term memory. This 'brain-based' theory explains the still defective declarative and procedural memory, as manifested in poor language and motor skills, and perhaps also the absence of more complex emotions in early childhood.
>
> Source: Bauer et al. (1986).

agnosia, implying that objects cannot be identified by vision, sounds or touch. A deficit in naming objects not only occurs in visual agnosia, but also in *anomia*. Anomia however is a linguistic disorder, manifested in problems with producing the verbal symbol, and not so much with recognizing the visual object. Agnosia patients differ from anomia patients in that they can neither name the confronted object, nor select it from a group or match it to a likeness.

Agnosia is considered to be 'conceptual': it cannot be attributed to a general memory disorder or impairment of specific sensory or language abilities. Conceptual disorders are highly complex, because they occur at the interface of memory, language, and perceptual functions. Agnosia patients often show category-specific deficits. They can, for example, easily identify natural objects but not man-made objects (Warrington & Shallice, 1984). Or a patient has a specific problem in recognizing faces of people, like in prosopagnosia (see also Chapter 5, Box 5.2). Remarkably, lesions in the inferior temporal gyrus were shown to be category specific: naming persons, for example, mostly activated the temporal pole, naming animals the middle portion, and naming tools the posterior portion, overlapping with the

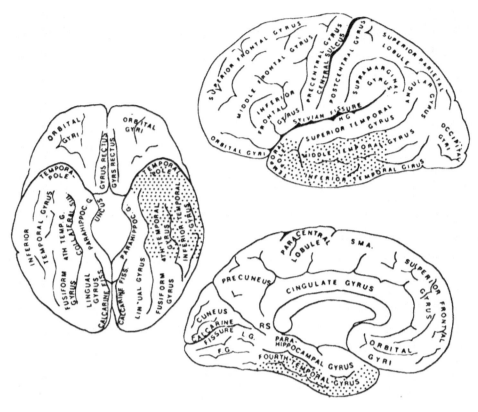

FIGURE 6.17
Dashed regions in the temporal lobe indicate the gyri where bilateral damage causes a deficit in recognizing or naming objects. Right: lateral (upper) and medial (lower) view of the left hemisphere. Left: bottom view.

Source: From: Damasio & Damasio (1994).

occipital area (Figure 3.4. in Chapter 3 provides an example of these category specific deficits).

Visual and auditory forms of agnosia reflect a deficit in the integrity of a network in the temporal lobes. An often-affected region is the border between the occipital and temporal cortex, which is part of the ventral pathway. Atrophies in the secondary – or association areas – within the ramifications of the ventral pathway might be the reason why agnostic symptoms are often manifested in a specific sensory modality. Voice agnosia, for example, often involves the secondary auditory areas in the superior temporal gyrus, and face agnosia the fusiform gyrus in the face area of the inferior temporal cortex. The inability to read, called *alexia*, often represents a complementary symptom of a facial-recognition deficit. Tactile agnosia however, is associated with the parietal regions of the cortex, adjacent to the somatosensory region (Banich, 1997; Kolb & Wishaw, 1998).

The category-specific character of agnostic symptoms has also led to new insights with regard to the organization of semantic memory (e.g. Martin et al., 1996). Connectionist network models have shown that conceptual knowledge depends on the two fundamentally different ways the semantic networks are organized; as categories (living versus non-living things), or as properties of objects (color, shape, visual and usage. In a wider context, the distinction between concrete and abstract concepts could be even more relevant for the way semantic networks and their neural correlates are organized. Concrete knowledge refers to real objects in our environment, living as well as non-living. The representation of a knife, for example, contains perceptual and action elements, like its sharpness, shape, the holding of it and cutting with it. These elements, in turn, correspond to specific local networks in the brain containing their respective codes (kinesthetic, form, movement). Categorical knowledge applies to higher-level abstract concepts, like lexical representations, the syntactic properties of words, associated with more distributed networks implementing language functions.

Frontal lesions

Evidence from lesions in animals as well as neuroimaging (fMRI) studies of normal humans have implicated the dorsolateral prefrontal cortex (DLPFC), as playing a critical role in working memory. Following lesions of the frontal cortex, monkeys were unable to perform the delayed-nonmatching-to-sample task, introduced earlier, even at very short delays. These effects were more severe when the lesions were in the DLPFC area (Goldman-Rakic 1988). Studies of intact humans, as well as of patients, have also corroborated the importance of DLPFC and the more ventral portion in the prefrontal cortex (VLPFC), in tasks making demands on working memory and executive functions. Frontal lesions and related executive functions might also lead to problems with retrieval of episodic and semantic memories (Buckner et al., 1999).

Implicit memory: priming, learning and mechanisms

Non-declarative, or implicit, memory is a mixed bag of memories that have one trait in common: that they do not depend on consolidation by medial temporal structures in the brain. All learning follows the principle of the gradual strengthening of synapses, either at the cortical or the subcortical level. The subsequent question is how this process is accomplished in the neural circuits involved in implicit memory. This concerns the site of its long-term memories, as well as learning: how the consolidation of new implicit memories takes place.

Priming

Priming refers to a change in the speed, bias or accuracy of the processing of a stimulus, following prior experience with the same, or a semantically related, stimulus. As such it can be seen as a specific form of implicit learning, based on change of neural activity as a function of repetition of a stimulus.

Priming and habituation

What priming and habituation paradigms have in common is that both produce effects that occur automatically and implicitly. Their underling neural mechanisms, however, differ substantially. Positive priming, for example, is based on pre-activation of a cortical circuitry, providing facilitation, or a 'head start', to a primed event. By contrast, habituation to a repeatedly presented task- irrelevant event reflects neural inhibition, manifested as a slowing of the behavioral response, and a decrement of the physiological response (Sokolov, 1963). It is possible though, that both effects occur simultaneously, in particular with short duration primes, when positive priming dominates habituation. Long duration primes are shown to result in a net slowing of behavioral response (negative priming), probably reflecting a shift in the balance of the two systems, with inhibition dominating pre-activation (Huber & O'Reilly, 2003).

Characteristics of positive priming

A finding of functional neuroimaging studies of repetition priming in visual tasks, is a *decreased* neural activity in the extrastriate and inferior prefrontal cortices for the second presentation of an object, relative to its first presentation. Effects of this 'repetition suppression' are usually interpreted as a more efficient processing of the second stimulus, due to pre-activated neural pathways. The suppression effects on the visual cortex were manifested most clearly when subjects were unaware of the content of the stimuli. In contrast to repetition priming, the posterior temporal region showed an *enhanced* response for primed words during semantic priming. This pattern could reflect more conscious selection processes in inferior frontal regions, that operate when semantic information is retrieved from temporal regions (Henson, 2003).

Priming, in general, appears to be a pre-semantic phenomenon, in the sense that a) it occurs whether or not subjects perform semantic encoding operations, and b) that it is quite sensitive to changes in perceptual properties of target information. Explicit memory, on the other hand, is generally dependent on, and greatly enhanced by, semantic encoding operations and less sensitive to changes in perceptual properties of target information (Schacter, 1992).

Priming tests often concern isolated perceptual characteristics of the stimulus. For example, priming effects are much stronger when study and test material appear in the same modality (visual-visual or auditory-auditory) than in different modalities (auditory-visual). The dependency of priming effects on elementary physical stimulus characteristics suggests that they are closely linked to perceptual systems in the posterior cortex, especially the primary sensory areas. Schacter and Moscovitch suggested that priming uses already existing structural anatomical connections within, and also between cortical modules.

In the same context, Schacter introduced the concept of a Perceptual Representation System (PRS), a system presumed to develop early in life, and to be resistant to the effects of aging. The involved regions are respectively the extrastriate, the inferotemporal and the auditory association areas lying near the temporal /parietal junction (Figure 6.18). The extrastriate system is sensitive to elementary visual features, while the system for storing perceptual objects in the inferotemporal cortex is more sensitive to global structure and dimensions. The auditory association area is especially active in the storage of spoken

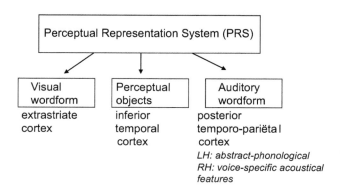

FIGURE 6.18
The three subsystems of the Perceptual Representation System, visual word form, perceptual objects, and auditory word form, and their corresponding cortical areas.

Source: Adapted from Schacter et al. (1990).

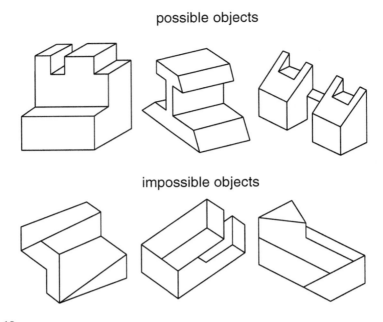

FIGURE 6.19
Schacter et al. (1990) found that when subjects were instructed to pay attention to the global form of previously presented perceptual objects, priming effects were stronger for possible than impossible 3D objects. Suggesting that the effects are mediated by the inferior temporal cortex (Schacter et al., 1991).

words. When priming spoken words (the effects of which mainly show in the parietal-temporal areas), there may be a further subdivision between two aspects. The first aspect relates to purely acoustic voice-specific features of spoken words, presumably associated with the right hemisphere. The second is the processing of abstract phonological characteristics, which would mainly take place in the left hemisphere. Priming effects also occur for abstract objects as drawings of three-dimensional figures, but only if they do not conflict with geometric rules (like an 'impossible figure': this does not work as a prime, see Figure 6.19).

In a PET study of Squire, presentations of full words were followed by word-stems, after which subjects had to name the first word which came into mind. The presentation of word-stems without prior presentation of the full versions served as the control condition. Interestingly, the extrastriate region showed a *reduced* blood flow compared with the control condition. However, when subjects received a 'recall' instruction (responding to the word-stem with a word from the previously presented series), the hippocampus and prefrontal regions showed a *stronger* activation compared to the priming and baseline condition. This result supported the idea that priming effects concern the selection of more efficient, pre-activated, synaptic connections in the cortical circuits.

Right-hemisphere and priming

The fact that priming often shows the most potent effects in the right hemisphere is a further indication that physical, form-specific characteristics of the stimulus play an essential role in repetition priming. Additional support for the role of the right hemisphere was found in the word-stem completion study of Squire, in which test stimuli were presented in the right and left visual hemifields, while the subject fixated the center of the display. In this set-up, the stimuli presented in the left and right left visual fields project respectively to the right and left visual cortical areas. Strongest effects of word-stem completion occurred for left visual field stimuli.

Habit learning

Some forms of visually presented verbal material also follow the implicit pathway. In contrast with flexible, context-dependent learning, habit learning is considered as an automatic, inflexible form of learning (Miskin et al., 1984). For example, the learning strategy could be based on a repeated presentation of words in paired-associates tasks. Subjects receive lists of different word pairs and are told to name the second word after the first. The instruction is not to pay any particular attention to the word pairs. Habit learning is another term for this automatic acquisition of stimulus-response associations. Amnesia patients with damage to the medial temporal cortex are still able to learn associations between objects or words, but the number of lists needed to reach a perfect score is much larger than for normal control subjects. These subjects associate the learned words – via the explicit route – with existing representations in their memory. If the learning material has little meaning or structure – for example when learning dot patterns – the learning curves of healthy subjects and patients show only a slight difference. These more associative forms of learning appear to be mainly controlled by the striatum and the motor areas. The cerebellum may also be involved in learning motor skills, especially with respect to the timing aspect of movements. It is evident, however, that the striatum is the key element in the acquisition of stereotypical behavioral repertoires, a process that is independent from the circuitry involved in acquisition of declarative memory (Sakai & Miyashita, 1991; Knowlton et al., 1996).

Sensorimotor learning

Motor skill acquisition refers to the process by which movements produced alone, or in a sequence, come to be performed effortlessly through repeated practice and interactions with the environment. An example is the serial four button pressing task, where subjects learn to press four buttons according to a repeated sequence. For example, subjects learn to push the buttons corresponding to four lights flashing in the complex repeated sequence 431342141. In this task, reaction time to the flashed lights becomes faster without subjects knowing that any pattern exists. In experiments of implicit learning of motor sequences it was crucial to isolate the implicit part of motor learning from the explicit (conscious) part. This was accomplished with a dual task condition, intended to prevent explicit learning or noticing the motor sequence. Considering the variety of the involved tasks of motor learning, the general picture emerging from these studies is far from being unequivocal.

Role of basal ganglia

A number of studies pointed to the additional role of the basal ganglia (in particular the striatum) and its projections to the cortex in supporting formation of new skills (see also Figure 5.8 in Chapter 5 illustrating the possibly involved 'motor loop' and 'cerebellar-cortical' loop). The striatum has many afferent connections with the sensory regions, and efferent connections with the premotor cortex and SMA. Which makes the striatal-cortical circuits ideally suited for linking input (perception) to output (action). From this perspective, it is tempting to compare the role of the striatum in establishing synaptic connections with the anterior motor regions, with that of the hippocampus in consolidating explicit learning (Doyon et al., 2009). Indeed, synaptic potentiation in the motor cortices during skill learning possibly also reflects the cellular mechanism of LTP in learning, as established in the hippocampus (Eichenbaum, 2012). Similar to explicit learning, the underlying circuitry would involve reciprocal pathways connecting the cerebral cortex with subcortical structures, which in implicit learning involve the striatum and amygdala, instead of the hippocampus.

Involvement of the striatum and the SMA was demonstrated in a PET study by Grafton in which subjects had to learn specific patterns of finger movements. They performed another task at the same time, to prevent them from paying attention to the learning task. The PET images in the dual task condition, were compared with images derived from the single task condition (allowing conscious processing). Interestingly, in the double-tasked condition, motor areas like the SMA and the motor cortex in the left cerebral hemisphere and the basal ganglia were most active. Another study by Knowlton and colleagues demonstrated the involvement of the striatum of the basal ganglia as well. In contrast to patients with medial temporal lesions, Parkinson's patients with lesions in the striatum performed poorly in associative tasks requiring gradual, incremental learning, characteristic of habit learning.

The time course of skill learning

Skill acquisition develops initially relatively fast and later more slowly, when further gains develop incrementally over multiple sessions of practice. The relative duration of what can be defined as fast and slow learning is highly task specific. For example, the fast stage of learning a simple four component key press sequence could last minutes, while the fast stage of learning to play a complex musical piece may last months. In humans, the neural substrates of these learning stages were studied with Positron Emission Tomography (PET) and functional magnetic resonance imaging (fMRI) (see Dayan & Cohen, 2011 for a comprehensive review). fMRI studies indicate that the functional connectivity of the cortical motor network is modulated with practice, and suggest that early skill learning is mediated by enhanced interregional coupling (Sun et al., 2007). Different patterns of cortical subcortical coupling were found during fast and slow learning phases. A more detailed account follows.

Fast learning A number of studies using PET and fMRI reported that skill learning in relatively simple tasks, like the serial four button pressing task explained earlier, is accompanied by contrasting patterns of the direction of activation. During the early phase of learning, brain activity *decreased* in the presupplementary motor area (preSMA), dorsolateral prefrontal cortex (DLPFC) and primary motor cortex (M1). The premotor cortex, supplementary motor area (SMA), parietal regions, striatum and the cerebellum however showed a concurrent *increase* of activation in the (Figure 6.20).

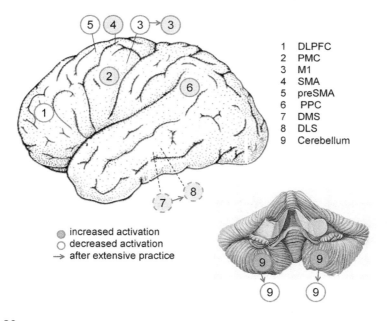

FIGURE 6.20
Effects of fast learning of a sequential motor task overlayed for a number of fMRI and PET studies. Increased activation reflects recruitment of additional cortical substrates with practice. Decreased activation suggests that less neuronal resources are needed as learning proceeds. Involved areas: dorsolateral prefrontal cortex (DLPFC), primary motor cortex (M1), premotor cortex (PMC), supplementary motor area (SMA) and pre-supplementary motor area (pre-SMA), posterior parietal cortex (PPC), dorsomedial striatum (DMS) (dorsolateral striatum (DLS) (striatal areas located in the medial surface) and the posterior cerebellum.

Source: Adapted from Dayan & Cohen (2011). Cerebellum (lower panel): adapted from Kandel et al., (1991). P. 629 Fig. B

One possible interpretation of these data is that decreasing activations of the preSMA and DLPFC, reflect a rapid decrease of the demands on attentional resources, provided by these areas during early learning (Poldrack, 2000). Interestingly, BOLD activity was also shown to decrease in M1, as motor skill learning progresses over a single training session in the learning of motor sequences.

The increase of fMRI activity in the SMA, the premotor cortex, the posterior parietal cortex (PPC) and the cerebellum might reflect the learning of spatial-motor aspects of the task. The premotor cortex receives massive input from the PPC, which provides the spatial coordinates of movements. The two contrasting activation patterns could thus reflect the differential engagement of the two systems of action control introduced earlier: the action programming and instructions generation systems respectively (Figure 5.12).

Slow learning Slow learning may follow different patterns, depending on whether it involves the learning of a simple finger movement sequence, or a difficult musical piece on the piano. The difference in complexity, and the much smaller behavioral gains of the involved tasks makes it difficult to evaluate the changes observed in the involved neural circuitries. Extended practice of simple sequential motor skills became manifest in a progressively increasing BOLD activity of the motor cortex (M1), as well of the size of its motor maps. Progressing from fast to slow motor skill learning was also accompanied by a shift in fMRI activation from the associative to the sensorimotor striatum, and a concomitant decrease of activation in the cerebellum. The stronger engagement of the primary motor cortex and neurons in the sensorimotor striatum during the advanced slower stages of learning when behavioral gains were minimal, has been proposed as a substrate for the acquisition of habitual and automatic behavior (Dayan & Cohen, 2011). The reported changes are also reminiscent of the movement execution stage of action control, as introduced earlier (Figure 5.12).

Motor sequence versus motor adaption learning Motor skill learning studies using fMRI, have also contrasted two different motor tasks: sequence learning and motor adaptation. Motor adaptation tasks typically require tracking of a moving visual target, which involves the hands as well as the oculomotor system. For instance, subjects manipulate a joystick with their dominant hand to follow an elliptical trajectory on the computer screen (Debas et al., 2010).

Doyon and Underleider (2002) proposed that motor sequence and motor adaptation tasks both recruit similar cerebral structures in the early 'cognitive' stage of learning. This involves the striatum, hippocampus, cerebellum and motor cortical regions, in addition to the prefrontal and parietal areas (Figure 6.21). During practice, two shifts of motor activity can be observed in subcortical structures. The first is a transition from the associative to the sensorimotor striatal regions in the sequence learning task. The second is additional activity in the cerebellar nuclei in the motor adaptation task. This trend becomes even more conspicuous in the slow learning stage, after consolidation and automatization of the two skills. In the sequence learning task, the striatum keeps playing a central role, together with the related cortical areas (see also Figure 6.21, illustrating the transitions of sequence learning in the slow learning stage). In the motor adaptation task, the striatum is no longer necessary for the retention and execution of the acquired skill; regions representing the skill now include the cerebellum and related cortical regions. Another finding was that in motor sequence learning, off-line consolidation is sleep dependent, and manifested in a differential increase of neural activity in this stage, within the corticostriatal system, whereas motor adaptation consolidation was not affected by sleep. A possible explanation is that sequence learning depended upon explicit mnemonic processes, as the subject had prior declarative knowledge of the sequence, whereas learning during motor adaptation was implicit in nature (Debas et al., 2010).

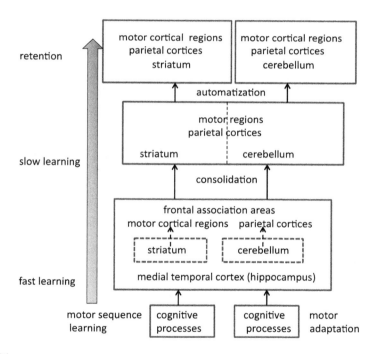

FIGURE 6.21
Model proposed by Doyon and Underleider (2002), to describe plasticity within the corticostriatal and corticocerebellar systems during the course of learning a motor sequence task (left column) and a motor adaptation task (right column). Both tasks recruit similar cerebral structures in the early learning phase. During fast learning, a selective shift of activity occurs to the motor areas and parietal areas of the cortex, in the motor sequence and adaptation tasks respectively. After consolidation, the sequence learning and motor adaptation tasks rely more strongly on representations in the striatum and the cerebellar nuclei, respectively. With identical additional activations in the cortex.

Cellular processes of elementary learning

Habituation and sensitization are two elementary forms of nonassociative learning that do not require an association between stimuli, but a change in responsiveness to repeated stimulation. Their underlying cellular mechanism has been described in detail by Eric Kandel and coworkers, using the sea slug Aplysia Californica as an animal model. Aplysia has a simple nervous system with a relatively small number (20,000) of very large neurons. Tactile stimulation of either the mantle or siphon leads to retraction of the gill, the respiratory tract (see Figure 6.22). This basic reflex appears to be sensitive to habituation, sensitization and classical conditioning.

Habituation

Repeated stimulation of the siphon results in a decrease in the strength of the gill retraction response. This effect is not the result of 'neural fatigue' of sensory or motor neurons,

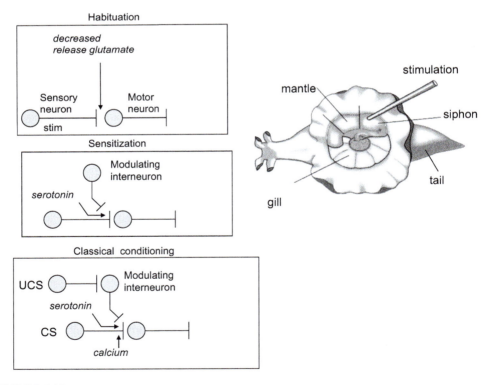

FIGURE 6.22
Three elementary forms of implicit learning in Aplysia: habituation, sensitization, and classical conditioning. Stimulation of the mantle causes the gill to withdraw.

as the amplitude of involved neurons shows no decrement when stimulated directly. The response decrement showed in habituation, results from of the decreased strength of the synaptic connection between the sensory and the motor neuron (Figure 6.22, upper left panel). This is initiated by a decreasing amount of the neurotransmitter glutamate in the presynaptic (sensory) neuron, which in turn results in a gradual blocking of calcium (Ca2+) channels in its axon terminal.

Sensitization

Sensitization is the enhancement of the connection between a sensory and a motor neuron, due to a prior strong or noxious stimulus. Here the cause lies in an increase in neurotransmitters in the presynaptic neuron, also referred to as presynaptic facilitation. The neural circuit is somewhat more complicated than that of habituation, due to the involvement of an interneuron (Figure 6.22, middle left). When a strong stimulus is applied to the head, tail or other parts of Aplysia, a modulating neuron produces serotonin, which spreads diffusely over the synapses of the sensory neurons. Serotonin affects synapses with motor neurons as well as with interneurons. It specifically blocks the potassium channels in the cell membrane, thereby delaying the outflow of potassium, and extending the action potential. As a result, calcium channels will remain open for a more extended period, causing more calcium to flow into the presynaptic (sensory) neuron, and increasing the amount of neurotransmitters.

Classical conditioning

In classical conditioning, coupling takes place between an unconditional stimulus (UCS) and a conditional stimulus (CS, Figure 6.22, lower left). For example, the UCS (a powerful electrical pulse) is presented at the tail of Aplysia, and the CS (a milder stimulus) at the siphon. Coupling of UCS and CS appears to lead to a gradual strengthening of the gill reflex to the CS, after a couple of trials. A stimulus applied on another part, the mantle, which is not coupled with the electrical pulse, acts as a control stimulus.

Conditioning involves the same presynaptic facilitation principle as for sensitization. The conditioning mechanism is based on a convergence of two types of substances, UCS-induced serotonin, and calcium generated by the CS, thereby releasing additional neurotransmitters in the presynaptic neuron. The timing of CS-UCS is crucial: reinforcement of the gill reflex to the CS only occurs at a 0.5-second CS-UCS interval. The joint action of UCS (via serotonin) and CS (via calcium) on molecules in the presynaptic neuron, results in the release of a large amount of transmitter substance. This will subsequently enhance synaptic transmission between pre- and post-synaptic (motor) neurons, and an increase of the CS reflex after a certain number of CS-USC trials.

An example of classical conditioning applied in humans is the conditioned eye-blink reflex. Here a tone is followed by an air puff to the eye, that elicits the blink reflex. After some trials, the subject will also blink his eye if only the tone is presented. Especially the cerebellum is involved in this form of conditioning. Classical conditioning has often been used in humans to gain insight into mechanisms underlying learned fear and startle reactions. However, these responses are primarily mediated by a circuit involving the amygdala and the orbitofrontal cortex, possibly also utilizing LTP as the cellular mechanism of synaptic plasticity (see Chapter 7 for more details). Startle responses have also been used to measure disturbances in sensory reactivity in schizophrenia. Schizophrenic subjects did demonstrate significantly reduced rates of habituation to repeated presentations of the acoustic startle probe (Geyer et al., 1990).

Notes

1 The question of where memory is localized is called *compartmentalization* by Howard Eichenbaum, which is supposed to occur at two levels, distinct modules and larger systems connecting the separate modules.

2 Note that this is merely a gross classification, given the caveats made in Chapter 2 that specialization of the cerebral hemispheres is relative rather than absolute, and more fine-grained than suggested by these global dichotomies.

3 'Access to' may be understood as a condition when all stimuli automatically reach long-term memory and activate some of its elements. Awareness of their content would require that sufficient elements are activated to reach a minimal threshold of activation.

4 This 'homuncular' metaphor is not meant to suggest that encoding, consolidation and retrieval are controlled by a single central agency in the brain.

5 Some theories, like relational memory theory have stated that the hippocampus could be site for storing relational representations, i.e. the kind of memory that stores and recalls the relationships and associations between two or more percepts, such as objects and/or events (Konkel & Cohen, 2009). However, in contrast with declarative memories, these relational hippocampal memories do not require conscious awareness.

6 The model outlined here largely corresponds to models of short-term memory as proposed by Donald Norman, Joachim Fuster, Nelson Cowan and Risto Näätänen.

7 An exception being Eichenbaum (2014) who proposed an alternative model of the time course of consolidation, in particular in the consolidation and retrieval of context-related information. He argued that the consolidation process is not restricted to the hippocampus but extends to an active dynamic interplay between the ventral hippocampus and the prefrontal cortex (see further in this chapter).

8 Nadel and Moscowitch proposed an alternative 'multiple trace' theory of long-term consolidation. The major element in their theory is the assumption that episodic and semantic

memories follow different temporal trajectories, with episodic memory remaining dependent on contextual detail and hippocampal involvement, and semantic memory becoming gradually more factual and less dependent on the hippocampus over time.

9   A schema is an 'active organization of memories whose structure determines the framework in which new memories are added, and can be employed during remembering to reconstruct the constituents of memory and their order', Eichenbaum (2012).

10 The precise neurochemical mechanisms in the postsynaptic cell are still a matter of debate. One assumption is that calcium activates specific enzymes *within* the postsynaptic neuron that feed back to, and increase the sensitivity of the non-NMDA receptors. This, in turn, may lead to stronger depolarization of the postsynaptic membrane. Another option is that the enzymes produce a retrograde messenger NO (nitric oxide) that cycles back *outside* the neuron to affect the dendrites of the presynaptic neuron, where it enhances the production of glutamate.

11 Suzanne Corkin (1997) re-examined HM's donated brain with MRI about 20 years after his surgery, and discovered that a much larger part of the hippocampus was spared (mostly the posterior parts) than was initially assumed, in contrast with the general belief that HM had his entire hippocampus removed.

7 Emotions

CONTENTS

- ▶ Introducing emotions
- ▶ Learning emotions
- ▶ Neuroaffective networks
- ▶ Neurotransmitters and emotions

Introducing emotions

Most stimuli capable of causing emotions do so without any conscious evaluation in the person that is affected by that emotion. These emotions occur through a mechanism that we are not aware of and that we cannot fully control. Emotion and cognition originate from separate but interacting neural systems in our brain. Emotions affect human consciousness and decision making, and conversely, the cognitive system controls the expression of emotions. Emotions and 'feelings', their subjective counterpart, are often accompanied by an increase in heart rate, production of stress hormones and somatic (muscle) activity. Initially, this gave rise to the debate about which aspect came first in the causal chain: feelings or bodily reactions?

Research of the last two decades shifted gradually to a greater emphasis on the brain and the neural substrates (hence called the 'neuroaffective network'), that regulate elementary and complex forms of emotions. The discovery of the role of neurotransmitters in modulating affective processes was another important factor. New theories emerged on how emotions influence human decision making, pointing at the significant role of the orbitofrontal cortex in regulating human reactions in a social and emotional world. Emotions were also conceived as information-processing functions, with research aimed at tracking down in greater detail the flow of information running from the senses to the brain.

The present chapter first considers some general characteristics and definitions of emotions, and how they relate to cognition and bodily reactions. The next paragraph then focuses on learning elementary emotions, and the role of reinforcers. The final paragraphs deal in more detail with the neural basis of emotions. This concerns the neuroaffective networks underlying primary and secondary emotions, explicit and implicit emotional memories, and the role of neurotransmitters in regulation affective processes.

Classification of emotions

A recurring theme in this book is the connection of complex cognitive functions to large-scale networks in the brain, each of which is composed of various subsystems and local networks. Like cognitive functions, emotions are not a unitary system, but can be partitioned into various subsystems which in turn correspond to specific structures and neural circuits. Emotions can globally be classified according to the following criteria: a) valence and intensity, b) level of neural organization, c) level of experience and d) their subprocesses (Figure 7.1).

Valence and intensity

The most common distinction between emotions is that between positive and negative emotions, also called the valence of emotions. Within the categories of positive and negative emotions, more fine-grained subdivisions are possible. These concern differences in their type or direction, and in their intensity. For example, hunger and thirst differ with respect to their underlying physiological condition, and the resulting drive for food or water. Emotions can also vary in intensity, such as a feeling of apprehension

Valence	Positive, negative
Intensity	High, low
Level of organization	Primary, secondary
Level of experience	Implicit, explicit
Sub-process	Perception, evaluation, action

FIGURE 7.1
Classification of emotions according to five criteria.

or severe anxiety. Differences in intensity are directly linked to arousal, the brain's activation state.

Peter Lang and Margaret Bradley developed standards for determining the valence and intensity (arousal value) of a variety of visual incentives, individually for men and women. Their system, called the International Affective Picture System (IAPS), has been an essential tool for investigators to select scenes meant to evoke a desired emotional response in experimental research.

At the level of brain functions, valence and arousal are difficult to separate from one another. The reason being that negative emotions often elicit stronger arousal, subjectively or physiologically, than positive emotions do. During evolution, avoiding a dangerous situation could possibly have acquired a higher adaptive value than approaching a pleasant situation, which in turn caused a stronger arousal.

Our language has a rich arsenal of words regarding emotion, which can be categorized along some separate dimensions (Osgood et al., 1957). The social psychologist Shaver (Shaver et al., 1987) asked people to judge a large number of words with emotional intent. They were also asked to compare words like joy, sadness, crying, laughing, fear, optimism, pessimism and screams in their emotional significance. A cluster analysis (a kind of correlation analysis) produced about six prototypical emotions, that could be ranked on one evaluative (positive-negative) dimension. These were: love – joy – surprise – anger – sadness – fear. Most negative is 'fear', most positive 'love' while 'surprise' takes a middle position. These prototypical emotions do not necessarily represent basic biological mechanisms, but reflect our intuitive knowledge of emotions and how people in everyday life experience and name them.

BOX 7.1 MOOD STATE AND EMOTION

Emotions are not always linked to external events, so it is important to distinguish between emotions and mood states. A change in mood can sometimes be the result of an emotion triggered by an external event. For example, getting a bad grade for an exam can spoil the student's temper for the rest of the day. However, moods can pop-up spontaneously, without any direct external cause. Examples are mood changes resulting from deviant states of the brain, such as a lack of sleep or fatigue, or in major depression. In certain neurological disorders like epilepsy, emotional experiences can be experienced as a sense of fear or a strangeness ('aura'). The neurotransmitter serotonin appears to play an important role in the regulation of mood states. Mood states also affect the cognitive evaluation of events and memories

The level of organization: primary versus secondary emotions

Emotions are often distinguished in primary ('lower' or innate) and secondary ('higher' or acquired) emotions. Primary emotions have deep bio-evolutionary roots; they have a direct function in the survival of the species and are thus strongly action-oriented. A classic example is the 'fight or flight' distinction. Secondary emotions are the product of later adult development and learning. They often represent a mix of rational processes and feelings, with cognitive evaluation of people and situations playing a more central role.

BOX 7.2 EMPATHY IN MAN AND ANIMAL

Empathy is the capability or trait to share feelings with others, to feel what others feel. It is as if our automatic appraisal system, when observing emotions in others, responds like something has happened to us (Ekman, 2004). It involves communication and interpretations in which an 'individual (animal or human) interprets signs produced by another, in a way that induces a corresponding emotional state' (Deacon, 1997). It could be expressed in language, facial expressions, the tone of voice, a hug, crying and laughing. Newborns already show a rudimentary form of empathy that shows in spontaneous mimicry of the laughing – or sad – face of an adult.

continued

> *Picture legend:*
>
> *Consolation behavior (i.e. comforting reaction to the distress of others) is common in humans and many other mammals. Here a juvenile chimpanzee puts an arm around a screaming adult male who has been defeated in a fight. Photograph and caption by Frans de Waal. Director, Living Links Center at the Yerkes National Primate Research Center. Picture reproduced with kind permission from Frans de Waal.*
>
> In tens of millions of years of evolution, these capacities may have evolved as a mechanism of social signaling, reflecting the mood state or state of arousal of who send the signs. These social capacities are not unique for man, but are found in various species of mammals, although they vary in complexity, depending on the species and type of social interactions, confirming the view of Darwin that 'many animals certainly sympathize with each other's distress or danger'. On a descriptive level, they have been frequently observed in elephants and dolphins. Dogs are notably clever in picking up implicit body signals of their masters that express the feeling of happiness or anxiety. In monkey and chimpanzee, it is not unusual for one individual to respond emotionally to the distress of others. Systematic studies verified that the chimpanzee may take great risks to rescue a buddy in distress, to seek reassurance from each other, and to console each other after fights (de Waal, 2004).

The primary-secondary distinction is also relevant from the perspective of the brain. Primary emotions are usually associated with lower structures in the brain stem and the limbic system, including the hypothalamus regulating basic instincts and drives like hunger and thirst. Regulation of secondary emotions, in turn, is attributed to higher areas in the neocortex.

Level of experience: explicit or implicit

Consciously experienced 'feelings' vary in aspects like happiness, sadness, fear or aversion. As such, they are often attributed to humans and not to nonhuman mammals.[1] These conscious or explicit forms of secondary emotions often represent a combination of affective and cognitive processes. Our impressions, thoughts, and experiences indeed often have an affective 'color'; they contain elements of feelings like happiness, aversion or anger.

Not all forms of emotions are consciously experienced feelings. In many animals emotions are manifested in reflexive behavior, in particular approach or avoidance behavior. These reactions are primarily mediated by direct neural pathways that transform the (emotional) perception into action. These direct forms of emotion also occur in humans, in the form of 'implicit' emotions that affect our behavior or physiological condition, without (or before) being aware of it. Implicit emotional reactions have their roots in the same bio-evolutionary mechanisms that underlie the emotional behavior of animals. Further sections in this chapter deal in more detail with the neural circuits that underlie these implicit and explicit forms of emotion.

Subprocesses of emotion

Practically all emotion theories are based on the assumption that an emotional experience results from a prior interpretation or evaluation of an antecedent event, which has a positive or a negative character. Following this assumption, an emotion can be defined as a state of the organism (or our brain) that results from an evaluation of a positive or negative event. Evaluation sometimes elicits a conscious experience (feeling), but may also occur implicitly without any conscious reflection. Emotions are not solely manifested as subjective experiences. They also serve a practical purpose and lead to action. In the latter sense, emotions are often conceived of as 'motivations', an internal drive that triggers goal-directed action. Finally, emotions are accompanied by physiological changes as well, such as an increase in heart rate, production of stress hormones or somatic (muscle) reactions, like a 'freezing' response during fear.

In summary, an emotion is a process (or state of the organism) that consists of three major components, a) evaluation, b) the explicit (feeling) or implicit processing of its emotional content and c) the expression, or action-related element.

Emotion and cognition

The long-lasting debate about the relative contribution of cognitive factors in human emotions, has become known as the 'emotion cognition' or the 'Lazarus-Zajonc' controversy. According to Lazarus emotional processes depend on cognitive processes, referred to as 'cognitive appraisal' (Lazarus, 1991). Zajonc defended the opposite view that emotions have an intrinsic function, and that conscious evaluation is not essential for their manifestation. He, therefore, pleaded for separate and independent roles of cognition and affect (see also Leventhal & Scherer, 1987).

Interactive model

The debate on 'what comes first', cognition or affect, perhaps seems somewhat outdated, from the perspective of modern neuroscience. That made it clear that separate but interacting neural systems are responsible for the regulation of emotional and cognitive processes. Within each of these systems, processes take place on their own timescale. For example, in some primary forms of emotion like fear, an early evaluation of stimuli is triggered in the amygdala without any conscious reflection. Affective processes can modulate our thoughts, and 'color' explicit memories. Conversely, cognitive processes may control and inhibit the 'feeling part', or expression of emotions.

Figure 7.2 sketches the interaction between emotion and cognition in a simple working model. A sensory stimulus activates the cognition and emotion systems in parallel. Perception of the stimulus by the emotion-system leads via route a, directly and without conscious perception (or cognitive modulations), to certain forms of affective behavior: a reflexive fear reaction or autonomic-physiological responses (the action box). In route b, an action is triggered by the cognition system, without interference of the emotion system. Route c (represented by dashed lines) depicts interactions between the cognition and emotion systems, which may take two forms. Cognitive processes can feed into (or 'penetrate') the emotion-system by providing an 'internal stimulus'. This could be an image or thought that elicits emotions without any external eliciting event (downward black dashed arrow; the 'cogni-emo' pathway). Another form of cognitive modulation lies in its ability to control emotions, like suppressing a feeling or an emotional expression. Note that the black interactive pathway (represented by the downward dashed line) provides an optional route, that comes into play when the source of stimulation is internal (cognitively mediated) or when the emotional content of the eliciting event has been acquired by learning rather than by innate mechanisms.

'Feelings', the conscious reflection of emotion, are also associated with the interaction route c, but now caused by upward projections (upward red dashed arrow, the 'emo-cogni' pathway), allowing the emotion-system to 'penetrate' the cognition-system. Put differently, feelings are the subjective-cognitive reflections of processes triggered from the emotion system.

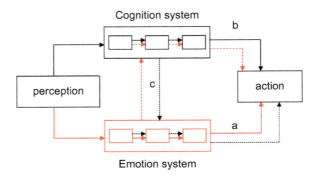

FIGURE 7.2
Simple working model of the interaction between the cognition system (in black) and emotion system (in red) converging on the action system. a = direct emotion route, b = direct cognition route, c = interaction routes (dashed lines). See text for clarification.

Although the neurobiological aspects of emotions will be discussed in more detail later in this chapter, an example serves to clarify how the interaction between cognitive and emotional systems may take place in the brain. The example shown in Figure 7.3 starts from the premise that emotional processing of visual impressions takes places at the object level, that is to say the visual perception of complete objects in the inferotemporal cortex. An example of visual objects that often trigger an emotional response are human faces, presumably stored in distributed networks of the inferior temporal lobe. Recognizing emotional expressions and their associated emotional components (e.g. a happy face eliciting a pleasant feeling, or an angry face an unpleasant feeling) is not restricted to the inferotemporal cortex. It more likely reflects the workings of a network within the temporal cortex, where visual representations are coactivated in parallel with affective representations in the amygdala and the orbitofrontal cortex. Backward projections from these regions to the temporal cortex then lend the objects their affective color (Adolphs et al., 1996).

The function and expression of emotions

The function of emotions varies according to the signals and environments that lead to its elicitation. This includes the release of an autonomic response and the neurotransmitters

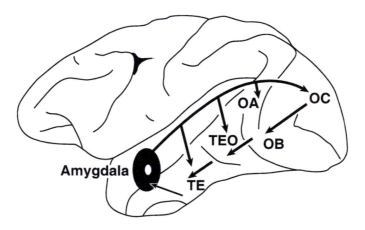

FIGURE 7.3
An example of a neural circuit that involves interaction between emotion and cognition in the monkey brain. The amygdala receives input from the inferior temporal cortex (TE), containing complex visual representations (for example, a face). The amygdala is assumed to contain representations of emotional states. Backward projections from the amygdala to the superior temporal cortex (TEO) and occipital regions (OA, OC) lend the observed object an affective color. The model also indicates how emotional context can be stored in the brain as part of memory representations.
Source: From Rolls & Treves (1998).

that prepare for a bodily reaction. It could also include the selection of behavioral responses to reinforcing stimuli, by directing attention to high valence aspects of these stimuli. Other functions include motivation, social communication, memory storage (by enhancing the input of neurotransmitters to the hippocampus and the cortex) and recall of memories by back projection of the amygdala to the cortex (Rolls & Treves, 1998).

The expression side of emotions is most evident from behavior that occurs in intense emotions like fear, rage and aggressive behavior when angry. In a less extreme form, these emotions are manifest in facial expressions. Paul Ekman conducted extensive research into the typical facial expressions of emotions. He discovered that humans from all over the world share the same facial expressions, which are also interpreted similarly, confirming Darwin's hypothesis that facial expressions are inborn (Darwin, 1872; Ekman,1993, 1994). Overt reactions triggered by noxious stimuli or potentially dangerous events often have a reflexive character. Think for example of withdrawing a hand when touching a painful stimulus, or a driver braking abruptly to obstacles in the city traffic. The conscious perception of fear, reflected for example in the awareness of heartbeat acceleration, follows a few seconds after the initial motor reaction.

Another example of an unconsciously triggered emotional response is the conditioned fear response, where a tone by association with an electrical shock automatically causes an autonomic physiological response. These examples also indicate that emotions either are expressed in fast circuits that translate the perception of a stimulus directly into a motor action, or in circuits associated with the slower conscious emotional experience.

In sum: emotions are expressed in overt behavioral as well as in more covert physiological reactions, characteristic of stress. Although these physiological responses also occur without apparent motor actions, their utility lies in providing the 'fuel for action' or 'energy mobilization'. In other words, the physiological responses reflect a state of the organism that facilitates rapid action, when required by environmental conditions.

The relationship between feelings and bodily reactions

The strong link between feelings and autonomic physiologic and somatic reactions stirred a lively debate in the early years of emotion research. The debate concerned the question what 'comes first': the (conscious) feeling or the bodily response. The four prevailing views are summarized in Figure 7.4 and briefly discussed next.

Feelings as the cause of bodily reactions

The traditional and intuitively appealing view that feelings are the cause of bodily reactions is contradicted by the fact that some physiological reactions, such as a startle response to loud sounds, occur rapidly, in less than 200 msec after a stimulus. The

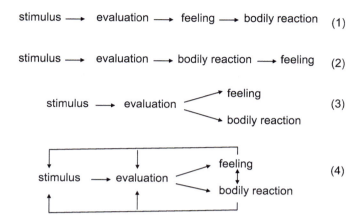

FIGURE 7.4
Four conceptualizations of the relationship between bodily reactions and feelings. 1) the traditional view, 2) James-Lange theory, 3) Cannon-Bard theory and 4) commonly accepted parallel hierarchical model. See text for clarification.

physiological reaction here clearly occurs before we could have become aware of the eliciting event.

Feelings as the result of bodily reactions

The second view became known as James-Lange theory. William James and Carl Lange independently developed this counter-intuitive theory at the beginning of the 20th century. Their theory, implying that the self-perception of bodily states produces an emotional experience, became widely popularized in expressions like 'we are afraid because we run', or 'we are sad because we cry'.

Later research showed that autonomic physiologic reactions cannot be the cause of feelings. Injection of noradrenaline, for example, does not affect the subjective emotional experience to a neutral stimulus, when presented in isolation. It is only effective, occurring in combination with an emotion-provoking setting, like an angry man entering the room (Schachter & Singer, 1962). These findings suggest that the physiologic arousal mechanisms underlying bodily reactions may enhance but do not cause emotional experiences.

Feelings and bodily reactions emitted as parallel reactions

A third possibility, shown in Figure 7.4 (panel 3) is that feelings and bodily reactions are emitted in parallel. This view was originally promoted by the physiologist Walter Cannon and his student Philip Bard in what became known as the Cannon-Bard theory of emotion (Cannon, 1927). They hypothesized that the evaluation of the emotion-provoking stimulus had to occur in the brain, in the hypothalamic-thalamic region. Later it was proved that their theory, although much closer to new insights based on knowledge of the brain, was wrong in one crucial aspect. Not the thalamus, but structures in the limbic system (such as the amygdala) appeared to be responsible for the evaluation of the emotional content of the stimulus.

A parallel hierarchical model

A more comprehensive model, which combines aspects of earlier models is sketched in panel 4 of Figure 7.4. Here, bodily reactions and feelings are not only emitted in parallel, but send feedback signals to earlier evaluative and perceptual stages as well. The model also implies that the evaluation of an emotion provoking event not only depends on external factors but also on internal emotional experiences and bodily reactions. The model thus combines elements from previous theories, taking into account early (implicit) and late (explicit) evaluation processes, as well as feedback from bodily reactions, as claimed in the James-Lange theory.

In summary, emotional processes can be unraveled in three significant subcomponents: a) evaluation of the content of elementary incentives, b) feelings, or subjective experiences and c) expression in overt behavior or covert physiological processes. Together they constitute the 'input', the 'central' and the 'output' functions of affective processing. This three-part structure is reminiscent of information processing models from cognitive psychology. In affective systems this primarily concerns information with a 'survival function' or, put in more operational terms, the processing of the reward or punishment value of information.

In the most general sense emotions can be described as a state of the organism that results from the evaluation of a positive or negative event. This can be an external event, like the perception of a dangerous animal, or an internal event, like a thought that makes us happy or unhappy. Feedback of bodily reactions is another example of an internal signal that can trigger a feeling. Importantly, the evaluation process that evokes an emotional reaction, is not always accompanied by consciously experienced and subjective feelings. Emotions can also implicitly trigger our behavior and our physiological state. Finally, explicit and implicit forms of emotion are regulated by different neural systems. to be described in more detail further in this chapter.

BOX 7.3 TO TICKLE OR NOT TO TICKLE

Primary reinforcers also include certain forms of touch. Tickling is the act of touching a part of a body, or another person or animal, in such a way that it causes involuntary twitching movements or laughter ('giggling'). 'Tickling' ourselves

continued

does not have the same effect, because the perceptual system of the brain already knows what to expect, which greatly reduces its impact. Tickling (or rather, stroking) usually leads to a pleasant, playful sensation when carried out in a consensual context. Non-consensual – or aggressive – tickling can be unpleasant and even painful for the recipient. The reaction to tickling is intrinsically related to the source of tickling.

(Inserted picture reproduced with kind permission of Dr. Ishiyama (Ishiyama & Brecht, 2016).

Primates like chimpanzees, gorillas, bonobos and orangutans when tickled also show laughter-like vocalizations that sound like alternating inhalations and exhalations. Similar reactions can be observed in domesticated dogs when tickled or stroked by their keepers. Even rats, supposed to be lower on the evolutionary scale, show reactions to tickling. When a rat is tickled (or stroked) on its favorite spot, being the back or belly (see insert), it may show two types of reactions. It first seems to resist the human intrusion by wildly moving its legs. Then it surrenders, and seems to enjoy the treatment. When tickling stops, they will first move away but quickly return to the hand, like it is 'asking for more'. During tickling, rats produce very high (ultrasonic) squeaking sounds. The same kind of sound is produced during spontaneous, playful contacts between young rats, suggesting these are a genuine expression of a pleasant, playful state, and not of distress or pain. German investigators found a brain region that generates these reactions. The

continued

> 'tickle area' lies deep in the somatosensory cortex, an area in the upper-posterior brain, that processes physical touch. Furthermore, microstimulation of this region evoked the same 'ticklish' behavior.
>
> Interestingly, they found that one cannot tickle rats in anxiety-inducing situations. This condition also suppressed the cell's firing, and the animal could no longer be tickled. So, just like humans, rats have to be in a good mood to enjoy tickling. Finally, laughter itself is seen as a reflection of emotional expression (not necessarily of feelings itself), regulated by neurons in the cerebellar-pontine regions.
>
> Sources: Panksepp & Burgdorf (2003), Ishiyama & Brecht (2016), Parvizi et al. (2001).

Learning emotions

Emotions have been classified as lists of experiences or expressions. Accordingly, Paul Ekman distinguished six basic types of emotional expressions: anger, fear, happiness, sadness, disgust and surprise (Ekman, 1993). Instead of creating lists of emotional experiences or expressions, others have attempted to describe and classify emotions according to their primary action goals, in particular the tendency to approach or withdraw from an eliciting situation. Positive stimuli usually elicit an approach, and negative stimuli a withdrawal response. Emotions originate from biologically determined innate mechanisms, or are acquired later in life. Primary emotions fall in the first, and secondary emotions in the latter category. Secondary emotions develop when the brain learns to associate objects or events with primary events that are innately set to cause emotions. Different pathways and structures are involved in the learning of implicit and explicit emotions, globally corresponding with primary and secondary emotions.

What triggers an emotion?

Emotions are often triggered by events, perceived or recalled from memory. Sometimes they occur spontaneously as part of certain mood states. Especially the valence (positive or negative value) of these events proved to be of importance for the systems involved in the evaluation of their affective value. But what are the characteristics of stimuli that determine their affective value inside our brain? Some events have automatically achieved the status of emotional stimulus in the course of our evolution. This applies in particular to stimuli that trigger innate mechanisms, an approach reaction to positive stimuli, and an avoidance reaction to negative stimuli. These primary forms of innate emotions later develop into secondary emotions, when other objects and events acquire emotion status by association with the primary events. The adult world then comes in 'shades of good and bad', with surprisingly little neutrality in between (Damasio, 2004).

Emotions often exist for the sake of action, in particular, physiological needs like hunger, thirst and sexuality, which function as elementary driving forces of our behavior. They also serve to avoid conditions that signal danger, discomfort or pain. Together they provide an internal signal that encourages us to act: to approach conditions that satisfy primary needs and avoid those that endanger survival and reproduction. Animal conditioning work, in particular, contributed to more detailed insights into conditions that shape emotional behavior, and well as the neural substrates of emotions.

Positive and negative reinforcers

The stimuli or conditions that result in the satisfaction of primary needs are referred to as primary reinforcers. If a reinforcer increases the probability of emission of a response on which it is contingent, it is called positive or reward. If it decreases the probability of such a response, it is called negative or punishment. There is a conversed contingency as well, that produces the opposite effects on behavior. Omission or termination of a positive reinforcer (called extinction) decreases the probability of responses. Responses followed by omission or termination of the negative reinforcer (called avoidance or escape) will increase the probability of their occurrence.

Animal research has shown that groups of cells in the limbic system, among which the amygdala, are capable in 'recognizing' the characteristics of these reinforcers (Gore et al., 2015). An interesting discovery in self-stimulating studies of rats was that cells in these areas not only fired if rats confronted the positive reinforcer. Rats also readily learned to electrically stimulate themselves, if a stimulation electrode was connected to critical cell regions which they could control by pushing a button. Artificial stimulation of these 'pleasure centers' evidently simulated the effect of a natural reinforcer: the taste of food or water or a particular drug (Olds & Milner, 1954).

BOX 7.4 INTERACTION BETWEEN MEMORY AND EMOTION

Although the amygdala is not critical for capturing new impressions in explicit memory (see the previous chapter), events that evoke strong emotions are better remembered. From an evolutionary perspective, this link is useful, as incentives and circumstances important for maintaining the species, such as danger, are also

continued

> better remembered. According to neurologist Cahill, the mechanism responsible for the interaction between emotions and memory rests on the neurotransmitter noradrenaline. This substance is released by emotional stimuli and strengthens the consolidation of impressions in the hippocampus and cortex. Administration of beta-blockers like propranolol that inhibit the action of noradrenaline, is shown to decrease the enhancing effect of emotions on memory. The same effect may also be responsible for the suppression of the effects of conditioned anxiety and stress reaction as in Posttraumatic Stress Disorder (PTSD). PTSD is believed to be associated with disrupted regulation of fear memories, and enhanced amygdala activity to stress. Administration of propranolol in patients with PTSD, is reported to reduce physiologic responses during mental imagery of the event, and to attenuate traumatic memories during reconsolidation.

Self-stimulation tests have shown that negative reinforcers also correspond with specific circuits in the brain. If the electrode is attached to an area associated with avoidance behavior, test animals rapidly learned to turn the current of by a button press. Evidently, there are neural circuits for processing positive, as well as negative reinforcers.

A classification of emotions based on reinforcers

Based on the idea that the state produced by reinforcing stimuli can define emotions, Rolls proposed a model based on two dimensions of emotions, their valence, and their intensity (Rolls, 2000). The valence dimension reflects the different values of positive versus negative reinforcers (Figure 7.5, vertical axis), called a contingency relation.

On the positive side of the valence dimension there are emotions like delight and happiness, on the negative side emotions like terror and fear. The horizontal axis reflects emotions elicited by omission and termination of a positive or negative reinforcer, called conversed contingency. They represent a different spectrum of emotions like anger and frustration (on the negative side) and relief (on the positive side).

Relative positions on the two axes reflect differences in intensity of positive and negative emotions, with the less intense emotions in the center, and more intense ones at the end of the axis. By combining these factors, the model can account for a broad range of emotions. It is worth emphasizing that emotions, as depicted in Figure 7.5, can be produced by external reinforcing stimuli as much as by recall of these stimuli. Some emotions may even require cognitive processing to determine the reinforcing valence of a particular event. For example, after a long period of brooding on the next holiday

EMOTIONS

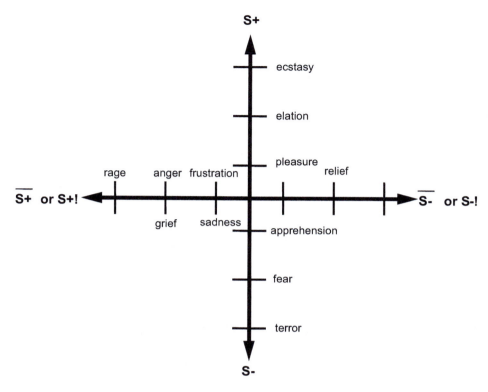

FIGURE 7.5
Classification of emotions according to two dimensions. Vertical axis: the presence of positive (S+) or negative (S−) reinforcer. Horizontal axis: the omission or termination of a positive reinforcer (S+!, $\overline{S+}$) or negative reinforcer (S−!, $\overline{S-}$).
Source: After Rolls (1999).

destination, a person may feel extremely relieved after deciding to stay at home, instead of visiting a foreign country.

Primary and secondary reinforcers

Examples of primary reinforcers are food when hungry (positive reinforcer) or a stimulus that causes pain (negative reinforcer). Novelty is sometimes regarded as a primary reinforcer, because something new drives animals to explore still unknown environments with better survival opportunities. In a more general sense, any stimulus that has acquired reward or punishment value in the course of evolution to increase man's chances of survival, may function as a primary reinforcer. According to Rolls, this would also include stimuli as flowers, sunshine, snakes, faces (happy or angry), beauty and voices (friendly or unfriendly) as primary reinforcers.

In turn, a secondary reinforcer is a neutral stimulus which receives reinforcing quality through association with a primary reinforcer. They are implicitly acquired via classical or instrumental condition procedures. For example, a tone becomes a negative reinforcer by association with an aversive stimulus like an electric shock. Experimental animals or subjects will, therefore, try to avoid this stimulus in future. Emotional learning can also be accomplished by instrumental (or operant) conditioning, which implies that reward and punishment are the outcome of certain forms of behavior. These forms of behavior are mediated by different circuits in the brain than those involved in classical conditioning. Secondary reinforcers established through instrumental learning are often action related. Think of the athlete driven to win a race, or the painter in pursuit of creating a great work of art. Other forms of secondary reinforcers are purely experiential, like the emotions we might experience when listening to Maria Callas singing a famous aria in Puccini's Tosca. These examples underline the important distinction between primary or innate and secondary or acquired reinforcers.

The drive for curiosity and information seeking

In the early 1950s Robert Butler and Harry Harlow performed a classical study with rhesus monkeys (Butler & Harlow, 1954). They found that mature monkeys enclosed in a small dimly lighted chamber would open and reopen a door hour after hour, for no other reward than that of looking outside the box. Although the monkeys received no external reward, the rate and frequency of door opening depended on the attractiveness of the scenes outside the chamber. Monkeys are also known to exhibit curiosity in solving mechanical puzzles, without extrinsic incentive. Similarly, children often show an increased interest in exploring new situations or tasks, like for example playing with new toys.

The function of curiosity in young children as well as in adult humans is comparable to hunger which motivates eating (Loewenstein, 1994, see Kidd & Hayden, 2015, for a recent general overview and critical discussion). This 'hunger for information' may serve an evolutionary purpose to explore new environments, in order to find new food resources necessary for survival and identification of conspecies. In humans, this could have taken form as 'epistemic curiosity', a term coined by Daniel Berlyne, to designate the drive to acquire knowledge and 'to get to the heart of things'. Berlyne also suggested a relationship between curiosity and functions like uncertainty reduction, orienting and conflict (Berlyne, 1957, 1960).[2]

Although a generally accepted definition of curiosity is still lacking, two elements seem to be crucial: a motivational and a memory element. The motivational element mainly incorporates a drive-information state, reflected in a continuous demand for information, manifested among other things in an almost compulsive need for news, checking of media, computers and mobile telephones in modern man. The information drive may be internal or external, conscious or unconscious. An example is scanning the visual environment with the eyes while driving a car or walking on the street. Although curiosity reflects intrinsic motivation, brain studies have revealed the involvement of the same mechanisms that underlie extrinsic reward conditions. This concerned dopamine circuits and structures like the oribitofrontal cortex, receiving dopamine reward signals originating in the reward centers in the nucleus accumbens of the basal ganglia (Rushworth et al., 2011; Kidd & Hayden, 2015).

The memory element of curiosity mostly reflects the outcome of the information drive state and relies on a circuitry in the brain involved in the detection of novel events and their subsequent consolidation in declarative memory. It incorporates, among other things, the hippocampus, the hippocampal gyrus, and the association areas in the posterior and frontal cortex. The cluster of processes underlying this circuitry is often described in terms of novelty detection, orienting, information delivery, uncertainty reduction and conflict resolution.[3]

Implicit emotional learning

Implicit emotional learning may occur when a neutral stimulus acquires aversive properties through pairing with an aversive event. Fear conditioning is a method of classical conditioning, in which the unconditional stimulus is aversive. The paradigm underlying fear condition is applicable across a wide range of species, from fruit flies to rats to humans. Recall that in the conditioning terminology CS and UCS stand for conditional and unconditional stimuli, and CR and UCR for the conditioned and unconditioned response, respectively. An example of fear conditioning is an unpleasant feeling (CR) that is triggered by a current event (CS) without any conscious awareness why this should happen. The reason might be that the event implicitly activated a representation held in long-term memory (UCR) that links to an unpleasant event experienced in the past (UCS).

Augmented startle

In experimental animals as rats, an aversive stimulus like an electrical shock follows a neutral stimulus (usually a tone or a light signal, see Figure 7.6).

Rats exhibit the typical characteristics of a fear response: heart rate acceleration, increase in blood pressure, startle or 'freezing' when after some trials only the light signal is presented. The startle reflex is often used as a vehicle to measure the strength of the established fear response. In humans, it is reflected in the blinking of the eyes or reflexive muscular movements, as a 'jump' after a loud noise. It shows little or no habituation (decrease in strength) with repeated presentation of the noise. Michael Davis, who has carefully mapped the neural circuit of the startle reaction, showed that

EMOTIONS

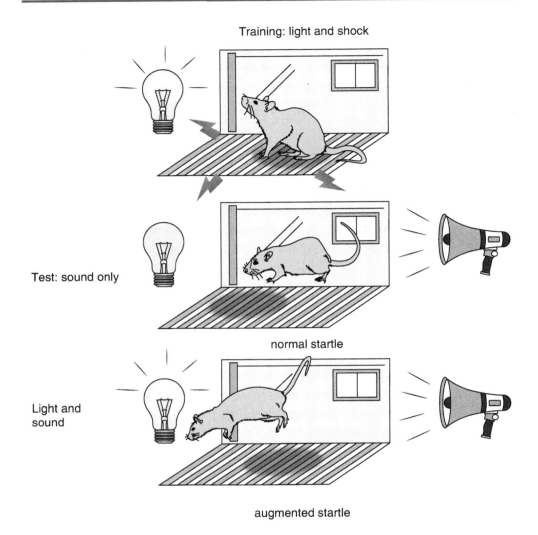

FIGURE 7.6
Three phases in the formation of the augmented startle reaction (after Davis (1992). Top: in the acquisition period a light (the conditioned stimulus, CS) is combined with an electrical shock (the unconditioned stimulus, US). Middle: normal startle to a loud noise stimulus. Bottom: light and sound combined: augmented startle reflects the condition fear response (CR).

peripheral auditory nuclei in the cochlear nucleus, and neurons in the pons of the brain stem are involved in its generation.

Augmented (or potentiated) startle means that an already conditioned fear response strengthens the startle action. Figure 7.6 depicts the three phases of the conditioning process. A natural fear response is learned by pairing a light stimulus (the CS) with an electric shock, the UCS (top panel). In the test phase, the standard startle response to loud noise is elicited (middle panel). When the light stimulus is presented simultaneously with the loud tone (light plus sound: lower panel), the startle response to the noise is significantly enhanced (CR), compared to the condition in which only noise was presented. The enhancement occurs because neurons in the pons that are part of the circuit underlying startle, are already in a state of increased activation due to the fear response mediated by the amygdala. The role of the amygdala could be the facilitation of the acquisition of the conditioned fear response, instead of producing the (unconditioned) fear response per se.

In humans, the startle response is manifested, among other things, in the eye blink reflex to a brief and loud tone. This reflex also increases in amplitude during a conditioned fear reaction, suggesting that startle in animals and humans depends on the same neural circuitry. The fear conditioning paradigm based on the startle reaction has been applied successfully in the assessment and treatment of anxiety disorders in humans, specifically the generalized anxiety disorder (see Ray et al., 2009).

Fear conditioning: direct and indirect afferent routes

Using the fear conditioning paradigm Joseph Le Doux has been able to map the neural circuitry of fear, from initial perception to the emotional response. A central structure in his model is the amygdala and its subnuclei. The lateral nuclei in particular are crucial for the binding of information, arriving from various regions involved in fear conditioning. In the fear conditioning paradigm, an auditory stimulus (the CS) is followed by an electric shock or loud noise (UCS). The subcortical circuits are less clearly mapped for visual stimuli than for auditory stimuli.

A critical element of Le Doux's model concerns the circuitry of fear conditioning. Information is channeled to the amygdala via two separate pathways: a direct and fast, and an indirect slower route. In the case of sound stimuli, the subcortical route passes directly from the medial geniculate nuclei of the thalamus to the lateral nuclei of the amygdala. Parallel with the direct route, the indirect routes run through the thalamus via the primary and secondary cortical areas to the amygdala. According to Le Doux, the direct route is fast and inaccurate, and the indirect route is slow and accurate. The direct route is part of a primitive evolutionary system, which enables animals lacking a highly developed cortex to react effectively to threatening stimuli. In higher-developed species, including humans, this route presumably plays a minor role, but still acts as an early warning system, enabling to respond to elementary but biologically relevant characteristics of stimuli from the environment. Figure 7.7 also illustrates the critical role of the lateral nucleus, as a convergence point for the direct (thalamic) and indirect (cortical) routes, in establishing the conditioned fear response. The input from the hippocampus (at the right) is only involved in fear conditioning situations involving complex, polymodal events.

EMOTIONS

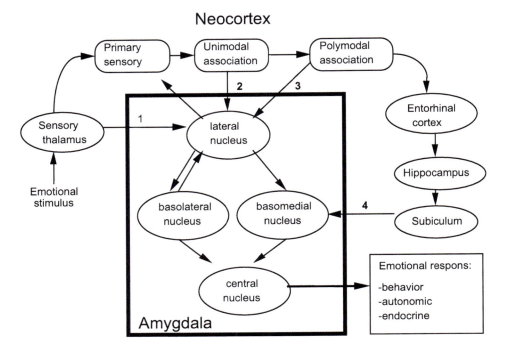

FIGURE 7.7
Circuit of fear conditioning after Le Doux. 1 = direct route of the thalamus to the amygdala (lateral nucleus). 2 and 3 = indirect routes from higher cortical areas to the amygdala (also to the lateral nucleus). 4 = input from the hippocampus to the basomedial nucleus of the amygdala. The central nucleus has output connections that lead to different types of autonomous, behavioral and endocrine responses.

Affective priming

According to the model proposed by Le Doux, emotional stimuli that are not consciously perceived by the subject may still influence behavior (Le Doux, 1991, 1994). This hypothesis seems to receive support from affective priming studies in humans. The affective primacy hypothesis (Zajonc, 1980) asserts that positive and negative affective reactions can be evoked with minimal stimulus input and virtually no cognitive processing. Affective priming studies have demonstrated that subliminal stimuli (i.e. very briefly presented visual prime words, or masked words and pictures) can exert an influence on responses to positive or negative target stimuli. Zajonc further claimed that the affective system responsible for preferences, is separate from the cognitive system responsible for inferences. This applies in particular to early affective processes, occurring automatically without any higher-order intervention.

Explicit emotional learning

Implicit memories of emotional events have been called emotional memories, and explicit memories 'memories about emotions' (Le Doux, 1996). The previous section clarified how affective memories influence our behavior and subjective experience implicitly, for example by eliciting a sense of familiarity, or autonomic physiological reactions to fearful events. But is there a separate explicit memory system for emotions, different from declarative memory? The advantage of conscious awareness of emotions is allowing emotional information to be integrated with cognitive processes like emotional control, to think ahead, and to generalize to other similar situations (Lane & Nadel, 2000). We indeed sometimes consciously recall emotional experiences that are part of our declarative memories, which suggests that explicit emotional learning may result from a process by which the brain associates perceived objects and experiences with more primary forms of affective memory. The medial temporal memory system thus 'learns' these emotionally colored events through association with primary emotions, stored in affective memory, e.g. in structures of the limbic system like the amygdala. The neural circuitry enabling these associations, consists of pathways between the anterior hippocampus and the limbic system (see Figure 6.7 for an example, further characteristics of explicit emotional memories and related networks are provided in the following sections in this chapter). The affective quality itself may not necessarily reside in declarative memory, but results from co-activation of the limbic structures as repositories of 'raw feelings'. For example, one may feel anxious or uneasy about dogs or an angry face (which would perhaps also show up as activation of the amygdala), because of a once experienced dog bite or an unpleasant, shouting person. Following the interaction model of Figure 7.2 we might say that the raw feeling 'penetrates' the cognitive system leading to a negative experience of the environmental event.

BOX 7.5 IS THE RIGHT-HEMISPHERE SUPERIOR IN RECOGNIZING EMOTIONAL EXPRESSIONS?

Visual perception of faces differs from normal perception of objects. For example, recognition of faces of familiar persons seems to correspond with a specific area in the inferior right temporal lobe (IT), called the fusiform face area, also described as a 'dedicated face module'. Other studies suggest involvement of the right half of the temporal cortex in recognizing emotional expressions in general, independent of the familiarity or valence (positive or negative) of expressed emotions. When right-handed subjects looked at chimerical stimuli (such as artificially composed faces), with left and right halves of a face

continued

showing different emotional expressions (see insert), right-handed subjects fixating on the nose of the face, tend to interpret the left face as sad, and the right face as happy. When fixating a point in the center of the visual field, the left and right halves of the visual field project to the contralateral (opposite) side of the brain.

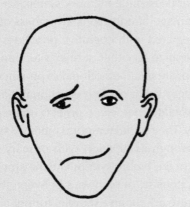 

Patients with lesions in the left side of the brain will usually experience problems with speech production, but not but with interpreting emotional expressions, whereas patients with lesions in the right side of the brain show impairment of the ability to recognize emotional expressions, but not in speech. The amygdala is crucial for processing facial expression, in particular for fearful faces, even in conditions when the subject is not aware of having seen these faces. The ability to (explicitly) recognize emotional expressions may depend not solely on the amygdala, but on pathways connecting the amygdala to the temporal cortex.

The property of the right half of the cortex probably originated from specific, innate mechanisms that developed in right-handed people, independently from the ability to learn to speak. Producing speech in right-handed adults is typically associated with the Broca area in the left frontal cortex. During infancy, emotional expressions and speech still take place independently from another. One speculation why speech and face recognition are neurally separable, is that in the course of human evolution, essential survival functions were assigned to different halves of the brain according to the principle of efficient division of functional brain space. When right-handedness and speech gradually co-evolved in the left hemisphere, perceptual-spatial abilities were probably channeled to networks in the right half of the brain.

Any primary or secondary negative reinforcer may elicit anxiety. A notorious example is the fear of wild predators like tigers, snakes and sharks. Sharks are a prototypical example of a primary negative reinforcer, stemming from the far evolutionary past when predators threatened the survival of our ancestors. In modern times many people (in particular children) still consciously experience fear of sharks without ever having been confronted with these animals. Their fears have been implanted in their hippocampal-amygdalic-cortical memory system, seeing TV documentaries in the tradition of Spielberg's epic movie *Jaws*. The gruesome images and commentaries probably activated structures like the amygdala, involved in the expression of fear, and concurrently affected explicit knowledge and the visual imagery system, creating a powerful aversive secondary reinforcer.

Whatever the way in which we learn about the threatening nature of stimuli, explicitly or implicitly, the amygdala will probably contribute to the indirect expression of the fear response to these stimuli. Internally and explicitly learned fear, activated by images of emotional events, may thus activate circuits in the brain connecting to the amygdala, eliciting the actual expression of fear in autonomic physiological reactions. The same circuitry possibly also contributes to the consolidation of novel non-fearful events, via enhancing the arousal state of the involved cortical area, thus strengthening explicit memories for these events (McGaugh et al., 2002; Phelps et al., 2001). In this way the amygdala modulates the storage and recall of emotional events, ensuring they will not be forgotten over time. Lesions of the amygdala, for example, have indeed shown to attenuate or even block arousal-induced enhancement of memories and their physiological expressions (Cahill & McGaugh, 1996). Explicit learning of emotions may also underlie 'feelings', that is to say, the consciously appraised or experienced content of affective memories, associated with secondary emotions. In these secondary emotions, the feeling and thinking part are evoked concurrently. Further in this chapter we shall highlight the neural basis of emotional memories in greater detail.

Neuroaffective networks

Research done in the last three decades has provided groundbreaking new insights into the neural substrates of emotions. This research established that more areas are involved in the regulation of emotional behavior than assumed in the pioneering theories of Papez and Maclean. The discovery of the vital role of neurotransmitters in the regulation of affective processes was another new element. The next section describes the characteristics of neuroaffective circuits and their structural components in more detail. The subsequent sections focus on the role of neurotransmitters in the regulation of emotional states.

Components of the neuroaffective network

At the most basal level of the neuroaffective network (Figure 7.8), the hypothalamic-pituitary-adrenal axis mediates responses to stressful events. For example, recording of neuronal activity in the paraventricular nucleus (PVN) CRF axis in freely behaving mice revealed neurons that encode the positive and negative valences of stimuli (Kim et al., 2019). These reactions to primary reinforcers are probably mediated directly, without intervention of the amygdala. Research in monkeys and humans made it clear that not only the hypothalamus and the amygdala, but also higher cortical regions of the prefrontal cortex like the orbitofrontal cortex constitute the principal structures in the network that controls primary and secondary emotions. Later research also confirmed the important role of the anterior cingulate area. The dense connections between various structures in the network, also form the basis of their close functional relationship. Activation of lower structures will thus also co-activate higher structures in the network's hierarchy. In a similar fashion, structures at the top of the hierarchy, the orbitofrontal and ventral medial cortices, automatically recruit mechanisms at lower levels, subserving more elementary forms of emotion. The major components of the network are described in more detail as follows.

Structure and function of the amygdala

The amygdala is situated deeply in the medial part of the temporal lobe. It forms a highly complex structure with several groups of nuclei participating in different neuroaffective

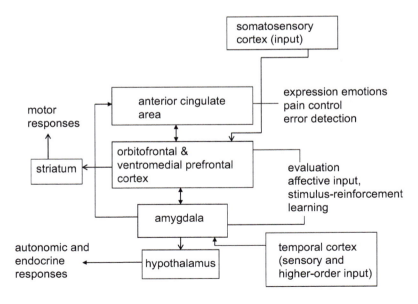

FIGURE 7.8
Schematic view of the components of the neuro-affective network in the brain and their function. Principal input functions are shown at lower right, output functions at the left.

circuits. The three main nuclei in the amygdala are the lateral nucleus, the basal nucleus and the central nucleus.

Globally they regulate three successive stages of affective processing, namely input, central processing and output (Figure 7.9). The first and second stages are responsible for the evaluation and preliminary formation of affective stimulus representations, in respectively the lateral and basal nuclei of the amygdala. The definite formation of affective stimulus-representations does not take place in the amygdala, but is accomplished in the limbic-cortical network, in which the lateral and basal nuclei of the amygdala connect through reciprocal pathways to the lateral and medial temporal cortices and the orbitofrontal cortex, respectively. Further sections in this chapter focus in more detail on the circuitries involved in formation of affective memories.

At this level of processing the social context of affective stimuli is also incorporated in memory representations. For example, in the chimpanzee the response to an aggressive face differs according to status of the other animal, high or low in rank. In a neuroimaging study, Schwartz et al. (2003) found that adults who were known to be shy as a young child showed a stronger activation of their amygdala to new faces than to familiar faces, as compared with adults who were known not to be shy when young. Taken together, the lateral and basal nuclei of the amygdala seem to be suitable candidates of the appraisal function of emotions. They form an input mechanism that evaluates the valence of emotional stimuli on the basis of which these are classified as negative or positive reinforcers.

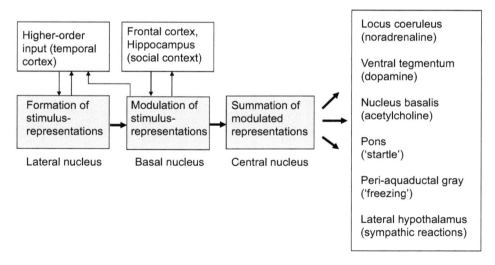

FIGURE 7.9
Structure and circuits within the amygdala. Left: (grey boxes) three hypothetical stages of processing, and related nuclei of the amygdala (lateral, basal and central nuclei). Right: output from the central nucleus.

Source: Derived from Pitkänen et al. (1997).

BOX 7.6   THE SAD TALE OF PHINEAS GAGE

Patient studies revealed much about the role of the orbitofrontal cortex in regulating of emotional behavior. The most 'famous' patient in this context may have been Phineas Gage. Gage was a railway worker, who in 1841 when placing dynamite in a rocky block was hit by an iron rod that passed through his head after an explosion (see reconstruction in the following figure). Later it became clear that this had destroyed a large part of the ventromedial prefrontal region in his brain. Miraculously, Gage was still conscious after the accident, an even able to chat with the men around him despite his severe head wounds. After two months he was declared cured by his physician.

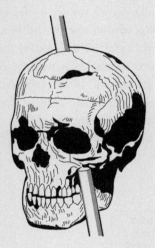

Gage was known as a serious, hardworking person with a high sense of responsibility. After the accident he seemed to have transformed to another human being; his behavior became childish and uninhibited. Gage also showed indifference to others, and occasional outbursts of anger and rage. He died at 38 years old, three years after the accident, as a victim of violent epileptic seizures, and was buried with the iron placed alongside his body.

In addition to a loss of inhibition in social behavior, patients with lesions in the orbitofrontal cortex make more perseveration errors in tasks in which the response schedule is reversed. For example, if they had responded to a figure like a triangle a number of times in a row, and not to a square, they would continue to respond to the triangles after the schedule changed to squares. The performance of frontal patients in this type of task, also correlated with indices derived from an assessment of their social behavior, such as the extent to which patients show socially inappropriate or emotionally disturbed behavior.

At the third level, the output of the basal nucleus is processed in the central nucleus, which integrates the summated affective representations from the two prior stages, and then generates the affective response via a number of output channels. In the earlier example, the aggressive face of a dominant male chimpanzee led to the release of a flight response in another male chimpanzee, via output to the striatum and motor centers, and (or) to the release of stress hormones via output to the hypothalamus. The central nucleus has many projections to subcortical regions that regulate autonomous physiological responses and release of neurotransmitters, as shown in Figure 7.9. As noted earlier, the central nucleus of the amygdala is especially important for the expression and learning of classically conditioned fear reactions.

The dense connections between the amygdala and other structures in the neuroaffective network make it difficult to determine the extent to which effects of stimulation or lesions of its nuclei are attributable to properties of the amygdala itself, or of other structures in the network. Damage to the amygdala in humans, unlike lesions in monkeys, rarely leads to drastic changes in behavior. The most critical effect reported, seems to be a reduced sensitivity to aversive stimulation. Nevertheless, in modern emotion theories, the intact amygdala is often considered to be the central 'computer', or modular system, where the emotional significance of stimuli from the environment is analyzed.

Orbitofrontal cortex

The orbitofrontal cortex developed most strongly in higher mammals like monkeys, the great apes and humans. As shown in Figure 7.8, this region has many reciprocal links with the amygdala and the anterior cingulate area. Anatomically it forms the most anterior part of the ventral prefrontal cortex. This area in turn contains two sub-regions, the ventromedial and ventrolateral prefrontal cortex. Similarly, the orbitofrontal cortex can also be subdivided in a lateral and a medial section. It receives input from the primary sensory areas for touch, smell, taste and sound, from the thalamus, and from the secondary visual and temporal cortex areas. These pathways mainly arrive in the ventral part of the orbitofrontal cortex. The connections with the anterior cingulate region originate in the dorsal part. Due to its numerous input connections, the orbitofrontal cortex seems ideally suited for the forming of associations between stimuli from different sensory modalities, as well as between inputs from the primary sensory areas (smell and taste for instance) and the secondary visual areas of the temporal cortex.

The functions of the amygdala and the orbitofrontal cortex have much in common. Both areas play a role in evaluating the affective character of stimuli, but the evaluation process in the orbitofrontal cortex is assumed to take place at a higher level. For example, cells in the orbitofrontal cortex react selectively to faces. Similar cells are also found in the amygdala and the inferior temporal cortex. The latency of firing of face-specific cells in the orbitofrontal cortex, however, is longer than that of cells in the temporal cortex, suggesting a later and possibly more advanced type of processing.

Further evidence suggests that positive and negative reinforcers and related mechanisms for approach and avoidance are lateralized in the left and right medial parts of the ventral prefrontal cortex (Davidon & Tomarken, 1989; Davidson, 1993). This hypothesis receives support from PET studies of depressed patients showing less activation in the left frontal areas than control subjects have. Davidson also found frontal asymmetries in the EEG of normal subjects, watching positive video films of dogs playing, and negative video films of surgery scenes. Positive videos elicited stronger activation in the left frontal area, while looking at negative images triggered stronger activation in the right frontal cortex. Research with macaque monkeys also shed more light on the function of the orbitofrontal cortex. Monkeys with lesions in this area continue to respond to objects that are no longer rewarded, after having received a food reward on preceding trials. According to Rolls, this is because lesions in the orbitofrontal cortex prohibit neurons to build memory representations of objects presented on non-rewarded trials, a phenomenon also designated as extinction.

Further evidence from animal studies suggests that the orbitofrontal cortex is crucial for recognizing secondary reinforcers in learning situations where different objects are coupled to primary reinforcers, and the animal needs to switch continuously between reinforcers. Similar problems with switching attention have also been observed in humans with lesions of the orbitofrontal region (see Box 7.6 for a human example).

BOX 7.7 THE CAPGRAS SYNDROME

The Capgras syndrome is the delusionary conviction that a 'double' or fraud has replaced a familiar and trusted person like a spouse, partner or family member. It is named after the French psychiatrist Jean Marie Joseph Capgras, and based on a case history of one of his patients. Recognizing a familiar trusted or loved person has an emotional and perceptual-cognitive aspect. Hirnstein and Ramachandran believe that the source of the Capgras delusion lies in the specific emotions triggered by the face of a trusted person (Hirnstein & Ramachandran, 1997; Hirnstein, 2010).The patients however are fully able to 'feel emotions', and to recognize familiar faces, which suggests that the problem lies in the interaction between memory and emotion. Thus, there may be damage to the connections between brain areas (such as the amygdala) and memory areas in the temporal lobe, containing face representations. Especially the affective component (the familiarity of the face) associated with the inferior temporal gyrus, could be responsible for the emotional experience. If its access is damaged or blocked, the emotional response cannot find its expression. According to the latter view, the misidentification in Capgras syndrome primarily reflects a specific disorder of episodic memory.

Anterior cingulate cortex

The anterior cingulate cortex (ACC) is often seen as the 'interface' between the rational and the emotional brain (Bush et al., 2000). The ACC contains two sub-areas, a posterior (or dorsal) part and an anterior (or rostral) part (Figure 7.10). The posterior part with connections to the dorsolateral prefrontal cortex is the 'cognitive division'. The anterior part (dubbed the 'affective division') is thought to be primarily responsible for processing and controlling emotional responses. It contains the most frontal curved part of the cingulate gyrus, and functionally links to three neighboring areas, the prefrontal cortical areas (important for cognitive control and working memory), the limbic system (amygdala and orbitofrontal cortex) and the motor areas.

A neuroimaging study by Lane showed that the most prominent part of the anterior cingulate area (the section underneath the frontal curved part, see Figure 7.10), was most strongly activated in tasks requiring subjects to pay attention to affective aspects of visual images. Interestingly, a recent human fMRI study established that information encoded by perigenual anterior cingulate cortex (pgACC: the most frontal curved part

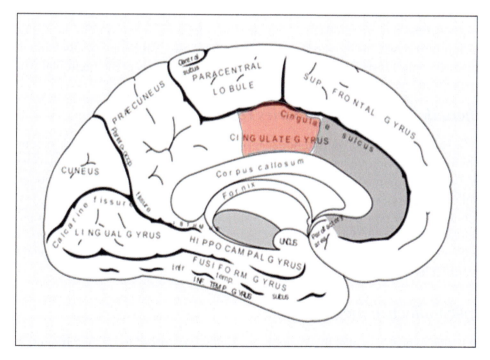

FIGURE 7.10
Medial view of the left half of the brain, showing the anterior cingulate cortex with the dorsal part in red and rostral part in grey.
Source: From: Gray 751.

of the ACC) tracks subjective sense of decision confidence in a choice reaction tasks. PgACC predicted both within-subject and between subject variation in explicit confidence estimates (Bang & Fleming, 2018). The study suggests that the brain maintains choice-dependent and choice-independent estimates of certainty, and why dysfunctional confidence often emerges following medial prefrontal lesions or dysfunctions.[4]

The ACC is also activated by conflicting trials in selective attention tasks. In the Stroop task (for example: say red to the word green printed in red), and after error trials in a reaction task. This suggests that activation of ACC could reflect processes that involve some form of response conflict. On a more fundamental level, the specific role of the ACC is to evaluate negative reinforcers. Its outcome then provides feedback to higher control processes in the prefrontal cortex, for triggering 'recovery actions'. A similar role of ACC was highlighted by studies examining event-related responses of the brain (ERPs). In reaction tasks, a negative ERP component called error-related negativity (ERN) is elicited just after movement initiation of error trials. The ERN is interpreted in terms of conscious detection of an error, some form of response competition between voluntary responses (Gehring et al., 1993), or of automatic detection or errors after involuntary saccades (Nieuwenhuis et al., 2001). The ERN has been localized in the ACC (Dehaene et al., 1994; Hollroyd et al., 2004) with its magnitude correlating to the intensity of the incorrect response. In sum, these findings seem to point to a specific function of the ACC in monitoring behavioral responses, probably to supplement the executive control system, implemented in dorsolateral regions of the prefrontal cortex.

Where do emotional memories reside?

In the earlier paragraph on emotional learning, we raised the question if emotional memories form a unique memory system, or are just modulations of declarative memories. There are arguments that both options are viable, and that emotional memories are manifested in what we shall here provisionally label as the explicit and implicit versions of neuroaffective representations. In the explicit version, the amygdala plays a neuromodulatory role in the formation of declarative memories, in the implicit version they are the core structure for establishing affective memories independently of declarative memory (Eichenbaum & Cohen, 2001).

Explicit affective memory

The explicit version of affective memory is usually considered to be the product of co-activating (or linking) declarative and affective memory representations, stored or reactivated in respectively the cortical and limbic structures. It is generally accepted that explicit learning of emotional events involves the establishment of a functional connection between the medial-temporal cortex and the amygdala, with the amygdala-produced neurotransmitter noradrenaline enhancing the respective synaptic connections (Emery & Amaral, 2000). In this case, the better retention of emotional events in declarative memory can be ascribed to an arousal-mediated effect on consolidation via the medial-temporal cortex. Support for this view is given by maze learning of rats, as well as by human studies showing that blocking of noradrenaline by a beta-blocker called propanolol diminishes the memory-enhancing effect (Morris et al., 1998; Cahill et al., 1994).

It is unlikely that noradrenergic input conveys the specific information stored in a synapse, like a reward or punishment value of stimuli. More likely noradrenaline increases the excitability of cells in the hippocampus and hence enhance consolidation of the event by affecting the voltage-dependent NMDA receptors in the hippocampus. Co-activation of limbic and cortical circuits that occur during consolidation or retrieval, is not necessarily restricted to primary reinforcers processed in the amygdala. It could also involve secondary reinforcers and emotions stored in a more extensive affective network (see also Figure 7.12 for an example). An unpleasant feeling, for example, elicited by an angry human face or an unpleasant social situation could involve a network, in which the basal and lateral nuclei of the amygdala connect with the superior temporal lobe and orbitofrontal cortex (see Figures 7.3 and 7.9). Figure 7.12 of the following section describes such a circuitry, responsible for production of 'feelings', the consciously experienced activated state of the circuit of secondary emotions.

In this case, the affective coloring of declarative memories would result from igniting in parallel a distinct affective network. For example, the sight of objects or the experience of situations linked to an earlier traumatic event (a traffic accident, for instance) might not only activate the recall of details of the event from episodic memory, but also concurrently elicit some indirect fear response from a network representing the conditioned fear reaction. A person who has once witnessed a severe traffic accident may still feel uneasy when driving on the freeway. Negative secondary reinforcers stored in the network of long-term memory could also include fear for objects that have never been linked to real unpleasant or traumatic events, experienced earlier in life.

Reconsolidation

Contrary to the classical hypothesis which regards consolidation as a one-time event, the reconsolidation hypothesis claims that events encoded into long-term memory experience a new period of consolidation, upon each recollection. Shortly after recollection of consolidated fixed memories, previously acquired memories are reactivated, turning their neural representations into an unstable state. Subsequent 'reconsolidation' then reorganizes and updates the content of the old memories, demonstrating post-reactivation memory plasticity (Nader et al., 2000; Nader & Einersson, 2010).

The reconsolidation hypothesis received support from experiments by Joseph Le Doux and Karim Nader on fear conditioning of rats. The rats were infused with a substance that inhibited protein synthesis in the amygdala, shortly after a retention test. The tests were administered after a period of 14 days, when conditioning was complete. It appeared that memory was impaired when the infusion occurred immediately after the retention test. The same infusion after a longer delay of the retention test had no effect on memory. Le Doux and Nader concluded that after the short interval, memory was still in a labile state which required protein synthesis for its reconsolidation. Other studies suggested that consolidation blockers did not erase but modify the original memories. In humans, competing memories or actions that cause distraction during a post-reminder period can also block expression of unwanted memories and lead to a reorganization of the content of these memories – a finding that has also opened therapeutic applications in patients suffering from fearful or unwanted memories.

BOX 7.8 ARE WOMEN MORE EMOTIONAL THAN MEN?

Women pick up emotional cues from others more easily than men, facilitate communication and social bonding. According to cross-cultural studies, women tend to report more negative emotionality and depression, a trend that was more conspicuous in high gender equity societies than in low gender equity societies. They also differ from men in the expression of their emotion, shed tears more easily, and smile more often than men, in particular in situations when they are expected to smile. A large scale study of facial muscle activity found that women show stronger zygomaticus (smiling) and frontalis (brow rising) than men (McDuff et al., 2017). These behaviors could have been socialized according to display rules regulating how, when and where emotions can or should be expressed (Fischer et al., 2004). However, the consistent finding that emotional expressions are the same across cultures, suggests that they must be deeply rooted, sculpted by a common evolutionary trajectory or biological factors. Other characteristics could more strongly reflect the influence of acquired current social-cultural factors (Brody & Hall, (2008).

When men and women are asked to evaluate pleasant and unpleasant slides, women react more negatively than men to unpleasant slides (mutilated bodies, physical violence) than pleasant slides. Women also tend to better recognize and process the negative emotions of others. Men, in contrast, were shown to be more strongly affected by pictures displaying aggression and in recognizing threatening cues from potential male competitors. They also showed a stronger physiological arousal during exposure to angry male faces than to angry female faces (Kret & de Gelder, 2012). At the level of the brain, aggressive scenes elicited a stronger activation in the bilateral amygdala and the left fusiform gyrus in men than in women. Exposure to angry male, as opposed to angry female faces, activated the visual cor-

continued

> tex and the anterior cingulate cortex more in men than in women. Sex differences in the amygdala response were valence-dependent: in studies where negative affect was induced the average amygdala response was larger in women, while studies of positive affect show larger responses in men (van Wingen et al., (2011).
>
> The steroid hormone testosterone, produced by the gonads, is known to influence the regulation of emotional responses and affective states, and to mediate some of the sex differences that are seen in emotional processes. Endogenous testosterone concentrations are generally positively correlated to activity in the amygdala and the orbitofrontal cortex. Studies also suggest that the ovarian hormones progesterone and estradiol have opposing effects on the amygdala and the prefrontal cortex. These substances also play an important role in emotional functions and probably influence behavior directly, or via brain plasticity and functionality.

Implicit affective memory

Consolidation of events in the affective network can also occur implicitly, using principles of Hebbian learning without the intervention of the hippocampus or the medial-temporal cortex. Many studies have confirmed that the implicit aspect of memory relates to a separate emotional memory system, parallel to the system of declarative memory. The best examples are brain systems that mediate classical conditioning (Le Doux, 1996; Davis, 1992). Fear conditioning, for instance, implies the coupling of pathways through the amygdala with the primary sensory as well as the secondary association cortex.[5]

Implicit emotional learning implies the association between perceptual inputs and a primary reinforcer, or between a primary and secondary reinforcer with its product stored in affective representations. Assumedly, these associations involve the same structures of the neuroaffective network that are involved in the processing of emotional stimuli. The amygdala, in particular, is well placed in the neural hierarchy to create associations between higher-order visual stimuli (visual objects) and primary reinforcers (Cahill & Mcgaugh, 1996). The emotional valence of stimuli depends on complete objects, and not so much on elementary physical characteristics as modality, color or shape. For example, we are not afraid of the color yellow, but of a yellow (toxic) snake.

Pattern association networks in the amygdala

Implicit learning in the amygdala and the orbitofrontal cortex may occur in pattern association networks, linking a primary reinforcer (like food) and a secondary reinforcer (the smell or sight of food). This process would involve enhancement of synaptic connections, using the same cellular processes (LTP) and receptors (NMDA) that are active during consolidation in the hippocampal-cortical memory system. Association learning in the amygdala can be disrupted by local application of NMDA receptor blockers (Davis et al., 1994), suggesting that learning in the amygdala and orbitofrontal cortex takes place in Hebb-modifiable synapses. These associative processes are not confined to the amygdala but comprise thalamus-amygdala-hippocampus pathways, forming the basis of long-term encoding and maintenance of implicit emotional memories.

According to Rolls three types of neurons are involved in these associative networks (displayed in Figure 7.11). In succession: a) a series of input axons associated with the primary reinforcer (UCS; e.g. the taste of food) that activate neurons through non-modifiable synapses, b) a series of input axons from the secondary reinforcer (or CS, the sight of food) connecting with the dendrites of output neurons through a modifiable synapse, and c) a series of output neurons. According to the rule of Hebb, learning strengthens the modifiable synapses between the input axons of the conditional CS and the dendrites of the output neurons. The summated activity of these synapses is then relayed to other regions through the axons of the output neurons.

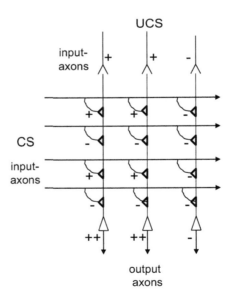

FIGURE 7.11
Prototypical pattern association network in networks of the amygdala and orbitofrontal cortex (Adapted from Rolls, 1999), with associations between primary reinforcers (UCS) and secondary reinforcers (CS). Primary reinforcers (UCS) utilize non-modifiable synapses. Secondary reinforcers (CS) utilize modifiable (Hebbian-style) synapses. Sum of activation of dendrites of output neurons expressed in its output axons is depicted below (++, ++, −).

Back projections

The central nucleus is of one of the output stations of the amygdala that routes information to various destinations. These include the ventral striatum, mediating the release of neurotransmitters, the hypothalamus eliciting autonomic reactions, and the striatum mediating instrumental responses. Other nuclei like the lateral and basal medial nuclei of the amygdala possibly also function as output neurons, with axons projecting to cortical and hippocampal neurons. Notice again that the amygdala has many back projections to adjacent higher association areas in the cortex, in particular in the temporal lobe, from where they also receive their input. These originate in the lateral and basal nucleus of the thalamus (see also Figure 7.9). These back projections implement the recall of neural activity in an earlier critical stage and operate on the basis of pattern association networks with modifiable synapses of the cortical pyramidal cells. They probably also provide the mechanism by which mood states generated in the amygdala affect cortical memories (Rolls, 1999).

In the hierarchy of the neuroaffective network the role of the orbitofrontal cortex and its more central neighbor, the ventromedial prefrontal cortex, could be to provide an additional route for some of the functions performed by the amygdala. This route would be effective in situations when a learning rule must be rapidly readjusted, with the reward shifting to other visual objects. The function of orbitofrontal cortex could then be to inhibit or suppress automatic learning of emotional information as established in networks of the amygdala.

Circuits of primary and secondary emotions

Within the hierarchical network of the affective system it is possible to roughly distinguish between two large-scale networks that regulate primary and secondary emotions. Primary emotions are the product of implicit learning, regulated by a circuit of the hypothalamus and the amygdala. Secondary emotions are the product of explicit learning and regulated by a more extended circuit that includes lower as well as higher cortical areas.

Primary emotions

Primary emotions such as anger, anxiety and joy are innate pre-organized emotions with the amygdala and hypothalamus functioning as prime players (Damasio, 1994, see the left panel of Figure 7.12). The hypothalamus is stimulated by the amygdala, which in turn receives perceptual input of primary characteristics of environmental stimuli, some of which may signal threat or danger. These stimuli often take shape as objects, or combinations of elementary features, derived from the secondary posterior and temporal

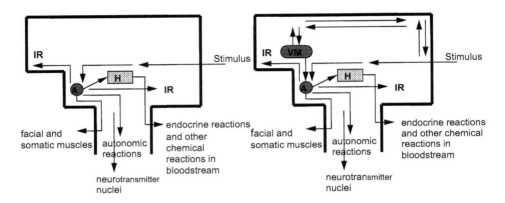

FIGURE 7.12
Two neural circuits, associated with the regulation of primary emotions (left) and secondary emotions (right) in a schematical view of the lateral-medial view of the brain. H = Hypothalamus, A = Amygdala; VM = Ventromedial prefrontal cortex; IR = internal response.
Sources: Adapted from Damasio (1994).

cortical areas. The detection of these stimuli still occurs at a relatively coarse level. For example, a bird in a nest watching the sky may respond to the form 'bird' (a creature with wings) without the need for full recognition of its species (a falcon or osprey). The hypothalamus then translates this initial evaluation in autonomic reactions, or in signals that lead to the production of neurotransmitters and certain hormones. The hypothalamus also triggers overt reactions, which are partly mediated through the basal ganglia. Primary emotions are normally emitted automatically and implicitly. They can also elicit conscious feelings, through pathways from the amygdala to higher cortical regions (referred to as IR: internal responses in Figure 7.12).

Secondary emotions

Secondary emotions (right panel in Figure 7.12) depend on a more complex circuit, with not only the hypothalamus and amygdala, but also the ventral medial prefrontal cortex functioning as the central elements.

That the amygdala not only receives input from external stimuli but also from the ventromedial prefrontal cortex is a significant extension of this circuit. These higher areas 'recruit' the lower more primitive structures, which involve the coupling of explicit declarative memories with implicit primary memories. They are responsible for production of 'feelings', the consciously experienced activated state of the circuit of secondary emotions. More specifically they could involve a circuitry between amygdala-dependent arousal and hippocampus-dependent explicit memory which are fused in working memory. The experience of fear then takes place in working memory, which in turn is controlled by the prefrontal cortex. This circuitry also allows comparing an immediate present visual stimulus, with long-term representations stored in declarative memory. Although the amygdala does not have many interconnections with the dorsolateral prefrontal cortex, it does communicate with its neighbors, the orbitofrontal and anterior cingulate areas that also participate in working memory operations (Lane & Nadel, 2000).

In short, feelings can be described as mental states which arise from the neural state residing in networks appropriate to store emotions. These mental states could involve emotional experiences elicited by the outside world (for example when listening to music), as well as internally generated processes, e.g. thinking of pleasant or unpleasant events once experienced. Feelings could also arise more autonomously as a change in the state of the brain itself, reflected for example in a change of mood. In addition, feelings are also affected by factors like neurotransmitters, drugs or implicitly experienced 'somatic markers'. The latter aspect forms an important element in Damasio's somatic marker theory, discussed in the following section.

Emotions and decision making

Interaction between rational thoughts and emotion is not only theoretically relevant, but has practical implications too, for example when choosing how to act in social situations. A wide range of factors affects everyday decision making. Even in routine actions like driving a car, we scan the environment for signals that make us decide to deviate from out fixed route or not. The orbitofrontal cortex, introduced earlier in this chapter, seems to be crucial for processing or prioritizing social or emotional information. Different theoretical models have been proposed to describe how the emotional brain interacts with the rational brain when utilizing emotional information in decision making. Two influential models which have attracted general interest from emotion researchers are discussed next.

Somatic markers

Body ownership and its impact on human consciousness, is a neglected area in cognitive psychology. Body ownership arises as an interaction between current multisensory input and internal models of the body (Tsakiris, 2010). The idea that peripheral-somatic factors have an impact on our consciousness – a critical aspect of the previously discussed James-Lange theory – is also an essential element in Damasio's somatic marker theory. Somatic markers are signals from the body informing the brain about physiological experiences. Damasio argued that these experiences are essential elements in decision making, because they narrow the options of the rational brain, and constrain the repertoire of decisions. The ventromedial cortex plays a central role in storing representations that link specific facts with emotional states. Damasio coined these representations as 'dispositional representations' because they do not store the experience of an event, but rather the potential to reactivate an emotion. They function, in short, as a binding site for memories stored elsewhere in the brain.

The ventromedial prefrontal cortex (also taken to include the more frontally located orbitofrontal cortex) plays a crucial role in mediating somatic markers (see Figure 7.13). This area forms the link with adjacent prefrontal areas, the dorsolateral and ventrolateral prefrontal cortex, typically engaged in cognitive processes as working memory, decision making, and preparation of action (Ridderinkhof et al., 2004). The ventromedial prefrontal cortex also receives input from the somatosensory area that contains a topographical map of body areas, and from neurotransmitter circuits that originate in the brain stem. The latter circuits are responsible for the delivery of the neurotransmitters noradrenaline, dopamine, serotonin and acetylcholine. These two circuits play a crucial role in Damasio's somatic-marker theory, with its emphasis on the peripheral-somatic input to the prefrontal cortex. After damage of ventromedial prefrontal areas, memory

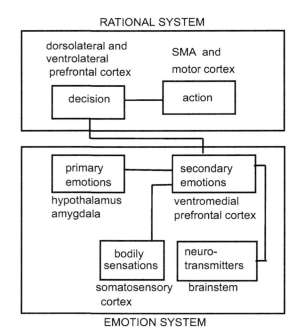

FIGURE 7.13
Schematical view of Damasio's somatic marker theory. The ventromedial prefrontal cortex (lower panel) regulates secondary emotions. It also influences decision and action processes controlled by the dorsolateral and ventrolateral prefrontal cortex (upper panel, SMA = supplementary motor area). The ventromedial prefrontal cortex also receives input from the somatosensory cortex (bodily feelings) and brainstem neurotransmitters (lower panel).

representations still guide and produce actions and recruit working memory, but are stripped of their emotional content. Patients may be preoccupied with an emotional event such as the death of a good friend, but their feelings are deprived of the emotional pain that normally accompanies such a loss. The lack of emotional content also becomes apparent in the reactions of the autonomic nervous system, like in the skin conductance response (SCR). Although the physiological system underlying SCR is still intact in frontal patients, it fails to respond to stimuli with emotional qualities. When confronted with decisions, prefrontal patients often seem to become entangled in the process of endless deliberation. According to Damasio, this is because they have lost their intuition or 'gut feeling' that usually supports rational decision making.

Somatic marker theory was verified in a card playing game, requiring subjects to choose between cards in two piles, a high risk and a low-risk pile. High-risk piles contain cards associated with large amounts of money to win or lose, while cards in low-risk piles contain cards that are associated with small amounts of money. Normal subjects showed a strong SCR response in the period preceding their choice of a card from the high-risk pile, while these anticipatory SCR reactions were absent in prefrontal patients. Prefrontal patients however favored the riskier card decks and showed a SCR response after they turned a selected card, and were confronted with a big loss.

Reinforcement guided decisions

Other theories relevant for emotional decision making emphasize the role of higher emotional centers, in particular the orbitofrontal cortex (OFC) and the anterior cingulate cortex (ACC), in guiding reinforcement learning and selection of actions. Roll's theory of decision making is an example. The core element of his theory is the ability of the OFC to adapt to changes in rewarding stimuli, like a reversal of choices in an instrumental condition paradigm (Rolls, 2008). Evidence to support his theory is both based on animal studies, and on studies of patients with frontal lesions, in a discrimination reversal task involving gaining or losing points. The task is a simplified version of the Wisconsin Card Sorting Task.[6] In the simplified version, normal and frontal (OFC lesioned) patients learned specific responses by touching one of two simultaneously presented figures (a triangle and square) on a screen, by gaining a bonus of one point. Touching the other stimulus, meant the loss of a point. After the patients had learned over a number of trials to respond to one figure (in this case, triangles), they perseverated with responding to triangles when the stimulus-reinforcement contingency unexpectedly changed from triangles to squares. The difficulty patients had to adapt to reversals, was also correlated with behavioral indices of uninhibited social behavior. Their OFC deficit specifically concerned perseveration to a previously rewarded stimulus, not forms of response perseveration that occur after damage to other parts of the prefrontal cortex (Rolls et al., 2000).

In contrast to the somatic marker theory, Roll's decision model does not incorporate feedback from the somatosensory cortex, and related dispositional representations. Instead, it is centered on the ability of the OFC to correct and flexibly guide actions, based on learned stimulus-reinforcement associations. When new information changes the social context, the OFC is essential to inhibit the prevailing action tendencies to adapt to the new situation. This suggests that the OFC must also contain or have access to representations of preferences.

In the macaque brain at least four frontal cortex regions can be identified with distinct roles in reward-guided behavior: the ventromedial prefrontal cortex, the medial and lateral orbitofrontal cortex, the anterior cingulate cortex (ACC) and the anterior prefrontal cortex, (Figure 7.14 presents a medial view of some of these areas in the macaque brain). A widely replicated finding is that the BOLD signals in the medial OFC and ventral PFC, are correlated with the reward value of the choice (reviewed by Rushworth et al., 2007). In humans, these signals probably reflect not only expectations of monetary gain but also expectations of monetary loss. Furthermore, lesion studies in macaques, have suggested that these neural signals could also be causally linked to guide decisions in choice reaction tasks.

Recent evidence further suggests that reinforcement guided decision making not just depends on the OFC but also the anterior cingulate cortex (ACC). An exciting aspect of the ACC function, supported by research including the recording of event-related potentials and fMRI, concerns its responsiveness to errors and the initiation of subsequent changes in behavior (Nieuwenhuis et al., 2004). Lesions of the ACC impair reinforcement guided action, in particular in conditions when performance is not directly mediated by a learned association between a stimulus and a reinforcer (Rushworth

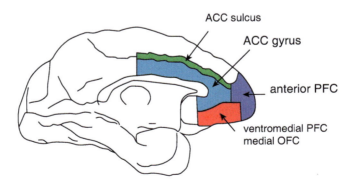

FIGURE 7.14
Frontal medial brain regions in the macaque involved in reward-guided learning and decision-making.

Source: Adapted from Rushworth et al. (2011).

et al., 2007). Since the ACC has access to a greater repertoire of representations than the OFC, it might also participate in exploratory behavior in natural environments, where decisions depend on consideration of the benefits, as well as of the costs of the actions involved. This requires a system in the brain, guided by the ACC that represents and possibly also updates the actual value of action itself. Such a system might also take into account the costs associated with the amount of effort needed to obtain a reward. In summary, these findings suggest that although the OFC and ACC are anatomically strongly connected, they have distinctive and supplementary functional roles in emotional decision making. While the OFC is bound to representations of the association between preferences and rewards, the ACC would be bound more strongly to representations of the action values and the task itself, and action to reward ratios.

Neurotransmitters and emotions

The regulation of emotional processes is based on interaction between structural and energetical factors. Structural factors relate to what the emotion system is 'doing' and involve 'computational' mechanisms situated in local networks of the amygdala, hypothalamus, and orbitofrontal cortex, as reviewed in the previous sections. Their primary task is to assess the quality of reinforcers (or the valence or affective stimuli), and to translate this into action programs. Energetical factors relate to the state of the brain, controlled by neurotransmitters and hormones that modulate, that is attenuate or enhance these processes during emotional learning and recall (Panksepp, 1993). Their primary role is to control the activational state of networks, where emotions are represented in their respective memories.

Neuroaffective circuits have a high degree of connectivity. For instance, the amygdala not only has connections with the hypothalamus and the orbitofrontal cortex, but also with lower brain structures like the ventral part of the tegmentum. There also are reciprocal links between the prefrontal cortex and these areas. The following sections first consider some of the specific neural nuclei and circuits involved in the release of neurotransmitters, and then focus more specifically on the four major classes of neurotransmitters, and their effect on behavior and emotions. Although some of these structures and circuits have already been dealt with in prior chapters, we focus here in particular on their significance in regulating affective states.

Medial forebrain bundle

The medial forebrain bundle (MFB) consists of axons in the medial plane of the brain, connecting parts of the ventral tegmentum through the lateral hypothalamus to structures in the basal part of the frontal brain and the orbitofrontal cortex (see Figure 7.15).

EMOTIONS

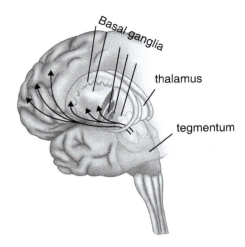

FIGURE 7.15
The medial forebrain bundle (MFB) with neurotransmitter pathways projecting to striatum in the basal ganglia and the forebrain.

Two major cell groups in the tegmentum are responsible for the production of dopamine, namely the ventral tegmentum and the substantia nigra ('black substance'). The ventral tegmentum has many connections to the ventral part of the striatum (also known as the nucleus accumbens), the substantia nigra to the dorsal part of the striatum.

The MFB consists of long ascending and descending axons. They receive input from the somatosensory area that contains a topographical map of body areas, and from neurotransmitter circuits that originate in the brain stem with short-branched axons to nearby structures.

Importantly, the MFB also contains ascending pathways from noradrenergic, serotonergic and dopaminergic neurons in the brainstem, that project to the frontal cortical areas. The mesolimbic dopamine pathway is essential for the regulation of emotions and of reward. Its origin is the ventral tegmentum, a collection of cells in the tegmentum next to the substantia nigra. It passes the hippocampus and the amygdala and then projects through the MFB via the ventral part of the striatum to the prefrontal cortex.

Locus coeruleus-noradrenergic system

When evaluating emotional events, noradrenaline is released after some initial appraisal of the valence of a stimulus. The lateral and basal nuclei of the amygdala are suitable candidates to fulfill this role. The amygdala evaluates incoming stimuli and classifies them as positive or negative reinforcers. This signal is then transmitted via the central nucleus to the hypothalamus that in turn activates the locus coeruleus in the brainstem to release noradrenaline (Bouret et al., 2003). Exposure to a single stressor assumedly causes adaptive changes in synapses of the hypothalamus that modify responses to subsequent stressors (Bains et al., 2015). The locus coeruleus-norepinephrine system innervates neocortical and subcortical structures, like cerebellum, hippocampus, and limbic system. It also feeds back to the amygdala where it further increases the noradrenaline level (McCall et al., 2017). At the cortical level, it leads to a diffuse facilitation of cortical synapses, also known as the arousal reaction.

Usually noradrenaline is released whenever some form of action is required, which implies approach to or avoidance of a reinforcer. Both positive 'stressors' (events associated with surprise, thrill, and novelty) and negative stressors (events associated with discomfort, fear and anxiety) also trigger the noradrenaline system. Experimental findings suggest that an increased release of noradrenaline is involved in the provocation of anxiety and fear in animals exposed to stress, as well as in humans. In rats, for example, benzodiazepine attenuated not only noradrenaline release but also anxiety-related behavior, while the effects were stronger when a benzodiazepine antagonist was applied (Tanaka et al., 2000). High arousal and noradrenaline normally enhance memory consolidation in the hippocampus (McGaugh et al., 2002). Anxiolytic drugs or beta-blockers like propanolol, in contrast, attenuate their effect. These substances lower blood pressure, but at the cortical level also diminish modulatory effects of noradrenaline on consolidation, or reconsolidation, in the hippocampus (Morris et al., 1998; Cahill et al., 1994).

Dopamine and emotions

The production of dopamine in the brain depends on specific opiate receptors, located in the ventral tegmentum and ventral striatum. Cells of these receptors are highly sensitive to substances like morphine and cocaine (called dopamine agonists) which block the inhibitory properties of the neurotransmitter GABA on dopamine, resulting in increased production of it.

Enhancement of positive reinforcers

Self-stimulation studies of rats and monkeys have revealed the role of dopamine as a reward neurotransmitter. In an instrumental learning paradigm, rats learn to stimulate themselves electrically with electrodes placed in the nucleus accumbens, or to administer themselves dopamine agonists. Spiroperidol, a dopamine antagonist, in turn, suppresses the frequency of self-stimulation or conditioned responses of rats and monkeys. This effect is not just a consequence of blocking the motor response, but of a reduction of the effect of the reward itself. Interestingly, studies using deep brain stimulation in an area near the nucleus accumbens in human patients suffering from obsessive compulsive disorder (OCD) have reported effects resembling those of positive reinforcers, manifested in a rapid increase of self-confidence ratings (Kiverstein et al., 2019).

Emotional learning and dopamine

Structures in the neuroaffective network and dopaminergic pathways regulate emotions in different but interacting ways.

The question then arises how dopamine affects neural processing, and emotional learning in this network (see also Figure 7.16). The amygdala, with its various nuclei and pathways, typically functions as a computational system in processing affective stimuli. It also receives visual and auditory input from the temporal lobe of higher order representations (objects, faces, voices). Effects of noradrenaline on the amygdala seem to involve an increase of sensitivity of detection, and a modulation of the effect of emotional events. In fear, for example, this affects the encoding and consolidation of the events in memory.

Dopamine however seems to affect more specifically the 'drive' system, and to mobilize energy via dopaminergic pathways to the striatum. A possible scenario is that after initial evaluation of the valence of a stimulus in lateral and medial nuclei, this information is transmitted via the central nucleus to the ventral tegmentum, which then causes a release of dopamine via the nucleus accumbens. This feeds back to structures in the emotion system, modulating its intrinsic connections. In particular, it could help to strengthen the neural connections associating a) primary and secondary reinforcers in the orbitofrontal cortex, and b) the response and secondary reinforcers in the basal ganglia (Figure 7.16, red arrows). In the primate dopaminergic neurons fluctuating output were even shown to signal changes or errors in the predictions of future salient and rewarding events (Schultz et al., 1997).

The involved neural connections assumedly recruit the same mechanism of long-term potentiation (LTP) that underlies learning processes in the hippocampus. In contrast to cognitive learning, the principal function of LTP in instrumental conditioning of emotional behavior could be the strengthening of synapses in action circuits, linking the anterior motor cortices with the striatum of the basal ganglia. The major effect of dopamine thus being on the selection of actions.

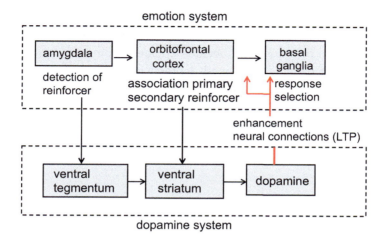

FIGURE 7.16
Schematic view of the possible interaction between the dopamine system and the emotion systems in emotional learning, and action selection.

Depression: the role of noradrenaline, serotonin and stress hormones

Depression is a widespread disorder, in psychiatric patients and in healthy persons. This illness is characterized by a sad mood and reduced interest and pleasure in daily activities. There often are feelings of fatigue, of insomnia and disturbances in thinking, memory and concentration. Severe depression can seriously affect cognitive functions such as memory, attention and awareness. Research of identical twins has pointed to a clear hereditary factor in the development of depression. The probability that identical twins both develop depression is much higher than in brothers and sisters. However, it is still unclear which chromosomes are the carrier of the genes for depression. Studies that focused on the role of biochemical factors suggested that noradrenaline and serotonin, two neurotransmitters that belong to the group of amino-acids (monoamines), are of principal importance (see also Nemeroff, 1998, for a review of biological factors).

Noradrenaline

Depressive patients often exhibit a reduced level of noradrenaline metabolites in their urine and cerebrospinal fluid. Post-mortem examination of the brain of depressed patients has further revealed a relatively large number of noradrenergic receptors in postsynaptic cortical cells. This is seen as a compensatory response to the decreased noradrenaline levels in the synaptic connections. The relationship between noradrenaline and depressive disorders also became apparent from research confirming that high blood pressure patients developed depressive complaints after treatment with Reserpine, a substance that not only reduces blood pressure but also inhibits the production of monoamines. Substances like Monoamine Oxidase Inhibitors that counteract the natural degradation of monoamines have the opposite effect: namely mood enhancement. These so-called 'MAO inhibitors' were the first antidepressants being marketed.

Serotonin

Depressive and suicidal patients often have reduced levels of serotonin in their brain. There also may be an increase in the number of receptors, which can be a compensatory response to the decreased serotonin levels in the synapses of cortical cells. Lower serotonin levels possibly also lead to a reduced production of noradrenaline, or to mitigate its effect on stress hormones. The important role of serotonin in depressive disorders was also revealed at the end of 1980 by the discovery of substances known as serotonin reuptake inhibitors (SRI's). These have proved to be effective in suppression of depressive states. SRI's work selectively on synaptic processes: they mainly affect reuptake of serotonin, and much less of noradrenaline and dopamine.

Stress hormones

Another symptom of depressive disorders is a disturbance in the hormonal regulation. Depressive patients often exhibit an increased production of CRF (corticotropic release factor) secreted by the hypothalamus, which in turn stimulates the pituitary gland to increase the production of ACTH (adrenal-cortical-thyroid hormone).

The paraventricular nucleus (PVN) of the hypothalamus contains cells with a certain plasticity, which enables them to 'recognize' characteristics of stressors. This occurs via neurotransmitters glutamate and GABA, which render PVN synapses more sensitive to new stress stimuli. This, in turn, leads to the production of CRF and cortisol via the hypothalamic-pituitary-adrenal axis (Figure 7.17). Normally, stress hormones like cortisol exert an inhibitory effect on the production of CRF and noradrenaline, helping these systems to maintain a state of balance, and to attenuate the neural response to stressful stimuli. In depression, this balance could be disturbed which requires an artificial intervention (in the form of an application of antidepressant drugs) to restore the balance.

Increased cortisol production maybe also be a factor leading to the reduced volume of the hippocampus, often observed in depressive patients. This is supported by the finding from animal research that chronic stress and cortisol production destroy cells

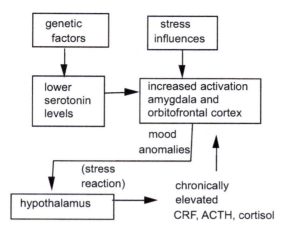

FIGURE 7.17
Diagram picturing the possible interaction between factors involved in the development of depression, and converging in the amygdala and orbitofrontal cortex. CRF= corticotropic releasing factor; ACTH= adrenal-cortical-thyroid hormone. See text for clarification.

in the hippocampus (Smith, 2005). Environmental factors contribute to increased CRF production (Nemeroff, 1998), as found in studies of young rats, deprived of their mother's care. Treatment with serotonin reuptake inhibitors was found to lead to the recovery of CRF production to the normal level. Researchers Plotsky and Meany suggested that early human childhood trauma, as well as childhood abuse and neglect, might trigger the same chronic stress reactions and depressive symptoms in children, who already have a higher genetic predisposition for depressive symptoms.

Importantly, the stress hormone cortisol has a complex effect on the serotonin receptors. In the hippocampus, it leads to a reduced activity of 5HT1a receptors, but in the cerebral cortex to greater activity of 5HT2 receptors. A disturbed balance between both types of receptors could possibly also be the basis of depression.

Summarizing neurotransmitters and depression

Despite the beneficial effect of antidepressants in the treatment of depression, there still is insufficient insight into brain mechanisms that cause depression (in particular into the discussed circuits that regulate emotion). There still is need for a comprehensive theory, that specifies how the different genetic, neural, biochemical and hormonal factors interact in causing depressive states.

The complex regulatory system underlying these neurochemical processes, suggests that depression does not have one but multiple causes (see also McEwen, 1995 for a general overview). For example, selective noradrenaline reuptake inhibition now seems a promising avenue in understanding the causal mechanisms of depression. The advent and success of the selective serotonin reuptake inhibitors have also led to a greater emphasis on the amygdala as the principal player in (unipolar) depressive disorders.

A scenario might be that genetic factors lead to a reduced production of critical neurotransmitters as serotonin. This creates a neurochemical signal, leading to an enhanced activation of groups of neurons in the amygdala and the orbitofrontal cortex. The resulting negative appreciation of the environment and greater sensitivity to stressful stimuli trigger the stress reaction, leading to the release of stress hormones via the hypothalamus (see Holmes, 2005). Feedback from the stress hormones to the amygdala, may then lead to a state of chronic overstimulation and chronic depressive complaints. The vicious circle thus created would be hard to break without drugs like SRIs.

Depression and disturbed functional connectivity in the brain

Significant cognitive deficits have been reported in first-episode major depression patients, in neuropsychological tests of psychomotor speed and executive functioning (Lee et al., 2012). Major depression patients were also characterized by a loss of global functional connectivity of networks in the medial frontal and medial temporal gyri of the brain as compared with normal subjects, in the resting state (Zhang et al., 2011). Disturbed neural connections between neurocognitive and affective networks in the brain in depressive patients, could have been the result, at least in part, of the neurochemical effects of various neurotransmitters and stress hormones. In the interaction model between emotion and cognition, sketched in our earlier working model (Figure 7.2), cognitive deficits occurring in major depression could result from 'bottom-up' effects from emotions regulated by the limbic system. As such, cognitive deficits would rather be a symptom, and not a cause of depression. A contrasting view was expressed by Michael Cole who suggested that disturbances in a frontal-parietal control network play a more causal role in generating mental illness like depression (Cole et al., 2014). When compromised, these networks could be responsible for emitting typical behavioral symptoms of depression: a lack of interest for the environment, withdrawal, and ruminations of thoughts and feelings. The latter view also fits with the notion that within the neuroaffective network (as sketched in Figure 7.8), the ventromedial prefrontal and orbitofrontal cortices with their brain-wide connectivity, also participate in 'top-down' control of affect and of emotional disturbances.

Inspired by this hypothesis, Kaiser and colleagues performed a meta-analysis of a number of resting-state fMRI functional connectivity studies of patients, suffering from Major Depression Disorder (MDD, Kaiser et al., 2015). Of interest here are three major networks involved in MDD: the frontal-parietal network (FPN) involved in top-down control of attention and emotion; the default network (DN), and the dorsal attention network (DAN), presumed to be involved in internally or externally oriented attention. The meta-analysis found two deviant connectivity pattern between patients and controls that were most conspicuous for these networks (Figure 7.18). The first pattern concerned *hypoconnectivity* within the frontal-parietal system and between the frontal-parietal system, and the dorsal attention network involved in attending to the external environment (solid arrows). The second pattern concerned *hyperconnectivity* within the default network, and between frontal parietal control systems and regions of the default network (white arrows). Recall that the default network supports internally oriented and self-referential thoughts. Taken together these findings seem to provide empirical support for the view that an imbalanced connectivity between control

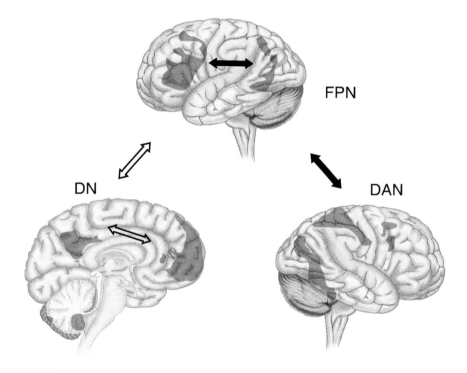

FIGURE 7.18
Neurocognitive network model of major depressive disorder relative to healthy control subjects. Increased connectivity between the frontal-parietal network (FPN) and default network (DN, white arrow), and reduced connectivity between the FPN and dorsal attention network (DAN, black arrow,) reflect a bias toward ruminative thoughts, at the cost of attending to the external world. Compressed data from meta-analysis showing significant differences between healthy control and Major Depression Disorder patients. See text for clarification.

systems and networks involved in internal or external attention may reflect depressive biases toward internal thoughts at the cost of engaging with the external world.

Notes

1. This common tendency of biological scientists, used to draw sharp boundaries between living species, may not apply to mammals like dogs and chimpanzees, and perhaps many more. Their capacity for expressing empathy, sadness and joy are not simple manifestations of conditioned behavior, but likely occur spontaneously, originating from the same neural affective networks as in humans.
2. Of the many curiosity quotes circulating in the media, Einstein's alleged quote: 'I have no special talent. I am only passionately curious', is perhaps worth mentioning in the present context.
3. Event-related potential (ERP) components, such as N2 and the novelty P300 have frequently been associated with the detection of significant or novel events, that are the outcome of search for information. Two different types of N2 are found in conditions of automatic detection of a negative outcome. One is the 'mismatch negativity' (MMN), a brain response to physically deviant auditory stimuli, the other is the 'error related negativity' (ERN) elicited in conditions when incorrect responses are automatically detected. P300 is elicited by unpredictable, novel and task relevant events, and often seen as reflecting processes like orienting, uncertainty reduction and information delivery. Frontal patients in particular show a reduction of the novelty P300 recorded on the frontal scalp sites (Løvstad et al., 2012).
4. Functional imaging studies have also reported with remarkable consistency hyperactivity in the orbitofrontal cortex (OFC), anterior cingulate cortex (ACC), and caudate nucleus of patients with obsessive compulsive disorder (OCD). These findings have often been interpreted as evidence that abnormalities in cortico-basal ganglia-thalamocortical loops involving the OFC and ACC are causally related to OCD (Maia et al., 2008).
5. Other implicit forms of memory, not discussed here, are priming and procedural memory, described in the previous chapter.
6. In this task, which contains special sets of cards, subjects learn to sort cards by trial and error into piles on the basis of criteria as color, form and number of elements on the card. Patients with lesions in the lateral prefrontal cortex often show perseveration errors (applying the initial rule over and over again) when a sorting rule (sorting according to color) is changed (into sorting according to form) without informing the subjects.

Epilogue

The purpose of this book was not to add another textbook to the growing number of excellent introductory books in the field of cognitive neuroscience. Instead, it is meant to supplement these books by choosing a more conceptual approach, and restricting its content to matters reflecting my personal interest. In sketching a picture of modern cognitive neuroscience I often leaned on classical 'anchor points': theories of attention, memory, and emotion, and perception-action systems, developed in earlier decades. I added more recent insights and methods whenever I felt they shed a new light on old problems or presented more refined techniques to unravel the networks underlying complex mind-brain interactions.

A recurring theme is the brain's functional organization. The prevailing view developed in the last decades, is the brain being a network with local structures operating in the context of larger distributed networks, through parallel and reciprocal circuits. This implied that the question of 'where' in the brain became subordinate to the question of 'which network' is recruited during cognitive performance. Another aspect of this development is that the principle of functional segregation of cortical regions, which dominated earlier research in cognitive neuroscience, gradually gave way to that of functional integration. This did not rule out the importance of more dedicated 'modular' structures. According to Marsel Mesulam, one of the great minds in the history of cognitive neuroscience, it is the combination of modularity and connectivity which makes our brain an extremely efficient information processing system.

Modern connectionist studies have mostly remained silent with respect to the brain's global functional architecture and the way it controls what 'goes on inside' the active or the resting brain. If indeed every structure connects with almost any other structure, it becomes tempting to embrace a distributed parallel model of brain organization. This in turn may end up in a 'pandemonium': an anarchy of structures linked by short- and long-ranging connections, depending on their intrinsic constraints. An increasing number of functional imaging studies however have pointed out that the brain has a distinct architecture, in which 'higher' and 'lower' structures engage in different functional roles. These findings favor a hierarchical parallel model compatible with the evolutionary principle that phylogenetically new structures control older structures, which we humans share with other mammals in the evolutionary tree.

Examples of functional hierarchies are the frontal-parietal and central executive networks, in which the prefrontal cortex constitutes an ideal station in establishing coherent activity in the network of surrounding, as well as more distant, subcortical areas. The role of higher areas like the prefrontal cortex in coordinating 'executive functions' does not necessarily mean a return to Daniel Dennett's famous 'Cartesian Theater' (Dennett,1995, 2005). During the evolution of Homo Sapiens, the strong development of the neocortex almost certainly was the basis for the emergence of unique functions, such as self-awareness and cognitive control. In line with this view, this book has provided several examples of domains of cognition that emerge from large-scale networks operating on the basis of higher cortical regions controlling lower structures in the limbic stem and brainstem.

The complexity of concepts and the tremendous variety of methods used in cognitive neuroscience could be the reasons why there is so little consensus on the definition of global theoretical concepts. A notorious example is consciousness, perhaps the most debated and controversial topic in the field (Crick & Koch, 1992). As such, consciousness is not a separate function, but rather a mode of functioning, depending on the state (explicit or implicit) of representations in the brain. Considered from this perspective, consciousness plays a central role in practically every domain of cognition, perception, memory, motor function, and emotions.

The present book also puts much emphasis on the role of neural representations as the analog of mental representations. They constitute the smaller and 'firmer entities' (a term used by Steven Pinker) that form the building blocks of complex memories, including their declarative and their non-declarative sub-varieties. The overarching term I used for their common architecture is functional cerebral space, which in my vision represents an elegant and parsimonious way to describe memory systems. Inspired by the thinking of Joachim Fuster, Neal Cowan, and Howard Eichenbaum I argued that within functional cerebral space neural representations vary in state and content. Their active versus inactive states correspond respectively with what we usually call short-term and long-term memories. The content of representations relates to anatomical sites in the brain, where larger and smaller networks are committed to specific forms of information processing.

Another concern writing this book was to not only speak to those with a professional interest in brain matters, but also to students in cognitive neuroscience who probably are still struggling with the big questions relating to mind-brain matters. This book does not provide clear-cut solutions to solving questions relating to the mind-brain relationship. It tries to clarify important elements of influential, and sometimes contrasting models of the functional architecture of the brain relating to cognitive functions as perception and action, attention, memory, and emotions. Here and there I also ventured into more fundamental questions concerning the mind-brain relationship by peeping behind the silvery curtains of neurophilosophy, the field so aptly introduced by Patricia Smith-Churchland.

The old and fundamental dualist dichotomy created by René Descartes still puzzles cognitive neuroscientists in their attempt to infer cognition from images of the brain. The dichotomy is also reflected in the view of some 'hard-boiled' cognitive psychologists, convinced that the study of the mind does not need the brain or, put even more strongly, should try to avoid the pitfalls of 'brain thinking'. The contrasting view comes from neuroscientists advocating a 'new phrenology', implying that with increasing knowledge of the brain, and the development of increasingly refined techniques to unravel its structure, brain science will ultimately make psychology superfluous (Uttal, 2001).

May this book support the view that cognitive science remains a valuable source of inspiration to guide research in neuroscience by providing a guideline in the form of cognitive blueprints or maps for those who wish to enter the labyrinth of the brain.

References

Adolphs, R., Damasio, H., Tranel, D. and Damasio, A.R. (1996). Cortical systems for the recognition of emotion in facial expression. *J. Neurosci.* 16: 7678–7687.

Aggleton, J.P. and Brown, M.W. (1999). Episodic memory, amnesia and the hippocampal-anterior thalamic axis. *Behav. Brain Sci.* 22: 425–489.

Albert, M.L., Butters, N. and Levin, J. (1979). Temporal gradients in the retrograde amnesia of patients with Korsakoff's disease. *Arch. Neurolog.* 36: 211.

Alcami, O. and Pereda, A. (2010). Beyond plasticitu: The dynamic impact of electrical synapses on neural circuits. *Nat. Rev. Neurosci.* 20: 253–271.

Alexander, G.E. and DeLong, M.R. (1985). Microstimulation of the primate neostriatum. I. Physiological properties of striatal microexcitable zones. *J. Neurophysiol.* 53: 1401–1416.

Alexander, G.E., DeLong, M.R. and Strick, P.L. (1986). Parallel organization of functionally segregated circuits linking basal ganglia and cortex. *Ann. Rev. Neurosci.* 9: 357–381.

Allen, M. (1994). Models of hemispheric specialization. *Psych. Bull.* 93: 73–104.

Allport, D.A. (1985). Distributed memory: Modular subsystems and dysphasia. In: S.K. Newman and R. Epstein (Eds.), *Current perspectives in dysphasia* (pp. 32–60). Edinburg: Churchill Livingstone.

Altikulac, S., Lee, N., van der veen, C. and van Atteveldt, N. (2019). The teenage brain: Public perceptions of neurocognitive development during adolescence. *J. Cogn. Neurosci.* 3: 339–359

Amedi, A., Raz, N., Pianka, P., Malach, R. and Zohary, E. (2003). Early visual cortex activation correlates with superior verbal memory in the blind. *Nat. Neurosci.* 6: 758–766.

Anderson, M.C., et al. (2004). Neural systems underlying the suppression of unwanted memories. *Science* 303: 232–235.

Andrews-Hanna, J.R. (2010). Functional-anatomic fractionation of the brain's default network. *Neuron* 75: 550–562.

Aron, A.R. (2007). The neural basis of inhibition in cognitive control. *Neuroscientist* 13: 214–228.

Ashby, F.G. and Waldschmidt, J.G. (2008). Fitting computational models to fMRI data. *Behav. Res. Meth.* 40: 713–721.

REFERENCES

Ashby, F.G., Turner, B.O. and Horvitz, J.C. (2010). Cortical and basal ganglia contributions to habit learning and automaticity. Perceptual learning, motor learning and automaticity. Review. *Cell* 3: 208–215.

Atkinson, R.C. and Shiffrin, R.M. (1968). Human memory: A proposed system and its control processes. In: K.W. Spence and J.T. Spence (Eds.), *The psychology of learning and motivation: Advances in research and theory*, vol. 2 (pp. 89–195). New York: Academic Press.

Baars, B.J. (1988). *A cognitive theory of consciousness*. Cambridge: Cambridge University Press.

Baars, B.J. (1997). *In the theater of consciousness: The workspace of the mind*. New York: Oxford University Press.

Baars, B.J. (2003). The global brainweb: An update on global workspace theory. Guest editorial. *Science and Consciousness Review* 2, October.

Baddeley, A. (2003). Working memory: Looking back and looking forward. *Nat. Rev. Neurosci.* 4: 829–839.

Baddeley, A.D. and Hitch, G.J. (1994). Developments in the concept of working memory. *Neuropsychology* 8: 485–493.

Baddeley, A.D., Emslie, H., Kolodny, J. and Duncan, J. (1998). Random generation and executive control of working memory. *Quart. J.`Exp. Psychol.* 51A: 819–852.

Bahrick, H.P. (1984). Semantic memory content in permastore: Fifty years of memory for Spanish learned in school. *J. Exp. Psychol. Gen.* 113: 1–29.

Bains, J.S., et al. (2015). Stress-related synaptic plasticity in the hypothalamus. *Nat. Rev. Neurosci.* 16: 377–388.

Ball, L., Beukelman, D. and Bardach, L. (2007). AAC intervention for ALS. In: D. Beukelman, K. Garrett and K. Yorkston (Eds.), *Augmentative communication strategies for adults with acute or chronic medical conditions* (pp. 287–316). Baltimore, MD: Paul H. Brookes.

Bang, D. and Fleming, S.M. (2018). Distinct encoding of decision confidence in human medial prefrontal cortex. *Proc. Natl. Acad. Sci.* 115: 6082–6087.

Banich, M.T. (1997). *Neuropsychology*. Boston: Houghton Mifflin Company.

Barlow, H. (1994). What is the computational goal of the neocortex? In: C. Koch and J.L. Davis (Eds.), *Large-scale neuronal theories of the brain* (pp. 1–22). Cambridge: MIT Press.

Baron-Cohen, S., et al. (1995). Are children with autism blind to the mentalistic significance of the eyes? *British J. Dev. Psychol.* 13: 379–398.

Bartlett, F.C. (1932). *Remembering: A study in experimental and social psychology*. Cambridge: Cambridge University Press.

Bartoli, E., Aron, A.R. and Tandon, N. (2018). Topography and timing of activity in right inferior frontal cortex and anterior insula for stopping movement. *Hum. Brain Mapp.* 39: 189–203.

Bartolomei, F., Barbeau, E., Gavaret, M., Guye, M., McGonigal, A., Régis, J. and Chauvel, P. (2004). Cortical stimulation study of the role of rhinal cortex in déjà vu and reminiscence of memories. *Neurology* 63: 858–864.

REFERENCES

Bauer, P.J. (2014). The development of forgetting: Childhood amnesia. In: P.J. Bauer and R. Fivush (Eds.), *The Wiley-Blackwell handbook on the development of children's memory* (pp. 519–544). Chichester: Wiley-Blackwell.

Bauer, P. Wetzler, S.E. and Sweeney, J.A. (1986). Childhood amnesia: An empirical demonstration. In: D.C. Rubin (Ed.), *Autobiographical memory* (pp. 191–201). New York: Cambridge University Press.

Beaton, A.A. (1997). The relation of planum temporale asymmetry and morphology of the corpus callosum to handedness, gender, and dyslexia: A review of the evidence. *Brain and Language* 60: 255–322.

Beckmann, C.F., DeLuca, M., Devlin, J.T. and Smith, S.M. (2005). Investigations into resting-state connectivity using independent component analysis. *Philos. Trans. R. Soc. Biol. Sci.* 360: 1001–1013.

Belin, P., et al. (2004). Thinking the voice: Neural correlates of voice perception. *Trends Cogn. Sci.* 8: 129–135.

Berlyne, D.E. (1957). Conflict and information-theory variables as determinants of human perceptual curiosity. *J. Exp. Psychol.* 53: 399–404.

Berlyne, D.E. (1960). *Conflict, arousal, and curiosity*. New York: McGraw-Hill Book Company.

Berns, G.S. and Sejnowski, T.J. (1998). A computational model of how the basal ganglia produce sequences. *J. Cogn. Neurosci.* 10: 108–121.

Bishop, S., Lau, M., Shapiro, S., Carlson, L., Anderson, N.D., Carmody, J., et al. (2004). Mindfulness: A proposed operational definition. *Clin. Psychol. Sci. Pract.* 11: 230–241.

Bisiach, E. and Luzzatti, C. (1978). Unilateral neglect of representational space. *Cortex* 14: 129–133.

Bliss, T.V.P. and Lømo, T. (1973). Long-lasting potentiation of synaptic transmission in the dentate area of the anaesthesized rabbit following stimulation of the perforant path. *J. Physiol.* 232: 331–356.

Bloom, F.E. and Lazerson, A. (1988). *Brain, mind and behavior*. 2nd edition. New York: Freeman.

Boring, E.A. (1929). *A history of experimental psychology*. New York: Appleton-Century Crofts.

Botvinick, M.M. and Cohen, J.D. (2014). The computational and neural basis of cognitive control: charted territory and new frontiers. *Cogn. Sci.* 38: 1249–1285.

Bouret, S., Duvel, A., Onat, S. and Sara, S.J. (2003). Phasic activation of locus ceruleus neurons by the central nucleus of the amygdala. *J. Neurosci.* 23: 3491–3497.

Braver, T.S. and Cohen, J.D. (2000). On the control of control: The role of dopamine in regulating pre-frontal function and working memory. In: S. Monsell and J. Driver (Eds.), *Control of cognitive processes* (pp. 713–737). Cambridge: MIT Press.

Bressler, S.L. and Menon, V. (2010). Large-scale brain networks in cognition: Emerging methods and principles. *Trends Cogn. Sci.* 14: 277–290.

Bressler, S.L., Tang, W., Sylvester, C.M., Shulman, G.L. and Corbetta, M. (2008). Topdown control of human visual cortex by frontal and parietal cortex in anticipatory visual spatial attention. *J. Neurosci.* 28: 10056–10061.

Brewer, J., Zhao, Z., Desmond, J.E., Glover, G.H. and Gabrieli, J.D.E. (1998). Making memories: Brain activity that predicts how well visual experience will be remembered. *Science* 281: 1185–1187.

Broadbent, D.E. (1958). *Perception and communication.* London: Pergamon Press.

Brodmann, K. (1909). *Vergleichende Lokalisationslehre der Grosshirnrinde.* Leipzig: Barth.

Brody, L.R. and Hall, J.A. (2008). Gender and emotion in context. In: M. Lewis, J.M. Haviland-Jones and L.F. Barrett (Eds.), *Handbook of emotions,* 3rd edition (pp. 395–408). New York: The Guilford Press.

Bruer, J. (1999). *The myth of the first three years: A new understanding of early brain development and lifelong learning.* New York: The Free Press.

Buckner, R.L., Andrews-Hanna, J.S. and Schacter, D.L (2008). The brain's default network anatomy, function, and relevance to disease. *Ann. N. Y. Acad. Sci.* 1124: 1–38.

Buckner, R.L., Kelley, W.M. and Petersen, S.E. (1999). Frontal cortex contributes to human memory formation. *Nat. Neurosci.* 2: 311–314.

Buhusi, C.V. and Meck, W.H. (2005). What makes us tick? Functional and neural mechanisms of interval timing. *Nat. Rev. Neurosci.* 6: 755–765.

Bullmore, E. and Sporns, O. (2009). Complex brain networks: graph theoretical analysis of structural and functional systems. *Nat. Rev. Neurosci.* 10: 186–198.

Bullmore, E. and Sporns, O. (2012). The economy of brain network organization. *Nat. Rev. Neurosci.* 13: 336–349.

Bullock, D. and Grossberg, S. (1988). Neural dynamics of planned arm movements: Emergent invariants and speed-accuracy properties during trajectory formation. *Psychol. Rev.* 95: 49–90.

Bundesen, C., Habekost, T. and Kyllingsbæk, S. (2005). A neural theory of visual attention: Bridging cognition and neurophysiology. *Psychol. Rev.* 112: 291–328.

Bunge, S.A., Klingberg, T., Jacobsen, R.B. and Gabrieli, J.D.E. (2000). A resource model of the neural basis of executive working memory. *Proc. Natl. Acad. Sci.* 97: 3573–3578.

Bush, G., Luu, P. and Posner, M.I. (2000). Cognitive and emotional influences in anterior cingulate cortex. *Trends Cogn. Sci.* 4: 215–222.

Butler, R. and Harlow, H.F. (1954). Persistence of visual exploration in monkeys. *J. Comp. Physiol. Psychol.* 46: 258.

Cabeza, R. and Nyberg, L. (2000). Imaging cognition II: An empirical Rev. 275 PET and fMRI studies. *J. Cogn. Neursci.* 12: 1–47.

Cabeza, R., Ciaramelli, E. Olson, I.R. and Moscovitch, M. (2008). The parietal cortex and episodic memory: An attentional account. *Nat. Rev. Neurosci.* 9: 613–625.

Cabeza, R., Nyberg, L. and Park, K. (2005). *Cognitive neuroscience of aging.* Oxford: Oxford University Press.

Cahill, L. and McGaugh, L. (1996). Modulation of memory storage. *Curr Op. Neurobiol.* 6: 237–242.

Cahill, L., Prins, B., Weber, M. and McGaugh, J.L. (1994). Beta-adrenergic activation and memory for emotional events. *Nature* 371: 702–704.

REFERENCES

Call, J. and Tomasello, M. (2008). Does the chimpanzee have a theory of mind? 30 years later. *Trends Cogn. Neurosci.* 12: 187–192.

Cannon, W.B. (1927). The James-Lange theory of emotions: A critical examination and an alternative. *Am. J. Psychol.* 239: 106–124.

Cantalupo, C. and Hopkins, W.D. (2001). Asymmetric Broca's area in great apes. *Nature* 414: 505.

Carlson, N.R. (2002). *Physiological psychology*. 7th edition. Boston: Allyn and Bacon.

Cavada, C. and Goldman-Rakic, P.S. (1989). Posterior parietal cortex in rhesus monkey: II. Evidence for segregated corticocortical networks linking sensory and limbic areas with the frontal lobe. *J. Compar. Neurolog.* 287: 422–445.

Cavanagh, J.F. and Frank, M.J. (2014). Frontal theta as a mechanism for cognitive control. *Trends Cogn. Sci.* 18: 414–421.

Chadwick, M.J. Anjum, R.S., Humaran, D., Schacter, D.J., Spiers, H.J. and Hassabis, D. (2016). Semantic representations in the temporal pole predict false memories *Proc. Natl. Acad. Sci. U.S.A.* 113: 10180–10185.

Changeux, J.P. (1985). *Neuronal man. The biology of mind*. New York: Oxford University Press.

Cherry, E.C. (1953). Some experiments on the recognition of speech with one and with two ears. *J. Acoustical Soc. America* 25: 975–979.

Christoff, K., Irving, Z.C., Fox, K.C.R., Spreng, R.N. and Andrews-Hanna, J.R. (2016). Mind-wandering as spontaneous thought: A dynamic framework. *Nat. Rev. Neurosci.* 17: 719.

Churchland, A.K., Kiani, R. and Shadlen, M.N. (2008). Decision-making with multiple alternatives. *Nat. Neurosci.* 11: 693–702.

Churchland, P.S. (1986). *Neurophilosophy. Toward a unified science of the mind-brain*. Cambridge: MIT Press.

Churchland, P.S. and Sejnowski, T.S. (1988). Perspectives in Cognitive Neuroscience. *Science* 242: 741–745.

Churchland, P.S. and Sejnowski, T.S. (1992). *The computational brain*. Cambridge: MIT Press.

Churchland, P.S., Ramachandran, V.S. and Sejnowski, T.S. (1995). A critique of pure vision. In: C. Koch and J.L. Davis (Eds.), *Large-scale neuronal theories of the brain* (pp. 23–60). Cambridge: MIT Press.

Cisek, P. (2006). Integrated neural processes for defining potential actions and deciding between them: A computational model. *J. Neurosci.* 26: 9761–9770.

Cisek, P. (2007). Cortical mechanisms of action selection: The affordance competition hypothesis. *Philos. Trans. R. Soc. Lond. B Biol. Sci.* 362: 1585–1599.

Cisek, P. and Kalaska, J.F. (2010). Neural mechanisms for interacting with a world full of action choices. *Ann. Rev. Neurosci.* 33: 269–298.

Cohen, L.G., et al. (1997). Functional relevance of cross-modal plasticity in blind humans. *Nature* 389: 180–183.

Cohen, N.J. and Eichenbaum, H. (1993). *Memory, amnesia, and the hippocampal system*. Cambridge, MA: MIT Press.

Colby, C.L. and Goldberg, M.E. (1999). Space and attention in parietal cortex. *Ann. Rev. Neurosci.* 22: 319–349.

Cole, M.W., Repovš, G. and Anticevic, A. (2014). The frontal parietal control system: A central role in mental health. *Neuroscientist* 20: 652–664.

Cole, M.W., Reynolds, J.R., Power, J.D., Repovš, G., Anticevic, A. and Braver, T.S. (2013). Multitask connectivity reveals flexible hubs for adaptive task control. *Nat. Neurosci.* 16: 1348–1355.

Cole, M.W., Yarkoni, T., Repovš, G., Anticevic, A. and Braver, T.S. (2012). Global connectivity of prefrontal cortex predicts cognitive control and intelligence. *J. Neurosci.* 32: 8988–8999.

Collignon, O., Lassonde, M. Lepore, F., Bastien, D. and Veraart, C. (2007). Functional cerebral organization for auditory spatial processing and auditory substitution of vision in early blind subjects. *Cereb. Cortex* 17: 457–465.

Collignon, O., Voss, P., Lassonde, M. and Lepore, F. (2009). Cross-modal plasticity for the spatial processing of sounds in visually deprived subjects. *Exp. Brain Res.* 192: 343.

Collins, A.M. and Loftus, E.F. (1975). Spreading-activation theory of semantic processing. *Psychol. Rev.* 82: 407–428.

Coltheart, M. (1999). Modularity and cognition. *Cog. Sci.* 3: 115–120.

Conway, R.A., Cowan, N., Bunting, M.F., Therriault, D.J. and Minkoff, S.R.B. (2002). A latent variable analysis of working memory capacity, short-term memory capacity, processing speed, and general fluid intelligence. *Intelligence* 30: 163–183.

Corballis, M.C. (1989). Laterality and human evolution. *Psych. Rev.* 96: 492–505.

Corballis, M.C. (1991). *The lopsided ape: Evolution of the generative mind*. New York: Oxford University Press.

Corbetta, M. and Shulman, G.L. (2002). Control of goal-directed and stimulus-driven attention in the brain. *Nat. Rev. Neurosci.* 3: 201–215.

Corbetta, M., Kincade, J.M., Ollinger, J.M., McAvoy, M.P. and Shulman, G.L. (2000). Voluntary orienting is dissociated from target detection in human posterior parietal cortex. *Nat. Neurosci.* 3: 292–297.

Corbetta, M., Sylvester, C.M. and Shulman, G.I. (2009). The frontal parietal attention network. In: M. Gazzzaniga (Ed.), *The cognitive neurosciences*, 4th edition (pp. 219–234). Cambridge: The MIT Press.

Cordes, S.P. (2005). Molecular genetics of the early development of hindbrain serotonergic neurons. *Clin. Genet.* 68: 487–494.

Corkin, S., Amaral, D., Gonzalez, R., Johnson, K., et al. (1997). H.M.'s medial temporal lobe lesion: Findings from magnetic resonance imaging. *J. Neurosci.* 17: 3964–3979.

REFERENCES

Cowan, N. (1995). *Attention and memory. An integrated framework*. New York: Oxford University Press.

Cowan, N. (2005). *Working memory capacity*. New York: Psychology Press.

Crammond, D.J. and Kalaska, J.F. (1996). Differential relation of discharge in primary motor cortex and premotor cortex to movements versus actively maintained postures during a reaching task. *Exp. Brain Res.* 108: 45–61.

Crick, F. and Koch, C. (1992). The problem of consciousness. *Scientific American* 167: 152–159.

Crovitz, H.F. and Schiffman, H. (1974). Frequency of episodic memories as a function of their age. *Bull. Psychon. Soc.* 4: 517–518.

Damasio, A. (1994). *Descartes' error. Emotion reason and the human brain*. New York: AVON Books.

Damasio, A.R. (2004). Emotions and feelings: A neurobiological perspective. In: A.S.R. Manstead, N. Frijda and A. Fischer (Eds.), *Feelings and emotions: The Amsterdam symposium* (pp. 49–57). New York: Cambridge University Press.

Damasio, A.R. and Damasio, H. (1994). Cortical systems for retrieval of concrete Knowledge: The convergence zone framework. In: C. Koch and J.L. Davis (Eds.), *Large-scale neuronal theories of the brain* (pp. 61–74). Cambridge: MIT Press.

Damasio, H., Grabowsky, T.J., Tranel, D., Hichwa, R.D. and Damasio, A.R. (1996). A neural basis for lexical retrieval. *Nature* 380: 499–505.

Darwin, C. (1859). *On the origin of species by means of natural selection*. London: John Murray.

Darwin, C. (1872). *The expressions of the emotions in man and animals*. Chicago: The University of Chicago Press.

Davachi, L. and Wagner, A.D. (2002). Hippocampal contributions to episodic encoding: Insights from relational and item-based learning. *J Neurophysiol.* 88: 982–990.

Davey, C.G., Pujol, J., and Harrison, B.J. (2016). Mapping the self in the brain's default mode network. *NeuroImage* 132: 390–397.

Davidson, R.J. (1993). Cerebral asymmetry and emotion: Conceptual and methodological conundrums. *Cognition and Emotion* 7: 115–138.

Davidson, R.J. and Tomarken, A.J. (1989). Laterality and emotion: An electrophysiological approach. In: F. Boller and J. Grafman (Eds.), *Handbook of neuropsychology*, vol. 3 (pp. 419–441). North Holland: Elsevier.

Davis, M. (1992). The role of the amygdala in fear potentiation and startle: Implications for animal models of anxiety. *Trends Pharmacol. Sci.* 13: 35–41.

Davis, M., Rainnie, D. and Cassell, M. (1994). Neurotransmission in the rat amygdala related to fear and anxiety. *Trends Neurosci.* 17: 208–214.

Dayan, E. and Cohen, L.G. (2011). Neuroplasticity subserving motor skill learning. *Neuron* 72: 443–454.

Deacon, T.W. (1997). *The symbolic species*. New York: W.W. Norton.

Debas, K., et al. (2010). Brain plasticity related to the consolidation of motor sequence learning and motor adaptation. *Proc. Natl. Acad. Sci.* 107: 17839–17844.

Dehaene, S., Hakwan, L. and Kouider, S. (2017). What is consciousness, and could machines have it? *Science* 358: 486–449.

Dehaene, S., Posner, M.I. and Tucker, D.M. (1994). Localizing of a neural system for error detection and compensation. *Psychol. Sci*. 5: 303–305.

DeLong, M. and Wichmann, T. (2017). Update on models of basal ganglia function and dysfunction. *Parkinsonism Rel. Disords*. 15: 237–240.

Dennett, D.C. (1995). *Darwin's dangerous idea: Evolution and the meanings of life*. New York: Simon and Schuster.

Dennett, D.C. (2005). *Sweet dreams. Philosophical obstacles to a science of consciousness*. Cambridge: Bradford book.

Desimone, R. and Duncan, J. (1995). Neural mechanisms of visual selective attention. *Ann. Rev. Neurosci*. 18: 193–222.

Desimone, R. and Ungerleiter, L.G. (1989). Neural mechanisms in visual processing in monkeys. In: F. Boller and J. Grafman (Eds.), *Handbook of neuropsychology*, 2 (pp. 267–269). Amsterdam: Elsevier Press.

Desimone, R., Miller, E.K. and Chelazzi, L. (1994). The interaction of neural systems for attention and memory. In: C. Koch and J.L. Davis (Eds.), *Large-scale neuronal theories of the brain* (pp. 75–91). Cambridge: MIT Press.

Desimone, R., Wessinger, M., Thomas, L. and Schneider, W. (1990). Attentional control of visual perception: Cortical and subcortical mechanisms. *Cold Spring Harb. Symp. Quant. Biol*. 55: 963–971.

DeYoe, E.A. and van Essen, D.C. (1988). Concurrent processing streams in monkey visual cortex. *Trends Neurosci*. 11: 219–226.

Diekelmann, S., Wilhelm, I. and Born, J. (2009). The whats and whens of sleep-dependent memory consolidation. *Sleep Med. Rev*. 13: 309–321.

Dolan, R.J. and Fletcher, P.F. (1999). Encoding and retrieval in human medial temporal lobes: An empirical investigation using functional magnetic resonance imaging (fMRI). *Hippocampus* 9: 25–34.

Donald, M. (1991). *Origins of the modern mind. Three stages in the evolution of culture and cognition*. Cambridge: Harvard University Press.

Donald, M. (1995). The neurobiology of human consciousness: An evolutionary approach. *Neuropychologia* 9: 1087–1102.

Donchin, E. (1981). Surprise! . . . Surprise? *Psychophysiology* 18: 493–513.

Donders, F.C. (1869). On the speed of mental processes. Translated by W.G. Koster (1969). *Acta Psychologica: Attention and Performance I* 30: 412–431.

Douglas, R.J. and Martin, K.A. (2004). Neuronal circuits of the neocortex. *Ann. Rev Neurosci*. 27: 419–451.

Doyon, J. and Ungerleider, L.G. (2002). Functional anatomy of motor skill learning. In: L.R. Squire and D.L. Schacter (Eds.), *Neuropsychology of memory*, 3rd edition (pp. 225–238). New York: The Guilford Press.

REFERENCES

Doyon, J., Bellec, P., Amsel, R., Penhunem, V., Monchi, O., Carrier, J., Lehericy, S. and Benali, H. (2009). Contributions of the basal ganglia and functionally related brain structures to motor learning. *Beh. Brain Res.* 199: 61–75.

Duncan, J. (1984). Selective attention and the organization of visual information. *J. Exp. Psychol. Gen.* 113: 501–517.

Duncan, J. and Humphreys, G.W. (1989). Visual search and visual similarity, *Psychol. Rev.* 96: 433–458.

Eagleman, D.M. (2008). Human time perception and its illusions. *Curr. Op. Neurobiol.* 18: 131–136.

Edelman, G.M. (1992). *Bright air, brilliant fire. on the matter of the mind.* New York: Basic Books, Harper Collins Publishers, Inc.

Edelman, G.M. and Gally, J.A. (2013). Reentry: A key mechanism for integration of brain function. *Front Integr. Neurosci.* 7: 63.

Eichenbaum, H. (2012). *The cognitive neuroscience of memory: An introduction.* Oxford: Oxford University Press.

Eichenbaum, H. and Cohen, N.J. (2001). *From conditioning to conscious recollection.* Oxford Psychology Series. Oxford: Oxford University Press.

Eichenbaum, H., Sauvage, M., Fortin, N., Komorowski, R. and Lipton, P. (2012). Towards a functional organization of episodic memory in the medial temporal lobe. *Neurosci. Biobehav. Rev.* 36: 1597–1608.

Eichenbaum, H., Yonelinas, A.R. and Ranganath, C. (2007). The medial temporal lobe and recognition memory. *Ann. Rev. Neurosci.* 30: 123–152.

Eichenbaum, H. (2014). Time cells in the hippocampus: A new dimension for mapping memories. *Nat. Rev. Neurosci.* 15: 732–743.

Eimer, M. (2004). Multisensory integration: How visual experience shapes spatial perception. *Curr Biol.* 14: 115–117.

Ekman, P. (1993). Facial expression and emotion. *Am. Psychologist* 48: 384–392.

Ekman, P. (1994). *The nature of emotion.* New York: Oxford University Press.

Ekman, P. (2004). What we become emotional about. In: A.S.D. Manstead, N. Frijda and A. Fischer (Eds.), *Feelings and emotions* (pp. 119–135). Cambridge: Cambridge University Press.

Eldridge, L.L., Knowlton, B.J., Furmanski, C.S., Bookheimer, S.Y. and Engel, S.A. (2000). Remembering episodes: A selective role for the hippocampus during retrieval. *Nat Neurosci.* 3: 1149–1152.

Emery, N.J. (2016). *Bird brain. An exploration of avian intelligence.* Princeton, NJ: Princeton University Press.

Emery, N.J. and Amaral, D.G. (2000). The role of the amygdala in primate social cognition. In: R.D. Lane and L. Nadel (Eds.), *Cognitive neuroscience of emotion* (pp. 156–191). New York: Oxford University Press.

Engel, A.K. and Singer, W. (2001). Temporal binding and the neural correlates of sensory awareness. *Trends Cogn. Sci.* 5: 16–25.

REFERENCES

Eriksen, B. and Eriksen, C. (1974). Effects of noise letters upon the identification of a target letter in a non search task. *Percept. Psychophys.* 16: 143–149.

Eriksen, C.W. and Schultz, D.W. (1979). Information processing in visual search: A continuous flow conception and experimental results. *Percept. Psychophys.* 25: 249–226.

Fanselow, M.S. and Dong, H.W. (2010). Are the dorsal and ventral hippocampus functionally distinct structures? *Neuron* 65: 1–23.

Farah, M.J. (1984). The neurological basis of mental imagery. *Cognition* 18: 245–272.

Farah, M.J. and McClelland, J.L. (1991). A computational model of semantic memory impairment: Modality specificity and emergent category specificity. *J. Exp. Psychol. Gen.* 120: 339–357.

Farroni, T., Csibra, G., Simion, F. and Johnson, M.H. (2002). Eye contact detection in humans from birth. *Proc. Natl. Acad. Sci. U.S.A.* 99: 9602–9605.

Farwell, L.A. (2012). Brain fingerprinting: A comprehensive tutorial review of detection of concealed information with event-related brain potentials. *Cogn. Neurodyn.* 6: 115–154.

Fazelpour, S. and Thompson, E. (2015). The Kantian brain: Brain dynamics from a neurophenomenological perspective. *Curr. Opin. Neurobiol.* 31: 223–229.

Feldman, J.A. and Ballard, D.H. (1982). Connectionist models and their properties. *Cogn. Sci.* 6: 205–254.

Felleman, D.J. and van Essen, D.C. (1991). Distributed hierarchical processing in primate cerebral cortex. *Cerebral Cortex* 1: 1–47.

Fernandez-Duque, D., Evans, J., Christian, C. and Hodges, S.D. (2015). Superfluous Neuroscience information makes explanations of psychological phenomena more appealing. *J. Cogn. Neurosci.* 27: 926–944.

Finney, E.M., Fine, O. and Dobkins, K.R. (2001). Visual stimuli activate auditory cortex in the deaf. *Nat. Neurosci.* 4: 1171–1173.

Fischer, A.H., Rodriguez Mosquera, P.M., Van Vianen, A.E. and Manstead, A.S. (2004). Gender and culture differences in emotion. *Emotion* 4: 87–94.

Fodor, J.A. (1985). Précis of the modularity of mind. *Beh. Brain Sci.* 8: 1–42.

Fodor, J.A. (2000). *The mind doesn't work that way*. Cambridge, MA: Bradford Books/MIT Press.

Foote, S.L. and Morrison, J.H. (1987). Extrathalamic modulation of cortical function. *Ann. Neurosci.* 10: 67–95.

Fornito, A., Harrison, B.J., Zalesky, A. and Simons, J.S. (2012). Competitive and cooperative dynamics of large-scale brain functional networks supporting recollection. *Proc. Natl. Acad. Sci.* 109: 12788–12793.

Forstmann, B.A., Anwander, A., Schäfer, A., Neumann, J., Brown, S., Wagenmaker, E.J., Bogaczd, R. and Turner, R.N (2010). Cortico-striatal connections predict control over speed and accuracy in perceptual decision making. *Proc. Natl. Acad. Sci.* 107: 15916–15920.

Frankenhaeuser, M. (1981). A psychobiological framework for research on human stress and coping. In: M.H. Apply and R. Trumbull (Eds.), *Dynamics of stress. physiological, psychological and social perspectives* (pp. 101–116). New York: Plenum Press.

REFERENCES

Freud, S. (1939). *Die Traumdeutung*. Franz Deuticke: Leipzig und Wien.

Frey, S., Hansen, M. and Marchal, N. (2014). Grasping with the press of a button: Grasp-selective responses in the human anterior intraparietal sulcus depend on nonarbitrary causal relationships between hand movements and end-effector action. *J. Cogn. Neurosci*. 27: 1–15.

Friederici, A.D. (2017). *Language in our Brain. The origins of a uniquely human capacity*. New York: MIT Press.

Friederici, A.D. (2018). The neural basis for human syntax: Broca's area and beyond. *Curr. Opin. Beh. Sci*. 21: 88–92.

Friedman, H.R. and Goldman-Rakic, P.S. (1994). Co-activation of prefrontal cortex and inferior parietal cortex in working memory tasks revealed by 2DG functional mapping in the rhesus monkey. *J. Neurosci*. 14: 2772–2788.

Friston, F.J. (2011). Functional and effective connectivity, a review. *Brain Connectivity* 1: 13–36.

Friston, F.J. and Dolan, R.J. (2010). Computational and dynamic models in neuroimaging. *Neuroimage* 52: 752–765.

Fuster J.M. (1990). Prefrontal cortex and the bridging of temporal gaps in the perception-action cycle. *Ann. N. Y. Acad Sci*. 1608: 318–29.

Fuster, J.M. (1995). *Memory in the cerebral cortex*. Cambridge: MIT Press.

Gabay, S., Pertzov, Y. and Henik, A. (2011). Orienting of attention, pupil size, and the norepinephrine system. *Att. Percept. Psychophys*. 73: 123–129.

Gabrieli, J., Fleischman, D., Keane, M., Reminger, S. and Morell, F. (1995). Double dissociation between memory systems underlying explicit and implicit memory in the human brain. *Psychol. Sci*. 6: 76–82.

Galaburda, A.M. (1990). The testosterone hypothesis: Assessment since Geschwind and Behan. *Ann. Dyslexia*. 40: 18–38.

Gall, F.J. and Spurzheim, J. (1810–1819). *Anatomie et Physiologie du Système Nerveux en géneral, et du Cerveaux en particulier*. Paris: F. Schoel.

Gallup, G.G. Jr. (1970). Chimpanzees: Self-recognition. *Science* 2: 86–87.

Gauthier, I. and Logothetis, N. (2000). Is face recognition not so unique after all? *Cogn. Neuropsychol*. 17: 125–142.

Gazzaniga, M.S. (1998). The split-brain revisited. *Sci. Am*. 297: 51–55.

Gazzaniga, M.S. and Sperry, R.W. (1967). Language after section of the cerebral hemispheres. *Brain* 90: 131–148.

Gazzaniga, M.S., Ivry, R.B. and Mangun, G.R. (2002). *Cognitive neuroscience the biology of the mind*. New York: Norton and Cie.

Gazzaniga, M.S., Ivry, R.B. and Mangun, G.R. (2014). *Cognitive neuroscience the biology of the mind*. New York: Norton and Cie.

Gehring, W.J.M., Goss, B., Coles, M.G.H., Meyer, D.E. and Donchin, E. (1993). A neural system for error detection and compensation. *Psychol. Sci*. 4: 385–390.

Georgopoulos, A.P. (1995). Motor cortex and cognitive processing. In: M.S. Gazzaniga (Ed.), *The cognitive neurosciences* (pp. 507–518). Cambridge: MIT Press.

Geschwind, N. (1979). Specializations of the human brain. In: *The brain: Scientific American* (pp. 108–119). San Francisco: Freeman and Company.

Geyer, M.A., Swerdlow, N.R., Mansbach, R.S. and Braff, D.L. (1990). Startle response models of sensorimotor gating and habituation deficits in schizophrenia. *Brain Res. Bull.* 25: 485–498.

Gibbon, J. and Church, R.M. (1984). Sources of variance in an information processing theory of timing. In: H.L. Roitblat et al. (Eds.), *Animal cognition* (pp. 465–488). Hillsdale, NJ: Erlbaum.

Gibbon, J., Church, R.M. and Meck, W.H. (1984). Scalar timing in memory. *Ann. N. Y Acad. Sci.* 423: 52–77.

Gibson, J.J. (1979). *The ecological approach to visual perception*. Boston: Houghton Mifflin.

Gillihan, S.J. and Farah, M.J. (2005). Is self special? A critical review of evidence from experimental psychology and cognitive neuroscience. *Psych. Bull.* 131: 76–97.

Glasser, M.F., et al., (2016). A multi-modal parcellation of human cerebral cortex. *Nature* 537: 171–176.

Goldberg, G. (1985). Supplementary motor area structure and function: Review and hypotheses. *Beh. Brain Sci.* 8: 567–616.

Goldman-Rakic, P.S. (1988). Topography of cognition. Parallel distributed networks in primate association cortex. *Ann. Rev. Neurosci.* 11: 137–156.

Goldman-Rakic, P.S. (1995). Architecture of the prefrontal cortex and the central executive. *Ann. N. Y. Ac. Sci.* 769: 71–83.

Goldman-Rakic, P.S. (2000). The prefrontal landscape: Implications of functional architecture for understanding human mentation and the central executive. In: A.C. Roberts, T.W. Robbins and L. Weiskrantz (Eds.), *The prefrontal cortex. Executive and cognitive functions* (pp. 87–102). Oxford: Oxford University Press.

Goldman-Rakic, P.S., Selemon, L.D. and Schwartz, M.L. (1984). Dual pathways connecting the dorsolateral prefrontal cortex with the hippocampal formation and parahippocampal cortex in the rhesus monkey. *Neurosci.* 12: 719–743.

Gopher, D. (1986). In defense of resources: On structures, energies, pools and allocation of attention. In: R.J. Hockey, A.W.K. Gaillard and M.G.H. Coles (Eds.), *Energetics and human information processing* (pp. 353–371). Dordrecht: Martinus Nijhoff.

Gore, F., et al., (2015). Neural representations of unconditioned stimuli in basolateral amygdala mediate innate and learned responses. *Cell* 162: 134–145.

Grafton, S., Hazeltine, E. and Ivry, R. (1995). Functional mapping of sequence learning in normal humans. *J. Cogn. Neurosci.* 7: 497–510.

Greenfield, P.M. (1991). Language, tools and the brain: The ontogeny and phylogeny of hierarchically organized sequential behavior. *Beh. Brain Sci.* 14: 531–595.

REFERENCES

Grefkes, G. and Fink, G.R. (2005). The functional organization of the intraparietal sulcus in humans and monkeys. *J. Anat.* 207: 3–17.

Greicius, M.D., Krasnow, B., Reiss, A.L. and Menon, V. (2003). Functional connectivity in the resting brain: A network analysis of the default mode hypothesis. *Proc. Natl. Acad. Sci. U.S.A.* 100: 253–258.

Greicius, M.D., Supekar, K., Menon, V. and Dougherty, R.F. (2009). Resting-state functional connectivity reflects structural connectivity in the default mode network. *Cereb. Cortex.* 19: 72–78.

Guilford, J.P. (1967). *The Nature of human intelligence.* McGraw-Hill, New York.

Haggard, P. and Eimer, M. (1999). On the relation between brain potentials and the awareness of voluntary movements. *Brain Res.* 126: 128–133.

Haggard, P., Clark, S. and Kalogeras, J. (2002). Voluntary action and conscious awareness. *Nat. Neurosci.* 5: 382–385.

Hagoort, P. (2005). On Broca, brain, and binding: A new framework. *Trends Cogn. Sci.* 9: 416–423.

Ham, T., Leff, A., de Boissezon, X., Joffe, A. and Sharp, D.J. (2013). Cognitive control and the salience network: An investigation of error processing and effective connectivity. *J. Neurosci.* 33: 7091–7098.

Hampson, R.E., et al. (2018). Developing a hippocampal neural prosthetic to facilitate human memory encoding and recall. *J. Neural Engin.* 15: 1–15.

Handy, T.C. (2004) *Event-related potentials – a methods handbook.* New York: MIT Press.

Harari, N.Y. (2014). *Sapiens: A brief history of humankind.* London: Harvill Secker.

Haxby, J.V., Hoffman, E.A. and Gobbini, M.A. (2000). The distributed human neural system for face perception *Trends Cogn. Sci.* 4: 223–233.

Hebb, D.O. (1949). *The organization of behavior. A neuropsychological theory.* New York: Wiley.

Heeger, D.J. and Ress, D. (2002). What does fMRI tell us about neural activity? *Nat. Neurosci. Rev.* 3: 142–151.

Henson, R.N. (2003). Neuroimaging studies of priming. *Prog. Neurobiol.* 70: 53–81.

Henson, R.N., Shallice, T. and Dolan, R.J. (1999). Right prefrontal cortex and episodic memory retrieval: a functional MRI test of the monitoring hypothesis. *Brain* 122: 1367–1381.

Hernandez-Péon, R. (1966). Physiological mechanisms in attention. In: R.W. Russel (Ed.), *Frontiers physiological psychology* (pp. 121–147). New York: Academic Press.

Hickok, G. (2009). Eight problems for the mirror neuron theory of action understanding in monkeys and humans. *J. Cogn. Neurosci.* 21: 1229–1243.

Hillyard, S.A. (1993). Electrical and magnetic brain recordings: Contributions to cognitive neuroscience. *Curr. Opin. Neurobiol.* 3: 710–717.

Hillyard, S.A. and Anllo-Vento, L. (1998). Event-related brain potentials in the study of visual selective attention. *Proc. Natl. Acad. Sci.* 95: 781–787.

Hillyard, S.A., Luck, S.J. and Mangun, G.R. (1994). The cuing of attention to visual field locations: Analysis with ERP recordings. In: H.J. Heinze and G.R. Mangun (Eds.), *Cognitive electrophysiology* (pp. 1–250). Boston: Birkhauser.

Hillyard, S.A., Mangun, G.R., Woldorff, M.G. and Luck, S.J. (1995). Neural systems mediating selective attention. In: M.S. Gazzaniga (Ed.), *The cognitive neurosciences* (pp. 665–682). Cambridge: MIT Press.

Hirshorn, E.A., Dye, M.W.G., Hauser, P.C., Supalla, T.R. and Bavelier, D. (2014). Neural networks mediating sentence reading in the deaf. *Front. Hum. Neurosci.* 8: 1–13.

Hirnstein, W (2010). The misidentification syndromes as mindreading disorders. *Cogn. Neuropsychiat.* 15: 233–260.

Hirnstein, W. and Ramachandran, V.S. (1997). Capgras syndrome: A novel probe for understanding the neural representation of the identity and familiarity of persons. *Proc. Royal Soc. B: Biol. Sci.* 264: 437–444.

Hobson, J.A. (1988). *The dreaming brain*. New York: Basic Books.

Hobson, J.A. and McCarley, R.W. (1977). The brain as a dream state generator: An activation-synthesis hypothesis of the dream process. *Am. J. Psychiatry* 134: 1335–1348.

Holmes, A. (2005). Genetic variation in cortico-amygdala serotonin function and risk for stress-related disease. *Nat. Neurosci.* 8: 20–21.

Holroyd, C.B., Nieuwenhuis, S., Yeung, N., Nystrom, L., Mars, R.B., Coles, M.G. and Cohen, J.D. (2004). Dorsal anterior cingulate cortex shows fMRI response to internal and external error signals. *Nat. Neurosci.* 7: 497–498.

Honey, C.J., Sporns, O., Cammoun, L., Gigandet, X., Thiran, J.P., Meuli, R. and Hagmann, P. (2009). Predicting human resting-state functional connectivity from structural connectivity. *Proc. Natl. Acad. Sci. U.S.A.* 106: 2035–2040.

Hopfinger, J.B. and Mangun, G.R. (1998). Reflexive attention modulates processing of visual stimuli in human extrastriate cortex. *Psychol. Sci.* 6: 441–447.

Hopfinger, J.B., Buonocore, M.H. and Mangun, G.R. (2000). The neural mechanisms of top-down attentional control. *Nat. Neurosci.* 3: 284–291.

Hopfinger, J.B., Woldorff, M.G., Fletcher, E.M. and Mangun, G.R. (2001). Dissociating top-down attentional control from selective perception and action. *Neuropsychologia* 39: 1277–1291.

Howard-Jones, P.A. (2014). Neuroscience and education: Myths and messages. *Nat. Rev. Neurosci.* 15: 817–824.

Hubel, D.H. (1979). The brain. *Scientific American*, September 1.

Hubel, D.H. and Wiesel, T.N. (1959). Receptive fields of single neurons in the cat's striate cortex. *J. Physiol.* 148: 574–591.

Huber, D.E. and O'Reilly, R.C. (2003). Persistence and accommodation in short-term priming and other perceptual paradigms: Temporal segregation through synaptic depression. *Cogn. Sci.* 27: 403–430.

REFERENCES

Ishiyama, S. and Brecht, M. (2016). Neural correlates of ticklishness in the rat somatosensory cortex. *Science* 354: 757–776.

Jacoby, L.L. and Whitehouse, K. (1989). An illusion of memory: False recognition influenced by unconscious perception. *J. Exp. Psychol. Gen.* 118: 126–135.

Jansari, A. and Parkin, A.J. (1996). Things that go bump in your life: Explaining the reminiscence bump in autobiographical memory. *Psychol. Aging* 11: 85–91.

Janssen, S.M.J. and Murre, J.M.J. (2008). Reminiscence bump in autobiographical memory: Unexplained by novelty, emotionality, valence, or importance of personal events. *Quart. J. Exp. Psychol.* 61: 1847–1860.

Jeannerod, M. (1994). The representing brain: Neural correlates of motor intention and imagery. *Beh. Br. Sci.* 17: 187–245.

Jerison, H.J. (1973). *The evolution of the brain and intelligence.* New York: Academic Press.

Johnson, A. and Proctor, R.W. (2004). *Attention: Theory and practice.* London: Sage Publications.

Johnson, J.D. and Rugg, M.D. (2007). Recollection and the reinstatement of encoding-related cortical activity. *Cerebral Cortex* 17: 2507–2515.

Jolles, D., et al. (2011). Whole-brain functional connectivity in children and young adults. *Cerebral Cortex* 21: 385–391.

Jonides, J. (1981). Voluntary versus automatic control over the mind's eye's movement. In: J.B. Long and A.D. Baddeley (Eds.), *Attention and performance IX* (pp. 187–203). Hillsdale, NJ: Lawrence Erlbaum Associates.

Jordan, M.I. (1996). Computational aspects of motor control and motor learning. In: H. Heuer and S. Keele (Eds.), *Handbook of perception and action,* vol. 2 (pp. 71–120). New York: Academic Press.

Just, M.A., Carpenter, P.A., Keller, T.A., Eddy, W.F. and Thulburn, K.R. (1996). Brain activation modulated by sentence comprehension. *Science* 274: 114–116.

Kafkas, A. and Montaldi, D. (2018). How do memory systems detect and respond to novelty? *Neurosci. Lett.* 680: 60–68.

Kahle, W. (1986). *Atlas van de Anatomie. Sesam, deel 3. Zenuwstelsel and Zintuigen.* Baarn: Bosch en Keuning B.V.

Kahneman, D. (1973). *Attention and effort.* Englewood Cliffs: Prentice-Hall Inc.

Kahneman, D. (2011). *Thinking fast thinking slow.* New York: Farrar et al.

Kahneman, D. Treisman, A. and Gibbs, B. (1992). The reviewing of object files: Object-specific integration of information. *Cogn. Psychol.* 24: 175–219.

Kaiser, M., Hilgetag, C.C. and Kötter, R. (2010). Hierarchy and dynamics of neural networks. *Front. Neuroinform.* 4: 112.

Kaiser, R.H., Andrews-Hanna, J.H., Wager, T.D. and Pizagalli, D.A. (2015). Large-scale network dysfunction in major depressive disorder. A meta-analysis of resting-state functional connectivity. *JAMA Psychiatry* 72: 603–611.

Kandel, E., Schwartz, J.H. and Jessel, T.M. (1991). *Principles of neural science.* 3rd edition. New York: Elsevier.

Kanwisher, N. (2000). Domain specificity in face perception. *Nature Neurosci.* 3: 759–763.

Kanwisher, N. and Wojciulik, E. (2000). Visual attention: Insights from brain imaging. *Nat. Rev. Neurosci.* 1: 91–100.

Kastner, S. and Ungerleider, L.G. (2001). The neural basis of biased competition in human visual cortex. *Neuropsychologia* 39: 1263–1276.

Kastner, S., de Weerd, P., Desimone, R. and Ungerleider, L.G. (1998). Mechanisms of directed attention in the human extrastriate cortex as revealed by functional MRI. *Science* 282: 108–111.

Kelly, A.M.C. and Garavan, H. (2005). Human functional neuroimaging of brain changes associated with practice. *Cerebral Cortex* 15: 1089–1102.

Kempermann, G. et al. (2018). Human adult neurogenesis: evidence and remaining questions. *Cell Stem Cell* 23: 25–30.

Kenemans, J.L., Kok, A. and Smulders, F.T.Y. (1993). Event-related potentials to conjunctions of spatial frequency and orientation as a function of stimulus parameters and response requirements. *Electroencephal. Clin. Neurophysiol.* 88: 51–63.

Kidd, C. and Hayden, B.Y. (2015). The psychology and neuroscience of curiosity. *Neuron* 88: 449–460.Kilner, J.M. and Lemon, R.N. (2013). What we know currently about mirror neurons. *Curr. Biol.* 23: 1057–1062.

Kim, J. et al. (2019). Rapid, biphasic CRF neuronal responses encode positive and negative valence. *Nat. Neurosci.* 22: 576–585.

King, A.J. (2004). Development of multisensory spatial integration. In: C. Spence and J. Driver (Eds.), *Crossmodal space and crossmodal attention* (pp. 1–24). New York: Oxford University Press.

Kinsbourne, M. and Hicks, R.E. (1978). Mapping cerebral functional space: Competition and collaboration in human performance. In: M. Kinsbourne (Ed.), *The asymmetrical function of the brain* (pp. 267–273). New York: Cambridge University Press.

Kiverstein, J., Rietveld, E., Slagter, H.A. and Denys, D. (2019). Obsessive compulsive disorder: A pathology of self-confidence? *Trends Cogn. Neurosci.* 23: 369–372.

Knight, R.T. and Grabowecki, M. (1995). Escape from linear time: Prefrontal cortex and conscious experience. In: M.S. Gazzaniga (Ed.), *The cognitive neurosciences* (pp. 1357–1371). Cambridge: MIT Press.

Knowlton, B.J., Mangels, J.A. and Squire, L.R. (1996). A neostriatal habit learning system in humans. *Science* 273: 1399–1402.

Koch, C. and Davis, J.L. (1994). *Large-scale neuronal theories of the brain*. Cambridge: MIT Press.

Koenigsberger, A.A., Misi, B. and Sporns, O. (2017). Communication dynamics in complex brain networks. *Nat. Rev. Neurosci.* 19: 17–33.

Kok, A. (2001). On the utility of P3 amplitude as a measure of processing capacity. *Psychophysiology* 38: 557–577.

Kok, A., Ridderinkhof, K.R. and Ullsperger, M. (2006). The control of attention and actions: Current Research and future developments. *Brain Res.* 1105: 1–6.

REFERENCES

Kolb, B. and Whishaw, I.Q (1998). Brain plasticity and behavior. *Ann. Rev Psychol.* 49: 43–64.

Konkel, A. and Cohen, N.J. (2009). Relational memory and the hippocampus: Representations and methods. *Front. Neurosci.* 3: 166–174.

Koppel, J. and Rubin, D.C. (2016). Recent advances in understanding the reminiscence bump: The importance of cues in guiding recall from autobiographical memory. *Curr. Dir. Psychol. Sci.* 25: 135–149.

Kosslyn, M., Thompson, W.L., Kim, I.J. and Alpert, N.M. (1995). Topographical representations of mental images in primary visual cortex. *Nature* 378: 496–498.

Kosslyn, S.M. and Koenig, O. (1992). *Wet mind. The new cognitive neurosciences.* New York: The Free Press.

Kosslyn, S.M. and Sussman, A.L. (1995). Roles of imagery in perception: or there is no such thing as immaculate perception. In: M.S. Gazzaniga (Ed.), *The cognitive neurosciences* (pp. 1035–1042). Cambridge: MIT Press.

Kostovic, I., et al. 2014. Perinatal and early postnatal reorganization of the subplate and related cellular compartments in the human cerebral wall as revealed by histological and MRI approaches. *Brain Struct. Funct.* 219: 231–253.

Krett, M. and De Gelder, B. (2012). A review on sex differences in processing emotional signals. *Neuropsychologia* 50: 1211–1221.

Kumaran, D. and Maguire, E.A. (2005). The human hippocampus: cognitive maps or relational memory? *J. Neurosci.* 25: 7254–7259.

Kumaran, D. and Maguire, E.A. (2007). Match mismatch processes inderlie human responses to associative novelty. *J. Neurosci.* 27: 8517–8524.

Kutas, M. and Hillyard, S.A. (1980). Reading senseless sentences: Brain potentials reflect semantic incongruity. *Science* 207: 203–205.

LaBerge, D. (1995). *Attentional processing.* Cambridge: Harvard University Press.

Lane, R.D. and Nadel, L. (2000). *Cognitive neuroscience of emotion.* New York: Oxford University Press.

Lang, P.J., Bradley, M.M. and Cuthbert, B.N. (1999). *International affective picture system (IAPS). Technical manual and affective ratings.* Gainesville, FL: The Center for Research in Psychophysiology, University of Florida.

Langeslag, S.J.E., Schmidt, M., Ghassabian, A. Jaddoe, V.W. and Hofman, A., (2013). Functional connectivity between parietal and frontal brain regions and intelligence in young children: The Generation R study. *Hum. Brain Mapp.* 34: 3299–3307.

Lashley, K.S. (1929). Functional determination of cerebral localization. *Arch. Neurol. and Psychiatry* 38: 371–387.

Lavie, N. (1995). Perceptual load as a necessary condition for selective attention. *J. Exp. Psychol.: Human Percep. Perform.* 21: 451–468.

Lazarus, R.S. (1991). *Emotion and adaptation.* New York: Oxford University Press.

Le Doux, J.E. (1994). Emotion, memory and the brain. *Sci. Am.* 270: 32–39.

Le Doux, J.E. (1996). *The emotional brain*. New York: Simon and Schuster.

Lee, R.S., Hermens, D.F, Porter, M.A. and Redoblado-Hodge, M.A. (2012). A meta-analysis of cognitive deficits in first-episode major depressive disorder. *J. Affect. Disord.* 140: 113–124.

Lepage, M., Habib, R. and Tulving, E. (1998). Hippocampal PET activations of memory encoding and retrieval: The HIPER model. *Hippocampus* 8: 313–322.

Leventhal, H. and Scherer, K. (1987). The relationship of emotion to cognition: A functional approach to a semantic controversy. *Cognition and Emotion* 3: 3–28.

Libet, B. (1985). Unconscious cerebral initiative and the role of conscious will in voluntary action. *Beh. Brain Sci.* 8: 529–566.

Libet, B., Wright, E.W. and Gleason, C.A. (1982). Readiness potentials preceding unrestricted 'spontaneous' vs. pre-planned voluntary acts. *Electroencephal. Clin. Neurophysiol.* 54: 322–335.

Lim, M., Metlzer, R. and Bar-Yam, U. (2007). Global pattern formation and ethnic/cultural violence. *Science* 317: 1540–1544.

Lindsley, D. (1961). The reticular activating system and perceptual integration. In: D.E. Sheer (Ed.), *Electrical stimulation of the brain*. Austin: University of Texas Press.

Llinás, R. and Churchland, P.S. (1996). *The mind-brain continuum*. Cambridge: MIT Press.

Loewenstein, G. (1994). The psychology of curiosity: A review and reinterpretation. *Psychol. Bull.* 116: 75–98.

Lomber, S.G., Meredith, M.A. and Kral, A. (2010). Crossmodal plasticity in specific auditory cortices underlies compensatory visual functions in the deaf. *Nat. Neurosci.* 13: 1421–1427.

Løvstad, M., et al. (2012). Contribution of subregions of human frontal cortex to novelty processing. *J. Cogn. Neurosci.* 24: 378–395.

Low, K.A. Leaver, E.E. Kramer, A.F., Fabiani, M. and Gratton, G. (2009). Share or compete? Load-dependent recruitment of prefrontal cortex during dual-task performance. *Psychophysiology* 46: 1069–1079.

Luck, S.J., Hillyard, S.A., Mangun, G.R. and Gazzaniga, M.S. (1994). Independent attentional scanning in the separated hemispheres of split-brain patients. *J. Cogn. Neurosci.* 6: 84–91.

Luria, A.R. (1973). *The working brain*. London: The Penguin Press.

Lv, H., et al. (2018). Resting-state functional MRI: Everything that nonexperts have always wanted to know. *AJNR Am. J. Neuroradiol.* 18: 1–10.

Lynch, G. (2002). Memory enhancement: The search for mechanism-based drugs. *Nat. Neurosci. Supplement* 5: 1035–1038.

Magoun, H.W. (1952). An ascending reticular activating system in the brain stem. *Am. Arch. Neurol. Psychiatry* 67: 145–154.

Mahncke, H.W., et al. (2006). Memory enhancement in healthy older adults using a brain plasticity-based training program: A randomized, controlled study. *Proc. Natl. Acad. Sci* 12523–12528.

REFERENCES

Maia, T.V., Cooney, R.E. and Peterson, B.S. (2008). The neural bases of obsessive-compulsive disorder in children and adults. *Devel. Psychopathol.* 20: 1251–1283.

Mangun, G.R. and Hillyard, S.A. (1995). Mechanisms and models of selective attention. In: M.D. Rugg and M.G.H. Coles (Eds.), *Electrophysiology of mind. Event-related potentials and cognition*. Oxford: Oxford University Press.

Martin, A., Wiggs, C.L., Ungerleider, L.G. and Haxby, J.V. (1996). Neural correlates of category specific knowledge. *Nature* 379: 649–652.

Matsuhashi, M. and Hallett, M. (2008). The timing of the conscious intention to move. *Euro. J. Neurosci.* 28: 2344–2351.

Mayr, U. (2008). Introduction to the special section on cognitive plasticity in the aging mind. *Psychol. Aging* 23: 681–683.

McCall, J.G., et al. (2017). Locus coeruleus to basolateral amygdala noradrenergic projections promote anxiety-like behavior. *eLife* 18247: 1–23.

McCarthy, M.M. and Arnold, A.P. (2011). Reframing sexual differentiation of the brain. *Nat. Neurosci.* 14: 677–683.

McClelland, J.L. and Rumelhart, D.E. (1988). *Parallel distributed processing: Explorations in the microstructure of cognition, volume 2: Psychological and biological models*. Cambridge, MA: MIT Press.

McDuff, D., Kodra, E., Kaliouby, R. and LaFrance, M. (2017). A large-scale analysis of sex differences in facial expressions. *PLoS ONE* 12: e0173942.

McEwen, B.S. (1995). Stressful experience, brain and emotions: developmental, genetic and hormonal influences. In: M.S. Gazzaniga (Ed.), *The cognitive neurosciences* (pp. 1117–1135). Cambridge: MIT Press.

McGaugh, J.L., McIntyre, C.K. and Power, A.E. (2002). Amygdala modulation of memory consolidation: Interaction with other brain systems. *Neurobiol. Learning Mem.* 78: 539–552.

Meck, W.H., Penney, T.B. and Pouthas, V. (2008). Cortico-striatal representation of time in animals and humans. *Curr. Opin. Neurobiol.* 18: 145–152.

Meeter, M., Jansen, S. and Murre, J. (2008). Reminiscence bump in memory for public events. *Eur. J. Cogn. Psychol.* 20: 738–764.

Meeter, M., Murre, J.M.J., Janssen, S.M.J., Birkhenhager, T. and van den Broek, W.W. (2011). Retrograde amnesia after electroconvulsive therapy: A temporary effect? *J. Affect. Dis.* 132: 216–222.

Menon, V. and Uddin, L.Q. (2010). Saliency, switching, attention and control: A network model of insula function. *Brain Struct. Funct.* 214: 655–667.

Mesulam, M.M. (1981). A cortical network for directed attention and unilateral neglect. *Ann. Neurolog.* 10: 309–325.

Mesulam, M.M. (1990). Large-scale neurocognitive networks and distributed processing for attention, language, and memory. *Ann. Neurol.* 28: 597–613.

Meunier, D., et al. (2009). Hierarchical modularity in human brain functional networks. *Front. Neuroinform.* 3: 37.

REFERENCES

Miller, E.K. and Cohen, J.D. (2001). An integrative theory of prefrontal cortex function. *Ann. Rev. Neurosci.* 24: 167–202.

Miller, J. (1988). Discrete and continuous models of human information processing: theoretical distinctions and empirical results. *Acta Psychologica* 67: 191–257.

Minsky, M. (1985). *The society of mind*. New York: Simon and Schuster.

Mishkin, M. (1982). A memory system in the monkey. *Philos. Trans. Royal Soc. of London* 298: 85–95.

Mishkin, M. and Appenzeller, T. (1987). The anatomy of memory. *Sci. Am.* 256: 62–71.

Mishkin, M., Malamut, B. and Bachevalier, J. (1984). Memories and habits: Two neural systems. In G. Lynch, J.L. McGaugh and N.M. Weinberger (Eds.), *Neurobiology of learning and memory* (pp. 65–77). New York: Guilford Press.

Mishkin, M., Ungerleider, L.G. and Macko, K.A. (1992). Object vision and spatial vision: Two cortical pathways. *Trends in neurosciences* 6: 414–417 (originally publsihed 1983). In: S.M. Kosslyn and R.A. Andersen (Eds.), *Frontiers in cognitive neuroscience* (pp. 19–23). Cambridge: MIT Press.

Mitchell, A.S. (2015). The mediodorsal thalamus as a higher order thalamic relay nucleus important for learning and decision-making. *Neurosci. Biobehav. Rev.* 54: 76–88.

Montaldi, D., Spencer, T.J., Roberts, N. and Mayes, A.R. (2006). The neural system that mediates familiarity memory. *Hippocampus* 16: 504–520.

Moran, J. and Desimone, R. (1985). Selective attention gates visual processing in exstrastriate cortex. *Science* 229: 782–784.

Mori, S. (2007). *Introduction to diffusion tensor imaging*. New York: Elsevier.

Morris, R.G.M., Anderson, E.G., Lynch, G.S. and Baudry, M. (1998). Selective impairment of learning and blockade of long-term potentiation by an N-methyl-D-aspartate receptor antagonist, AP5. *Nature* 319: 774–776.

Morris, R.G.M., Davis, S. and Butcher, S.P. (1990). Hippocampal synaptic plasticity and NMDA receptors: a role in information storage? *Phil. Trans. R. Soc. London* 329: 187–204.

Moruzzi, G. and Magoun, H. (1949). Brainstem reticular formation and activation of the EEG. *Electroencephal. Clin. Neurophysiol.* 1: 455–473.

Moscovitch, M., Goshen-Gottstein, Y. and Vriezen, E. (1994). Memory without conscious recollection: A tutorial review from a neuropsychological perspective. In: C. Umilta and M. Moscovitch (Eds.), *Conscious and nonconscious information processing. Attention and performance XV* (pp. 619–660). Cambridge: MIT press.

Mountcastle, V.B. (1978). An organizing principle for cerebral function: The unit module and the distributed system. In: G.M. Edelman and V.B. Mountcastle (Eds.), *The mindful brain* (pp. 7–51). Cambridge: MIT Press.

Mountcastle, V.B., et al. (1975). Posterior parietal association cortex of the monkey: Command functions for operations within extrapersonal space. *J. Neurophysiol.* 38: 71–908.

Mummery, C.J., Patterson, K., Price, C.J., Ashburner, J., Frackowiak, R.S. and Hodges, J.R. (2000). A voxel-based morphometry study of semantic dementia: Relationship between temporal lobe atrophy and semantic memory. *Ann. Neurol.* 47: 36–45.

REFERENCES

Murakami, M., Vicente, M.I., Costa, G.M. and Mainen Z.F. (2014). Neural antecedents of self-initiated actions in secondary motor cortex. *Nat. Neurosci.* 17: 1574–1582.

Murre, J.M.J. (1997). Implicit and explicit memory in amnesia: Some explanations and predictions by the TraceLink model. *Memory* 5: 213–232.

Näätänen, R. (1992). *Attention and brain function*. Hillsdale, NJ: Lawrence Erlbaum.

Nadel, L. and Moscovitch, M. (1997). Memory consolidation, retrograde amnesia and the hippocampal complex. *Curr. Op. Neurobiol.* 7: 217–222.

Nader, K. and Einarsson, E.Ö. (2010). Memory reconsolidation: An update. *Ann. N.Y. Ac. Sci.* 1191: 27–41.

Nader, K., Schafe, G.E. and Le Doux, J.E. (2000). Fear memories require protein synthesis in the amygdala for reconsolidation after retrieval. *Nature* 406: 722–726.

Nambu, A. (2008). Seven problems on the basal ganglia. *Curr. Opin. Neurobiol.* 18: 595–604.

Neisser, U. and Harsch, N. (1992). Phantom flashbulbs: False recollections of hearing the news about Challenger. In: E. Winograd and U. Neisser (Eds.), *Affect and accuracy in recall: studies of 'flahsbulb' memories* (pp. 9–31). New York: Cambridge University Press.

Nemeroff, C.B. (1998). The neurobiology of depression. *Scientific American* June: 28–35.

Newman, M.E.J. (2006). Modularity and community structure in networks. *Proc. Natl. Acad. Sci.* 103: 8577–8582.

Niebur, E., Hsiao, S.S. and Johnson, K.O. (2002). Synchrony: A neuron mechanism for selective attention? *Curr. Op. Neurobiol.* 12: 190–194.

Nieuwenhuis, S., Holroyd, C.B., Mol, N. and Coles, M.G. (2004). Reinforcement-related brain potentials from medial frontal cortex: origins and functional significance. *Neurosci. Biobehav. Rev.* 28: 441–448.

Nieuwenhuis, S., Ridderinkhoff, K.R., Blom, J., Band, G.P. and Kok, A. (2001). Error-related brain potentials are differentially related to awareness of response errors: Evidence from an antisaccade task. *Psychophysiology* 38: 752–760.

Nobre, A.C. and van Eede, F. (2018). Anticipated moments: Temporal structure in attention. *Nat. Rev. Neurosci.* 19: 34–48.

Nolde, S.F., Johnson, M.K. and D'Esposito, M. (1998). Episodic remembering: An event-related fMRI study. *NeuroReport* 9: 3509–3514.

Norman, D. and Bobrow, D. (1975). On data-limited and resource-limited processes. *Cogn. Psychol.* 7: 44–64.

Nyberg, L. (1998). Asymmetric frontal activation during episodic memory. What kind of specificity? *Trends Cogn. Sci.* 2: 419–420.

Nyberg, L., Cabeza, R. and Tulving, E. (1996). PET studies of encoding and retrieval: The HERA model. *Psychon. Bull. Rev.* 3: 134–147.

O'Connor, C., et al. (2012). Neuroscience in the Public Sphere. *Neuron* 74: 220–226.

Oberauer, K. (2009). Design for a working memory. *Psychol. Learn. Motiv.* 51: 45–100.

Öhman, A. (1979). The orienting reflex, attention and learning: an information processing perspective. In: H.D. Kimmel, E.H. van Olst and J.F. Orlebeke (Eds.). *The orienting reflex in humans.* Hillsdale, NJ: Lawrence Erlbaum Associates, Inc.

Okita, A.A., Mulder, G. and Mulder, L.J.M. (1985). Memory search and visual spatial attention: An event-related brain potential analysis. *Acta Psychologica* 60: 263–292.

Olds, L. and Milner, P. (1954). Positive reinforcement produced by electrical stimulation of septal area and other regions in the rat brain. *J. Compar. Physiol. Psychol.* 47: 419–427.

Olkowicz, A., et al. (2016). Birds have primate-like numbers of neurons in the forebrain. *Proc. Natl. Acad. Sci. U.S.A.* 113: 7255–7260.

O'Madagain, C., Kachel, G. and Strickland, B. (2019). The origin of pointing: Evidence for the touch hypothesis. *Sci. Adv.* 5: 1–8.

Oprisan, S.A. and Buhusi, C.V. (2014). What is all the noise about interval timing? *Phil. Trans. R. Soc. B* 369: 20120459.

Osgood, C.E., Suci, G.J. and Tannenbaum, G.H. (1957). *The measurement of meaning.* Urbana, IL: University of Illinois Press.

Ouyang, G., Sommer, W. and Zhou, C. (2016). Reconstructing ERP amplitude effects after compensating for trial-to-trial latency jitter: A solution based on a novel application of residue iteration decomposition. *Int. J. Psychophysiol.* 109: 9–20.

Owen, A.M., Hampshire, A., Grahn, J.A., Stenton, R., Dajani, S., Burns, A.S., Howard, R.J. and Ballard, C.G. (2010). Putting brain training to the test. *Nature* 465: 775–778.

Panksepp, J. (1993). Neurochemical control of moods and emotions: Aminoacids to neuropeptides. In: M. Lewis and J.M. Havilland (Eds.), *Handbook of emotions* (pp. 87–107). New York: Guilford.

Panksepp, J. and Burgdorf, J. (2003). "Laughing" rats and the evolutionary antecedents of human joy? *Physiol. Behav.* 79: 533–547.

Parvizi, J., Anderson, S.W., Martin, C.O., Damasio, H. and Damasio, A.R. (2001). Pathological laughter and crying: A link to the cerebellum. *Brain* 24: 1708–1719.

Pascual-Leone, A., et al. (1994). Induction of visual extinction by rapid-rate transcranial magnetic stimulation of parietal lobe. *Neurolog.* 44: 494–498.

Pashler, H. (1994). Dual-task interference in simple tasks: Data and theory. *Psychol. Bull.* 116: 220–224.

Passingham, R.E. (1982). *The human primate.* San Francisco: Freeman.

Passingham, R.E. (2002). The frontal cortex: Does size matter? *Nat. Neurosci.* 5: 190–192.

Paulesu, E., Frith, C.D. and Frackowiak, R.S.J. (1993). The neural correlates of the verbal component of working memory. *Nature* 362: 342–345.

Pavani, F., Spence, C. and Driver, J. (2000). Visual capture of touch: Out-of body experience with rubber gloves. *Psychol. Sci.* 11: 353–359.

Pearson, J. Naselaris, T., Holmes, E.A. and Kosslyn, S.M. (2015). Mental imagery: Functional mechanisms and clinical application. *Trends Cogn. Sci.* 19: 590–602.

Penfield, W. and Jasper, H. (1954). *Epilepsy and the functional anatomy of the human brain.* Boston: Little, Brown.

REFERENCES

Penfield, W. and Perot, P. (1963). The brain's record of auditory and visual experience. *Brain* 86: 595–696.

Petersen, S.E., Robinson, D.L. and Keys, W. (1985). Pulvinar nucleus of the behaving rhesus monkey. Visual responses and their modulation. *J. Neurophysiol.* 54: 867–886.

Peterson, L.R. and Peterson, M.J. (1959). Short-term retention of individual verbal items. *J. Exp. Psychol.* 58: 193–198.

Phelps, E.A., O'Connor, K.J., Gatenby, J.C., Gore, J.C., Grillon, C. and Davis, M. (2001). Activation of the left amygdala to a cognitive representation of fear. *Nat. Neurosci.* 4: 437–441.

Pinker, S. (1997). *How the mind works*. New York: Norton and Company Inc.

Pitkänen, A., Savander, V. and Le Doux, J.E. (1997). Organization of intra-amygdaloid circuitries in the rat: An emerging framework for understanding functions of the amygdala. *Trans. Neurosci.* 20: 517–523.

Plotkin, H. (1997). *Evolution in mind. An introduction to evolutionary psychology*. London: Allen Lane, the Penguin Press.

Plotsky, P.M. and Meaney, M.J. (1993). Early, postnatal experience alters hypothalamic corticotropin-releasing factor (CRF) mRNA, median eminence CRF content and stress-induced release in adult rats. *Mol. Brain Res.* 18: 195–200.

Poldrack, R.A. (2000) Imaging brain plasticity: Conceptual and methodological issues – a theoretical review. *Neuroimage* 12: 1–13.

Polich, J. and Kok, A. (1995). Cognitive and biological determinants of P300: An integrative review. *Biol. Psychol.* 41: 103–146.

Posner, M.I. and Cohen, Y. (1984). Components of visual orienting. In: H. Bouma and D.G. Bouwhuis (Eds.), *Attention and performance X*, 32 (pp. 531–556). Hillsdale, NJ: Lawrence Erlbaum Associates.

Posner, M.I. and Raichle, M.E. (1994). *Images of mind*. New York: Scientific American Library.

Premack, D. and Woodruff, G. (1978). Does the chimpanzee have a theory of mind? *Beh. Brain Sc.* 1: 515–526.

Preston, A.E. and Eichenbaum, H. (2013). Interplay of hippocampus and prefrontal cortex in memory. *Curr Biol.* 23: 764–773.

Prince, S.E, Daselaar, S.M. and Cabeza, R. (2005). Neural correlates of relational memory: Successful encoding and retrieval of semantic and perceptual associations. *J. Neurosci.* 25: 1203–1210.

Pulvermüller, F. (1999). Words in the brain's language. *Beh. Brain Sci.* 22: 253–336.

Quintana, J. and Fuster, J.M. (1999). From Perception to Action: Temporal Integrative Functions of Prefrontal and Parietal Neurons. *Cerebral Cortex* 9: 213–221.

Raichle, M.E., MacLeod, A.M., Snyder, A.Z., Powers, W.J., Gusnard, D.A., et al. (2001). A default mode of brain function. *Proc. Natl. Acad. Sci. U.S.A.* 98: 676–682.

Ramachandran, V.S. and Hubbard, E.M. (2001). Psychophysical investigations into the neural basis of synaesthesia. *Proc. Biol. Sci.* 268: 979–983.

Ramautar, J.R., Slagter, H.A., Kok, A. and Ridderinkhof, K.R. (2006). Probability effects in the stop-signal paradigm: The insula and the significance of failed inhibition. *Brain Res.* 1105: 143–154.

Ranganath, C. and Ritchey, M. (2012). Two cortical systems for memory guided behavior. *Nat. Rev. Neurosci.* 13: 713–726.

Ranganath, C., Yonelinas, A.P., Cohen, M.X., Dy, C.J., Tom, S.M. and D'Esposito M. (2004). Dissociable correlates of recollection and familiarity within the medial temporal lobes. *Neuropsychologia* 42: 2–13.

Rao, S.M., et al. (2007). Distributed neural systems underlying the timing of movements. *J. Neurosci.* 17: 5528–5535.

Ray, W.J., et al. (2009). Startle response in generalized anxiety disorder. *Depression and Anxiety* 26: 147–154.

Requin, J., Riehle, A. and Seal, J. (1992). Neuronal networks for movement preparation. In: D.E. Meyer and S. Kornblum (Eds.), *Attention and performance XIV* (pp. 745–769). Cambridge: MIT Press.

Ribot, R. (1882). *Diseases of memory*. New York: Appleton.

Ridderinkhof, K.R., Ullsperger, M., Crone, E.A. and Nieuwenhuis, S. (2004). The role of the medial frontal cortex in cognitive control. *Science* 306: 443–447.

Ritchie, S.J., et al. (2018). Sex differences in the adult human brain: Evidence from 5216 UK biobank participants. *Cereb. Cortex* 28: 2959–2975.

Rizzolatti, G. and Craighero, L. (2004). The mirror-neuron system. *Annual Rev. Neurosci.* 27: 169–192.

Rizzolatti, G., Fadiga, L., Gallase, V. and Fogassi, L. (1996). Premotor cortex and the recognition of motor actions. *Cogn. Brain Res.* 3: 131–141.

Robbins, T.W. and Everitt, B.J. (1994). Arousal systems and attention. In: M.S. Gazzaniga (Ed.), *The cognitive neurosciences* (pp. 703–720). Cambridge: MIT Press.

Robinson, D.L. (1993). Functional contributions of the primate pulvinar. *Progr. Brain Res.* 95: 371–380.

Robinson, D.L. and Petersen, S. (1992). The pulvinar and visual salience. *Trends Neurosci.* 15: 127–132.

Robinson, P.A., Henderson, J.A., Matar, E., Riley, P. and Gray, R.T. (2009). Dynamical reconnection and stability constraints on cortical network architecture. *Phys. Rev. Lett.* 103: 108–104.

Röder, B., Stock, O., Bien, S., Neville, H. and Rösler, F. (2002). Speech processing activates visual cortex in congenitally blind humans. *Eur. J. Neurosci.* 16: 930–936.

Roediger, H.L., Balota, D.A. and Watson, J.M. (2001). Spreading activation and the arousal of false memories. In: H.L. Roediger, J.S. Nairne, I. Neath and A.M. Surprenant (Eds.), *The nature of remembering: Essays in honor of Robert G. Crowder* (pp. 95–115). Washington, DC: American Psychological Association.

Rolls, E.T. (1999). *The brain and emotion*. New York: Oxford University Press.

Rolls, E.T. (2000). Précis of the brain and emotion. *Beh. Brain Sci.* 2: 177–191.

REFERENCES

Rolls, E.T. (2008). *Memory, attention, and decision-making: A unifying computational neuroscience approach*. Oxford: Oxford University Press.

Rolls, E.T. and Treves, A. (1998). *Neural networks and brain function*. New York: Oxford University Press. Inc.

Rosenbaum, D.A. (1991). *Human motor control*. San Diego: Academic Press.

Rosenfeld, J.P. (Ed.) 2018. *Detecting concealed information and deception: Recent developments*. London: Academic Press.

Rösler, F., Heil, M. and Hennighausen. E. (1996). Distinct cortical activation patterns during long-term memory retrieval of verbal, spatial and color information. *J. Cogn. Neurosci.* 7: 53–67.

Rossini, P.M. and Rossi, S. (2007). Transcranial magnetic stimulation: Diagnostic, therapeutic, and research potential. *Neurolog.* 68: 484–488.

Rubin, D.C., Rahhal, T.A. and Poon, L.W. (1998). Things learned in early adulthood are remembered best. *Psychol. Aging* 17: 636–665.

Ruchkin, D.S., Johnson, R., Mahaffey, D. and Sutton, S. (1988). Toward a functional categorization of slow waves. *Psychophysiology* 25: 339–353.

Rugg, M.D. and Vilberg, K.L. (2013). Brain networks underlying episodic memory retrieval. *Curr Op. Neurobiol.* 23: 255–260.

Ruigrok, A.N.V., et al. (2014). A meta-analysis of sex differences in human brain structure sex differences in the brain. *Neurosci. Biobehav. Rev.* 39: 34–50.

Rushworth, M.F., Buckley, M.J., Behrens, T.E, Walton, M.E. and Bannerman, D.M. (2007). Functional organization of the medial frontal cortex. *Curr. Op. Neurobiol.* 17: 1–8.

Rushworth, M.F., Noonan, M.P., Boorman, E.D., Walton, M.E. and Behrens, T.E. (2011). Frontal cortex and reward-guided learning and decision-making. *Neuron* 70: 1054–1069.

Ryan, J.D., Althoff, R.R., Whitlow, S. and Cohen, N.J. (2000). Amnesia is a deficit in relational memory. *Psychol Sci.* 11: 454–461.

Sacks, O. (1985). *The man who mistook his wife for a hat, and other clinical tales*. New York: Summit Books.

Sakai, M. and Miyashita, Y. (1991). Neural organization for the long-term memory of paired associates. *Nature* 354: 533–536.

Sanders, A.F. (1983). Towards a model of stress and human performance. *Acta Psychol.* 53: 61–97.

Sapolsky, R.M. (1992). *Stress, the aging brain, and mechanisms of neuron death*. Cambridge, MA: MIT Press.

Schachter, S. and Singer, J. (1962). Cognitive, social, and physiological determinants of emotional state. *Psychol. Rev.* 69: 379–399.

Schacter, D.J., Cooper, L. and Delaney, S. (1990). Implicit memory for unfamiliar objects depends on access to structural descriptions. *J. Exp. Ps. Gen.* 119: 5–24.

Schacter, D.L. (1992). Priming and multiple memory systems: Perceptual mechanisms of implicit memory. *J. Cogn. Neurosci.* 4: 244–256.

Schacter, D.L. (1995). Implicit memory: A new frontier for Cognitive Neuroscience. In: M.S. Gazzaniga (Ed.), *The cognitive neurosciences* (pp. 815–824). Cambridge: MIT Press.

Schacter, D.L., et al. (1993). Implicit memory: A selective review. *Ann. Rev. Neurosci.* 6: 159–182.

Schacter, D.L., Cooper, L.A., Delaney, S.M., Peterson, M.A. and Thoran, M. (1991). Implicit memory for possible and impossible objects: Constraints on the construction of structural descriptions. *J. Exp Psychol: Learning Mem. Cogn.* 17: 3–19.

Schacter D.L. and Wagner, A.D. (1999). Medial temporal lobe activations in fMRI and PET studies of episodic encoding and retrieval. *Hippocampus* 9: 7–24.

Scherg, M. and Von Cramon, D. (1985). Two bilateral sources of the late AEP as identified by a spatio-temporal dipole model. *Electoenceph. Clin. Neurophysiol.* 62: 32–44.

Schultz, A., Dayan, P. and Montague, P.R. (1997). A neural substrate of prediction and reward. *Science* 275: 159.

Schulz, M.A., Schmalbach, B., Brugger, P. and Witt, K. (2012). Analysing Humanly Generated Random Number Sequences: A Pattern-Based Approach. *PLoS ONE* 7: e41531.

Schwartz, C.E., Wright, C.I., Shin, L.M., Kagan, J. and Rauch, S.L. (2003). Inhibited and uninhibited infants 'grown up': Adult amygdalar response to novelty. *Science* 300: 1952–1953.

Schweinberger, S.R., et al. (2011). Neural correlates of adaptation to voice identity. *British J. Psychol.* 102: 748–764.

Schweinberger, S.R., Kloth, N. and Robertson, D.M. (2011). Hearing facial identities: Brain correlates of face-voice integration in person identification. *Cortex* 47: 1026–1037.

Scott, H.F., Hansen, M. and Marchal, N. (2015). Grasping with the press of a button: Grasp-selective responses in the human anterior intraparietal sulcus depend on nonarbitrary causal relationships between hand movements and end-effector actions. *J. Cogn. Neurosci.* 27: 1146–1160.

Scoville, W.B. and Milner, B. (1957). Loss of recent memory after bilateral hippocampal lesions. *J. Neurolog. Neurosurg. Psychiat.* 20: 11–21.

Seeley, W.W., et al. (2007). Dissociable intrinsic connectivity networks for salience processing and executive control. *J. Neurosci.* 27: 2349–2356.

Semendeferi, K., Lu, A., Schenker, H. and Damasio, H. (2002). Humans and great apes share a large frontal cortex. *Nat. Neurosci.* 5: 272–276.

Semmes, I. (1968). Hemispheric specialization: A possible clue to mechanism. *Neuropsychologia* 3: 295–315.

Senju, A., et al. (2015). Early social experience affects the development of eye-gaze processing. *Curr. Biol.* 25: 1–6.

Seth, A., Barret, A.B. and Barnett, L. (2015). Granger causality analysis in neuroscience and neuroimaging. *J. Neurosci.* 35: 3293–3297.

Shadmehr, R. and Holcomb, H.H. (1997). Neural correlates of motor memory consolidation. *Science* 277: 821–825.

Shallice, T. (1984). More functionally isolable subsystems but fewer "modules"? *Cognition* 17: 243–252.

Shaver, P., Schwartz, J., Kirson, D. and O'Connor, C. (1987). Emotion knowledge: Further exploration of a prototype approach. *J. Pers. Soc. Psychol.* 52: 1061–1086.

Shepard, R.N. and Cooper, L.A. (1982). *Mental images and their transformations*. Cambridge, MA: MIT Press.

REFERENCES

Sherman, L.E. (2014). Development of the default mode and central executive networks across early adolescence: A longitudinal study. *Devel. Cogn. Neurosci.* 10: 148–159.

Shiffrin, R.M. and Schneider, W. (1977). Controlled and automatic human information processing, II: Perceptual learning, automatic attending and a general Theory. *Psychol. Rev.* 84: 127–189.

Shiffrin, R.M., Dumais, S.T. and Schneider, W. (1981). Characteristics of automatism. In: J.B. Long and A. Baddeley (Eds.), *Attention and performance IX* (pp. 223–238). Hillsdale, NY: Lawrence Erlbaum Associates.

Shulman, R.G. and Rothman, D.L. (2019). A non-cognitive behavioral model for interpreting functional neuroimaging studies. *Front. Hum. Neurosci.* 13: 1–18.

Siebner, H.R. (2000). Consensus paper: Combining transcranial stimulation with neuroimaging. *Brain Stimul.* 2: 58–80.

Simon, H.A. (1962). The architecture of complexity. *Proc. Am. Philosophical Soc.* 106: 467–482.

Skinner, J.E. and Yingling, C.D. (1977). Central gating mechanisms that regulate event-related potentials and behavior. In: J.E. Desmedt (Ed.), *Attention, voluntary contraction and event-related cerebral potentials: Progress in clinical neurophysiology*, vol. 1 (pp. 30–69). Basel: Karger.

Slagter, H.A., Giesbrecht, B., Kok, A., Weissman, D.H., Kenemans, J.L., Woldorff, M.G. and Mangun, G.E. (2007). fMRI evidence for both generalized and specialized components of attentional control. *Brain Res.* 1177: 90–102.

Slagter, H.A., Kok, A., Mol, N. and Kenemans, J.L. (2005). Spatial versus nonspatial preparatory attention: An ERP study. *Psychophysiology* 42: 428–439.

Slagter, H.A., Weissman, D.H., Giesbrecht, B., Kenemans, J.L., Mangun, G.R., Kok, A. and Woldorff, M.G. (2006). Brain regions activated by endogenous preparatory set-shifting as revealed by fMRI. *Cogn. Aff. Beh. Neurosci.* 6: 175–189.

Smith Churchland, P. (2002). *Brain-wise. Studies in neurophilosophy*. Cambridge: MIT Press.

Smith, E.E. and Jonides, J. (1995). Working memory in humans: Neuropsychological evidence. In: M.S. Gazzaniga (Ed.), *The cognitive neurosciences* (pp. 1009–1020). Cambridge: MIT Press.

Smith, M.E. (2005). Bilateral hippocampal volume reduction in adults with post-traumatic stress disorder: a meta-analysis of structural MRI studies. *Hippocampus* 15: 798–807.

Smith, S.M., et al. (2011). Network modelling methods for FMRI. *Neuroimage* 54: 875–891.

Sokolov, E.N. (1963). *Perception and the conditioned reflex*. New York: Pergamon Press.

Sokolov, E.N. and Vinograda, O.S. (1975). *Neuronal mechanisms of the orienting reflex*. New Jersey: Erlbaum.

Song, D., Robinson, B., Hampson, R., Marmarelis, V., Deadwyler, S. and Berger, T. (2018). Sparse large-scale nonlinear dynamical modeling of human hippocampus for memory prostheses. *IEEE Trans. Neural Syst. Rehabil. Eng.* 26: 272–280.

Song, M., et al. (2008). Brain spontaneous functional connectivity an intelligence. *Neuroimage* 41: 1168–1176.

Soon, C.S., et al. (2008). Unconscious determinants of free decisions in the human brain. *Nat. Neurosci.* 11: 543–545.

Spaniol, J., Davidson, P.S.R., Kim, A.S.N., Han, H., Moscovitch, M. and Grady, C.L. (2009). Event-related fMRI studies of episodic encoding and retrieval: Meta-analyses using activation likelihood estimation. *Neuropsychologia* 47: 1765–1779.

Spataro, R., Ciriacono, M., Manno, C. and La Bella, V. (2014). The eye-tracking computer device for communication in amyotrophic lateral sclerosis. *Acta Neurol Scand*. 130: 40–45.

Spence, C. and Driver, J. (Eds.) (2004). *Crossmodal space and crossmodal attention*. Oxford: Oxford University Press.

Sperling, G. (1960). The information available in brief visual presentations. *Psychol. Monogr. Gen. Appl*. 74: 1–29.

Sporns, O. (2014) Contributions and challenges for network models in cognitive neuroscience. *Nat. Neurosci*. 17: 652–660.

Sporns, O., et al. (2007). Identification and classification of hubs in networks. *PLos ONE* 2: e 1049.

Sporns, O., Tononi, G. and Kötter, R. (2005). The human connectome: A structural description of the human brain. *PLOS Comput Biol*. 1: 42.

Spunt, R.P. and Adolphs, R. (2017). A new look at domain specificity: Insights from social Neuroscience. *Nat. Rev. Neurosci*. 18: 559–567.

Squire, L.R (1992). Declarative and nondeclarative memory: Multiple brain systems supporting learning and memory. *J. Cogn. Neurosci*. 4: 232–243.

Squire, L.R. (1992). Memory and the hippocampus: A synthesis from findings with rats, monkeys and humans. *Psychol. Rev*. 99: 195–231.

Squire, L.R. and Zola Morgan, S. (1991). The medial temporal lobe memory system. *Science* 253: 1380–1386.

Squire, L.R., Wixted, J.T. and Clark, R.E. (2007). Recognition memory and the medial temporal lobe: a new perspective. *Nat. Rev. Neurosci*. 11: 872–883.

Steriade, M.M. (1996). Arousal: Revisiting the reticular activating system. *Science* 272: 225–226.

Steriade, M.M. and McCarley, R.W. (1990). *Brainstem control of wakefulness and sleep*. Boston: Springer.

Sternberg, S. (1969). The discovery of processing stages: Extensions of Donders method. *Acta Psychologica* I 30: 276–315.

Strange, B.A., Witter, M.P., Lein, E.S. and Moser, E.I. (2014). Functional organization of the hippocampal longitudinal axis. *Nat. Rev. Neurosci*. 15: 655–669.

Strayer, D. and Kramer, A.F. (1990). Attentional requirements of automatic and controlled processing. *J. of Exp. Psychol.: Learning, Mem. Cogn*. 16: 67–82.

Sun, F.T., Miller, L.M., Rao, A.A. and D'Esposito, M. (2007) Functional connectivity of cortical networks involved in bimanual motor sequence learning. *Cereb. Cortex* 17: 1227–1234.

Sutton, S., Braren, M., Zubin, J. and John, E.R. (1965). Evoked-Potential Correlates of Stimulus Uncertainty. *Science*. 150: 1187–1188.

Tanaka, K. (1992). Inferotemporal cortex and higher visual functions. *Curr. Op. Neurobiol*. 2: 502–505.

Tanaka, M., Yoshida, M., Emoto, H. and Ishii, H. (2000). Nornoradrenaline systems in the hypothalamus, amygdala and locus coeruleus are involved in the provocation of anxiety: Basic studies. *Eur. J. Pharmacol.* 29: 397–406.

Thompson-Schill, S.L., D'Esposito, M., Aguirre, G.K. and Farah, M.J. (1997). Role of left inferior prefrontal cortex in retrieval of semantic knowledge: A reevaluation. *Proc. Natl. Acad. Sci. U.S.A.* 94: 14792–14797.

Thura, D. and Cisek, P. (2017). Modulation of premotor and primary motor cortical activity during volitional adjustments of speed-accuracy trade-offs. *J. Neurosci.* 36: 938–956.

Tipper, S.P. (1985). The negative priming effect: Inhibitory priming by ignored objects. *Quart. J. Exp. Psychol.* 37A: 571–590.

Touroutoglou, A., Hollenbeck, M., Dickerson, B.C. and Feldman Barrett, L. (2012). Dissociable large-scale networks anchored in the right anterior insula subserve affective experience and attention. *Neuroimage* 60: 1947–1958.

Tranel, D., Damasio, H. and Damasio, A.R. (1997). A neural basis for the retrieval of conceptual knowledge. *Neuropsychologia* 35: 1319–1327.

Tranel, D., Kemmerer, D., Adolphs, L., Damasio, H. and Damasio, A.R. (2003). Neural correlates of conceptual knowledge for actions. *Cogn. Neuropsychol.* 20: 409–432.

Treisman, A.M. and Gelade, G. (1980). A feature-integration theory of attention. *Cogn. Psychol.* 12: 97–136.

Treisman, M. (1963). Temporal discrimination and the indifference interval: Implications for a model of the "internal clock". *Psychol. Mon.: Gen. Appl.* 77: 1–31.

Tsakiris, M. (2010). My body in the brain: A neurocognitive model of body-ownership. *Neuropsychologia* 48: 703–712.

Tulving, E. (1994). Hemisperic encoding/retrieval asymmetry in episodic memory. PET findings. *Proc. Natl. Acad. Sci. U.S.A.* 91: 2016–2020.

Turgeon, M., Lustig, C. and Meck, H. (2016). Role of Bayesian optimization and degeneracy. *Frontiers in Aging* 8: 1–17.

Tversky, A. and Kahneman, D. (1981). The framing of decisions and the psychology of choice. *Science* 211: 453–458.

Umilta, M.A., Escola, L., Intskirveli, I., Grammont, F., Rochat, M. and Caruana, F. (2008). When pliers become fingers in the monkey motor system. *Proc. Natl. Acad. Sci. U.S.A.* 105: 2209–2213.

Uddin, L.Q., Supekar, K.S., Ryali S. and Menon V. (2011). Dynamic reconfiguration of structural and functional connectivity across core neurocognitive brain networks with development. *J Neurosci.* 31:18578-89.

Uttal, W.R. (2001). *The new phrenology. The limits of localizing cognitive processes in the brain.* Cambridge: MIT Press.

Valdez-Sosa, P.A., Roebroeck, A., Daunizeau, J. and Friston, K. (2011). Effective connectivity: Influence, causality and biophysical modeling. *Neuroimage* 58: 339–361.

Van den Heuvel, M.P. (2009). *The connected brain*. Dissertation. UMC. Utrecht.

Van den Heuvel, M.P. and Hulshoff Pol, H.E. (2010). Exploring the brain network: A review on resting-state fMRI functional connectivity. *Eur. Neuropsychopharmacol.* 20: 519–534.

Van den Heuvel, M.P. and Sporns, O. (2011). Rich-club organization of the human connectome. *J. Neurosci.* 31: 15775–15786.

Van den Heuvel, M.P. and Sporns, O. (2013). Network hubs in the human brain. *Trends Cogn. Sci.* 17: 683–696.

Van Essen, D.C. (2013). Cartography and connectomes. *Neuron* 80: 775–779.

Van Essen, D.C., et al. (2012). The human connectome project: A data acquisition perspective. *Neuroimage* 62: 2222–2231.

Van Olst, E.H. (1971). *The orienting reflex*. The Hague: Mouton.

Van Wingen, G.A., Ossewaarde, L., Bäckström, T., Hermans, E.J. and Fernández, G. (2011). Gonadal hormone regulation of the emotion circuitry in humans. *Neurosci.* 191: 38–45.

Van Zoest, W., Donk, M. and Theeuwes, J. (2004). The role of stimulus-driven and goal-driven control in saccadic visual selection. *J. Exp. Psychol. Hum. Perc. Perf.* 30: 746–759.

Von der Malsburg, C. (1996). The binding problem of neural networks. In: R. Llinás and P.S. Churchland (Eds.), *The mind-brain continuum* (pp. 131–146). Cambridge: MIT Press.

Von Kriegstein, K. and Giraud, A.L. (2006). Implicit multisensory associations influence voice recognition. *PLoS Biol.* 4: e326.

Vossel, S., Weidner, S.R., Driver, J., Friston, K.J. and Fink, G.R. (2012). Cognitive deconstructing the architecture of dorsal and ventral attention systems with dynamic causal modeling. *J. Neurosci.* 32: 10637–10648.

Voytek, B., et al. (2015). Oscillatory dynamics coordinating human frontal networks in support of goal maintenance. *Nat. Neurosci.* 18: 1318–1324.

Waal de, F.B.M. (2004). On the possibility of animal empathy. In: A.S.D. Manstead, N. Frijda and A. Fischer (Eds.), *Feelings and emotions* (pp. 381–401). Cambridge: Cambridge University Press.

Wagner, A.D., Maril, A., Bjork, R.A. and Schacter, D.L. (2001). Prefrontal contributions to executive control: fMRI evidence for functional distinctions within lateral prefrontal cortex. *Neuroimage* 14: 1337–1347.

Wagner, A.D., Poldrack, R.A., Eldridge, L.L., Desmond, J.E., Glover, G.H. Gabrieli, E. and John, D. (1998). Material-specific lateralization of prefrontal activation during episodic encoding and retrieval. *NeuroReport* 9: 3711–3717.

Wagoner, B. (2017) *The constructive mind: Frederic Bartlett's psychology in reconstruction*. Cambridge: Cambridge University Press.

Walker, M.P., Brakefield, T., Hobson, J.A. and Stickgold, R. (2003). Dissociable stages of human memory consolidation and reconsolidation. *Nature* 425: 616–620.

Warrington, E.K. and Shallice, T. (1984). Category specific semantic impairments. *Brain* 107: 829–853.

Weiskrantz, L. (1986). *Blindsight: A case-study and implications*. Oxford: Oxford University Press.

REFERENCES

Weiskrantz, L. (2000). Blindsight: Implications for the conscious experience of emotion. In: R.D. Lane and L. Nadel (Eds.), *Cognitive neuroscience of emotion* (pp. 277–295). New York: Oxford University Press.

Wheeler, M.E., Petersen, S.E. and Buckner, R.L (2000). Memory's echo: Vivid remembering reactivates sensory-specific cortex. *Proc. Natl. Acad. Sci. U.S.A.* 97: 11125–11129.

Wichmann, T. and DeLong, R. (1996). Functional and pathological models of basal ganglia. *Curr. Op. Neurobiol.* 6: 751–758.

Wickens, C.D. (1986). Gain and energetics in information processing. In: R.J. Hockey, A.W.K. Gaillard and M.G.H. Coles (Eds.), *Energetics and human information processing* (pp. 373–384). Dordrecht: Martinus Nijhoff.

Wickens, C.D. (2008). Multiple resources and mental workload. *Human Factors* 50: 449–455.

Wijers, A.A., Mulder, G., Okita, T. and Mulder, L.J.M. (1989). Event-related potentials during memory search and selective attention to letter size and conjunctions of letter size and color. *Psychophysiology* 26: 529–547.

Woldorff, M.G. and Hillyard, S.A. (1991). Modulation of early auditory processing during selective attention to rapidly presented tones. *Electroenc. Clin. Neurophysiol.* 79: 170–191.

Xiao, X., Dong, Q., Gao, J., Men, W., Poldrack, R.A. and Xue, G. (2017). Transformed neural pattern reinstatement during episodic memory retrieval. *J. Neurosci.* 37: 2986–2998.

Yantis, S. and Jonides, J. (1984). Abrupt visual onsets and selective attention: Evidence from visual search. *J. Exp. Psychol.: Hum Perc. Perf.* 10: 601–621.

Yarbus, A.L. (1967). *Eye movements and vision*. New York: Plenum Press.

Young, C.B., Raz, G., Everaerd, D., Beckmann, C.F., Tendolkar, I., Hendler, T., Fernández, G. and Hermans, E.J. (2017). Dynamic shifts in large-scale brain network balance as a function of arousal. *J. Neurosci.* 37: 281–290.

Zajonc, R.C. (1980). Feelings and thinking: Preferences need no inferences. *Am. Psychol.* 35: 151–175.

Zamora-López, M., et al. (2010). Cortical hubs form a module for multisensory integration on top of the hierarchy of cortical networks. *Front. Neuroinform.* 4: 1–10.

Zeki, S. (1993). *A vision of the brain*. Cambridge, MA: Blackwell Scientific Publications.

Zhang, J., Wang, J., Wu, Q., Kuang, W., Huang, X., He, Y., et al. (2011). Disrupted brain connectivity networks in drug-naive, first-episode major depressive disorder. *Biol. Psychiatry* 70: 334–342.

Zhong, L., Zhang, Y., Duan, C.A., Deng, J., Pan, J. and Xu, N. (2019). Causal contribution of parietal cortex to perceptual decision-making during stimulus-categorization. *Nat. Neurosci.* 22: 963–973.

Ziemann, U. (2010). TMS in cognitive Neuroscience: Virtual lesion and beyond. *Cortex* 46: 124–127.

Index

acetylcholine 129
action potential 56
action programming system 191
activation hierarchy 123
activity distributions (attention) 158–159
affective control 164, 320
affective priming 300
affordance 204
affordance competition model 205
aging and memory 236
aging and time perception 217–218
agnosia 188–189, 264
alertness and wakefulness 122, 165
alexia 266
Ames room illusion 183
amnesia: animal studies 262–263; anterograde and retrograde amnesia 259; childhood amnesia 265; consolidation deficits 258; Korsakoff's disease 260; priming effects 258
amygdala 305; animal studies 263; back projections 305–315; cognitive appraisal 130, 285, 305; detecting fearful stimuli 46; expression of fear 46, 210; fear conditioning 300; functions and orbitofrontal cortex 307; implicit learning 313; nuclei 305; pattern association networks 313–314; structure and circuits 300, 304–305; temporal cortex interaction 287
anomia 265
anterior cingulate cortex (ACC) 43, 304, 307, 309, 319–320; decision making 164, 310; dorsal and rostral sections 309; response conflict and monitoring 319; reward based decision making and learning 319–320
anxiety 283, 294, 299, 303, 323; depression 227; noradrenaline 323
apraxia 208–209
arcuate fasciculus (language) 84
arousal 10, 50, 53–54, 124, 128, 167; consolidating emotional memory 311
artificial intelligence (AI) 25, 31
ascending reticular activation system (ARAS) 126–127
asymmetry of the brain *see* laterality
attention: attentional blink 156; attentional neglect 144, 146; attention capture 134; attention spotlight 7, 133, 139, 141, 146; attentional trace 108, 175; automatic detection 136; bottleneck *vs*. resource theories 139–140; central executive 232, 238; cocktail party phenomenon 123, 139; control mechanisms 154, 159; covert attention 138; cued attention tasks 138; divided attention 134–136; dual tasks 136; early attentional modulation (ERP) 153; early *vs*. late selection 141; executive attentional control 116, 141, 147; expression and control 133, 150–154; extinction 144–145; fate of unattended 155–156; focused attention 137, 166; goals of attention 131–132; hierarchical classification 134; inattentional blindness 156; inhibition of return 138, 158;

INDEX

maintenance 133; and memory 146; mental effort 137; mnemonic filter 107; neglect 144–146; performance trade-off 137; pulvinar 150, 157; reflexive attention (orienting) 134; resource theory 140; role of spatial attention 102, 116, 139, 143, 167; selection as core element of attention 131; selective attention network 150; selective inhibition 152; selective voluntary attention 132; source and site of attention 142, 155; theory of visual attention (TVA) 143; vigilance 133; visual attention in the brain 154; visual search 135–136; voluntary attention 134
augmented startle 298
autistic children 211
awareness 46, 91, 92, 121, 133, 297

basal ganglia 46–49, 193, 197–198, 272; action biasing 204–205; complex and motor loops 193; direct and indirect pathways 194; inhibitory circuits 157, 193–195; learning new skills 272–273, 275; motivation 48; nuclei 47; urgency signal 111, 204
behaviorism 2–3
behavioral-cognitive continuum 124–125
beta-blockers 294, 323
biased competition 104, 143, 206
binding 102–104; amygdala 299; convergence 102; hippocampus 102, 103–104, 243; interaction 103; language areas 84, 105; location map 143; medial-temporal region 243; posterior parietal cortex 174; synchronicity 103; temporal binding 104; units 187
blindsight 179, 180–181
blind subjects 187
Blood Oxygenation Level Dependent (BOLD) signal 22, 27, 105
bottleneck theories 139
brainstem 51
Brodmann regions 61

Cannon-Bard theory 289–290
Capgras syndrome 308

caudate nucleus 46–48
central executive network (CEN) 67, 117, 147; see also memory
cerebellar-cortical loops 192
cerebellum 53, 116, 191, 193, 197, 199, 210, 230, 233, 273–274, 275
cerebral cortex: anatomy 37; appendages 71; areas motor control 196; columns 62; cytoarchitecture 60–61; large-scale networks 67; layers 61; lesions 264–267; receptive fields 64–65; spatial divisions 35; structural and functional connectivity 69
cerebral lateralization 72; see also laterality
childhood amnesia see amnesia
chimpanzee 40–41, 80, 284
cingulate gyrus 43
circadian rhythms 122
circuit of fear conditioning 294–300
circuitry of consolidation 245
classical conditioning 277
coding 98; coarse coding 98–99; ensemble coding 101; location coding 98; temporal coding 104; vector coding 98–100
cognitive appraisal 130, 285
cognitive control 162, 172, 169
cognitive neuroscience 5
cognitive neuroscience triangle 6
cognitive psychology 4
cognitivism 4, 17
colliculi 8, 51
communication efficiency 71
comparator mechanism 107, 166, 214, 216
complex loop see motor system
computational ('connectionist') model 25
computations 7, 90
computing in the brain 105
conceptual knowledge 94–95
conditioned blink reflex 278
conditioned fear response 288
conjunction search 104
connectionist model 112
connectivity 14, 18, 25–26; effective connectivity 28; functional connectivity 26, 29, 69; structural connectivity 26, 60

connectomy (connectome) 68–70
consciousness 165, 332; access to consciousness 93, 121; free will 200–201; global workspace 167; levels of 165; manifestations of 165; neural self 168; unrestrained mind 168
consolidation: decreasing function with age 236; deficits 258; general recollection network 248; via medial-temporal cortices 243–245; via striatum 272; time-course 246
constraints (thoughts) 172–173
control functions of the brain 115
control of movements 62, 110
convergence 102, 277, 294
convergence zones 97
core networks (Mesulam) 66
corpus callosum 75, 77–78
crossmodal links 186
curiosity drive 296

deaf subjects 187
decision confidence 310
decision making 202, 204, 206
decomposition 12, 14
default mode network 67, 124, 168–169
déjà vu 109
delayed non-matching-to-sample task 263
depression: and the brain 328–329; hypothetical model 327; neurocognitive model 328–329; and neurotransmitters 325–326
Descartes, René 12
Desimone 151
dichotic listening 156
diencephalon lesions 260–261
differential activation 140
diffusion tensor imaging (DTI) 26
dipole modeling 21
dispositional representations 97, 118, 318
distributed hierarchical network 118, 205
distributed representation 88
divergent thinking 39
divided visual field paradigm 78

domain specificity 17
dopamine 48, 322–323; demand for information 297; dopamine release 216, 322; dopaminergic pathways 51–52; emotions 323, 325; memory consolidation 324; motor control 191, 193; positive reinforcers 323–324; time perception 215–216
dorsal and ventral routes 181
dorsal striatum 46, 216–217
dorsolateral prefrontal cortex (DLPFC) 38, 141, 159
dorsomedial prefrontal cortex (DMPFC) 38–39
double dissociation 22–23, 231, 258
dreams 96; activation-synthesis theory 125–126; functions of 125–126; as synthesizer 126
DRM test of false memory 253
dynamic causal modeling (DCM) 27, 29–30, 161–162, 175
dyslexia 146

electroencephalogram (EEG) 18, 124, 164
embodied cognition 204
emotion: affect and dopamine 323; affective control 164; affective priming 300; appraisal (neural sites) 305; augmented startle 297–298; classification of emotions 281, 294–295; and cognition 285; cognition-emotion interaction model 286–287; cognitive appraisal 103, 305; decision making 317–320; definitions 290, 296; dopamine in emotion learning 324; emotional memories 310; empathy 283; energy mobilization 288; explicit memory and learning 300; facial expressions 288; fear conditioning 299–300; feelings 286; feelings and bodily reactions 288–289; frontal asymmetries 308; function and expression 287–288; gut feelings 319; memory interaction 293; mood states 282; neuroaffective network 304; neurotransmitters and emotions 323; primary and secondary emotions 316; reinforcers 293–294; reward based

decision making 319–320; subcomponents of 285; testosterone 313; triggers of 292; valence and intensity 281, 281–282, 294–295; valence evaluation (neural site) 131, 264, 304–305, 313, 322; women and 312
empathy in man and animal 283
encephalization 41–42
encoding, definition 225–226
encoding and consolidation 225
encoding and retrieval 238
ensemble coding principle 100
entorhinal cortex 244
episodic encoding and semantic retrieval 177
episodic memory temporal structure 213
episodic retrieval see memory
EPSP/IPSP 57
equivalent dipoles 21
Eriksen flanker task 5
error-related negativity (ERN) 300, 310
event-related fields (ERFs) 21
event-related potentials (ERPs) 20
evolution 40–42; chimpanzee 284; development neocortex 332; direct route emotions 299; emotion-memory links 293; face-voice coupling 188; handedness and language 64, 74; hierarchical brain structure 118; huger for information 296; laterality 73, 84, 302; self representations 97, 167
executive control network 115, 170, 238
exogenous vs. endogenous orienting 133
explicit emotional learning 301
extinction see attention
extrathalamic pathways 50, 127
eye contact and gaze detection 211
eye-tracker 212

face-voice interaction 188
facial expressions 203
false memories see memory
fate of the unattended see attention
fear conditioning 297–300
feature integration model 102, 143

feelings see emotions
flashbulb memories 184, 264
Fodor, J. 17–18
forgetting, causes of 228–229
forgetting curve 228–229, 262
free will 200–201
Freud, Sigmund 125
frontal eye fields (FEF) 161
frontal lesions 267
frontal-parietal attention network 67, 160, 241
functional cerebral space 92–93, 223, 332
functional magnetic imaging (fMRI) 22, 27
functional plasticity 72, 120
fusiform face area (FFA) 101, 188, 301
Fuster, J. 93, 110, 163, 202

Galton-Crovitz method 226–227
gate and gain systems 117, 128–129
Generative Assembly Device (GAD) 84–85
generativity 82, 84
general linear model (GLM) 27
general recollection network 248
genetic envelope 57
geniculostriate pathway 178
global-local debate 14–17
global workspace 167
globus pallidus 46
gnostic cells 97
Goldman-Rakic, P. 110, 163, 227
grain size 219
grandmother cell 98
granger causality analysis (GCA) 27, 30
graph theory 28, 114
grasping 199
guided activation model 163
guilty knowledge 19–20

habit learning 27; see also learning
habituation 276
handedness 80–81
Hawking, Stephen 212
Hebb's rule 16, 58, 113, 220, 314
hemispheric specialization see laterality
HERA model 239

hierarchical distributed networks 118–119, 205, 331
hierarchical modularity 71, 119
higher-order vision 183
hippocampus: anatomy and circuit 44, 244, 255; anterior and posterior regions 248; consolidation circuitry 244–245; depression 326; episodic encoding 241; fear conditioning 300; long-term potentiation (LTP) 244–245; major sections 255; novelty detection 108, 245; prefrontal connections 250–251; prosthesis 247; retrieval 242; time cells 249; time–course of consolidation 246, 248
homunculus 12, 74
hubs 114
Human Connectome Project 70
Huntington's and Parkinson's diseases 195
hypothalamus 49, 116, 129–130, 284, 304–305, 315–316, 326–327

inattentional blindness *see* attention
independent component analysis (ICA) 28
inferior temporal cortex (naming) 95
information processing: components 108; models 106
inhibition of return *see* attention
insula 46, 169; *see also* salience network
internal capsule 47
internal clock and oscillatory mechanism 213–214
International Affective Picture System (IAPS) 282
interval timing network 160
intraparietal sulcus (IPS) 110, 207
intrinsic connectivity network 67

James-Lange theory 289

Korsakoff's disease 226, 248, 260, 262
Kosslyn S.M. 4, 6, 81, 111

LaBerge, D. 132, 150, 159
language circuit 84–86

large-scale networks 66–67, 114, 150, 170; and flexibility 120, 174
Lashley-Penfield controversy 18
lateral inhibition 157
lateral intra-parietal sulcus (LIP) 202
laterality 72; absolute *vs.* relative specialization 85; asymmetry 79–80; divided visual field task 78; emotions 86; General Assembly Device (GAD) 85; handedness 80–81; language circuit 86; retrieval (HERA model) 239–241; snowball effect 81; split brain 82–83; symmetry 73; words 88
Lateralized Readiness Potential (LRP) 5, 51
learning: elementary learning 276; emotional learning 292, 297, 301; fast and slow learning 273–274; habit learning 271; implicit learning, 267, 271–272; reward guided learning and decision 320; role of striatum 273–275; sensorimotor learning 271–272; skill learning 272–275
Le Doux model 299–300
lesions in the orbitofrontal cortex 217
levels of cortical activation 98
lexical decision task 227
limbic system 43
locus coeruleus-noradrenergic system 53, 129, 305, 323
long-term depression 255
long-term memory and the brain 229
long-term potentiation (LTP) 17, 244–255; amygdala 278, 314, 324–325; associative LTP 256; striatum 216, 272
looking 211

magnetic encephalogram (MEG) 21
magnetic resonance imaging (MRI) 21
Major Depression Disorder (MDD) 328–329
medial forebrain bundle 321–322
medial-temporal cortex network 244
memory: anterior temporal system (AT) 251; central executive 232, 235, 237; comparison and filter models 107–108; declarative memory 230, 243; emotion

interaction 293–294; encoding and retrieval 225, 241; episodic encoding and semantic retrieval 241; episodic retrieval 242; executive control 238; explicit memory (see declarative memory); explicit vs. implicit memory 225–230; false memories 253; forms of memory 221–222; forms of retrieval 226; functional cerebral space 92–93, 222–223; grandmother cell 98; guided behavior model 251; implicit memory (see non-declarative memory); long-term memories and brain 229–230; medial temporal cortical areas 244; memory-attention interaction 146–147, 226; memory for faces 188; memory guided behavior model 251; memory representations (see representations); mnemonic filter 107; motor adaptation network 274; multiple trace theory 278; network 244; non-declarative memory 178, 267; pattern associating network 112–114; pill 256; posterior medial system (PM) 251; priming 231, 268 (see also priming); procedural memory 72, 222, 272; relational memory 252; retrieval and forgetting 228; sensory memory 234; sequence learning (see learning); short-long-term memory interaction 223; short-term memory 224–225, 234, 235; skill learning (see learning); standard consolidation theory 246; and state of the brain 166; working memory 235–237
mental effort see attention
mentalizing 169
Mesulam, M. 66, 333
mild cognitive impairment (MCI) 256
mimesis 82
mind-brain dualism 9
mindfulness 171
mirror-drawing test 260
mirror neurons 96, 110, 208
mirror test 97
Mishkin, M. 263
mnemonic filter 107–108, 116
modularity (modules) 17, 114, 206

mood state 20; see also emotion
motor system: action programming 117; action selection 206; basal ganglia 46; cerebellum 53; cerebral-cortical loop 193; complex loop 193; global organisation 191; grasping an object 199; instructions-generating system 197–198; motor loop 193; movement execution system 197–198; population vector 99–100; sequence vs. adaptation learning 274; striatum 46, 271; subcortical loops 193
multiple trace theory 298

negative priming see priming
neglect see attention
neglect and mental imagery 148
neostriatum 46–48, 129
network flexibility 72, 119
network neuroscience 68
neural network modeling 24, 27
neural self 168
neuroaffective networks 304
neurogenesis 59, 120
neuromyths 87
neuronal model theory 108–109
neurophilosophy 333
neurotransmitters 129
neurotransmitters and emotions 321
nigrostriate pathway 51–52, 217
NMDA receptors 257
Non-cognitive Behavioral Model (NBM) 31
noradrenaline 50, 116, 129–131, 244, 255, 280, 294, 305, 311, 322–323
novelty detection 108, 245, 297
novelty P300 330
nucleus accumbens see ventral striatum

object recognition network 82
obsessive compulsive disorder (OCD) 324, 330
oculomotor neurons 210
oculomotor pathways 208–210
orbitofrontal cortex 38, 304, 306–308, 320; emotional decision making 319; extinction 308; inhibition prevailing actions 320

orientation sensitivity 54
orienting 133–134
orienting response model 108–109, 124

P300 19–20
parahippocampal gyrus 244
parallel distributed processing 25
parallel hierarchical model 333
parietal cortex role 206–207
Parkinson's patients 195
Patient Henry Gustav Molaison (HM) 259
patient MS 258
Patricia Churchland 6, 13, 31, 333
pattern association network 113
PDP systems 25
perception-action cycle 202–203
perceptual illusions 182
perceptual-representation-system (PRS) 234, 269
performance-trade off *see* attention
permastore 236
PGO waves 123, 126
Phineas Gage 306
phonological loop 237
phrenology 333
place cells 44
planum temporale 74
plasticity 120, 186, 274–275
pleasure centre 293
population vector 100
positive and negative reinforcers 293
posterior parietal cortex (PPC) 206; areas 154; attentional control 159; grasping an object 147, 152; lateral intra parietal cortex (LIP) 202; neglect 113; oculomotor pathways 153; perception-action cycle 147; position module 158, 252; visual spatial attention 116
Posttraumatic Stress Disorder (PTSD) 209, 294
prefrontal cortex (PFC): anatomy 38–39; attentional control 159, 166; cognitive control 162–163; decision making 318–320; emotion control 318, 325; episodic and semantic retrieval 240–241, 245; executive control 238; guided activation model 163–164; lesions 267; schema updating 250; self 168; working memory 237
premotor cortex 191, 193, 196–197
primary and secondary reinforcers 295
priming: affective priming 300; and habituation 268; negative priming 142, 231; perceptual priming 222; priming methods 227–228; semantic priming 268
procedural memory 72, 231, 272; and fast learning 176
prosopagnosia 185
pruning 57, 59
pulvinar *see* thalamus
putamen 47–48, 193; *see also* basal ganglia

random generation test 232
raphe nuclei 53–54
readiness potential 200–201
receptive fields 60
reconsolidation 248, 311
recursive synthesis 66
reductive integration 12–13
re-entry 182
reflexive orienting *see* attention
reinforcers 295; contingency relation 294; reversed contingency relation 294
reinforcement guided decisions 319
relational memory 252
reminiscence bump 236
REM sleep 54, 123
repeated encapsulation 119, 206
representations 91; action representations 96; active and passive representation 93; complex representations 94; dispositional representations 97; perceptual representation system (PRS) 234, 269; self-representations 97
resource theory *see* attention
response competition and affordance 203–206
response conflict 310
reticular activating system (RAS) 50, 126
reticular nucleus (RN) 127–128, 156; *see also* thalamus

retinotopic organization 60, 142
retrieval: and forgetting 228; forms of 226; hippocampus 242, 245; prefrontal cortex 239–241, 248; and 'tip of the tongue' phenomenon 228
retrosplenial cortex 252
reverberating circuits 16
reward-guided decisions 319–320
Ribot gradient 229, 262
rich-club networks 26
right-hemisphere emotional expressions 301
ROI analysis see seed-based (ROI) analysis
Rolls, E.T. 112–113, 252, 294–295
rubber hand effect 190

salience network 68, 169–170
scalar expectance theory 214
scan–path 210
schema 279
schema updating model 240, 250
scotoma 179
search negativities 162
seed-based (ROI) analysis 26–28
selective elimination and stabilization 59
self-reflection 167–168
semantic dementia 264
semantic hub 254
semantic retrieval 240–241
sense of self 168
sensitization 277
sensorimotor learning 232
sensory-gain (ERPs) 153
serotonin 53–54, 129, 244, 276–277, 284, 318, 325–326
serotonin reuptake inhibitors 326
sex differences and brain 45
short-term memory as: activated long-term memory 234; portal to long-term memory 234; working memory 234
Simon task 171
skill learning 272; fast 273; sequence and motor adaptation 275; slow 274
sleep 123
slow electrical potentials 136, 161
small-world organization 70

snowball effect 81
somatic markers 168, 317–318
somatotopic organization 52, 60
spatial cueing task 138
split-brain patients 82–83
spontaneous thoughts 172
spreading activation 253–254
Squire, L. 220, 229, 245–46, 262
standard consolidation model 246
startle 278, 288, 297–298
Statistical Parametric Mapping (SPM) 28
stop-signal paradigm 169
stress 129–131
stress hormones 326
striatal beat frequency model 215–216
striatum 46, 194, 216, 271–272, 275, 322, 325
stroop task 310
subcortical nuclei 64
subprocesses of emotion 201
subsequent memory paradigm 239
substantia nigra (SN) 46–48, 51, 216; SNc (pars compacta) 194, 216; SNr (pars reticulata) 194
superior colliculus 157–158, 179
supplementary motor area (SMA) 196–197
suprachiasmatic nucleus (SCN) 122
synapses 56, 58
synchronicity 103
synesthesia 189
syntactic working memory 86
system neuroscience 67–68

task-irrelevant thoughts 173
tectum and tegmentum 52
tectopulvinary pathways 179
temporal coding mechanism 103
temporal binding see binding
temporal gradient (forgetting) 229
temporal lobe bilateral damage 266
temporal voice area (TVA) 189
testosterone 45, 75, 313
thalamus 49; lateral geniculate nucleus (LGN) 49, 128, 180; medial dorsal nuclei 49, 230, 260; pulvinar 156–158, 178; reticular nucleus (RN) 156; thalamic

'gate'-model 128; thalamic nuclei 49, 127, 260; thalamic visual pathways 178; thalamocortical circuits 177–178
theory of mind 97, 209
theory of visual attention (TVA) 104
tickling and laughter 290–291
time–course of consolidation 246
time perception 213; coincidence detection 216; dorsal striatum 217; internal clock 213–214; scalar expectancy model 214; striatal beat frequency model 215, 217; substantia nigra (SNc) 216; time-cells 247
tonotopy 60
tractography 26–27, 68, 70
transcranial magnetic stimulation (TMS) 23–24
transmitters 54
turing machine 14

unrestrained mind 168

vector coding 98–100
ventral striatum 46–48, 51, 315
ventral tegmentum 52, 216–217, 321–322, 324–325

ventriloquist effect 189
ventromedial prefrontal cortex (VMPFC) 38–39, 130, 159, 166, 168, 249, 304, 306, 308, 319
visual search *see* attention
visual agnosia 183
visual illusions 182
visual pathways: dorsal (where) and ventral (what) 181; geniculostriate and tectopulvinar 177–178; ipsi- and contralateral 78, 178–180; magno- and parvocellular 178–180
von Neumann architecture 4

Wisconsin Card Sorting Task 319, 330
working memory 66, 234–237; and attention 158–159, 165–166; Baddeley's model 237; central executive 237–238; cognitive control 162, 165; Goldman–Rakic's animal model 237; memory retrieval 249; pathways 235–237; prefrontal cortex 158, 267, 318; preparation 155, 159; resources 140–141; time-perception 214–216

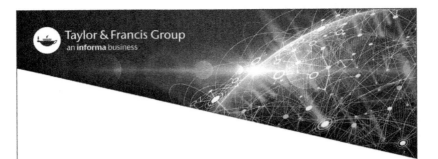